ALSO BY THE EDITORS AT AMERICA'S TEST KITCHEN

**FOR A FULL LISTING OF ALL OUR BOOKS
OR TO ORDER TITLES:**

CooksIllustrated.com

AmericasTestKitchen.com

or call 800-611-0759

COMFORT FOOD

ALL YOUR FAVORITES
MADE LIGHTER

FOOD
Makeovers

BY THE EDITORS AT
America's Test Kitchen

PHOTOGRAPHY BY
Daniel J. van Ackere

ADDITIONAL PHOTOGRAPHY BY
Carl Tremblay

AMERICA'S TEST KITCHEN
17 Station Street, Brookline, MA 02445

Library of Congress
Cataloging-in-Publication Data
Comfort food makeovers : all your favorites
made lighter / by the editors at America's Test
Kitchen ; photography by Daniel J. van Ackere ;
additional photography by Carl Tremblay.

      pages cm
  Includes index.
  ISBN 978-1-936493-42-5
  1. Comfort food. 2. Low-calorie diet--
Recipes. 3. Low-fat diet--Recipes. I.
America's Test Kitchen (Firm)
  TX740.C645 2013
  641.5'635--dc23
                              2012038539
Paperback: $26.95 US

Manufactured in the United States
of America
10 9 8 7 6 5 4 3 2

DISTRIBUTED BY
America's Test Kitchen
17 Station Street, Brookline, MA 02445

EDITORIAL DIRECTOR: Jack Bishop
EDITORIAL DIRECTOR, BOOKS: Elizabeth Carduff
EXECUTIVE EDITOR: Lori Galvin
EXECUTIVE FOOD EDITOR: Julia Collin Davison
ASSOCIATE EDITORS: Kate Hartke, Christie Morrison, Dan Zuccarello
ASSISTANT EDITOR: Alyssa King
TEST COOKS: Danielle DeSiato-Hallman, Ashley Moore, Rebecca Morris
ASSISTANT TEST COOK: Stephanie Pixley
ART DIRECTOR: Greg Galvan
DESIGNER: Taylor Argenzio
FRONT COVER PHOTOGRAPH: Carl Tremblay
STAFF PHOTOGRAPHER: Daniel J. van Ackere
ADDITIONAL PHOTOGRAPHY: Carl Tremblay, Keller + Keller,
and Steve Klise
FOOD STYLING: Catrine Kelty, Marie Piraino
PHOTOSHOOT KITCHEN TEAM:
     ASSOCIATE EDITOR: Chris O'Connor
     ASSISTANT TEST COOKS: Daniel Cellucci, Sara Mayer
PRODUCTION DIRECTOR: Guy Rochford
SENIOR PRODUCTION MANAGER: Jessica Quirk
SENIOR PROJECT MANAGER: Alice Carpenter
PRODUCTION AND TRAFFIC COORDINATOR: Brittany Allen
WORKFLOW AND DIGITAL ASSET MANAGER: Andrew Mannone
PRODUCTION AND IMAGING SPECIALISTS: Heather Dube, Lauren Pettapiece,
Lauren Robbins
COPYEDITOR: Jeffrey Schier
PROOFREADER: Elizabeth Wray Emery
INDEXER: Elizabeth Parson

PICTURED ON FRONT COVER: Baked Macaroni and Cheese (page 108)
PICTURED OPPOSITE TITLE PAGE: Chocolate Cupcakes (page 246)
PICTURED ON BACK OF JACKET: Buffalo Wings (page 14), New York–Style
Cheesecake (page 290), Meat and Cheese Lasagna (page 100)

Contents

Welcome to America's Test Kitchen

This book has been tested, written, and edited by the folks at America's Test Kitchen, a very real 2,500-square-foot kitchen located just outside of Boston. It is the home of *Cook's Illustrated* magazine and *Cook's Country* magazine and is the Monday-through-Friday destination for more than three dozen test cooks, editors, food scientists, tasters, and cookware specialists. Our mission is to test recipes over and over again until we understand how and why they work and until we arrive at the "best" version.

We start the process of testing a recipe with a complete lack of conviction, which means that we accept no claim, no theory, no technique, and no recipe at face value. We simply assemble as many variations as possible, test a half-dozen of the most promising, and taste the results blind. We then construct our own hybrid recipe and continue to test it, varying ingredients, techniques, and cooking times until we reach a consensus. The result, we hope, is the best version of a particular recipe, but we realize that only you can be the final judge of our success (or failure). As we like to say in the test kitchen, "We make the mistakes, so you don't have to."

All of this would not be possible without a belief that good cooking, much like good music, is indeed based on a foundation of objective technique. Some people like spicy foods and others don't, but there is a right way to sauté, there is a best way to cook a pot roast, and there are measurable scientific principles involved in producing perfectly beaten, stable egg whites. This is our ultimate goal: to investigate the fundamental principles of cooking so that you become a better cook. It is as simple as that.

You can watch us work (in our actual test kitchen) by tuning in to *America's Test Kitchen* (AmericasTestKitchenTV.com) or *Cook's Country from America's Test Kitchen* (CooksCountryTV.com) on public television, or by subscribing to *Cook's Illustrated* magazine (CooksIllustrated.com) or *Cook's Country* magazine (CooksCountry.com). We welcome you into our kitchen, where you can stand by our side as we test our way to the "best" recipes in America.

Curious to see what goes on behind the scenes at America's Test Kitchen? The Feed features kitchen snapshots, exclusive recipes, video tips, and much more. **AmericasTestKitchenFeed.com**

f **facebook.com/AmericasTestKitchen**
t **twitter.com/TestKitchen**
You Tube **youtube.com/AmericasTestKitchen**

Preface

Makeovers are the very essence of the American experience, from *Queer Eye for the Straight Guy* to *This Old House,* but, in Vermont, makeovers are less popular. I am reminded of the story of a kindhearted lady from Cavendish who was always on the lookout to invite a less fortunate soul over for a good meal during the holidays. One Christmas, she invited the local handyman, who was a bit eccentric—he wore several suits of long underwear during the winter along with two pairs of pants and several shirts, and he lived in squalid quarters. She met him on the street and extended the invitation, at which point he said that he would have to think it over. A few days later, he gave his reply as follows: "I thank you for your kindness but I've been thinking it over and I just don't know. I'd have to take off my clothes, take some kind of bath, and then try to find something else to wear. And I've about decided that it ain't worth it!"

In the test kitchen, recipe makeovers have been controversial. One group of cooks, including myself, wondered if it would be best to let comfort food classics alone. Do we really want to replace fat in a chocolate cake with prunes or applesauce? But when our own test kitchen undertook makeover projects (without silly substitutions), I found myself reaching for more. In fact, many of these recipes were so good that I actually preferred them to the originals. It wasn't about reducing fat or calories; it was about creating something that I actually liked more. That extra fat was often obscuring the flavor of the food itself—the leaner cupcake, muffin, or lasagna was, in fact, better.

To achieve truly revelatory makeovers, however, requires that one discard the easy and sometimes fraudulent methods employed by many test kitchens. No more tiny servings—the classic ruse used by food manufacturers—and no silly and off-putting ingredients such as the aforementioned prunes and applesauce in chocolate cake. Just because it looks like a chocolate cake doesn't mean that it tastes like one!

We had lofty goals for our makeovers. We aimed to cut calories by a third (we ended up averaging 41 percent) and fat by half (final average was 65 percent).

But the major rule was that the food had to taste good and be as similar as possible to, for instance, the Fettuccine Alfredo or Whoopie Pies that we had started with. We had to love it or leave it—if the latter, we simply moved on to the next recipe challenge.

Many of these recipes started their lives in restaurants and fast-food establishments, so we slimmed down and improved dishes such as McDonald's Quarter Pounder with Cheese (our Drive-Through Cheeseburgers use lean ground beef and turkey with a milk-bread panade) and KFC's Original Recipe Fried Chicken (try our lean but tasty version, Oven-Fried Chicken). We also did makeovers of Stuffed Shells with Meat Sauce (pureed cottage cheese helped to thicken the sauce, and soy sauce increased meatiness), a low-fat Eggs Benedict (cornstarch for thickening), Chocolate Cupcakes (canola oil instead of butter and more cocoa and espresso powder for an intense chocolate flavor), and Pecan Bars (a strange but successful use of Honey Nut Cheerios!).

In the end, I think of these recipes as my new comfort food repertoire, not my go-to versions only when I am watching my weight. I prefer cleaner, leaner recipes that still have a good level of fat but use it wisely and to best effect. Since the culinary arts are a work in progress—one generation revises the recipes from the prior one—this makes perfect sense. In the past 50 years, my tastes have changed and I want my food to step up to the plate and deliver big flavors that are not obscured with thick layers of cheese, cream, and butter. I want my chocolate cake to taste, well, like chocolate cake. And that's the essence of this book—if it doesn't taste good, if it doesn't satisfy, then you won't find it on these pages. A simple rule but one that ensures that a comfort food makeover is the real deal, not an ersatz imitation! (Try the Chocolate Cupcakes and you will see what I mean.)

CHRISTOPHER KIMBALL

Founder and Editor,

Cook's Illustrated and *Cook's Country*

Host, *America's Test Kitchen* and

Cook's Country from America's Test Kitchen

Our editors and test cooks examining baked low-fat cheeses to find out which varieties melt the best.

Behind the Makeovers

Introduction

For many cooks, classic home-style meals like creamy baked lasagna, hearty enchiladas, and crispy chicken Parmesan are the ones that always satisfy friends and family—the same goes for decadent treats like red velvet cupcakes and warm chocolate fudge cakes. The reality, though, is that these dishes—the comfort food classics we like to make at home as well as the ones we love to enjoy at restaurants (like a blue cheese wedge salad or fettuccine Alfredo)—are loaded with an astounding amount of fat and calories. Short of banishing these dishes from your diet, what's a responsible cook to do? Enter the recipe makeover.

Test cook Ashley Moore taking notes after one of many casserole tastings.

SETTING THE BAR HIGH

If you think "recipe makeovers" means tofu lasagna or carob-chip cookies, think again—our recipes had to taste good and stay as true to the original as possible. If a revamped recipe didn't hew closely to the full-fat original and didn't cut it with our tasters, then that dish didn't make it into the book. Period. Whereas other light recipes are quick to sacrifice flavor for the sake of nutrition numbers, we put flavor first and used our test kitchen experience, smart ingredient substitutions, and clever techniques to trim the fat. But before going into the test kitchen, we set some clear goals for our recipe development process. Our aim was to cut calories by at least 33 percent, total fat by at least 50 percent, and saturated fat by at least 50 percent. For example, if a serving of a traditional recipe contained 600 calories, 24 grams of fat, and 12 grams of saturated fat, our goal was to produce a recipe with no more than 400 calories, 12 grams of fat, and 6 grams of saturated fat. But before we could get cooking, we needed a place to start.

BEFORE AND AFTER

With every single recipe, you'll find "before" and "after" calorie, fat, and saturated fat counts (complete nutritional information, along with portion size information where relevant, can be found on pages 302–307). Where did our "before" recipes come from? Over the years, the test kitchen has developed countless recipes for everyone's favorite comfort foods, including everything from baked ziti and shepherd's pie to chocolate mousse and lemon squares, so we used these dishes as a point of comparison with our lightened versions. Other cookbooks or reputable online sources provided us with benchmarks for many other recipes. But since many comfort-food favorites are the sorts of dishes most people eat only at restaurants (think crab rangoon, cheesy nachos, or New York-style cheesecake), we turned to the nutritionals published on the websites or menus of national restaurant chains (we found one restaurant, Ruby Tuesday, that does not provide saturated fat counts, so these are listed as N/A throughout the book). This process was more revealing than we could ever have imagined. (Note that we rechecked the nutritional information for all restaurant dishes just prior to publication, but for the most up-to-date numbers, you should consult the restaurants' websites or contact them directly.)

ORDERING IN

It turns out that simply checking the nutritionals on restaurant websites for dishes like coconut shrimp, lasagna, macaroni and cheese, and cheesecake was not enough to ensure that we were comparing apples to apples. Very often these websites don't list the portion sizes, or they include a side dish as part of the nutritional info. So we took matters into our own hands and ordered hundreds of take-out dishes from these restaurants. Before long we were filling the test kitchen with take-out containers, weighing chicken, beef, sauces, and pasta, scraping crumb coatings off food, and more, all in an effort to be sure that the portion sizes of our makeovers matched the restaurant servings. We're well aware that restaurant portions are generous—who hasn't taken home a doggie bag?—but once we got the scales out, we truly understood the disparity between what you'd be served in a restaurant versus what you'd eat at home. These restaurant portions were downright astounding. In some instances the restaurant dinner portions were so huge that we found it more accurate to compare our recipes to their (smaller) lunch portions.

Our team spent many afternoons sorting through take-out boxes and weighing the contents.

Also, we found that the restaurants were usually pretty generous and tended to add some extra food—a few extra shrimp, spoonfuls of sauce, or scoops of pasta—into the take-out containers. So when the take-out portions just didn't make sense when compared with their nutritional information, we picked up the phone and talked directly to the restaurants' managers, chefs, and corporate headquarters to get the scoop on what the portion sizes should have been to match their published nutritional numbers. And, of course, if a dish arrived with an unexpected side dish, we made sure that this extra food was not reflected in its nutritional analysis.

THE BOTTOM LINE

So, how did we do in terms of meeting our goals? Quite well. Looking at the 178 recipes in the book as a whole, we succeeded in trimming calories by an average of 41 percent. We cut total fat by an average of 65 percent and trimmed saturated fat by an average of 66 percent. That said, there are a handful of recipes in the book where we just missed our stated goals. For instance, the pasta is the main source of calories in most pasta dishes, while the sauce is generally the main source of fat. Since we didn't want to reduce portion size, our test kitchen work focused on reworking the sauce—not cutting back on the amount of pasta in each serving. As a result, we fell a few points shy of our calorie reduction target of 33 percent in some pasta recipes. However, as you will see, for the vast majority of recipes in this book, we hit all three goals for reducing calories, total fat, and saturated fat—and those that didn't came reasonably close. With dishes like cheese pizza, stuffed shells, and peanut butter pie seriously lightened and still tasting every bit as good as their full-fat originals, we'd call that a win.

How did we do it? In the following pages, you'll find our most often used makeover techniques, the ingredients that worked best, tips on measuring (it can make a dramatic difference in the results), and equipment that's useful when preparing lighter dishes.

The Test Kitchen's Top Recipe Makeover Techniques

Sure, subbing reduced-fat cheese for the full-fat variety is an obvious way to trim the fat from rich, cheesy dishes, but will this change alone deliver a great-tasting, lighter dish? Not likely. We found that retooling our favorite comfort-food recipes to meet our guidelines took a bit more work—and some clever strategizing. Here are the techniques that we turned to time and again to revamp these classics into lighter dishes that are just as flavorful as their full-fat counterparts.

1. REPLACE HIGH-FAT COOKING METHODS WITH LOWER-FAT ONES: Deep frying definitely isn't a low-fat cooking method, so we turned to the oven instead. To get an ultra-crisp exterior on traditionally fried foods, we baked them; when coated with the right low-fat breading and baked, our "fried" chicken and shrimp delivered the same crisp crust as the full-fat versions. For a number of salads and casseroles, we opted to poach our chicken rather than pan-sear it so we could cut back on the oil but still enjoy moist, ultra-tender chicken.

2. MAKE A LITTLE GO A LONG WAY: There's no doubt about it—bacon and butter are fat-laden ingredients. But in many cases, cutting them entirely would compromise the flavor or texture of a dish. To keep these high-fat but high-flavor ingredients in certain recipes, we used smaller amounts but found ways to maximize their impact. For our New England clam chowder, we used just a couple slices of bacon, but chopped it finely so it would be evenly distributed and its flavor would permeate the dish. For a rich-tasting chicken Piccata, we cut back to a single pat of butter and stirred it into the sauce at the end of cooking; this way, it provided noticeable richness and flavor.

3. USE LOW-FAT AND NONFAT INGREDIENTS WISELY: Low-fat and nonfat ingredients were key in our makeovers—but it's all about knowing which ones to use and when to use them. For example, after a number of tests of various low-fat, reduced-fat, and nonfat cheese brands, we found a few we preferred over others, but these varied according to application. For casseroles, 50 percent light cheddar provided a creamy texture and ultra-cheesy flavor, but for cheeseburgers and tuna melts, which needed a gooey, melty topping, reduced-fat American cheese (which contains 25 percent less fat than the full-fat version) worked best.

4. ADD RICH, SAVORY FLAVOR WITH MEATY, GLUTAMATE-RICH INGREDIENTS: Here in the test kitchen, we've come to rely on a number of glutamate-rich ingredients, such as mushrooms, Parmesan cheese, soy sauce, anchovies, and tomato paste, to add meaty, savory depth to recipes. For our makeovers, these power-hitters were key to bumping up the meaty flavor of many dishes without using a lot of meat. For example, our Bolognese trims fat and calories by using ground turkey, but for more intense flavor, we added dried porcini and an anchovy and doubled up on the tomato paste.

5. USE LEAN GROUND BEEF OR POULTRY AND FIND WAYS TO KEEP IT MOIST AND TENDER: Using leaner cuts of ground beef or ground poultry can slash fat, but these substitutions can also make for dry, flavorless dishes. Lean ground beef and ground turkey helped us lighten our cheeseburgers, but a panade (a paste of milk and bread) was essential for moist, tender patties. In our shepherd's pie, a small amount of baking soda kept the lean beef tender and juicy.

Measuring for Makeover Success

When you are trying to lighten recipes, there is less room for error—you need to make sure that you are using the right volume of ingredients, otherwise what you might think is a low-fat dish may not be. Here are some helpful measuring tips that are specific to certain ingredients.

MEAT AND FISH
Be sure to buy the right amount of meat or fish that's called for in the recipe, but if you're not sure you have the right amount, you can double-check it at home with a digital scale. To keep the scale clean, place a sheet of plastic wrap on it before setting the food on top.

CHEESE
When it comes to cheese, the volume you end up with can vary based on how you grate it. For example, 1 ounce measures ½ cup when grated on a rasp-style grater and ¼ cup when shredded on a standard grater. You'll find both weight and volume in most recipes, so you can make sure you've got the right amount.

MESSY INGREDIENTS
Malleable ingredients like mayonnaise and yogurt can be hard to measure using a dry measuring cup; the ingredient may get trapped in the corner, and a rubber spatula will get you only so far. To measure these ingredients accurately, simply add them to an adjust-able measuring cup and level it off, then push them right out.

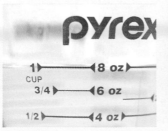

LIQUIDS
To measure broth or larger amounts of oil or other liquids, set a liquid measuring cup on a level surface and bend down to read it at eye level. Be sure to read the measurement from the bottom of the concave arc at the liquid's surface (this arc is known as the meniscus line).

OIL
When you measure small amounts of oil, it's easy to overfill the teaspoon and have oil spilling into your skillet or sauce. For more control and accuracy, fill a plastic squeeze bottle with oil, then squeeze it into measuring spoons. Or, pour the oil into a small bowl and dip your spoon into it.

DRY INGREDIENTS
We recommend weighing flour, sugar, and other dry ingredi-ents, but we've found that the dip-and-sweep method is also reliable. To measure with this method, dip the measuring cup into the ingredient and sweep away the excess with a straight-edged object, like the back of a butter knife.

Stocking Your Kitchen

Here is a list of ingredients that helped us lighten or add flavor to the recipes in this book.

1. GREEK YOGURT: Thicker, creamier, lower in carbohydrates, and higher in protein than regular yogurt, Greek yogurt made a great stand-in for sour cream. We used nonfat Greek yogurt as a topping for tostadas and nachos and even used it in our potato salad so we could cut back on the light mayo. Our favorite brand of Greek yogurt, both full-fat and nonfat, is **Olympus Authentic Greek Strained Yogurt**.

2. LIGHT MAYONNAISE: Mayonnaise is a big offender when it comes to fat and calories—not a shock given that it's made from egg yolks and vegetable oil, plus a few other ingredients—so we recommend using light mayo. But you can't use just any jar; brands vary widely in taste and fat content and the labeling can be confusing. In our taste tests, we found **Hellmann's Light** worked best; it offered a creamy texture and good flavor comparable to that of the full-fat variety. We call for it in creamy dips, salad dressings, and pasta and potato salads.

3. LIGHT CREAM CHEESE: One of the secret weapons in our makeover arsenal is ⅓ less fat cream cheese (also labeled neufchatel in the supermarket). We used this reduced-fat ingredient to impart a creamy richness in dishes like chicken fricassee, shrimp scampi, and green bean casserole.

4. LOWER-FAT CHEESES: For ultra-cheesy pizza and calzones, we used part-skim mozzarella; it melts well and adds a nice, subtle tangy flavor. As for lower-fat cheddar, we found the 50 percent light variety melted best and offered good flavor, making it perfect for macaroni and cheese and chicken enchiladas, which need a bold, cheesy presence. When we needed cheese for its melting abilities alone, not its rich flavor, we reached for reduced-fat American cheese. Boar's Head 25 Percent Lower Fat American Cheese (found at the deli counter) worked especially well in our burgers and tuna melts.

5. NONFAT COTTAGE CHEESE: To lighten lasagna, baked ziti, and calzones, we opted for nonfat cottage cheese instead of nonfat ricotta cheese. When processed until smooth, it gave the filling in these dishes an ultra-creamy texture and clean flavor, unlike nonfat ricotta, which lent a gummy texture and imparted off-flavors. Adding a few saltines to the food processor helped to absorb the extra moisture from the cottage cheese so the filling wasn't runny.

6. LOW-FAT BREADINGS: Though homemade bread crumbs are a test kitchen go-to for breaded dishes, we turned to panko bread crumbs, reduced-fat Ritz crackers, and cornflakes for our makeovers. Panko helped us achieve a crunchy coating in our baked (not fried) mozzarella sticks and chicken nuggets. Our favorite brand is **Ian's Panko Bread Crumbs**. Reduced-fat Ritz crackers came in handy when we need a breaded coating that offered a crispy texture and ultra-buttery flavor, without a lot of fat (think chicken Kiev). To replicate the super-crunchy coating of fried chicken and fried shrimp in our oven-fried chicken and oven-fried shrimp, we turned to cornflakes, which kept their crisp texture and didn't become soggy in the oven the way other coatings did.

7. VEGETABLE OIL SPRAY: After coating our breaded foods with panko, cracker crumbs, or cornflakes, we had to find a way to ensure they'd stay crisp in the oven. A light coating of vegetable oil spray did the trick every time, without costing much in the way of calories or fat. We also used it to help crisp tortillas for the taco bowls in our beef taco salad.

8. TURKEY BACON: Many dishes just wouldn't be the same without the smoky flavor and crunchy texture of bacon. Fortunately, we found we could swap in turkey bacon in some recipes; cooked until crisp, a few slices of turkey bacon delivered just the right smoky flavor and crunchy texture in our cobb salad.

9. GROUND POULTRY: Burgers and chili usually rely on ground beef for their meaty flavor and texture, but we supplemented or substituted 93 percent lean ground turkey, which is comprised of both light and dark meat (do not use 99 percent lean ground turkey, which is all breast meat and will cook up dry). Cooking our lean burgers covered helped them retain moisture, while adding our turkey incrementally to the chili guaranteed it offered big, meaty bites.

10. MUSHROOMS: To amp up the meaty, hearty flavor and texture in dishes like meatloaf and shepherd's pie while still cutting the fat, we replaced some of the meat with mushrooms, which added heft and a hearty texture. Chopping them finely or grinding them in the food processor ensured that they practically disappeared into the dish.

11. LOW-SODIUM SOY SAUCE: One secret weapon we turn to often in the test kitchen to boost savory, meaty flavor is soy sauce. And when you're cutting back on fat, you need to add depth and big flavor any way you can.

In this book, we call for it in everything from meatloaf to stuffed shells—even chicken pot pie. We also use it as a flavorful marinade for steak tips. Be sure to use low-sodium soy sauce to keep the salt level of your dishes in check.

12. LOW-SODIUM CHICKEN BROTH: We found that adding a bit of chicken broth to dishes like turkey tacos and scalloped potatoes was an easy way to add moisture and savory flavor to low-fat dishes. Our favorite brand is **Swanson Certified Organic Free Range Chicken Broth**.

13. CANOLA AND OLIVE OILS: Canola oil, one of the lowest in saturated fats, is our go-to oil for cooking, and olive oil is also a healthful choice. Canola oil has a high smoke point, making it great for sautéing. Extra-virgin olive oil adds rich flavor to salad dressings, sauces, and marinades, and when added judiciously to a dish before serving. Our favorite brand of extra-virgin olive oil is **Columela Extra-Virgin Olive Oil**; we also like **Lucini Italian Premium Select Extra-Virgin Olive Oil**. Canola oil has a neutral flavor so brand selection isn't terribly important.

14. COCOA POWDER: For big, chocolate flavor and intensity, without using a lot of chocolate, we turn to cocoa powder. Our chocolate cookies and warm fudge cakes call for a full cup for big flavor but not a ton of fat. Our favorite brand of cocoa powder is **Hershey's Cocoa Natural Unsweetened**.

Equipment Essentials

Sure, we keep the test kitchen well-stocked with a variety of pots and pans, good, sharp knives, and other essential tools. But when we had to revamp the recipes in this collection, these were our go-to items that we turned to again and again, plus our top-rated brands.

1. NONSTICK SKILLET: A nonstick skillet is a must-have in any kitchen, but especially when cooking lighter dishes. That's because the non-stick surface means you can use a minimum of oil while still developing a nicely golden exterior on your pork, beef, chicken, or anything else you're cooking. Our top-rated skillet is the **T-Fal Professional Total Non-Stick 12½-Inch Fry Pan** ($34.99), which has a wide cooking surface and a comfortable, oven-safe handle.

2. FOOD PROCESSOR: Many of our techniques for lightening recipes made use of the food processor. For example, to make a lighter meatloaf, we substituted mushrooms for some of the ground beef, but to ensure they disappeared into the loaf, we broke them down in the food processor. For our baked ziti and calzones, we used the food processor to turn cottage cheese and crackers into a smooth, creamy, and low-fat filling. Our favorite model is the **Cuisinart Custom 14-Cup Food Processor** ($199), which is easy to use and has a large capacity.

3. DIGITAL SCALE: A digital scale is an indispensable tool when watching fat and calories; we used it to weigh not only meat, fish, and poultry, but also flour and other baking ingredients.

In the test kitchen, our favorite digital scale is the **OXO Food Scale** ($49.99). We also like the Soehnle 65055 Digital Scale, which is our best buy and costs $34.95.

4. INSTANT-READ THERMOMETER: When you're cooking poultry and beef using less fat, taking the meat off the heat when it hits the right temperature is especially important and ensures that the interior stays tender and moist. Our top-rated thermometer is the **ThermoWorks Splash-Proof Super-Fast Thermapen** ($89); for a best buy, we like the ThermoWorks Super-Fast Pocket Thermometer ($19).

5. WIRE RACK: For oven-baked chicken, shrimp, and fish with crunchy, golden exteriors that mimic those of their deep-fried cousins, a wire rack is key; when elevated on a wire rack, these breaded foods stay crisp because the air circulates around them and they aren't left sitting in a pool of fat. The test kitchen's favorite brands are the **CIA Bakeware 12 by 17-Inch Cooling Rack** ($15.95) and the Libertyware Half-Size Sheet Pan Grate ($5.25), both of which fit into a standard 18 by 13-inch rimmed baking sheet.

Calculating the Nutritional Values of Our Recipes

Analyzing recipes for their nutritional values is a tricky business, and we did our best to be as realistic and accurate as possible throughout this book. When cooking and when calculating portion size, we were absolutely strict about measuring and never resorted to guessing or estimating. And we never made the portion sizes unreasonably small to make the nutritional numbers appear lower. We also didn't play games when analyzing the recipes in the nutritional program to make the numbers look better. We just tell it like it is.

Since for many of us our favorite comfort foods are the ones we splurge on when we order out, we decided to take a look at how the nutritional information for some of these recipes stacked up. Whether this means pizza, meaty lasagna, cobb salad, or New York–style cheesecake, we compared our makeover dishes with those from national restaurant chains, making sure our portion size and the components of the dish were similar, so we could be sure our makeovers were valid and sensible. To obtain the nutritional values of restaurant dishes, we either consulted the various restaurants' corporate web sites or requested these figures directly from their headquarters.

To calculate the nutritional values of our recipes, we used The Food Processor SQL by ESHA Research. When using this program, we entered all the ingredients in their raw form and used weights for important ingredients such as meat, cheese, and most vegetables. We also used all of our preferred brands in these analyses, and in some recipes have called out specific brands in the ingredient list. Yet there are two tricky ingredients to be mindful of when analyzing a recipe—salt and fat—and they require some special rules of their own.

Salt is tricky when analyzing a recipe because it is often used in unspecified amounts, or is added to cooking water that is then drained away. Here are the rules we used in order to be as accurate as possible. When the recipe called for seasoning food with an unspecified amount of salt and pepper (often for raw meat), we added ¼ teaspoon salt and ⅛ teaspoon pepper to the analysis. For food that was boiled in salted water then drained (as with pasta or blanched vegetables), we added ¼ teaspoon salt to the analysis to account for any that was absorbed during the boiling time. And if some of the salted cooking water was reserved and added back to the recipe, we added yet another ¼ teaspoon salt to the analysis. We did not, however, include additional salt or pepper in our analysis when the food was "seasoned to taste" at the end of cooking, or if the reserved salted cooking water was "added as needed."

As for fat, it can add up from some unexpected sources. For instance, take vegetable oil spray; we use it in lots of ways in this book—such as to coat bread crumbs (instead of browning them in oil), and to grease a baking dish. To account for its use, we added three seconds of vegetable oil spray to the analysis whenever it was used (except if specified otherwise in the recipe). Meat is another problematic source of fat because how you trim it has a big impact on the numbers; unless otherwise specified in the recipe, we trimmed away all visible fat.

So if you follow our ingredient lists and recipes carefully and accurately, and if you adhere to the portion sizes indicated by the yields and the serving specifics indicated in many of the recipes, we feel confident that our nutritional analyses will give you an accurate measurement of what you are consuming. You will find calorie and fat counts included with each recipe; for the complete nutritional information for all of our recipes, see pages 302–307.

BUFFALO WINGS

Appetizers
and Snacks

Nachos

Serves 8

☑ **WHY THIS RECIPE WORKS:** Nachos are typically piled high with cheese, refried beans, and sour cream. Tempting, yes, but a killer on the diet. Substituting reduced-fat cheddar for the full-fat version was one way to lighten our nachos. To make sure the cheese was evenly distributed, we found it best to lay out the chips and top each one separately. Swapping store-bought baked tortilla chips for the standard fried tortilla chips seemed like another obvious move, but the baked chips not only tasted like cardboard, they also became soggy once we added a few toppings. Our solution? Make our own. We cut corn tortillas into wedges, sprayed them with vegetable oil spray, sprinkled them with salt, and baked them until crisp. Topped with fat-free refried beans, sliced scallions, and jalapeños in addition to the cheese, our homemade chips stayed crunchy and offered great flavor. Greek yogurt made a great stand-in for the sour cream, providing a creamy counterpoint to the heat of the jalapeños, and just-made salsa added brightness.

12	**(6-inch) corn tortillas**
	Vegetable oil spray
	Salt
1	**(16-ounce) can fat-free refried beans**
4	**scallions, sliced thin**
8	**ounces 50 percent light cheddar cheese, shredded (2 cups)**
⅔	**cup jarred jalapeño slices**
2	**cups fresh tomato salsa**
½	**cup 0 percent Greek yogurt**

1. Adjust oven racks to upper-middle and lower-middle positions and heat oven to 350 degrees. Line 2 rimmed baking sheets with aluminum foil. Cut each tortilla into 4 wedges and arrange in single layer on prepared baking sheets. Evenly spray chips with oil spray for 5 seconds; flip chips over and spray second side with oil spray for 5 seconds. Season with salt. Bake chips until golden and crisp, about 20 minutes, switching and rotating sheets halfway through baking. Let cool.

2. Top each chip with refried beans, scallions, cheddar, and jalapeños (in that order). Bake nachos until cheese is melted, about 7 minutes. Transfer to platter; serve with salsa and yogurt.

ON THE SIDE FRESH TOMATO SALSA
Place 1 pound tomatoes, cored and cut into ½-inch dice, in large colander and let drain for 30 minutes. As tomatoes drain, layer 1 minced jalapeño, seeds reserved, ⅓ cup minced red onion, ½ teaspoon minced garlic, and 3 tablespoons minced fresh cilantro on top. Shake colander to drain off excess juice, then transfer to serving bowl. Season with salt, pepper, sugar, lime juice, and reserved chile seeds to taste. Makes 2 cups.

BEFORE NUMBERS BASED ON: **Classic Nachos from Chili's Grill and Bar**	BEFORE → **AFTER** 1 SERVING = 6 NACHOS	605 → **270** CALORIES	42.5 → **8** GRAMS FAT	22 → **3.5** GRAMS SAT FAT

Buffalo Wings

Serves 4

✔ **WHY THIS RECIPE WORKS:** Fried to a golden brown and tossed in a buttery hot sauce, Buffalo wings are about as far from health food as you can get. Luckily, we found a way to slash the fat and calories by about half—turning this barroom and game-day staple into a guilty pleasure we wouldn't feel so guilty about. Tossing the wings with baking powder helped to dry out the skin so it became crisp when roasted in a super-hot oven; baking the wings on a wire rack let the rendered fat drip away. A quick stint under the broiler crisped the skin even further and ensured a flavorful char. To lighten the sauce, we cut back on the butter. A single tablespoon was enough to temper the hot sauce and give it a glossy sheen. A spoonful of molasses added depth and richness to our made-over yet still finger-licking-good Buffalo wings. The mild flavor of Frank's RedHot Original Cayenne Pepper Sauce is crucial to the flavor of this dish; we don't suggest substituting other brands of hot sauce here.

3   pounds chicken wings, halved at joint and wingtips removed, trimmed

1   tablespoon baking powder

½   teaspoon salt

⅔   cup Frank's RedHot Original Cayenne Pepper Sauce

1   tablespoon unsalted butter, melted

1   tablespoon molasses

1. Adjust oven rack to middle position and heat oven to 475 degrees. Line rimmed baking sheet with aluminum foil and top with wire rack. Pat wings dry with paper towels, then toss with baking powder and salt in bowl. Arrange wings in single layer on wire rack. Roast wings until golden on both sides, about 40 minutes, flipping wings over and rotating sheet halfway through roasting.

2. Meanwhile, whisk hot sauce, butter, and molasses together in large bowl.

3. Remove wings from oven. Adjust oven rack 6 inches from broiler element and heat broiler. Broil wings until golden brown on both sides, 6 to 8 minutes, flipping wings over halfway through broiling. Add wings to sauce and toss to coat. Serve.

BEFORE NUMBERS BASED ON: Traditional Wings from Buffalo Wild Wings	BEFORE → **AFTER** 1 SERVING = 6 WINGS	670→**370** CALORIES	55→**25** GRAMS FAT	22→**8** GRAMS SAT FAT

MAKEOVER SPOTLIGHT: BUFFALO WINGS

1. CUT UP THE WINGS: Cutting up the wings made it easier to work with them and made them easier to eat. Using kitchen shears or a sharp chef's knife, cut through the wing at the two joints and discard the wingtip. (Sometimes, the butcher will even do this for you.)

2. USE BAKING POWDER TO GET CRISP SKIN: Before cooking our wings, we tossed them with baking powder and salt. The baking powder helped draw moisture from the skin so that it became super-crisp in the oven; the salt simply added flavor.

3. ELEVATE THE WINGS ON A RACK AND ROAST—DON'T FRY: To cook our Buffalo wings, we bypassed the vat of hot oil called for in traditional recipes and roasted our wings in a 475-degree oven instead. Cooking them on a wire rack set in a rimmed baking sheet ensured that the wings cooked through evenly and made it easy for the rendered fat to drain away.

4. BROIL FOR A CRISP FINISH AND TOSS WITH LOWER-FAT SAUCE: After roasting our wings in a hot oven, we turned to the broiler to guarantee super-crisp, well-browned skin before tossing them in our sauce. Though most recipes call for at least half a stick of butter in the sauce, we found that just a pat provided plenty of richness and sheen. Frank's RedHot Original Cayenne Pepper Sauce offered a mild, vinegary tang, while a bit of molasses added complexity.

Coconut Shrimp with Orange Dipping Sauce

Serves 6

✓ **WHY THIS RECIPE WORKS:** Take naturally low-fat shrimp, add a thick batter, a pile of sweetened coconut, and fry it all. The result? Coconut shrimp, a fat and calorie bomb with a tropical twist. To bring this dish back from the dark side, we knew we'd need to find another way to get that crisp, coconut-scented coating. Since frying was out, we opted for baking. Flaky panko, which we tossed with canola oil and toasted, baked up golden and crunchy in just minutes. As for the coconut, we found a little went a long way. Just ⅓ cup, mixed with the panko and toasted in the oven, did the trick. An orange dipping sauce, made with orange juice, marmalade, honey, and ginger, provided the perfect bright and tangy counterpoint to our crisp, golden coconut shrimp.

ORANGE DIPPING SAUCE

- ¾ **cup orange juice (2 oranges)**
- ¼ **cup orange marmalade**
- 1 **tablespoon honey**
- 2 **teaspoons cornstarch**
  Pinch ground ginger
  Pinch garlic powder
  Lemon juice
  Salt

COCONUT SHRIMP

- 1¾ **cups panko bread crumbs**
- 1 **tablespoon canola oil**
- ⅓ **cup sweetened shredded coconut**
- ⅓ **cup all-purpose flour**
- 4 **large egg whites**
- ½ **teaspoon salt**
- ¼ **teaspoon cayenne pepper**
  Vegetable oil spray
- 1½ **pounds extra-large shrimp (21 to 25 per pound), peeled and deveined**

1. FOR THE ORANGE DIPPING SAUCE: Whisk juice, marmalade, honey, cornstarch, ginger, and garlic powder together in small saucepan. Bring to simmer over medium-high heat, whisking constantly. Reduce heat to medium-low and simmer gently, whisking often, until slightly thickened, 3 to 5 minutes. Off heat, season with lemon juice and salt to taste; let cool.

2. FOR THE COCONUT SHRIMP: Adjust oven rack to middle position and heat oven to 475 degrees. Toss panko with oil, spread onto rimmed baking sheet, and bake until light golden, about 7 minutes. Stir in coconut and continue to bake until crumbs and coconut are deep golden, about 2 minutes longer; let cool slightly.

3. Spread flour into shallow dish. In second shallow dish, lightly beat egg whites until foamy. In third shallow dish, combine panko-coconut mixture, salt, and cayenne. Line rimmed baking sheet with aluminum foil, top with wire rack, and spray rack with oil spray.

4. Pat shrimp dry with paper towels. Working with several shrimp at a time, dredge in flour, dip in egg whites, then coat with panko-coconut mixture, pressing gently to adhere; lay on prepared wire rack. Spray shrimp with oil spray and bake until shrimp are just cooked through, 5 to 7 minutes. Serve with orange dipping sauce.

BEFORE NUMBERS BASED ON:	BEFORE → **AFTER**	530 → **290**	36 → **5**	9 → **2**
Parrot Isle Jumbo Coconut Shrimp from Red Lobster	1 SERVING = 6 SHRIMP	**CALORIES**	**GRAMS FAT**	**GRAMS SAT FAT**

Mozzarella Sticks

Serves 4

✔ **WHY THIS RECIPE WORKS:** Most recipes for mozzarella sticks call for simply breading the cheese and tossing it in the deep-fryer. We found that ditching the deep-fryer in favor of the oven was an easy fix, but further reducing the fat and calories required some ingenuity. Neither part-skim nor reduced-fat block mozzarella delivered the salty, tangy flavor and gooey, stretchy texture we wanted in our makeover mozzarella sticks. Luckily, we found another alternative: string cheese. With its cylindrical shape, string cheese made prep super-easy, and in the oven the sticks held their shape longer than cheese we'd cut ourselves. Light, crispy panko, tossed with dried basil and oregano, gave us a crisp, flavorful exterior, and egg whites (we ditched the yolks) helped the coating adhere and kept fat to a minimum. A quick hit of vegetable oil spray ensured the panko baked up ultra-crunchy. Serve with Low-Fat Tomato Sauce (page 135).

¼ **cup all-purpose flour**
¾ **teaspoon garlic powder**
⅛ **teaspoon cayenne pepper**
2 **large egg whites**
1 **cup panko bread crumbs, toasted**
½ **teaspoon dried basil**
¼ **teaspoon dried oregano**
¼ **teaspoon salt**
8 **ounces reduced-fat mozzarella string cheese sticks, cut into 2-inch lengths**
Vegetable oil spray

1. Adjust oven rack to middle position and heat oven to 475 degrees. Combine flour, garlic powder, and cayenne in shallow dish. In second shallow dish, whisk egg whites until foamy. In third shallow dish, combine toasted panko, basil, oregano, and salt.

2. Working with several pieces of cheese at a time, dredge in flour mixture, dip in egg whites, then coat with panko mixture, pressing gently to adhere; lay on large plate. Freeze breaded mozzarella until chilled and firm, about 30 minutes.

3. Line rimmed baking sheet with aluminum foil and spray with oil spray. Lay chilled cheese on prepared sheet and spray with oil spray. Bake until cheese is hot, 8 to 10 minutes. Serve.

QUICK PREP TIP **TOASTING PANKO**
We use toasted panko bread crumbs in a number of recipes in this book. Not only does toasted panko make a terrific coating for faux fried foods (as in our Mozzarella Sticks), but it also is a great binder in fillings and stuffings (as in our Clams Casino, page 26, and Baked Stuffed Shrimp, page 160). Although panko has a super-crisp texture right out of the package, it is both pale and bland-tasting. Luckily, this is easily remedied by toasting it. When toasting panko, you have two options: the stovetop or the oven. To toast panko on the stovetop, place it in a 12-inch nonstick skillet and toast it over medium-high heat, stirring often, until well browned, 5 to 10 minutes. To toast panko in the oven, spread it over a rimmed baking sheet and bake in a 475-degree oven until well browned, 7 to 10 minutes.

BEFORE NUMBERS BASED ON: Fried Cheese Sticks from Pizza Hut	BEFORE → **AFTER** 1 SERVING = 4 MOZZARELLA STICKS	310 → **230** **CALORIES**	19.5 → **7** **GRAMS FAT**	7.3 → **4** **GRAMS SAT FAT**

Herbed Deviled Eggs

Serves 6

✔ **WHY THIS RECIPE WORKS:** An essential part of any picnic or cookout, deviled eggs are easy to make, requiring just a handful of ingredients. But those few ingredients—eggs, mayonnaise, mustard, and a few flavorings—don't leave many opportunities for lightening. Swapping in light mayonnaise for the full-fat stuff was an easy starting point, but we knew we could do better than that. For our next move, we took out some of the egg yolks and replaced them with low-fat cottage cheese. Pressing the cottage cheese through a fine-mesh strainer ensured our filling stayed smooth and creamy. A pinch of turmeric reinforced the golden hue of the yolks, and chopped herbs added fresh flavor. For a traditional look, dust the filled eggs with paprika.

6	**large eggs**
¼	**cup 1 percent low-fat cottage cheese**
2	**tablespoons light mayonnaise**
1	**tablespoon minced fresh parsley, chives, or cilantro**
1	**tablespoon warm tap water**
½	**teaspoon white wine vinegar**
½	**teaspoon Dijon mustard**
⅛	**teaspoon turmeric**
⅛	**teaspoon ground coriander**
⅛	**teaspoon salt**
⅛	**teaspoon pepper**

1. Place eggs in medium saucepan, cover with 1 inch water, and bring to boil over high heat. Remove pan from heat, cover, and let stand for 10 minutes. Fill large bowl with ice water. Pour off water from saucepan and gently shake pan back and forth to lightly crack shells. Transfer eggs to ice water, let cool for 5 minutes, then peel.

2. Halve eggs lengthwise. Transfer 3 yolks to fine-mesh strainer set over medium bowl (reserve remaining yolks for another use or discard). Arrange whites on large serving platter. Using spatula, press yolks and cottage cheese through fine-mesh strainer into bowl.

3. Stir in mayonnaise, parsley, water, vinegar, mustard, turmeric, coriander, salt, and pepper until well combined and smooth. Transfer mixture to pastry bag fitted with star tip (or zipper-lock bag with corner snipped off) and pipe mixture into whites. Serve.

QUICK PREP TIP
MAKING DEVILED EGGS
A piping bag can make quick work of filling deviled eggs. But if you don't have one, simply substitute a zipper-lock bag. Spoon the filling into the bag and push it down into one corner. Use scissors to snip off the corner of the bag, then squeeze the filling into each egg.

BEFORE → **AFTER**	130 → **60**	11 → **3.5**	2.5 → **1**
1 SERVING = 2 DEVILED EGGS	**CALORIES**	**GRAMS FAT**	**GRAMS SAT FAT**

Crab Rangoon

Serves 8

✔ **WHY THIS RECIPE WORKS:** Now a staple in Chinese restaurants, crab rangoon was first made famous at the Polynesian-style restaurant Trader Vic's in San Francisco. But no matter its ethnicity, the crispy fried wonton pouches, stuffed with a filling of cream cheese and crabmeat, have become a takeout favorite. Most restaurants go heavy on the cream cheese and minimize the crab—a strategy that ups the fat and calorie counts—but we switched the proportions and packed our version with sweet, delicate crabmeat and a lesser amount of reduced-fat cream cheese. Achieving a crispy exterior was a challenge. Deep-frying was out from the get-go, and baking the rangoon was a flop because the rounded shape of the filled wonton wrappers prevented even browning and kept our rangoon from becoming crisp in the oven. Our unconventional twist was to make wonton "cups" that we baked in a mini muffin tin before filling them with our cream cheese and crab mixture. Sprinkled with sliced scallion greens, our open-faced crab rangoon were a fresher, lighter take on a typically heavy takeout dish.

Vegetable oil spray
16 wonton wrappers
4 ounces lump crabmeat, picked over for shells
3 ounces ⅓ less fat cream cheese (neufchatel), softened
1 scallion, white part sliced thin, green part sliced thin on bias
1 teaspoon grated fresh ginger
¾ teaspoon low-sodium soy sauce

1. Adjust oven rack to middle position and heat oven to 350 degrees. Spray mini muffin tin with oil spray. Gently press wonton wrappers into tins, making sure bottoms and sides are flush with tin; let edges of wrapper extend out of cups. Lightly spray wrappers with oil spray and bake until lightly browned, 6 to 9 minutes; let cool slightly.

2. Combine crabmeat, cream cheese, scallion whites, ginger, and soy sauce in bowl. Using small spoon, fill each wonton cup with 2 teaspoons filling. Bake until filling is heated through, 6 to 8 minutes. Sprinkle with scallion greens and serve.

QUICK PREP TIP
MAKING WONTON CUPS
Gently press each wonton wrapper into greased mini muffin tin until flush with bottom and sides of tin; press out any air bubbles and unnecessary folds. Then lightly spray wonton cups with vegetable oil spray and bake until lightly browned.

BEFORE NUMBERS BASED ON:	BEFORE → **AFTER**	163 → **80**	10 → **3**	4 → **1.5**
Crab Wontons from **P.F. Chang's China Bistro**	1 SERVING = 2 CRAB RANGOON	CALORIES	GRAMS FAT	GRAMS SAT FAT

Stuffed Jalapeños

Serves 8

✓ **WHY THIS RECIPE WORKS:** Classic bar food, stuffed jalapeños are spicy chiles that are loaded up with cheese before being battered and deep-fried. To make this appetizer more figure-friendly, we replaced the batter with bread crumbs and turned to the oven. A blanket of panko, toasted and sprinkled over the filling, provided so much crunch that tasters didn't even notice that our stuffed jalapeños were coated on the top only. A blend of reduced-fat cheeses delivered the best flavor and texture: Cheddar gave our filling its savory, cheesy flavor, while cream cheese contributed creaminess and a hint of tang. Scallions and chili powder livened things up, and a bit of lime juice added brightness to this revamped bar snack.

12   medium jalapeño chiles, preferably with stems

6   ounces 50 percent light cheddar cheese, shredded (1½ cups)

4   ounces ⅓ less fat cream cheese (neufchatel), softened

2   scallions, chopped fine

2   teaspoons lime juice

1   teaspoon chili powder

½   teaspoon salt

½   cup panko bread crumbs, toasted (see page 18)

    Vegetable oil spray

1. Adjust oven rack to middle position and heat oven to 350 degrees. Line rimmed baking sheet with aluminum foil.

2. Cut each jalapeño in half lengthwise through stem; remove ribs and seeds. Combine cheddar, cream cheese, scallions, lime juice, chili powder, and salt in bowl. Spoon cheese mixture evenly into jalapeños and transfer to prepared sheet. Top with toasted panko and spray lightly with oil spray. Bake until hot, 15 to 20 minutes. Serve.

QUICK PREP TIP
SEEDING JALAPEÑOS
To remove seeds and ribs from jalapeño, cut it in half lengthwise. Then, starting at end opposite stem, use melon baller to scoop down inside of each half.

BEFORE NUMBERS BASED ON: Cream Cheese Stuffed Jalapeños from T.G.I. Friday's	BEFORE → **AFTER** 1 SERVING = 3 STUFFED JALAPEÑOS	220 → **120** CALORIES	15 → **7** GRAMS FAT	6 → **4.5** GRAMS SAT FAT

Vegetable Egg Rolls

Serves 8

☑ **WHY THIS RECIPE WORKS:** Super-crisp and golden brown, egg rolls seem to be the ultimate takeout dish. But in reality, they tend to have an overly greasy exterior and a filling that's lackluster and soggy. Our challenge in remaking this dish was twofold: get a crisp exterior without the aid of a deep-fryer or copious amounts of oil, and build a flavorful filling that retained some bite. Starting with the filling, we skipped the fatty pork found in many egg rolls and stuck with just veggies. Napa cabbage, carrot, and scallion provided a nice crunch and freshness. Precooked fillings ended up soggy and bland in our egg rolls, so we simply tossed the vegetables with a warm dressing—this was enough to wilt them slightly. When attempts at baking the egg rolls failed to achieve a crisp exterior, we took a hint from recipes for pan-fried dumplings: We sautéed the egg rolls in a small amount of oil so they'd brown, added water and steamed them until cooked through, and finally uncovered the pan so the moisture could evaporate and the egg rolls could become crisp. Serve with duck sauce or sweet and sour sauce.

3   **cups finely shredded napa cabbage**
1   **small carrot, peeled and shredded**
1   **scallion, sliced thin**
1½   **tablespoons low-sodium soy sauce**
1½   **teaspoons Chinese rice wine or dry sherry**
1   **teaspoon toasted sesame oil**
1   **teaspoon sugar**
1   **garlic clove, minced**
½   **teaspoon grated fresh ginger**
8   **egg roll wrappers**
5   **teaspoons canola oil**
½   **cup hot tap water**

1. Combine cabbage, carrot, and scallion in large bowl. In separate bowl microwave soy sauce, rice wine, sesame oil, sugar, garlic, and ginger until hot, about 30 seconds; stir to dissolve sugar. Pour hot soy mixture over vegetables and toss to combine.

2. Working with 1 egg roll wrapper at a time, place wrapper on cutting board with 1 corner pointing toward you. Place 3 tablespoons cabbage mixture in center of wrapper. Fold bottom of wrapper over filling, then fold in sides. Brush remaining corner of wrapper with water, then roll egg roll up into tight, tidy bundle.

3. Heat canola oil in 12-inch nonstick skillet over medium-high heat until shimmering. Add egg rolls, seam side down, and cook until lightly browned on all sides, about 2 minutes. Carefully pour hot water around egg rolls. Cover and cook until most of liquid is absorbed, about 3 minutes. Uncover and continue to cook until rolls are crisp on all sides, 3 to 5 minutes longer. Serve.

BEFORE NUMBERS BASED ON: Vegetable Egg Roll from Asian Chao	BEFORE → **AFTER** 1 SERVING = 1 EGG ROLL	170 → **100** CALORIES	10 → **3.5** GRAMS FAT	2 → **0** GRAMS SAT FAT

MAKEOVER SPOTLIGHT: EGG ROLLS

1. LOAD UP ON VEGGIES FOR A LIGHTER, YET STILL FLAVORFUL, FILLING: Most egg rolls include pork, which can rack up the fat grams, but we opted for an all-vegetable filling of carrot, cabbage, and scallion. Instead of cooking the mixture beforehand, which can lead to a soggy, limp filling, we tossed our vegetables in a warm dressing (made in just seconds in the microwave) to wilt them slightly. Garlic, ginger, soy sauce, and sesame oil added big flavor to the dressing.

2. MAKE TIGHT AND TIDY EGG ROLLS: Assembling an egg roll is easy, but it's important to use authentic egg roll wrappers (found at most grocery stores in either the refrigerated or produce sections) and make uniform egg rolls so that they cook through properly. After positioning the wrapper with one corner pointing toward you, place the cabbage mixture in the center of the wrapper. Fold the bottom of the wrapper up over the filling, then fold in the sides.

3. SEAL EGG ROLLS WITH WATER: To hold the egg roll together in the pan, brush the remaining corner of the wrapper with water, then roll the egg roll up into a tight, tidy bundle. The water acts like glue to keep the egg roll tightly sealed during cooking and prevent it from unraveling.

4. SKIP THE DEEP-FRYER—COOK THE EGG ROLLS IN A PAN: Eggs rolls are usually deep-fried, which turns the wrapper crisp and cooks the filling. But we found that a combination of browning and steaming the rolls in a nonstick skillet worked just as well. The key was to brown the rolls first, while the wrappers were still firm and dry. Once they were browned, we simply added some hot water to the pan and covered it to steam the egg rolls and make them tender. Then, we removed the lid to evaporate the excess water and allow the wrappers to become crisp before serving.

Clams Casino

Serves 6

✔ **WHY THIS RECIPE WORKS:** A popular dish found on many a steakhouse menu, clams casino is a broiled appetizer topped with butter, bacon, and bread crumbs. But most of the time, the clams take a backseat in this dish—one recipe we found called for a cup of butter and almost half a pound of bacon. The problem with all this richness (besides the shockingly high fat and calorie counts) is that the sweet, briny flavor of the clams is completely obscured. We found we could scale back to just a few tablespoons of butter for our version; this reduction allowed the flavor of the clams to really take center stage. Minced bell pepper and shallots further amplified the fresh feel of our dish. Rather than covering our clams with bland bread crumbs, we added toasted panko to the topping to help bring the elements together. Finally, we trimmed the fat (literally) by ditching the traditional bacon in favor of lean turkey bacon, which gave every bite a hit of smoky, salty flavor. Baking the clams on a wire rack kept them from tipping over when moved to the oven.

3 slices turkey bacon, chopped fine

⅓ cup minced green bell pepper

2 shallots, minced

⅓ cup minced fresh parsley

¼ cup panko bread crumbs, toasted (see page 18)

3 tablespoons unsalted butter, softened

2 teaspoons lemon juice

⅛ teaspoon salt

¼ teaspoon pepper

24 littleneck clams, scrubbed, shucked, and left on the half shell

1. Cook bacon in 10-inch nonstick skillet over medium-high heat until crisp, about 5 minutes. Stir in bell pepper and shallots and cook until softened, 3 to 5 minutes. Transfer to bowl and let cool briefly. Stir in parsley, toasted panko, butter, lemon juice, salt, and pepper.

2. Adjust oven rack 8 inches from broiler element and heat broiler. Line rimmed baking sheet with aluminum foil and top with wire rack. Arrange clams on wire rack, top with bacon mixture, and pack mixture down gently. Broil until top is browned and clams are heated through, 3 to 5 minutes. Serve.

QUICK PREP TIP SHUCKING CLAMS

Place clam in kitchen towel-lined hand with hinge side facing fingers. Using clam knife (or butter knife), press side of blade through center of hinge; use your towel-wrapped fingers to help apply force to knife. Once blade breaks through hinge, swing knife down through clam and rotate blade to pry apart shells. Carefully cut clam free of shells, then twist off and discard top shell. Try to keep bottom shell level to reserve flavorful clam liquor.

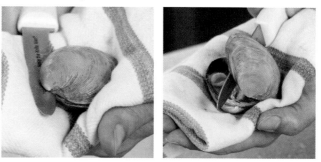

BEFORE → **AFTER**	370 → **160**	33 → **9**	20 → **4.5**
1 SERVING = 4 CLAMS	CALORIES	GRAMS FAT	GRAMS SAT FAT

Hot Spinach Dip

Serves 12

✓ **WHY THIS RECIPE WORKS:** Rich, creamy, and topped with a layer of buttery bread crumbs, spinach dip rarely has time to cool down before it's devoured at parties. But with an ingredient list that includes mayonnaise, sour cream, and cream cheese, this dip was in serious need of an overhaul. First, we looked to amp up the flavor with aromatics. Sautéing our spinach with onion, bell pepper, garlic, and fresh thyme gave our dip a nice foundation. For the creamy base, we found a combination of reduced-fat cream cheese and light mayonnaise added just the right blend of creaminess and tang—no need for sour cream. Reduced-fat cheddar added more cheesy flavor. For the topping, we liked super-crisp panko bread crumbs, but the butter had to go. Tossing the panko with Parmesan cheese gave it some nutty, savory oomph, and coating it with vegetable oil spray contributed richness.

Vegetable oil spray
2 teaspoons olive oil
1 onion, chopped fine
1 red bell pepper, stemmed, seeded, and chopped fine
1 (16-ounce) package frozen spinach (do not thaw)
2 garlic cloves, minced
2 teaspoons minced fresh thyme
1 cup light mayonnaise
4 ounces ⅓ less fat cream cheese (neufchatel), softened
2 ounces 50 percent light cheddar cheese, shredded (½ cup)
2 tablespoons lemon juice
   Pinch cayenne pepper
   Salt and pepper
½ cup panko bread crumbs, toasted (see page 18)
2 tablespoons grated Parmesan cheese

1. Adjust oven rack to middle position and heat oven to 375 degrees. Lightly spray 8-inch square baking dish with oil spray.

2. Heat oil in 12-inch nonstick skillet over medium-high heat until shimmering. Add onion and bell pepper and cook until softened, about 6 minutes. Add spinach and cook until defrosted and liquid evaporates, about 10 minutes. Stir in garlic and thyme and cook until fragrant, about 1 minute; transfer to food processor.

3. Pulse spinach mixture, mayonnaise, cream cheese, cheddar, lemon juice, and cayenne together in food processor until coarsely chopped, about 10 pulses. Season with salt and pepper to taste.

4. Scrape mixture into prepared dish. Toss toasted panko with Parmesan in bowl, then sprinkle over top and spray with oil spray. Bake until hot, about 20 minutes. Serve.

| BEFORE → **AFTER** | 220 → **120** | 18 → **9** | 12 → **3** |
| 1 SERVING = ⅓ CUP | CALORIES | GRAMS FAT | GRAMS SAT FAT |

Roasted Artichoke Dip

Serves 10

✓ **WHY THIS RECIPE WORKS:** For a flavorful artichoke dip that would fool partygoers into thinking it was the real full-fat deal, we began by putting the artichokes front and center. Opting for frozen artichokes (canned artichokes have a tinny flavor, and fresh artichokes are too much work for such a simple starter), we built flavor from the get-go by roasting them to a golden brown. After they cooled, we chopped them into bite-size pieces—perfect for being scooped up with a cracker. Sautéed onion and garlic added even more flavor. A combination of light mayo and reduced-fat cream cheese gave our dip some richness and a creamy texture, while a bit of grated Parmesan offered nutty, cheesy flavor. A spoonful of lemon juice added a bit of acidity to our rich and creamy artichoke dip.

Vegetable oil spray
2　(9-ounce) boxes frozen artichokes (do not thaw)
2　teaspoons olive oil
　　Salt and pepper
1　onion, chopped fine
2　garlic cloves, minced
1　cup light mayonnaise
4　ounces ⅓ less fat cream cheese (neufchatel), softened
1　ounce Parmesan cheese, grated (½ cup), plus 2 tablespoons
1　tablespoon lemon juice
1　tablespoon minced fresh thyme
　　Pinch cayenne pepper
½　cup panko bread crumbs, toasted (see page 18)

1. Adjust oven rack to middle position and heat oven to 450 degrees. Lightly spray 8-inch square baking dish with oil spray.

2. Line rimmed baking sheet with aluminum foil. Toss artichokes with 1 teaspoon oil, ½ teaspoon salt, and ¼ teaspoon pepper in bowl and spread over prepared sheet. Roast until artichokes are browned at edges, 20 to 25 minutes, rotating baking sheet halfway through baking. Let artichokes cool, then chop coarse. Reduce oven temperature to 400 degrees.

3. Meanwhile, heat remaining 1 teaspoon oil in 12-inch nonstick skillet over medium-high heat until shimmering. Add onion and ½ teaspoon salt and cook until softened, about 5 minutes. Stir in garlic and cook until fragrant, about 30 seconds; transfer to large bowl and let cool slightly.

4. Stir mayonnaise, cream cheese, ½ cup Parmesan, lemon juice, thyme, and cayenne into onion mixture. Gently fold in chopped artichokes and season with salt and pepper to taste. Scrape mixture into prepared baking dish.

5. Toss toasted panko with remaining 2 tablespoons Parmesan in bowl, then sprinkle over top and spray with oil spray. Bake until hot, about 20 minutes. Serve.

BEFORE → **AFTER**	310 → **150**	28 → **11**	7 → **3.5**
1 SERVING = ¼ CUP	CALORIES	GRAMS FAT	GRAMS SAT FAT

Seven-Layer Dip

Serves 12

✔ **WHY THIS RECIPE WORKS:** With its Tex-Mex flavors and contrasting textures, this classic dip is a regular on the party circuit. But hang out by the bowl too long, and you'll quickly run up a high tab of fat and calories before you know it. To make over our seven-layer dip, we started by ditching two of the usual layers, which we found to be unnecessary: shredded cheese seemed an extraneous element in such a rich dip, and canned black olives had a tinny, metallic flavor no matter how many times we rinsed them. We then focused on infusing our dish with bright, fresh flavors, and made our own refried beans and pico de gallo instead of using canned or jarred varieties. Rather than omit the fat-laden guacamole entirely, we simply used a little less—two avocados, mashed with lime juice and salt, provided plenty of richness. For the creamy layer, we reached for low-fat sour cream and amped up its flavor with spicy chipotles. Finally, we topped the whole thing with thinly sliced scallions. Sure, our revamped dip is two layers short—but it's so good, no one will even notice.

2 pounds tomatoes, cored, seeded, and chopped
  Salt
6 scallions, 2 minced and 4, green parts only, sliced thin
5 tablespoons plus 2 teaspoons lime juice (3 limes)
3 tablespoons minced fresh cilantro
2 jalapeño chiles, stemmed, seeded, and minced
1 (15-ounce) can black beans, drained (do not rinse)
2 garlic cloves, minced
¾ teaspoon chili powder
2 avocados, halved, pitted, and cubed
1½ cups low-fat sour cream
1 tablespoon minced canned chipotle chile in adobo sauce

1. Toss tomatoes with ½ teaspoon salt in bowl and let drain in fine-mesh strainer until tomatoes begin to soften, about 30 minutes; discard drained liquid. Transfer drained tomatoes to medium bowl and stir in minced scallions, 2 tablespoons lime juice, cilantro, and jalapeños. Season with salt to taste.

2. Pulse 2 teaspoons lime juice, beans, garlic, and chili powder together into chunky paste in food processor, about 7 pulses; season with salt to taste. In separate bowl, mash avocados, remaining 3 tablespoons lime juice, and ¼ teaspoon salt together with potato masher until smooth; season with salt to taste. In separate bowl, whisk sour cream and chipotle together.

3. Spread processed bean mixture evenly over bottom of 8-inch square baking dish or 1-quart glass bowl. Spread avocado mixture evenly over top, followed by sour cream mixture. Top with tomato mixture and sprinkle with sliced scallions. Serve.

BEFORE → **AFTER**	310 → **130**	25 → **7**	11 → **0.5**
1 SERVING = ⅓ CUP	CALORIES	GRAMS FAT	GRAMS SAT FAT

Pita Chips

Serves 8

✔ **WHY THIS RECIPE WORKS:** Pita chips may sound like a healthy alternative to potato chips, but some packaged brands can be just as high in fat and calories as regular old chips made from spuds. Luckily, making pita chips at home is fast and easy, and we found that baking gave us the same crisp texture as frying. Brushing the chips with oil before popping them in the oven to encourage crisping and browning didn't work—we ended up using too much oil, and it was hard to make sure the pitas were evenly covered. Switching to olive oil spray enabled us to coat our chips evenly and kept the fat count down. A sprinkling of salt gave us flavorful pita chips that were just as hard to resist as the store-bought variety.

4 (6- to 7-inch) pita breads
Olive or vegetable oil spray
Salt

1. Adjust oven racks to upper-middle and lower-middle positions and heat oven to 350 degrees. Using kitchen shears, cut around perimeter of each pita to yield 2 thin rounds. Cut each pita round into 6 wedges and arrange in single layer over 2 rimmed baking sheets. Evenly spray chips with oil spray for 5 seconds; flip chips over and spray second side with oil spray for 5 seconds. Season with salt.

2. Bake chips until they begin to crisp and brown lightly, 8 to 10 minutes. Remove sheets from oven, flip chips over, and continue to bake until chips are fully toasted, 8 to 10 minutes longer. Let cool before serving.

QUICK PREP TIP MAKING PITA CHIPS
Using kitchen shears, cut around perimeter of each pita bread to yield 2 thin rounds. Stack pita rounds and, using chef's knife, cut into 6 wedges each.

BEFORE NUMBERS BASED ON: Stacy's Naked Pita Chips	BEFORE → **AFTER** 1 SERVING = 6 CHIPS	130→**80** CALORIES	5→**0** GRAMS FAT	0.5→**0** GRAMS SAT FAT

Caramelized Onion Dip

Serves 12

✔ **WHY THIS RECIPE WORKS:** To make over this popular dip, we switched to low-fat sour cream and ditched the mayo in favor of cottage cheese, which we processed until smooth. Cider vinegar and Worcestershire sauce added depth of flavor. When browning the onion in step 1 be careful to watch for scorching.

2	tablespoons extra-virgin olive oil
1	onion, chopped fine
½	teaspoon light brown sugar
	Salt and pepper
8	ounces (1 cup) 1 percent low-fat cottage cheese
¼	cup boiling water
1	cup low-fat sour cream
1	tablespoon cider vinegar
⅛	teaspoon Worcestershire sauce
2	scallions, sliced thin

1. Heat 1 tablespoon oil in 8-inch nonstick skillet over medium-high heat until shimmering. Add onion, sugar, and ¼ teaspoon salt; cook until softened, about 5 minutes. Reduce heat to medium-low and cook, stirring often, until onion is golden and caramelized, about 20 minutes. Let cool slightly.

2. Process cottage cheese and boiling water together in blender until smooth, about 30 seconds. Add remaining 1 tablespoon oil, sour cream, vinegar, Worcestershire, ¼ teaspoon salt, and ⅛ teaspoon pepper; process until combined, about 30 seconds.

3. Transfer processed cheese mixture to bowl; stir in caramelized onion and scallions. Cover; refrigerate until flavors have blended, about 1 hour. Season with salt and pepper to taste. Serve.

BEFORE → **AFTER**	170 → **60**	16 → **3.5**	4 → **0**
1 SERVING = 3 TABLESPOONS	CALORIES	GRAMS FAT	GRAMS SAT FAT

Ranch Dip

Serves 12

✔ **WHY THIS RECIPE WORKS:** Cottage cheese and sour cream, blended until smooth, made the perfect creamy base for another low-fat dip. The trio of dill, cilantro, and scallions, plus a bit of garlic powder, gave this lightened starter that utterly addictive ranch flavor.

8	ounces (1 cup) 1 percent low-fat cottage cheese
2	tablespoons boiling water
1	cup low-fat sour cream
2	scallions, sliced thin
1	tablespoon extra-virgin olive oil
1	teaspoon garlic powder
	Salt and pepper
2	tablespoons minced fresh cilantro
1	tablespoon minced fresh dill

1. Process cottage cheese and boiling water together in blender until smooth, about 30 seconds. Add sour cream, scallions, oil, garlic powder, ¼ teaspoon salt, and ⅛ teaspoon pepper; process until combined, about 30 seconds.

2. Transfer processed cheese mixture to bowl and stir in cilantro and dill. Cover and refrigerate until flavors have blended, about 1 hour. Season with salt and pepper to taste. Serve.

BEFORE → **AFTER**	180 → **50**	19 → **2.5**	4.5 → **0**
1 SERVING = 3 TABLESPOONS	CALORIES	GRAMS FAT	GRAMS SAT FAT

Bacon-Scallion Cheese Ball

Serves 16

✔ **WHY THIS RECIPE WORKS:** For a modern-day take on the classic retro cheese ball, we decided to incorporate the flavors of bacon and scallions. Most cheese balls call for a mix of cheddar cheese, mayonnaise, and cream cheese, but when we subbed in the reduced-fat versions, we ended up with a crumbly, not smooth and creamy, cheese ball. Swapping out the cheddar for goat cheese, a naturally lower-fat cheese, solved the problem. The duo of goat cheese and reduced-fat cream cheese gave our cheese ball a creamy, spreadable texture and nice, tangy flavor—and allowed us to cut the mayo from our recipe altogether. A clove of minced garlic and some onion powder amped up the savory notes. While bacon sounds ominous in terms of fat—especially when paired with cheese—a little proved to go a long way. We needed only one slice, crumbled, to provide identity and smoky flavor to this lightened appetizer. As for the scallions, we saved them until the end for coating our cheese ball. This picture-perfect starter was now ready for any get-together.

1	**slice bacon**
8	**ounces goat cheese, crumbled (2 cups)**
8	**ounces ⅓ less fat cream cheese (neufchatel), softened**
3	**tablespoons minced fresh parsley**
3	**tablespoons minced fresh cilantro or dill**
1	**garlic clove, minced**
1	**teaspoon lemon juice**
½	**teaspoon onion powder**
⅛	**teaspoon salt**
	Pinch sugar
4	**scallions, sliced thin**

1. Cook bacon in 10-inch nonstick skillet over medium-high heat until crisp, about 5 minutes; transfer to paper towel–lined plate, let cool slightly, then crumble.

2. Process goat cheese, cream cheese, parsley, cilantro, bacon, garlic, lemon juice, onion powder, salt, and sugar together in food processor until smooth, about 20 seconds. Transfer cheese mixture to center of large sheet of plastic wrap. Holding 4 corners of plastic in one hand, twist cheese with other hand to seal plastic and shape cheese into rough ball. Place in small bowl and refrigerate until firm, about 4 hours.

3. Once cheese ball is firm, reshape as necessary to form smooth ball. Unwrap and roll in scallions to coat. Let sit at room temperature for 15 minutes. Serve.

QUICK PREP TIP
SHAPING A CHEESE BALL
Transfer processed cheese mixture to center of large sheet of plastic wrap. Holding 4 corners of plastic in one hand, twist cheese with other hand to shape into rough ball. Place in bowl and put in refrigerator to firm up.

BEFORE → **AFTER**	140 → **80**	13 → **6**	7 → **4**
1 SERVING = 2 TABLESPOONS	CALORIES	GRAMS FAT	GRAMS SAT FAT

Pimento Cheese

Serves 12

✔ **WHY THIS RECIPE WORKS:** Nothing says Southern comfort food like pimento cheese slathered on white bread or buttery crackers. Trading the full-fat cheddar for the reduced-fat variety gave us a spread lacking in creaminess. To smooth it out, we turned to an unconventional ingredient: nonfat Greek yogurt. Light mayonnaise added richness, while garlic, Worcestershire sauce, and hot sauce brought some complexity and a touch of heat. If you can't find jarred pimentos, an equal amount of roasted red peppers may be substituted.

1 (4-ounce) jar pimento peppers, drained and patted dry (½ cup)

6 tablespoons light mayonnaise

2 garlic cloves, minced

1½ teaspoons Worcestershire sauce

1 teaspoon hot sauce, plus extra for serving

1 pound 50 percent light cheddar cheese, shredded (4 cups)

½ cup 0 percent Greek yogurt

Salt and pepper

Process pimento peppers, mayonnaise, garlic, Worcestershire, and hot sauce together in food processor until smooth, about 20 seconds. Add cheddar and yogurt and pulse until uniformly blended, with fine bits of cheese throughout, about 25 pulses. Season with salt, pepper, and extra hot sauce to taste. Serve.

BEFORE → **AFTER** 1 SERVING = ¼ CUP	290 → **120** CALORIES	25 → **8** GRAMS FAT	14 → **4.5** GRAMS SAT FAT

Parmesan Popcorn

Serves 5

✔ **WHY THIS RECIPE WORKS:** We found a way to add real cheese flavor to our popcorn without making this snack a high-fat no-no. To cook the popcorn, we simply combined it with a tablespoon of water in a pot on the stovetop—no oil necessary—and shook the pot over the heat while the kernels popped away. For the cheese, we preferred grated Parmesan; a mere half-cup contributed plenty of nutty, savory flavor. A spritz of olive oil spray added some much-needed richness. Stirring in the cheese and then covering the pot trapped residual heat so that the Parmesan melted evenly and gave every bite intense cheesy flavor.

1 ounce Parmesan cheese, grated (½ cup)

¾ teaspoon salt

1 tablespoon water

½ cup popcorn kernels

Olive or vegetable oil spray

1. Combine Parmesan and salt in bowl. Heat Dutch oven over medium-high heat for 2 minutes. Add water and popcorn, cover, and cook, shaking pot frequently, until first few kernels begin to pop. Continue to cook, shaking vigorously, until popping has mostly stopped.

2. Off heat, remove lid and spray popcorn with oil spray for 6 seconds, stirring to coat. Quickly stir in Parmesan mixture, then cover and let sit until cheese melts, about 3 minutes. Serve.

BEFORE NUMBERS BASED ON: Smartfood White Cheddar Cheese Flavored Popcorn	BEFORE → **AFTER** 1 SERVING = 2⅓ CUPS	160 → **90** CALORIES	10 → **2** GRAMS FAT	2 → **1** GRAMS SAT FAT

THIN-CRUST CHEESE PIZZA

Salads, Sandwiches, and Pizza

Spinach Salad with Warm Bacon Dressing

Serves 4

✓ **WHY THIS RECIPE WORKS:** This indulgent salad can be found on many a bistro menu, and though it sounds tempting you'll most likely be disappointed by the excessive amount of dressing weighing down the spinach. We wanted to keep this salad fresh and light, but it still had to be infused with the rich flavor of bacon. We began with the rendered bacon fat, which is what gives this dressing its rich character and flavor, and found we could cut back on the amount—to just one spoonful—without sacrificing its identity. A surprise ingredient—chicken broth—helped amp up the savory notes and added volume in lieu of more bacon fat. Cider vinegar, balanced by a bit of sugar, added a nice bright tang to the dressing. Trimming the amount of bacon to just one slice per serving ensured a few crunchy bites, but allowed the spinach to take center stage. The warm dressing comes together quickly, so be sure to have your spinach ready. It's a good idea to step back from the stovetop when adding the vinegar mixture to the skillet—the aroma is quite potent.

8	ounces (8 cups) baby spinach
3	tablespoons cider vinegar
½	teaspoon sugar
	Salt and pepper
4	slices bacon, cut into ½-inch pieces
½	red onion, chopped fine
¼	cup low-sodium chicken broth
1	small garlic clove, minced
2	large hard-cooked eggs, peeled and sliced

1. Place spinach in large bowl. In small bowl, whisk vinegar, sugar, pinch salt, and ¼ teaspoon pepper together until sugar dissolves; set aside. Cook bacon in 12-inch nonstick skillet over medium-high heat until crisp, about 5 minutes; transfer to paper towel–lined plate.

2. Pour off all but 1 tablespoon fat left in skillet, add onion and broth, and cook over medium heat until onion is softened and liquid is thick and syrupy, about 2 minutes. Stir in garlic and cook until fragrant, about 15 seconds.

3. Stir in vinegar mixture, let it warm through briefly, then pour over spinach; toss gently to coat. Divide salad among 4 plates and garnish with cooked bacon and eggs. Serve.

BEFORE → **AFTER**	260 → **150**	20 → **9**	7 → **3**
	CALORIES	GRAMS FAT	GRAMS SAT FAT

Chicken Caesar Salad

Serves 4

✔ **WHY THIS RECIPE WORKS:** Most people think salads are good-for-you eating. But consider one of the most popular salads: the chicken Caesar. Sure, it's made up of crunchy romaine and moist, tender, white-meat chicken, but they're always heavily coated in a rich dressing made from, among other things, egg yolks and olive oil. To revamp the classic Caesar dressing without compromising its taste or richness, we swapped the egg yolks and a portion of the olive oil for buttermilk, which provided the same silky texture and tang of the yolks, and light mayonnaise, which contributed additional richness. Stirring some of the grated Parmesan into the dressing, rather than sprinkling it all on top, ensured that the cheese's salty, nutty flavor permeated the whole dish, so we could get away with using less. Thinly sliced poached chicken and low-fat croutons completed our made-over chicken Caesar salad. Parmesan cheese is a key ingredient in this classic salad, so be sure to use authentic Parmigiano-Reggiano and grate it yourself.

⅓ cup buttermilk

3 tablespoons light mayonnaise

2 tablespoons lemon juice

2 tablespoons water

2 teaspoons Dijon mustard

1 teaspoon Worcestershire sauce

2 garlic cloves, minced

3 anchovy fillets, rinsed and patted dry
Salt and pepper

2 tablespoons extra-virgin olive oil

1 ounce Parmesan cheese, grated (½ cup)

1 large head romaine lettuce (14 ounces), torn into bite-size pieces

18 ounces poached chicken breast (see page 42), sliced ½ inch thick

2 cups Low-Fat Croutons

1. Process buttermilk, mayonnaise, lemon juice, water, mustard, Worcestershire, garlic, anchovies, ½ teaspoon pepper, and ¼ teaspoon salt in blender until smooth, about 30 seconds. With blender running, add oil in steady stream. Transfer dressing to bowl and stir in all but 1 tablespoon Parmesan.

2. Gently toss lettuce with all but 2 tablespoons of dressing and divide among four plates. Toss chicken with remaining 2 tablespoons dressing and arrange on top of salads. Garnish with croutons and remaining 1 tablespoon Parmesan. Serve.

ON THE SIDE LOW-FAT CROUTONS
Adjust oven rack to middle position and heat oven to 350 degrees. Cut 2 slices hearty white sandwich bread into ½-inch pieces and spread onto rimmed baking sheet. Coat pieces generously with olive oil spray and season with salt and pepper. Bake, stirring occasionally, until golden, 20 to 25 minutes; let cool. Makes 2 cups.

| BEFORE NUMBERS BASED ON: Grilled Chicken Caesar Salad from Applebee's Neighborhood Grill and Bar | BEFORE → **AFTER** | 820 → **390** CALORIES | 57 → **18** GRAMS FAT | 11 → **4** GRAMS SAT FAT |

Classic Wedge Salad with Blue Cheese Dressing

Serves 6

✔ **WHY THIS RECIPE WORKS:** The pairing of crunchy iceberg lettuce and creamy, tangy, blue cheese dressing is what makes this steakhouse staple so popular. But that thick, rich dressing presents a huge problem for those watching their waistline. Typically loaded with mayonnaise, sour cream, and blue cheese, the dressing turns an otherwise light starter into a calorie bomb. Replacing the full-fat dairy ingredients with their lighter counterparts was a no-brainer, but there really isn't a good low-fat substitute for blue cheese. Reducing the amount of cheese helped us trim fat and calories, but what truly worked was trading the mild blue cheese usually called for in this salad with more pungent Roquefort or Stilton. Now our lightened dressing offered all the big, bold, blue cheese flavor we were craving.

4	slices bacon, cut into ¼-inch pieces
1½	ounces strong blue cheese, such as Roquefort or Stilton, crumbled (⅓ cup)
⅓	cup buttermilk
⅓	cup light mayonnaise
⅓	cup low-fat sour cream
3	tablespoons water
1	tablespoon white wine vinegar
¼	teaspoon garlic powder
¼	teaspoon salt
¼	teaspoon pepper
1	head iceberg lettuce (9 ounces), cored and cut into 6 wedges
3	tomatoes, cored and cut into wedges

1. Cook bacon in 12-inch nonstick skillet over medium-high heat until crisp, about 5 minutes; transfer to paper towel–lined plate.

2. Mash blue cheese and buttermilk together with fork in small bowl until mixture resembles cottage cheese with small curds. Stir in mayonnaise, sour cream, water, vinegar, garlic powder, salt, and pepper until well combined.

3. Divide iceberg wedges and tomatoes among 6 plates. Spoon blue cheese dressing over top and garnish with bacon. Serve.

BEFORE NUMBERS BASED ON: Classic Wedge Salad from T.G.I. Friday's	BEFORE→ **AFTER**	620→**130** CALORIES	59→**8** GRAMS FAT	15→**2.5** GRAMS SAT FAT

Chinese Chicken Salad

Serves 4

✔ **WHY THIS RECIPE WORKS:** With its shredded cabbage, bright vegetables, and tender chicken, all tossed in a lively toasted sesame oil vinaigrette, Chinese chicken salad offers an enticing variety of tastes, textures, and visual appeal. But many versions take it a step too far, weighing down the dish with too much oil and high-fat garnishes like cashews or peanuts. A simple vinaigrette, punched up with rice vinegar, fresh ginger, and hoisin sauce, kept our salad bright and fresh-tasting, while a mere 2 tablespoons of oil (we chose canola oil, which is low in saturated fat) provided ample richness. Tossing our chicken and vegetables in the vinaigrette, instead of drizzling it over the top, ensured that every bite offered big flavor. As a final touch, a sprinkle of crispy chow mein noodles lent a welcome crunch—and added far fewer calories and less fat than cashews or peanuts. Chow mein noodles, often sold in 5-ounce canisters, can be found in most supermarkets with other Asian ingredients; La Choy is the most widely available brand.

⅓ cup rice vinegar

¼ cup hoisin sauce

2 tablespoons canola oil

1½ tablespoons low-sodium soy sauce

1 tablespoon grated fresh ginger

½ teaspoon toasted sesame oil

12 ounces poached chicken breast, shredded (2 cups)

½ head green or napa cabbage, cored and sliced thin (6 cups)

1 carrot, peeled and shredded

½ large red bell pepper, cut into ¼-inch-wide strips

2 ounces (1 cup) bean sprouts

2 scallions, sliced thin on bias

1 tablespoon minced fresh cilantro

1 cup chow mein noodles

Whisk vinegar, hoisin sauce, canola oil, soy sauce, ginger, and sesame oil together in small bowl. In large bowl, toss chicken, cabbage, carrot, bell pepper, sprouts, scallions, and cilantro with dressing. Divide salad among four plates and garnish with chow mein noodles. Serve.

QUICK PREP TIP **EASY POACHED CHICKEN**

For convenience's sake, we call for shredded or cubed chicken in a number of recipes in this book. We've found that poaching is an easy—and low-fat—way to prepare it. Here's how to do it. Start by trimming boneless, skinless chicken breasts of all visible fat. Combine the chicken, 1½ cups water, 2 peeled and smashed garlic cloves, 2 bay leaves, and 2 teaspoons low-sodium soy sauce in a 12-inch skillet and bring to a simmer over medium-low heat, 10 to 15 minutes. When the water is simmering, flip the chicken over, cover, and continue to cook until the chicken registers 160 degrees, 10 to 15 minutes longer. Transfer to a carving board, let rest for 5 minutes, then cut or shred into pieces as desired. This chart will help you figure out how much uncooked chicken you need to start with in order to end up with the amount of meat called for in the recipe.

UNCOOKED WEIGHT	COOKED WEIGHT
8 ounces	6 ounces
12 ounces	9 ounces
1 pound	12 ounces
1½ pounds	18 ounces
2 pounds	1½ pounds

BEFORE → **AFTER**   500 → **350** CALORIES   31 → **14** GRAMS FAT   4 → **2** GRAMS SAT FAT

Buffalo Chicken Salad

Serves 4

✔ **WHY THIS RECIPE WORKS:** This chain restaurant favorite suffers from a few major high-fat culprits: deep-fried chicken, a buttery hot sauce, and blue cheese dressing. We wanted to reinvent this dish and lighten it up while also keeping all the bold flavors and appealing textures. Starting with the chicken, we knew deep-frying was out. To replicate that addictive crisp-coated chicken, we turned to the considerably less oily pan-searing method. Coating the chicken in a combination of cornstarch and cornmeal delivered the crisp exterior we expected. As for the sauce, we lowered the amount of butter to just 1 tablespoon and added molasses for depth of flavor along with the hot sauce. Finally, we tackled the dressing, reducing the amount of blue cheese until we couldn't go lower. Light mayo helped us lop off serious fat and calories while providing a rich creaminess, and low-fat yogurt contributed a nice tanginess. To serve the salad, we tossed our veggies—romaine lettuce, thinly sliced celery, and shredded carrots—with the dressing, then topped them with slices of tender chicken, which had been coated with the hot sauce. Either a strong or a mild-flavored blue cheese will work here. The mild flavor of Frank's RedHot Original Cayenne Pepper Sauce is crucial to the flavor of buffalo sauce; we don't suggest substituting other brands of hot sauce here.

⅔ cup plain low-fat yogurt

¼ cup light mayonnaise

1 ounce blue cheese, crumbled (¼ cup)

3 tablespoons water

1 tablespoon lemon juice

2 garlic cloves, minced
Salt and pepper

½ cup Frank's RedHot Original Cayenne Pepper Sauce

1 tablespoon unsalted butter, melted

1 tablespoon light or mild molasses

½ cup cornmeal

1 tablespoon cornstarch

4 (6-ounce) boneless, skinless chicken breasts, trimmed of all visible fat

1 tablespoon canola oil

3 romaine lettuce hearts (18 ounces), torn into bite-size pieces

3 celery ribs, sliced thin

2 carrots, peeled and shredded

1. Whisk yogurt, mayonnaise, blue cheese, water, lemon juice, garlic, ¼ teaspoon salt, and ⅛ teaspoon pepper together in small bowl. In separate bowl, whisk hot sauce, butter, and molasses together.

2. Combine cornmeal and cornstarch in shallow dish. Pat chicken dry with paper towels and season with salt and pepper. Dredge chicken in cornmeal mixture, pressing on coating to adhere. Heat oil in 12-inch nonstick skillet over medium-high heat until just smoking. Add chicken and cook until well browned on first side, 6 to 8 minutes. Flip chicken, reduce heat to medium-low, and continue to cook until chicken registers 160 degrees, 6 to 8 minutes longer. Transfer chicken to carving board, let rest for 5 minutes, then slice crosswise into ½-inch-thick pieces.

3. Toss lettuce, celery, and carrots with blue cheese dressing and divide among four plates. Toss chicken with hot sauce mixture and arrange on top of salads. Serve.

BEFORE NUMBERS BASED ON: Boneless Buffalo Chicken Salad from Chili's Grill and Bar	BEFORE → **AFTER**	920 → **470** CALORIES	63 → **17** GRAMS FAT	14 → **5** GRAMS SAT FAT

Classic Cobb Salad

Serves 4

✓ **WHY THIS RECIPE WORKS:** To lighten our cobb salad, we kept the main players—tender chicken, hard-cooked eggs, avocado, tomatoes, bacon, and blue cheese—but made a few small changes. Swapping turkey bacon for regular bacon delivered the same salty, smoky flavors and crunch, and the salad included so many other elements that tasters didn't even notice. Relying on potent Roquefort or Stilton allowed us to cut back on the amount of cheese, while poaching proved a low-fat way to prepare the chicken. Tossing the chicken, tomatoes, and greens with a bit of our boldly flavored vinaigrette ensured that each one was well-seasoned. When it came to the avocado, tasters liked the richness it provided, but it increases the overall fat substantially (though it is largely monounsaturated fat), so we leave the choice up to you. Watercress is traditional in cobb salad, but an equal amount of arugula, chicory, or curly endive can be substituted.

DRESSING

- 3 tablespoons extra-virgin olive oil
- 2 tablespoons rice vinegar
- 2 tablespoons minced shallot
- 2 tablespoons water
- 1 tablespoon lemon juice
- 1 tablespoon Dijon mustard
- 1 garlic clove, minced
- 1 teaspoon minced fresh thyme
- ¼ teaspoon salt
- ¼ teaspoon pepper

SALAD

- 2 slices turkey bacon
- 9 ounces poached chicken breast (see page 42), cut into ½-inch cubes
- 8 ounces grape or cherry tomatoes, halved
- 2 romaine lettuce hearts (12 ounces), cut into 1-inch pieces
- 4 ounces (4 cups) watercress
- 2 large hard-cooked eggs, chopped
- 1 ounce strong blue cheese, such as Roquefort or Stilton, crumbled (¼ cup)
- 1 avocado, halved, pitted, and cut into ¼-inch cubes (optional)

1. FOR THE DRESSING: Whisk all ingredients together in bowl.

2. FOR THE SALAD: Cook bacon in 12-inch nonstick skillet over medium-high heat until crisp, about 5 minutes; transfer to paper towel–lined plate, let cool slightly, then crumble.

3. Rewhisk dressing to combine. Toss cubed chicken with 2 tablespoons dressing in bowl. In separate bowl, toss tomatoes with 1 tablespoon dressing. In another bowl, toss romaine and watercress with remaining dressing. Arrange greens on four individual plates or large platter and top with rows of chicken, tomatoes, and eggs. Garnish with cooked bacon, blue cheese, and avocado, if using. Serve.

BEFORE NUMBERS BASED ON: Chicken Cobb Salad from Fresh City	BEFORE→**AFTER** (WITHOUT AVOCADO)	738→**320** CALORIES	51→**19** GRAMS FAT	17→**4.5** GRAMS SAT FAT

Beef Taco Salad

Serves 4

WHY THIS RECIPE WORKS: Golden and ultra-crunchy, the fried taco "bowl" in a taco salad makes the perfect contrast to the saucy, spicy beef filling and crisp salad fixings. But with that fried shell, this heavyweight salad can contain almost 50 grams of fat. To create a lighter shell with the same crispy appeal, we swapped the deep-fryer for the oven. Softening flour tortillas in the microwave made them pliable enough that we could shape them into bowls and bake them until set. An even coating of vegetable oil spray helped them crisp up nicely. For our salad, we topped lettuce, cherry tomatoes, and black beans with a quick yet flavorful beef taco filling. To avoid dried-out taco filling, be careful not to cook the meat beyond pink before adding the liquid ingredients, or it will overcook as it simmers. Serve with lime wedges and nonfat Greek yogurt.

TACO MEAT

- **1 teaspoon canola oil**
- **1 onion, chopped fine**
- **2 tablespoons chili powder**
- **3 garlic cloves, minced**
- **1 pound 93 percent lean ground beef**
- **1 (8-ounce) can tomato sauce**
- **½ cup low-sodium chicken broth**
- **2 teaspoons cider vinegar**
- **1 teaspoon packed light brown sugar**
- **Salt and pepper**

SALAD

- **4 (10-inch) flour tortillas**
- **Vegetable oil spray**
- **2 romaine lettuce hearts (12 ounces), shredded**
- **1 (15-ounce) can black beans, rinsed**
- **8 ounces cherry or grape tomatoes, quartered**
- **2 scallions, sliced thin**
- **¼ cup chopped fresh cilantro**
- **2 tablespoons lime juice**
- **Salt and pepper**
- **2 ounces reduced-fat shredded Mexican cheese blend (½ cup)**

1. FOR THE TACO MEAT: Heat oil in 12-inch nonstick skillet over medium-high heat until shimmering. Add onion and cook until softened, about 5 minutes. Stir in chili powder and garlic and cook until fragrant, about 30 seconds. Add ground beef and cook, breaking up meat with wooden spoon, until almost cooked through but still slightly pink, about 2 minutes. Stir in tomato sauce, broth, vinegar, and sugar and simmer until slightly thickened, about 5 minutes; mixture will be saucy. Off heat, season with salt and pepper to taste.

2. FOR THE SALAD: Adjust oven racks to upper-middle and lower-middle positions and heat oven to 425 degrees. Arrange 4 ovensafe soup bowls (or 4 slightly flattened, 3-inch aluminum foil balls) upside down on 2 rimmed baking sheets. Place tortillas on plate, cover with damp paper towel, and microwave until warm and pliable, about 30 seconds.

3. Generously spray both sides of warm tortillas with oil spray. Drape tortillas over soup bowls, pressing top flat and pinching sides to create 4-sided bowl. Bake until tortillas are golden and crisp, 10 to 15 minutes, switching and rotating sheets halfway through baking. Let cool upside down.

4. Combine lettuce, beans, tomatoes, scallions, and 2 tablespoons cilantro in large bowl; toss with lime juice and season with salt and pepper to taste. Place tortilla bowls on individual plates. Divide salad among bowls, top with taco meat, and sprinkle with cheese and remaining 2 tablespoons cilantro. Serve.

BEFORE NUMBERS BASED ON:
Taco Salad with Seasoned Ground Beef from Qdoba Mexican Grill

BEFORE → AFTER	875 → **500** CALORIES	48 → **19** GRAMS FAT	17.5 → **6** GRAMS SAT FAT

MAKEOVER SPOTLIGHT: BEEF TACO SALAD

1. USE LEAN GROUND BEEF AND DITCH THE DUSTY SEASONING PACKET: For a leaner, yet still flavorful, ground beef filling, we reached for 93 percent lean ground beef and set about infusing it with big flavor. Bypassing the usual dusty, flavorless store-bought taco spices called for in taco salad recipes, we flavored our meaty filling with sautéed aromatics, tomato sauce, chicken broth, cider vinegar, and brown sugar. A whopping 2 tablespoons of chili powder added heat and bold flavor.

2. BAKE TORTILLAS FOR THE TACO BOWLS AND SKIP THE DEEP-FRYER: The shells in taco salads are usually deep-fried, but deep frying is definitely not a low-fat cooking method. So we baked our shells. Warming the tortillas in the microwave made them pliable enough to shape, and spraying them with vegetable oil spray helped them crisp and turn golden in the oven. Draping the tortillas over ovensafe soup bowls, placed upside down on a rimmed baking sheet, then pressing the tops flat and pinching the sides created the typical multi-sided taco shells, which set after 10 minutes in a 425-degree oven.

3. MAKE A HEARTY SALAD WITH HEALTHY INGREDIENTS: In lieu of the shredded cheese, guacamole, and sour cream often found in taco salads, we kept ours light and filled it with healthy, and filling, ingredients. Canned black beans gave the dish substance, and shredded lettuce, quartered cherry tomatoes, thinly sliced scallions, and chopped cilantro added textural interest while keeping this salad squarely in the light and fresh category. Just 2 tablespoons of reduced-fat shredded Mexican cheese per salad provided plenty of cheesy flavor.

4. FORGO THE HEAVY DRESSINGS IN FAVOR OF LIME JUICE: We found heavy, oil-based dressings unnecessary in this salad—they weighed down the vegetables and obscured their fresh flavors. Instead of using an oil-laden vinaigrette to dress the vegetables, we simply tossed them with a small amount of lime juice and let the juices from the meaty filling drip down and add flavor.

Niçoise Salad

Serves 4

✓ **WHY THIS RECIPE WORKS:** Tossing each ingredient in a niçoise salad—including the green beans, potatoes, tomatoes, and tuna—with a bit of the dressing ensures that every bite offers bright, fresh flavor, but this requires using a lot of olive oil. Supplementing the olive oil in our dressing with a couple spoonfuls of the water we used to simmer the potatoes proved a clever, and low-fat, way to stretch our dressing. Not only did this cooking water contribute rich flavor, but, like olive oil, it also worked to thicken the dressing, thanks to the starches released from the spuds. To boost the flavor of the mild-tasting tuna, we seasoned it with a sprinkle of lemon juice and some minced parsley. The classic garnish of tiny, briny, piquant niçoise olives is a hallmark of this salad, but if they're not available, substitute another small, black, brined olive such as kalamata (do not use canned olives).

DRESSING

- ¼ cup extra-virgin olive oil
- 2 tablespoons lemon juice
- 2 tablespoons minced shallot
- 1 tablespoon white wine vinegar
- 2 teaspoons Dijon mustard
- 1 teaspoon minced fresh thyme
- 1 garlic clove, minced
- 1 anchovy fillet, rinsed, patted dry, and minced to paste
- ¼ teaspoon pepper
- ⅛ teaspoon salt

SALAD

- 1 pound red potatoes, cut into 1-inch pieces
   Salt
- 12 ounces green beans, trimmed and cut into 1½-inch lengths
- 8 ounces grape or cherry tomatoes, halved
- 8 ounces (8 cups) mesclun greens
- 2 (5-ounce) cans solid white tuna in water, drained thoroughly and flaked
- 1 tablespoon minced fresh parsley
- 2 teaspoons lemon juice
- 2 large hard-cooked eggs, peeled and quartered
- ¼ cup niçoise olives

1. FOR THE DRESSING: Whisk all ingredients together in bowl.

2. FOR THE SALAD: Bring 6 cups water, potatoes, and 1 tablespoon salt to gentle simmer in large saucepan, then cook until potatoes are tender, 5 to 8 minutes. Using slotted spoon, transfer potatoes to bowl. Whisk 2 tablespoons potato cooking water into dressing. Toss hot potatoes with 2 tablespoons dressing; let cool.

3. Return water to boil over high heat, add green beans, and cook until crisp-tender, about 5 minutes. Fill large bowl with ice water. Drain beans, transfer to ice water, and let chill for 3 minutes; drain and pat dry. Toss cooked beans and tomatoes with 1 tablespoon dressing in bowl.

4. Toss greens with ¼ cup dressing in bowl and arrange greens on individual plates or large platter. Toss tuna with remaining dressing, parsley, and lemon juice. Arrange tuna, potatoes, bean-tomato mixture, and eggs on top of greens and sprinkle with olives. Serve.

BEFORE → **AFTER**	790 → **410** CALORIES	58 → **21** GRAMS FAT	9 → **3.5** GRAMS SAT FAT

Open-Faced Tuna Melts

Serves 4

✔ **WHY THIS RECIPE WORKS:** We've seen pressed panini-style tuna melts, bagel tuna melts, and oven-baked, open-faced tuna melts. But no matter the style, they all seem to have one thing in common: the tuna is swimming in mayo. Not only does all that mayo make for a fat-laden sandwich, but it also obscures the tuna flavor and causes the bread to become soggy. For our tuna melt, we set out to create an open-faced sandwich using hearty rustic bread, which we pretoasted to ensure that it would hold its own under a big scoop of our lightened tuna salad. We couldn't ditch the mayo completely because our tuna still needed a binder, but we did switch to a light mayonnaise and cut back to a modest ⅓ cup. Minced red onion, lemon juice, and parsley added bright, fresh notes to the mild-mannered tuna, and thin slices of tomato contributed sweetness. We topped our tuna melts with reduced-fat American cheese, which melted, and tasted, best in our tests; we've had good luck using Boar's Head 25 Percent Lower Fat American Cheese, which can be found at the deli counter.

4	(1-inch-thick) slices rustic bread
3	(5-ounce) cans solid white tuna in water, drained thoroughly and flaked
⅓	cup light mayonnaise
1	celery rib, minced
¼	cup minced red onion
2	tablespoons minced fresh parsley
1	tablespoon lemon juice
2	teaspoons Dijon mustard
1	garlic clove, minced
	Salt and pepper
1	tomato, cored and cut into 8 thin slices
8	slices reduced-fat American cheese

1. Adjust oven rack to middle position and heat oven to 450 degrees. Line baking sheet with aluminum foil. Arrange bread on prepared sheet and toast until golden on both sides, about 8 minutes.

2. Combine tuna, mayonnaise, celery, onion, parsley, lemon juice, mustard, and garlic together in bowl. Season with salt and pepper to taste.

3. Spoon tuna on top of toast, then top each toast with 2 slices tomato and 2 slices cheese. Bake until tuna is heated through and cheese is melted, 5 to 10 minutes. Serve warm.

BEFORE → **AFTER**	610 → **320**	45 → **13**	10 → **5**
	CALORIES	GRAMS FAT	GRAMS SAT FAT

Drive-Through Cheeseburgers

Serves 4

✓ **WHY THIS RECIPE WORKS:** We love a good fast-food burger as much as anyone, but what we don't love is the heavy feeling and greasy fingertips we're left with afterward. Combining lean ground beef with a little ground turkey ensured that our quarter-pounders were leaner and less greasy than the drive-through version. A bit of Worcestershire sauce reinforced the savory, meaty notes. Since our patties included ground turkey, we had to cook them until well-done, which dried them out. So to keep them moist, we employed a trick we often use with meatballs, and mixed the meat with a panade, a paste of bread and milk, then covered the skillet during cooking to ensure that the burgers stayed juicy. For the cheese, we went the traditional route with classic American, but switched to the reduced-fat variety, which offered the same cheesy flavor and melty topping for our tender patties. Our cheeseburgers were now way better—and better for you—than anything we'd ever gotten out of a paper bag. Serve with your favorite burger toppings. For the cheese, we like Boar's Head 25 Percent Lower Fat American Cheese, which can be found at the deli counter.

1	slice hearty white sandwich bread, crusts removed, chopped
2	tablespoons skim milk
4	ounces 99 percent lean ground turkey breast
2	teaspoons Worcestershire sauce
¼	teaspoon salt
½	teaspoon pepper
12	ounces 93 percent lean ground beef
1	teaspoon canola oil
4	slices reduced-fat American cheese
4	hamburger buns, toasted

1. Mash bread and milk together in large bowl with fork until uniform. Add ground turkey, Worcestershire, salt, and pepper and mix until smooth.

2. Break up ground beef into small pieces and sprinkle over turkey mixture. Using hands, gently combine meats until uniform. Divide meat into 4 equal portions. Working with one portion of meat at a time, toss meat back and forth between hands to form loose ball, then gently flatten into ½-inch-thick patty, about 4½ inches wide.

3. Heat oil in 12-inch nonstick skillet over medium heat until just smoking. Lay patties in skillet, cover, and cook, without moving them, until well-browned, about 3 minutes. Flip burgers, cover, and continue to cook 2 minutes longer. Top each burger with 1 slice cheese, cover, and continue to cook until cheese is melted and burgers register 160 degrees, about 1 minute. Transfer burgers to buns and serve.

BEFORE NUMBERS BASED ON: Quarter Pounder with Cheese from McDonald's	BEFORE → **AFTER**	520 → **360** CALORIES	26 → **14** GRAMS FAT	12 → **6** GRAMS SAT FAT

MAKEOVER SPOTLIGHT: CHEESEBURGERS

1. USE 93 PERCENT LEAN GROUND BEEF AND GROUND TURKEY: We usually call for 85 percent lean ground beef in burgers, but that wouldn't do in our lightened recipe. But we also couldn't just substitute ground turkey for the ground beef—when we tried this, the patties didn't taste meaty enough. Instead, we kept most of the beef—switching to 93 percent lean—and combined it with a small amount of ground turkey. A ratio of 3:1 gave us burgers that were hearty and offered big meaty flavor, but allowed us to cut the fat grams almost in half. A small amount of Worcestershire sauce amped up the beefy flavor of our patties.

2. ADD A PANADE FOR MOIST, JUICY BURGERS: To ensure that our turkey and beef patties were plenty moist and juicy, we added a panade, which is a paste of milk and bread typically used to help meatballs hold their shape and retain their moisture. When a panade is added to ground meat, starches from the bread absorb the milk to form a gel that, like fat, coats and lubricates the protein molecules, keeping them moist. The bread also absorbs and holds on to juices from the meat, so they stay in the burger instead of draining away.

3. MAKE THE BURGERS THE RIGHT THICKNESS: We found it essential to form the burgers so they're the right thickness; this ensures that they'll cook through in the right amount of time and be tender and juicy. We found it best to shape our cheeseburgers into patties that are ½ inch thick. If they're any thinner than this, they will cook through more quickly and have a dry interior and burnt exterior. If the patties are any thicker, they will be underdone at the end of the cooking time and unsafe to eat due to the ground turkey.

4. COOK THE BURGERS COVERED AND TOP WITH REDUCED-FAT CHEESE: To ensure the patties stayed moist, we cooked them covered. Also, we let them cook without moving them to enable the formation of a well-browned crust. Once there was a nicely browned crust on both sides (we flipped the burgers after a few minutes in the pan), we topped the patties with cheese. Slices of reduced-fat American cheese melted nicely and offered ultra-cheesy flavor without a lot of fat, and covering the pan helped melt the cheese quickly so the burgers wouldn't overcook.

Philly Cheesesteaks

Serves 4

☑ **WHY THIS RECIPE WORKS:** You don't have to hail from the City of Brotherly Love to appreciate the combination of tender, thinly sliced beef, browned onions, and gooey cheese found in this famed sandwich. After selecting top round for the meat—among the leaner cuts we tried, top round was preferred for both its beefy flavor and its tender texture—we cut the steak into 1-inch-wide strips, then froze them so they'd be easy to slice thinly. Though we were able to slice the meat paper-thin using a very sharp knife, a food processor made much quicker work of this task. After sautéing a chopped onion, we added our shaved beef to the pan and cooked it briefly. Just a few slices of reduced-fat American cheese provided plenty of cheesy flavor and richness. We laid the slices on the meat in the pan so they would melt, then stirred them in to ensure that everything was nicely coated. Don't overfreeze the beef or it will be difficult to shave in the food processor. Serve with pickled hot peppers, sautéed bell peppers, sweet relish, and hot sauce. For the cheese, we like Boar's Head 25 Percent Lower Fat American Cheese, which can be found at the deli counter.

1   **(1-pound) top round steak, trimmed of all visible fat and cut into 1-inch-wide strips**
1   **onion, chopped**
2   **teaspoons canola oil**
    Salt and pepper
5   **slices reduced-fat American cheese**
4   **(6-inch) sub rolls, slit partially open and lightly toasted**

1. Place steak on large plate and freeze until exterior hardens but interior remains soft, about 30 minutes. Using food processor fitted with slicing disk, shave partially frozen steak.

2. Combine onion, 1 teaspoon oil, and ¼ teaspoon salt in 12-inch nonstick skillet. Cover and cook over medium-low heat, stirring occasionally, until softened, 8 to 10 minutes. Uncover, increase heat to medium-high, add remaining 1 teaspoon oil, shaved meat, ¼ teaspoon salt, and ⅛ teaspoon pepper, and cook until meat is no longer pink, 2 to 3 minutes.

3. Reduce heat to low, lay cheese slices on top of meat, and continue to cook until cheese has melted, about 1 minute. Stir melted cheese and meat together to combine. Divide meat mixture among toasted rolls and serve.

QUICK PREP TIP SHAVING MEAT FOR PHILLY CHEESESTEAKS
For an authentic Philly cheesesteak, the meat should be paper thin. To accomplish this, first cut the trimmed meat into 1-inch-wide strips, then spread the meat out on a large plate and freeze it until the exterior hardens but the interior remains soft, about 30 minutes. Using a food processor fitted with a slicing disk, shave the partially frozen meat as thin as possible. Alternatively, slice the meat thinly by hand using a sharp chef's knife.

BEFORE NUMBERS BASED ON: Regular Prime Rib Philly Steak Sub Sandwich from Quiznos	BEFORE → **AFTER**	785 → **400** CALORIES	37.5 → **15** GRAMS FAT	13 → **6** GRAMS SAT FAT

Sloppy Joes

Serves 4

✔ **WHY THIS RECIPE WORKS:** A kid and an adult favorite alike, Sloppy Joes make for a quick and easy skillet supper. But though they may be convenient, they're definitely not light. For a makeover of this casual classic, we tried replacing the typical ground beef with an assortment of nontraditional ingredients, like wheat berries, tofu, and textured vegetable protein, but none of these held a candle to the flavor and texture of real meat. So we kept the beef—93 percent lean helped us shave off a good amount of fat and calories—and looked for vegetables that we could use to supplement it. Mushrooms proved to be a great secret ingredient. Not only did they add heft, allowing us to use less total meat overall, they also added a deeply flavorful, meaty dimension. Chopping them in the food processor ensured that they had the texture and appearance of ground meat, and adding a splash of Worcestershire sauce to the filling helped boost the sandwich's meaty flavor even further. If the beef mixture becomes too dry during cooking, add water, 1 tablespoon at a time, to reach the desired consistency.

6	ounces white mushrooms, trimmed and sliced thin
2	teaspoons canola oil
	Salt and pepper
1	onion, chopped fine
1¼	teaspoons chili powder
1	(8-ounce) can tomato sauce
¼	cup ketchup
¼	cup water
1	tablespoon Worcestershire sauce
1	teaspoon packed brown sugar
1	teaspoon cider vinegar
10	ounces 93 percent lean ground beef
4	hamburger buns

1. Combine mushrooms, 1 teaspoon oil, and ¼ teaspoon salt in 12-inch nonstick skillet. Cover and cook over medium-low heat until softened, 8 to 10 minutes. Uncover, increase heat to medium-high, and cook, stirring occasionally, until mushrooms are well browned, 8 to 12 minutes. Transfer mushrooms to food processor and pulse until finely ground, about 6 pulses.

2. Heat remaining 1 teaspoon oil in now-empty skillet over medium heat until shimmering. Add processed mushrooms and onion, cover, and cook until onion is softened, 8 to 12 minutes. Stir in chili powder and cook until fragrant, about 30 seconds. Add tomato sauce, ketchup, water, Worcestershire, sugar, and vinegar. Bring to simmer, then reduce heat to medium-low and cook until slightly thickened, about 15 minutes.

3. Stir in ground beef, breaking up meat with wooden spoon, and simmer until no longer pink, about 5 minutes. Season with salt and pepper to taste. Divide meat mixture among buns and serve.

BEFORE → **AFTER**	500 → **310**	26 → **9**	8 → **2.5**
	CALORIES	GRAMS FAT	GRAMS SAT FAT

Reuben Sandwiches

Serves 4

✓ **WHY THIS RECIPE WORKS:** Towering high on the plate, the average New York–style Reuben sandwich is stuffed to the gills with corned beef, Swiss cheese, and sauerkraut. The meat is slathered with a thick, creamy dressing, and the bread—only rye will do—is buttered before the whole thing hits the griddle. Sounds great, right? Not when you consider the fat and calories that must be in this deli classic. The real diet-killers in this dish are easy to spot: the dressing, cheese, and butter. First things first, we swapped out the Swiss and the full-fat mayo in the dressing for their lighter counterparts. Shredded cheese had more of a presence in our sandwiches than sliced cheese once melted, so we opted for shredded. Finally, instead of slathering our sandwiches with melted butter before cooking them on a griddle or in a skillet, we simply pressed them between two ripping-hot baking sheets in the oven. After 15 minutes, the cheese was melted and the bread had crisped nicely.

½   **cup light mayonnaise**
¼   **cup dill relish**
3   **tablespoons ketchup**
1   **tablespoon lemon juice**
1   **garlic clove, minced**
¼   **teaspoon salt**
¼   **teaspoon pepper**
8   **slices rye bread**
6   **ounces reduced-fat Swiss cheese, shredded (1½ cups)**
1⅓   **cups sauerkraut, rinsed, drained, and squeezed dry**
1   **pound thinly sliced deli corned beef**
    Vegetable oil spray

1. Adjust oven racks to middle and lower-middle positions and heat oven to 450 degrees. Place 1 baking sheet on each rack. Mix mayonnaise, relish, ketchup, lemon juice, garlic, salt, and pepper together in bowl.

2. Spread 1 tablespoon mayonnaise mixture onto 1 side of each bread slice. Assemble 4 sandwiches by layering following ingredients on 4 slices of bread, with mayonnaise mixture inside: half of Swiss, sauerkraut, remaining mayonnaise mixture, corned beef, and remaining Swiss. Top with remaining 4 slices of bread and press gently on sandwiches to compact, then spray both sides with vegetable oil spray.

3. Carefully lay sandwiches on hot sheet on middle rack, then top with second hot sheet. Bake sandwiches until heated through and bread is toasted, 12 to 15 minutes. Serve warm.

BEFORE NUMBERS BASED ON: **Reuben from Arby's**

BEFORE → **AFTER**   640 → **430**   30 → **15**   8 → **5**
                              CALORIES   GRAMS FAT   GRAMS SAT FAT

Broccoli and Sausage Calzones

Makes 2 calzones; serves 4

✔ **WHY THIS RECIPE WORKS:** For lighter calzones, part-skim mozzarella offered gooey appeal. Pureed nonfat cottage cheese made our filling creamy; cracker crumbs helped to absorb the extra moisture. You can substitute 1 pound store-bought pizza dough if desired. Serve with Low-Fat Tomato Sauce (page 135).

DOUGH

- 2 cups (11 ounces) bread flour
- 1 teaspoon instant or rapid-rise yeast
- 1 teaspoon salt
- 1 tablespoon olive oil
- ¾ cup water, heated to 110 degrees

FILLING

- 4 ounces hot or sweet Italian chicken sausage, casings removed, broken into ½-inch pieces
- 6 ounces broccoli florets, cut into 1-inch pieces
- ¼ cup water
- 6 saltines, broken into pieces
- 10 ounces (1¼ cups) nonfat cottage cheese
- 4 ounces part-skim mozzarella cheese, shredded (1 cup)
- ¼ cup grated Parmesan cheese
- 1 garlic clove, minced
- ¼ teaspoon salt
- ⅛ teaspoon red pepper flakes
- 1 large egg white, lightly beaten

1. FOR THE DOUGH: Process flour, yeast, and salt together in food processor until combined, about 2 seconds. With processor running, slowly add oil, then water, until dough forms rough ball, 30 to 40 seconds. Let rest for 2 minutes, then process for 30 seconds longer.

2. Transfer dough to lightly floured counter. Knead into smooth, round ball, about 4 minutes, dusting with extra flour as needed. Place in greased bowl, cover tightly with greased plastic wrap, and let rise in warm place until doubled in size, 1 to 1½ hours. (Alternatively, refrigerate bowl of unrisen dough for 8 to 16 hours; let sit at room temperature for 30 minutes before using.)

3. FOR THE FILLING: Adjust oven rack to middle position and heat oven to 450 degrees. Cook sausage in 12-inch nonstick skillet over medium-high heat until lightly browned, about 4 minutes. Add broccoli and water, cover, and cook until broccoli is just tender, about 3 minutes. Drain mixture, transfer to paper towel–lined plate, and let cool.

4. Pulse crackers in food processor until finely ground. Add cottage cheese, mozzarella, Parmesan, garlic, salt, and pepper flakes; process until smooth. Combine with sausage mixture in bowl.

5. To make calzones, cut out two 10-inch squares from parchment paper. Place dough on lightly floured counter, divide in half, and press and roll each half into 10-inch round; lay each round on parchment square. Spread filling over bottom half of each dough round, leaving 1-inch border at edge. Brush bottom edge lightly with water. Fold top half of dough over filling, leaving ½-inch border of bottom layer uncovered. Lightly press dough around filling to remove air and seal dough.

6. Starting at one end of seam, place index finger across dough edge, gently pull bottom layer of dough over tip of finger, and press to seal. Brush calzones with egg white; cut steam vents in top. Slide calzones (still on parchment) onto baking sheet. Bake until golden, about 15 minutes, rotating sheet halfway through baking. Transfer calzones to wire rack; let cool slightly. Serve.

BEFORE → **AFTER**	740 → **540** CALORIES	33 → **15** GRAMS FAT	13 → **5** GRAMS SAT FAT

Thin-Crust Cheese Pizza

Makes two 13-inch pizzas; serves 8

✔ **WHY THIS RECIPE WORKS:** For a standout parlor-quality pie with a chewy crust, we let the dough rest overnight in the refrigerator. Shredded part-skim mozzarella and grated Parmesan offered plenty of gooey appeal and rich flavor. Be sure to wait until just before baking to top the pizzas. You can substitute a rimless baking sheet or inverted rimmed baking sheet, preheated for 30 minutes, for the baking stone. Also, you can substitute a floured rimless or inverted baking sheet for the peel.

- 3 **cups (16½ ounces) bread flour**
- 2 **teaspoons sugar**
- ½ **teaspoon instant or rapid-rise yeast**
- 1⅓ **cups ice water**
- 1½ **tablespoons canola oil**
  Salt and pepper
- 1 **(14.5-ounce) can whole peeled tomatoes, drained**
- 1 **garlic clove, minced**
- ½ **teaspoon red wine vinegar**
- ½ **teaspoon dried oregano**
- 1 **ounce Parmesan cheese, grated (½ cup)**
- 8 **ounces part-skim mozzarella cheese, shredded (2 cups)**

1. Process flour, sugar, and yeast together in food processor until combined, about 2 seconds. With processor running, slowly add water until dough is just combined and no dry flour remains, about 10 seconds. Let dough sit for 10 minutes.

2. Add 1 tablespoon oil and 1¼ teaspoons salt and process until dough forms satiny, sticky ball that clears sides of bowl, 30 to 60 seconds. Transfer to lightly greased counter and knead briefly until smooth, about 1 minute. Shape dough into ball, place in greased bowl, and cover tightly with greased plastic wrap. Refrigerate for at least 24 hours or up to 3 days.

3. Position oven rack 4½ inches from top of oven, set pizza stone on rack, and heat oven to 500 degrees; let stone heat for 1 hour. Meanwhile, divide dough in half. Shape each piece into smooth ball; place on greased baking sheet, at least 3 inches apart. Cover loosely with greased plastic and let stand for 1 hour.

4. Process tomatoes, remaining 1½ teaspoons oil, garlic, vinegar, and oregano together in food processor until smooth, about 20 seconds. Season with salt and pepper to taste.

5. Coat 1 ball of dough generously with flour and place on well-floured counter. Using fingertips, gently flatten into 8-inch disk, leaving 1 inch of outer edge slightly thicker than center. Using hands, gently stretch disk into 12-inch round, working along edges and turning dough as needed. Transfer dough to well-floured peel and stretch into 13-inch round.

6. Spread ½ cup tomato sauce over dough, leaving ¼-inch border around edge. Sprinkle with ¼ cup Parmesan, followed by 1 cup mozzarella. Slide pizza carefully onto hot stone and bake until crust is well browned and cheese is bubbly, 10 to 12 minutes, rotating pizza halfway through baking. Let cool on wire rack for 5 minutes, then slice and serve. Repeat steps 5 and 6 to make second pizza.

BEFORE NUMBERS BASED ON: **Large Thin Crust Cheese Pizza** from Papa John's	BEFORE→**AFTER** 1 SERVING = 2 SLICES	460→**350** CALORIES	24→**10** GRAMS FAT	10→**4.5** GRAMS SAT FAT

MAKEOVER SPOTLIGHT: CHEESE PIZZA

1. DEVELOP FLAVOR IN THE DOUGH WITH AN OVERNIGHT RISE: For the best thin-crust pizza, we let the dough rest and rise in the refrigerator for at least 24 hours. This sitting time not only allows the dough to develop a deep, hearty flavor and a sturdy texture, but it also makes the dough more flexible and easy to stretch thinly without it tearing or snapping back.

2. USE YOUR HANDS TO STRETCH THE DOUGH: Getting the pizza to the right size is important not only for portion control, but also to ensure that the crust will be the right thickness so it bakes through evenly. Since the dough is well rested, it can be easily stretched into a pizza using just your hands. On a well-floured surface, gently flatten the dough into an 8-inch disk, leaving the outer edge slightly thicker to create a "handle." Continue to stretch the dough into a 12-inch round, working along the edges and giving the dough quarter turns. Transfer to a well-floured peel, then finish stretching it into a 13-inch round.

3. TOP THE PIZZA SPARINGLY: Spread no more than ½ cup of the pizza sauce over the dough, leaving a ¼-inch edge of dough uncovered, then sprinkle it with ¼ cup Parmesan and 1 cup mozzarella. Don't overload the pizza with sauce and cheese or the crust won't bake through properly. Also, don't be tempted to substitute nonfat mozzarella here, or else the cheese will have a rubbery, plasticky texture after it is baked.

4. BAKE ON A BAKING STONE AT THE TOP OF THE OVEN: Baking the pizza on the top rack—rather than the usual approach of placing it near the bottom of a home oven—means the oven heat will hit the top of the pie, browning the toppings before the crust has a chance to overcook. After baking the first pizza, shape, top, and bake the second pizza.

ALL-AMERICAN CHILI

The Soup Bowl

French Onion Soup

Serves 6

✔ **WHY THIS RECIPE WORKS:** Restaurant versions of this soup cook the onions in tons of oil and cover the bowl with a pile of cheese, taking a naturally light soup into ultra-fatty territory. To revamp ours, we traded the oil for vegetable oil spray and cut back on the Gruyère. Cooking the onions in the oven was easy and also allowed us to go light on the oil spray since we didn't have to worry about the onions scorching as they might on the stovetop. Use broiler-safe crocks and keep the rims of the bowls 4 to 5 inches from the heating element to obtain a nice layer of melted, bubbly cheese. If using ordinary soup bowls, sprinkle the toasted bread with Gruyère, return toasts to the broiler until the cheese melts, then float them on the soup.

4	pounds yellow onions, halved and sliced ¼ inch thick
	Salt and pepper
3	cups water, plus extra as needed
½	cup dry sherry
4	cups low-sodium chicken broth
2	cups beef broth
6	sprigs fresh thyme, tied with kitchen twine
1	bay leaf
1	(4-inch) piece baguette, cut into 6 slices on bias
1½	ounces Gruyère cheese, shredded (⅓ cup)

1. Adjust oven rack to lower-middle position and heat oven to 400 degrees. Spray inside of Dutch oven with vegetable oil spray, then stir in onions and ½ teaspoon salt. Cover, transfer pot to oven, and cook for 1 hour (onions will be moist and slightly reduced in volume).

2. Stir onions thoroughly, scraping bottom and sides of pot. Partially cover pot and continue to cook in oven until onions are deep golden brown, 1½ to 1¾ hours longer, stirring onions and scraping bottom and sides of pot every 30 minutes.

3. Remove pot from oven and place over medium-high heat. Cook, stirring onions and scraping bottom and sides of pot often, until liquid evaporates and pot is coated with dark crust, 20 to 28 minutes; reduce heat if onions brown too quickly.

4. Stir in ¼ cup water and scrape pot bottom to loosen crust. Cook until water evaporates and another dark crust has formed on pot bottom, 6 to 8 minutes. Repeat 2 or 3 more times, until onions are very dark brown.

5. Stir in sherry and cook, stirring often, until evaporated, about 5 minutes. Stir in remaining 2 cups water, chicken broth, beef broth, thyme, and bay leaf. Bring to simmer, cover, and cook for 30 minutes. Remove thyme and bay leaf. Season with salt and pepper to taste.

6. Meanwhile, arrange baguette slices in single layer on baking sheet. Bake until edges are golden, about 10 minutes; set aside.

7. Adjust oven rack to upper-middle position and heat broiler. Set 6 individual broiler-safe crocks on baking sheet and fill each with soup. Top with toasted baguette slices and sprinkle with Gruyère. Broil until cheese is melted and bubbly around edges, 3 to 5 minutes. Let soup cool for 5 minutes before serving.

BEFORE NUMBERS BASED ON: **Too Right French Onion Soup from Outback Steakhouse**	BEFORE → **AFTER**	466 → **250** CALORIES	31 → **3.5** GRAMS FAT	15 → **1.5** GRAMS SAT FAT

Creamless Creamy Tomato Soup

Serves 6

✔ **WHY THIS RECIPE WORKS:** We've had too many bowls of tomato soup weighed down by a big dose of heavy cream—which is neither good for the soup's flavor, nor good for our waistline. We wanted a creamy tomato soup that truly tasted of bright, fresh tomatoes—without the cream. Our solution? Use bread instead. After cooking two cans of tomatoes (we prefer canned, which offer bright tomato flavor year-round) with a chopped onion, minced garlic, and pinch of red pepper flakes, we stirred in our bread pieces and let everything simmer. Once the bread started to break down, we pureed the soup in the blender, then stirred in some chicken broth and a touch of brandy. The bread not only provided creaminess and tempered the acidity of the tomatoes (without muting their flavor), but it also helped to thicken the soup to just the right consistency. To prevent our lightened creamy tomato soup from tasting too lean, we pureed the soup with two tablespoons of extra-virgin olive oil. Garnish with Low-Fat Croutons (page 39) if desired.

¼   cup extra-virgin olive oil
1   onion, chopped fine
3   garlic cloves, minced
1   bay leaf
    Pinch red pepper flakes
2   (28-ounce) cans whole peeled tomatoes
1   tablespoon packed brown sugar
3   slices hearty white sandwich bread, crusts removed, torn into 1-inch pieces
2   cups low-sodium chicken broth
2   tablespoons brandy
    Salt and pepper
¼   cup minced fresh chives

1. Heat 2 tablespoons oil in Dutch oven over medium heat until shimmering. Add onion and cook until softened, 5 to 7 minutes. Stir in garlic, bay leaf, and pepper flakes and cook until fragrant, about 30 seconds.

2. Stir in tomatoes and their juice. Using potato masher, mash until no pieces larger than 2 inches remain. Stir in sugar and bread and bring to simmer. Reduce heat to medium and cook, stirring occasionally, until bread is completely saturated and starts to break down, about 5 minutes. Remove bay leaf.

3. Working in batches, process soup with remaining 2 tablespoons oil in blender until smooth. Return soup to clean pot and stir in chicken broth and brandy. Reheat soup gently over medium-low heat. Season with salt and pepper to taste. Garnish individual bowls with chives before serving.

QUICK PREP TIP
PUREEING SOUP SAFELY
To prevent getting sprayed or burned by an exploding blender top when pureeing hot soup, puree in batches, filling the blender so it is never more than two-thirds full. Hold the lid in place with a folded kitchen towel and pulse rapidly a few times before blending continuously.

BEFORE → **AFTER**	400 → **190**	24 → **10**	15 → **1.5**
	CALORIES	GRAMS FAT	GRAMS SAT FAT

MAKEOVER SPOTLIGHT: TOMATO SOUP

1. USE WHOLE PEELED TOMATOES FOR A SHORTER COOKING TIME: We found that whole peeled tomatoes worked better in this soup because they are softer and break down more quickly than diced tomatoes, which are treated with a firming agent during processing that keeps them from breaking down readily. The whole tomatoes don't need a long simmering time and so offer a fresher flavor in the finished soup. To help the tomatoes cook down in just minutes, we used a potato masher to mash them into pieces no larger than 2 inches.

2. SKIP THE CREAM—USE BREAD INSTEAD: For a lower-fat, but still silky, soup that doesn't require any heavy cream, we added 3 slices of sandwich bread to the pot. Once blended, the bread also helped thicken the soup to just the right consistency. Be sure to use a high-quality white sandwich bread and remove the crusts before adding it to the soup.

3. ADD RICHNESS WITH EXTRA-VIRGIN OLIVE OIL: Without any cream, tomato soup can taste overly lean and a little raw. To fix this, we found it crucial to add extra-virgin olive oil to the soup. We used some of the oil to cook the aromatics and added the rest to the soup during blending (which ensures that it is fully incorporated into the soup) so that its flavor remained clean and fresh.

4. STIR IN THE BROTH AT THE END: Adding the chicken broth during blending didn't work because the blender became so full that the bread chunks were swimming in the broth and resisted being pulled down to the blades. Instead, we found it best to add the broth after the soup had been pureed, because the thicker mixture was easier to blend to a silky-smooth consistency.

Creamy Mushroom Soup

Serves 6

✔ **WHY THIS RECIPE WORKS:** For a lightened creamy mushroom soup that boasted all the deep, woodsy flavor and luxurious, velvety texture of the full-fat version, we started with a good amount of mushrooms. We cooked them, covered, in a single pat of butter, then removed the lid so the moisture could evaporate and the mushrooms could brown. Thinly sliced leeks added a delicate sweetness and an element of creaminess to the finished soup. Beef broth and Madeira were the perfect combination for the broth—the beef broth accentuated the meaty, savory notes, while the Madeira complemented the earthy mushroom flavor. As for the dairy, we knew heavy cream was out. Milk—no matter if it was 1 percent, 2 percent, or whole—only thinned out the soup. Half-and-half proved to be the happy medium, giving our soup the right richness and silky texture without overwhelming the mushroom flavor. A small amount of finely chopped mushrooms, which we stirred in after pureeing the soup, added textural interest, while a squeeze of lemon juice cut through the richness. Use the blender, not a food processor, for the smoothest soup. You can use brandy or dry sherry in place of the Madeira. Garnish with minced fresh chives and Low-Fat Croutons (page 39) if desired.

1	tablespoon unsalted butter
2	pounds white mushrooms, trimmed and quartered
1	pound leeks, white and light green parts only, halved lengthwise, sliced thin, and washed thoroughly
	Salt and pepper
4	garlic cloves, minced
2	teaspoons minced fresh thyme or ½ teaspoon dried
5	cups beef broth
½	cup Madeira, plus extra for serving
½	cup half-and-half
2	teaspoons lemon juice

1. Melt butter in Dutch oven over medium-low heat. Add mushrooms, leeks, ½ teaspoon salt, and ¼ teaspoon pepper, cover, and cook until mushrooms are softened and wet, 8 to 10 minutes. Uncover, increase heat to medium-high, and cook, stirring occasionally, until mushrooms are dry and well browned, 8 to 12 minutes. Transfer ⅔ cup of mushroom mixture to cutting board and chop fine; set aside.

2. Stir garlic and thyme into pot and cook until fragrant, about 30 seconds. Stir in broth and Madeira, bring to simmer, and cook until mushrooms and leeks are completely tender, about 20 minutes.

3. Working in batches, process soup in blender until smooth. Return soup to clean pot and stir in chopped mushroom mixture, half-and-half, and lemon juice. Reheat soup gently over medium-low heat and season with salt and pepper to taste. Drizzle individual bowls with extra Madeira before serving.

BEFORE → AFTER	270 → **130**	20 → **5**	12 → **2.5**
	CALORIES	GRAMS FAT	GRAMS SAT FAT

Classic Corn Chowder

Serves 6

✓ **WHY THIS RECIPE WORKS:** Corn chowder is a summertime favorite, since it tastes best when fresh corn is plentiful and bursting with flavor. But though it sounds like a healthy meal, most versions are weighed down with pork and cream, making them decidedly unhealthy. To make over this classic, we started with the bacon. Just one slice was all we needed to give it a nice, smoky flavor. Moving on to the cream, we tried substituting a few low-fat dairy options, ultimately settling on a small amount of half-and-half. But the real trick to eliminating a lot of the cream was how we handled the corn. Grating most of the corn and then milking it (using a butter knife to scrape any remaining pulp from the cob) helped give our chowder a creamy texture. Cutting the kernels off the remaining cobs ensured that every spoonful was full of big bites of fresh, sweet corn. The flavor of this soup depends on fresh corn; don't substitute frozen corn.

10	ears corn, husks and silk removed
1	tablespoon canola oil
1	slice bacon, chopped fine
1	onion, chopped fine
2	garlic cloves, minced
1	teaspoon minced fresh thyme or ¼ teaspoon dried
3	tablespoons all-purpose flour
3	cups low-sodium chicken broth
1	cup 1 percent low-fat milk
1	pound red potatoes, unpeeled, cut into ¼-inch cubes
1	bay leaf
½	cup half-and-half
2	tablespoons minced fresh parsley
	Salt and pepper

1. Cut kernels from 4 ears of corn into large bowl. In separate bowl, grate remaining 6 ears of corn over large holes of box grater. Using back of butter knife, scrape any remaining pulp from cobs into bowl with grated corn.

2. Heat oil in Dutch oven over medium heat until shimmering. Add bacon and cook until rendered and crisp, about 3 minutes. Stir in onion and cook until softened, 5 to 7 minutes. Stir in garlic and thyme and cook until fragrant, about 30 seconds. Stir in flour and cook for 1 minute.

3. Slowly whisk in broth and milk, scraping up any browned bits. Stir in potatoes, bay leaf, and grated corn mixture. Bring to simmer, partially cover, and cook until potatoes are tender, about 15 minutes.

4. Stir in remaining corn kernels and half-and-half and simmer gently until corn kernels are tender yet still slightly crunchy, about 5 minutes. Remove bay leaf, stir in parsley, and season with salt and pepper to taste. Serve.

QUICK PREP TIP
PREPARING FRESH CORN
To remove kernels from ear of corn, stand cob upright inside large bowl; this will help catch any flying kernels. Then, using paring knife, slice down along sides of cob to remove kernels.

BEFORE → **AFTER**	420 → **320** CALORIES	25 → **12** GRAMS FAT	12 → **2.5** GRAMS SAT FAT

Loaded Baked Potato Soup

Serves 6

☑ **WHY THIS RECIPE WORKS:** Rich, creamy, and hearty, and topped with shredded cheese, crisp bacon, and sour cream, baked potato soup is the picture of comfort food. But though it's immensely popular, it's definitely not diet-friendly. For our makeover version, we found a few ways to keep the same rich flavors and textures of the full-fat original. First, we scaled back the bacon and used the rendered fat to sauté our aromatics, which infused our soup with savory, smoky flavor. We also swapped the cream in the soup for half-and-half. Dried mustard and thyme punched up the flavors slightly, but what really put this dish over the top was adding two of the toppings to the soup itself. Instead of saving the grated cheese for a last-minute garnish, we stirred it right into the pot, which added irresistible cheese flavor to every spoonful. And rather than dollop individual bowls with sour cream, we subbed in nonfat Greek yogurt and added it directly to the soup. Supplementing the crumbled bacon topping with crispy potato peels, cooked in the rendered bacon fat, upped the crunch factor but kept the fat and calories to a minimum.

3	slices bacon, chopped
1½	pounds russet potatoes, peeled, peels reserved from 2 potatoes and chopped coarse, and potatoes cut into ¾-inch pieces
1	large onion, chopped
2	garlic cloves, minced
1	tablespoon all-purpose flour
4	cups low-sodium chicken broth
¼	teaspoon mustard powder
1	sprig fresh thyme
1	cup half-and-half
½	cup 0 percent Greek yogurt
2	ounces 50 percent light cheddar cheese, shredded (½ cup)
	Salt and pepper
2	scallions, sliced thin

1. Cook bacon in Dutch oven over medium heat until rendered and crisp, about 3 minutes. Using a slotted spoon, transfer bacon to paper towel–lined plate. Add reserved potato skins to fat left in pot and cook until browned and crisp, about 8 minutes. Transfer to plate with bacon.

2. Add onion to fat left in pot and cook over medium heat until softened, 5 to 7 minutes. Stir in garlic and cook until fragrant, about 30 seconds. Stir in flour and cook for 1 minute. Gradually whisk in broth, scraping up any browned bits, until smooth. Stir in potatoes, mustard, and thyme and bring to simmer. Reduce heat to medium-low, cover, and cook until potatoes are tender, about 7 minutes.

3. Remove thyme. Process half of soup in blender until smooth, about 2 minutes, then return to pot. Whisk in half-and-half. Stir ½ cup hot soup into yogurt in small bowl to temper, then whisk yogurt mixture into soup. Stir in cheddar and season with salt and pepper to taste. Sprinkle individual portions with scallions and bacon–potato skin mixture. Serve.

BEFORE → **AFTER**	560 → **270**	40 → **13**	23 → **6**
	CALORIES	GRAMS FAT	GRAMS SAT FAT

Broccoli-Cheddar Soup

Serves 5

✔ **WHY THIS RECIPE WORKS:** With all the cheese and heavy cream, it's easy to see how a bowl of broccoli-cheddar soup can clock in at over 600 calories. We wanted to transform this lunchtime favorite into a lighter dish and started by nixing the cream. But to get the same velvety texture, we'd have to find a substitute. Simply replacing the cream with milk or half-and-half resulted in a thin, watery soup. Fat-free evaporated milk, on the other hand, worked like a charm, producing a perfectly rich and satiny soup. As for the cheddar, some recipes call for as much as a pound. But we found that switching to a bolder cheese—extra-sharp cheddar—infused our soup with so much flavor that we were able to cut back to just 4 ounces. For more broccoli flavor, instead of discarding the stalks, we saved them and added them to the pot. Once pureed, our made-over broccoli-cheddar soup offered all the rich, creamy texture, sweet, subtle broccoli flavor, and bold cheddar taste that we were craving.

1	tablespoon unsalted butter
1½	pounds broccoli, florets cut into 1-inch pieces, stalks peeled and sliced ¼ inch thick
1	pound leeks, white and light green parts only, halved lengthwise, sliced thin, and washed thoroughly
2	garlic cloves, minced
3	cups low-sodium chicken broth
1	cup water
¾	cup fat-free evaporated milk
4	ounces extra-sharp cheddar cheese, shredded (1 cup)
1	tablespoon Dijon mustard
	Salt and pepper

1. Melt butter in Dutch oven over medium heat. Add broccoli stalks and leeks and cook until softened, 8 to 10 minutes. Stir in garlic and cook until fragrant, about 30 seconds.

2. Stir in broth and water and bring to simmer. Reduce heat to medium-low, cover, and simmer until broccoli stalks are soft, about 8 minutes. Stir in broccoli florets and continue to simmer, covered, until tender, about 5 minutes.

3. Working in batches, process soup with evaporated milk, cheddar, and mustard in blender until cheese is melted and soup is smooth. Return soup to clean pot and reheat gently over medium-low heat. Season with salt and pepper to taste. Serve.

QUICK PREP TIP CLEANING LEEKS
After trimming and discarding root ends and dark green parts of leek, halve it lengthwise, then chop into pieces. Rinse cut leeks in bowl of water (or salad spinner) to remove any grit or dirt.

BEFORE NUMBERS BASED ON: Broccoli and Cheese Soup from Ruby Tuesday	BEFORE → **AFTER**	650 → **260** CALORIES	44 → **11** GRAMS FAT	N/A → **6** GRAMS SAT FAT

New England Clam Chowder

Serves 6

✔ **WHY THIS RECIPE WORKS:** One bite of this seaside favorite and you just know it's not diet food. We wanted a lighter take on clam chowder that offered the rich, savory flavor and ultra-creamy texture of the full-fat version. Bacon is a given in chowder recipes—it's cooked at the outset and the rendered fat is combined with flour to thicken the soup. But adding several slices to the pot can ratchet up the fat and calories in a heartbeat. While we found we couldn't eliminate it altogether, we reduced the amount to just two slices, chopped finely so the smoky, meaty flavor dispersed into every spoonful. But now we didn't have enough fat in the pot to cook the flour and thicken our chowder. We tried pureeing some of the potatoes and stirring them back into the pot, but that didn't work. Luckily, we found something else that did: instant potato flakes. Microwaving them with some clam broth ensured that they dissolved fully in the chowder, and a little cornstarch gave the soup a silky finish. Half-and-half added much-needed richness. As for the clams, we opted for the canned variety—they made prep a snap. And incorporating the juice from the cans, rather than pouring it down the drain, added even more rich, briny flavor to our chowder.

2	slices bacon, chopped fine
1	onion, chopped fine
2	garlic cloves, minced
¼	teaspoon dried thyme
1	pound russet potatoes, peeled and cut into ½-inch chunks
¼	cup dry white wine
2	bay leaves
4	(6.5-ounce) cans chopped clams, drained, juice reserved
¾	cup instant potato flakes
1	tablespoon cornstarch
1	(8-ounce) bottle clam juice
¾	cup half-and-half
1	tablespoon minced fresh parsley
	Salt and pepper

1. Cook bacon in Dutch oven over medium heat until rendered and crisp, about 3 minutes. Stir in onion and cook until softened, 5 to 7 minutes. Stir in garlic and thyme and cook until fragrant, about 30 seconds. Stir in potatoes, wine, bay leaves, and reserved clam juice. Bring to simmer and cook until potatoes are tender, 10 to 12 minutes.

2. Whisk potato flakes, cornstarch, and bottled clam juice together in bowl and microwave until thickened and smooth, about 1 minute. Stir potato-flake mixture into pot and simmer until thickened, about 3 minutes. Stir in half-and-half, parsley, and chopped clams and simmer gently until clams are heated through, about 2 minutes; do not boil. Remove bay leaves and season with salt and pepper to taste. Serve.

BEFORE NUMBERS BASED ON: New England Clam Chowder from Panera Bread	BEFORE → AFTER	630 → **240** CALORIES	54 → **8** GRAMS FAT	35 → **3.5** GRAMS SAT FAT

Shrimp Bisque

Serves 7

✓ **WHY THIS RECIPE WORKS:** Shrimp bisque is a refined soup with an ultra-creamy, velvety texture imparted by generous amounts of cream and butter. To lighten this sophisticated soup, we swapped the heavy cream for half-and-half, which provided richness while allowing the clean flavor of the shrimp to shine through. We also cut back, little by little, on the butter, until we were down to a single tablespoon. To ensure our bisque offered intense shrimp flavor, we sautéed a pound of shrimp with their shells on before flambéing them with brandy. Bottled clam juice provided a savory, briny backbone, and white wine contributed some acidity. Processing and straining the soup ensured a silky-smooth texture. For sweet, tender bites of shrimp, we reserved some to stir in at the end, heating them just long enough to cook through. Before flambéing, be sure to roll up long shirtsleeves, tie back long hair, and turn off the exhaust fan and any lit burners.

2	pounds medium-large shrimp (31 to 40 per pound)
⅓	cup brandy or cognac
1	onion, chopped coarse
1	carrot, peeled and chopped coarse
1	celery rib, chopped coarse
1	garlic clove, peeled
⅓	cup all-purpose flour
1	cup dry white wine
4	(8-ounce) bottles clam juice
1	(14.5-ounce) can diced tomatoes, drained
1	cup half-and-half
1	tablespoon lemon juice
1	sprig fresh tarragon
1	tablespoon unsalted butter
	Salt and pepper
2	tablespoons minced fresh chives

1. Peel and devein 1 pound shrimp, reserving shells, and cut each shrimp into 3 pieces; refrigerate until needed.

2. Heat 12-inch skillet over medium-high heat until just smoking. Add remaining 1 pound shrimp and reserved shrimp shells and cook until lightly browned, about 5 minutes. Off heat, add brandy and let warm through, about 5 seconds. Wave lit match over pan until brandy ignites, then shake pan to distribute flames.

3. When flames subside, transfer flambéed shrimp mixture to food processor and process until mixture resembles fine meal, 10 to 20 seconds; transfer to bowl. Pulse onion, carrot, celery, and garlic in food processor until finely chopped, about 5 pulses.

4. Combine processed shrimp and vegetables in Dutch oven. Cover and cook over medium-low heat, stirring occasionally, until softened and fragrant, 5 to 7 minutes. Stir in flour and cook for 1 minute. Gradually whisk in wine and clam juice, scraping up any browned bits and smoothing out any lumps. Stir in tomatoes, bring to simmer, and cook until thickened and flavors meld, about 20 minutes.

5. Strain broth through fine-mesh strainer, pressing on solids to release as much liquid as possible. Discard solids and wipe pot clean.

6. Combine strained broth, half-and-half, lemon juice, and tarragon in now-empty pot and bring to simmer. Stir in reserved shrimp pieces and simmer until shrimp are bright pink, 1 to 2 minutes. Off heat, remove tarragon, stir in butter, and season with salt and pepper to taste. Sprinkle individual portions with chives before serving.

BEFORE → **AFTER**	390 → **190**	24 → **6**	12 → **3.5**
	CALORIES	GRAMS FAT	GRAMS SAT FAT

All-American Chili

Serves 8

✓ **WHY THIS RECIPE WORKS:** For a lighter riff on the classic, thick beef chili, we replaced the ground beef with ground turkey. But because of its low fat content, the turkey needed special treatment so it didn't break down into small, overcooked bits. Sautéing just half of the ground poultry at the start, and breaking it up into little pieces with a spoon, worked to distribute the flavor while it simmered, ensuring the finished chili had a hearty, meaty flavor. For big bites of moist, tender meat, we added the remaining ground turkey toward the end of the simmering time; pinching the turkey into small pieces before stirring it in mimicked the crumbled appearance of ground beef. A mix of crushed and diced tomatoes gave us a thick chili with tender bites of tomato throughout. Using a heavy hand with the chili powder—a whopping ¼ cup—and supplementing it with cumin, coriander, red pepper flakes, oregano, and cayenne pepper produced a chili with big, bold flavor. This chili is fairly spicy; for a milder chili, use less red pepper flakes and cayenne, or omit them altogether. Serve with diced tomato, diced avocado, sliced scallions, chopped red onion, shredded low-fat cheddar cheese, plain Greek yogurt, lime wedges, and/or chopped fresh cilantro.

1	tablespoon canola oil
2	onions, chopped fine
1	red bell pepper, stemmed, seeded, and cut into ½-inch pieces
6	garlic cloves, minced
¼	cup chili powder
1	tablespoon ground cumin
2	teaspoons ground coriander
1	teaspoon red pepper flakes
1	teaspoon dried oregano
½	teaspoon cayenne pepper
2	pounds 93 percent lean ground turkey
2	(15-ounce) cans kidney beans, rinsed
1	(28-ounce) can diced tomatoes
1	(28-ounce) can crushed tomatoes
2	cups low-sodium chicken broth Salt and pepper

1. Heat oil in Dutch oven over medium heat until shimmering. Add onions, bell pepper, garlic, chili powder, cumin, coriander, pepper flakes, oregano, and cayenne and cook, stirring often, until vegetables are softened, 8 to 10 minutes.

2. Add 1 pound turkey, increase heat to medium-high, and cook, breaking up meat with wooden spoon, until no longer pink and just beginning to brown, about 4 minutes. Stir in beans, diced tomatoes and their juice, crushed tomatoes, and broth and bring to simmer. Reduce heat to medium-low and simmer until chili has begun to thicken, about 1 hour.

3. Pat remaining 1 pound turkey together into ball, then pinch off teaspoon-size pieces and stir into chili. Continue to simmer, stirring occasionally, until turkey is tender and chili is slightly thickened, about 40 minutes longer. (If chili begins to stick to bottom of pot, stir in ½ cup water.) Season with salt and pepper to taste. Serve.

BEFORE NUMBERS BASED ON: Chili Bowl from Johnny Rockets	BEFORE → **AFTER**	610 → **320** CALORIES	48 → **10** GRAMS FAT	24 → **2** GRAMS SAT FAT

MAKEOVER SPOTLIGHT:
ALL-AMERICAN CHILI

1. BLOOM THE SPICES FOR DEEPER FLAVOR: In the test kitchen, we often call for blooming spices as a way to add deeper flavor to a variety of dishes, especially longer-cooking ones, because the spices' flavor can become dull over time. Sautéing the spices with the aromatics helped to boost their potency, ensuring maximum flavor in the finished chili, and using just a tablespoon of oil helped to keep the fat down. A mix of chili powder, cumin, coriander, oregano, red pepper flakes, and cayenne pepper provided warmth and complexity.

2. USE GROUND TURKEY AND ADD IT IN BATCHES: Most chili recipes call for ground chuck, but to lighten this dish the fatty beef would have to go. Instead, we used 93 percent lean ground turkey. It ensured our chili was still hearty and meaty-tasting, but allowed us to cut the fat and calories substantially. Be sure not to use 99 percent lean ground turkey, or ground turkey breast; either will result in an overly lean chili.

3. FORTIFY THE FLAVOR WITH BROTH: To amp up the savory flavor of our turkey chili in the absence of any beef, we added some chicken broth. Most chili recipes simply rely on the canned tomatoes and their juice, and sometimes a little water, for volume, but this can result in an overly thick chili. We found that 2 cups of chicken broth, stirred in with the tomatoes and beans, offered significant complexity and savory depth and ensured the chili wasn't too thick.

4. PINCH THE MEAT FOR A HEARTY TEXTURE: Because the turkey added at the outset of cooking breaks down into tiny pieces, we found it important to reserve some of the meat and add it to the chili later. To give this second addition of ground turkey an appealing chunky, crumbled texture similar to ground beef (ground turkey naturally has a stringy appearance), we packed the meat into a ball, then pinched off bits and stirred them into the simmering chili.

Beef and Vegetable Stew

Serves 6

✔ **WHY THIS RECIPE WORKS:** Few things are as comforting as a steaming bowl of beef stew, chock-full of tender meat, carrots, and potatoes. But in reality, most beef stews we've had go heavy on the beef and light on the veggies. To make over this classic, we limited the beef to just 4 ounces per person (using beef chuck roast, which we've found to be the best cut for stew), and added plenty of extra vegetables—this kept the portion sizes ample but allowed us to trim fat and calories substantially. Besides the traditional carrots and potatoes, we included parsnips, kale, and peas. To deepen the meaty flavor of our veggie-laden stew, we made sure to brown the beef (this left flavorful, dark bits behind on the bottom of the pot) and added tomato paste to the mix (a single tablespoon enhanced the savory notes of our stew). Make this stew in a Dutch oven, preferably one with a capacity of 7 or 8 quarts. After trimming the beef, you should have 1½ pounds of usable meat and ½ pound of scraps and fat.

2	pounds boneless beef chuck-eye roast, trimmed of all visible fat, and cut into 1½-inch pieces
	Salt and pepper
5	teaspoons canola oil
1	large portobello mushroom cap, cut into ½-inch pieces
2	onions, chopped fine
3	garlic cloves, minced
1	tablespoon minced fresh thyme or 1 teaspoon dried
3	tablespoons all-purpose flour
1	tablespoon tomato paste
1½	cups dry red wine
2	cups low-sodium chicken broth
2	cups beef broth
2	bay leaves
12	ounces red potatoes, unpeeled, cut into 1-inch pieces
4	carrots, peeled, halved lengthwise, and sliced 1 inch thick
4	parsnips, peeled, halved lengthwise, and sliced 1 inch thick
1	pound kale, stemmed and sliced into ½-inch-wide strips
½	cup frozen peas
¼	cup minced fresh parsley

1. Adjust oven rack to lower-middle position and heat oven to 300 degrees. Pat beef dry with paper towels and season with salt and pepper. Heat 1 teaspoon oil in Dutch oven over medium-high heat until just smoking. Brown half of meat on all sides, 5 to 10 minutes; transfer to bowl. Repeat with 1 teaspoon oil and remaining beef; transfer to bowl.

2. Add portobello pieces to fat left in pot, cover, and cook over medium heat until softened and wet, about 5 minutes. Uncover and continue to cook until portobello pieces are dry and browned, 5 to 10 minutes.

3. Stir in remaining 1 tablespoon oil and onions and cook until softened, about 5 to 7 minutes. Stir in garlic and thyme and cook until fragrant, about 30 seconds. Stir in flour and tomato paste and cook until lightly browned, about 1 minute.

4. Slowly whisk in wine, scraping up any browned bits. Slowly whisk in broths until smooth. Stir in bay leaves and browned meat and bring to simmer. Cover, transfer pot to oven, and cook for 1½ hours.

5. Stir in potatoes, carrots, and parsnips and continue to cook in oven until meat and vegetables are tender, about 1 hour. Stir in kale and continue to cook in oven until tender, about 10 minutes. Remove stew from oven and remove bay leaves. Stir in peas and parsley and let stew sit for 5 to 10 minutes. Season with salt and pepper to taste. Serve.

BEFORE → **AFTER**	620 → **440**	19 → **10**	4.5 → **2**
	CALORIES	GRAMS FAT	GRAMS SAT FAT

Pork and Hominy Stew

Serves 8

✔ **WHY THIS RECIPE WORKS:** *Posole* is a Mexican stew that's big on flavor, thanks to a long simmer and an assortment of hard-to-find dried chiles. But it's also fairly fatty, due to the pork shoulder roast traditionally called for. For our lightened version, we looked to trim the fat but keep the flavor. We turned to easy-to-find dried ancho chiles and toasted them to deepen their flavor. For the pork, we selected lean tenderloin, which cooks quickly. To keep it moist and juicy, we sliced it thinly and tossed it with cornstarch, flour, and oil (a technique called velveting) prior to browning. Poaching two slices of bacon in the stew, then removing them at the end of cooking, added plenty of smoky flavor. Toasting the hominy made it sweet and chewy. Don't use store-bought chili powder; dried ancho chiles make all the difference. Serve the stew with sliced radishes, chopped avocado, chopped cilantro, hot sauce, and lime wedges.

3	dried ancho chiles, stemmed and seeded
7	cups low-sodium chicken broth
5	teaspoons canola oil
1	tablespoon cornstarch
1	tablespoon all-purpose flour
2	teaspoons water
2	(1-pound) pork tenderloins, trimmed of all visible fat and sliced thin
3	(15-ounce) cans white hominy, rinsed
2	onions, chopped fine
5	garlic cloves, minced
2	slices bacon
1	tablespoon minced fresh oregano
	Salt and pepper
1	tablespoon lime juice

1. Toast ancho chiles in 12-inch skillet over medium-high heat, stirring often, until fragrant, 4 to 6 minutes; reduce heat if chiles begin to smoke. Transfer to bowl and let cool. Add 1 cup broth to cooled chiles, cover, and microwave until bubbling, about 2 minutes; let stand until chiles are softened, 10 to 15 minutes.

2. Whisk 2 teaspoons oil, cornstarch, flour, and water together in medium bowl until smooth, then stir in pork until evenly coated. Heat 1 teaspoon oil in Dutch oven over medium-high heat until just smoking. Add half of pork, breaking up any clumps, and cook, without stirring, for 1 minute. Stir pork and continue to cook until lightly browned, 1 to 2 minutes longer; transfer to clean bowl. Repeat with 1 teaspoon oil and remaining pork; transfer to bowl.

3. Add hominy to now-empty pot and cook, stirring often, until hominy begins to darken, 2 to 3 minutes; transfer to separate bowl.

4. Heat remaining 1 teaspoon oil in now-empty pot over medium-low heat until shimmering. Add onions, cover, and cook, stirring occasionally, until softened, 5 to 7 minutes. Stir in garlic; cook until fragrant, about 30 seconds. Combine onion mixture and chile mixture in blender; puree until mostly smooth.

5. Combine remaining 6 cups broth, onion-chile mixture, bacon, oregano, and ½ teaspoon pepper in now-empty pot and bring to boil. Reduce heat to low, add hominy to pot, and simmer, covered, until tender, about 30 minutes.

6. Stir in pork and any accumulated juices and let heat through, 2 to 3 minutes. Off heat, remove bacon. Stir in lime juice and season with salt and pepper to taste. Serve.

BEFORE → **AFTER**	370 → **290** CALORIES	20 → **9** GRAMS FAT	3 → **1.5** GRAMS SAT FAT

Creole-Style Gumbo

Serves 6

✓ **WHY THIS RECIPE WORKS:** A hearty stew starring chicken, shrimp, and vegetables—with a little sausage thrown in for good measure—gumbo wouldn't seem to need a makeover. But dig a little deeper, and you'll see that at the heart of every gumbo recipe is a roux—a mixture of vegetable oil and flour, cooked to copper brown, that adds an unmistakable richness and flavor. For a lightened version of this bayou favorite, we tried cutting back on both the oil and the flour, but this gave us a lean-tasting, too-thin gumbo. So we decided to employ a technique often used in the test kitchen to boost the flavor of nuts and spices: toasting. Toasting our flour until it was brown gave our stew such complexity that we were able to reduce the oil to just 1 tablespoon, down from ¾ cup called for in other recipes. To punch up the flavor even more, we looked to an untraditional ingredient: fish sauce. Just a few tablespoons added significant depth without tasting out of place in our gumbo. The color of the toasted flour in step 1 should be slightly paler than a brown paper bag. Fish sauce can be found in the international section of most grocery stores. Since the salt content of fish sauce varies among brands, taste the finished gumbo before seasoning with salt. Serve with rice.

½ cup all-purpose flour

1 tablespoon canola oil

4 ounces andouille sausage, halved lengthwise and sliced thin

1 onion, chopped fine

1 green bell pepper, stemmed, seeded, and chopped fine

1 celery rib, chopped fine

5 garlic cloves, minced

1 teaspoon minced fresh thyme

¼ teaspoon cayenne pepper

4 cups low-sodium chicken broth

1 (14.5-ounce) can diced tomatoes, drained

3 tablespoons fish sauce

2 (12-ounce) bone-in split chicken breasts, skin removed, trimmed of all visible fat

1 pound medium shrimp (41 to 50 per pound), peeled, deveined, and tails removed

2 cups frozen okra, thawed
Salt and pepper

1. Toast flour in Dutch oven over medium heat, stirring constantly, until light brown and fragrant, 7 to 10 minutes; transfer to bowl.

2. Heat oil in now-empty pot over medium heat until just smoking. Add sausage and cook until browned, about 5 minutes. Stir in onion, bell pepper, and celery and cook until softened, about 8 minutes. Stir in toasted flour, garlic, thyme, and cayenne and cook until fragrant, about 1 minute. Slowly whisk in broth, scraping up any browned bits and smoothing out any lumps. Stir in tomatoes and fish sauce.

3. Add chicken, bring to simmer, then reduce heat to medium-low and cook until chicken registers 160 degrees, about 25 minutes. Transfer chicken to carving board, let cool slightly, then shred into bite-size pieces, discarding bones.

4. Stir shredded chicken, shrimp, and okra into pot and cook gently over medium heat until heated through, about 5 minutes. Season with salt and pepper to taste. Serve.

BEFORE → **AFTER**	540 → **300**	29 → **8**	4.5 → **2**
	CALORIES	GRAMS FAT	GRAMS SAT FAT

CHICKEN POT PIE

Classic Casseroles

Chicken Divan

Serves 8

✓ **WHY THIS RECIPE WORKS:** Once an elegant dish starring tender broccoli and moist chicken in a velvety sauce, chicken Divan has morphed into a heavy meal that's definitely bad for the waistline thanks to copious amounts of cream and butter. We set out to trim the fat and also turn it into a satisfying one-dish dinner by adding rice to the mix. A good amount of reduced-fat cheddar gave us a sauce with ultra-cheesy flavor, but finding just the right dairy to give it a rich, creamy texture took some work. After a number of tests, we hit on low-fat evaporated milk, which gave the sauce a silky texture; a bit of cornstarch helped to thicken it nicely. Parcooking both the broccoli and the chicken was key to ensuring tender, moist bites in the finished dish. A final sprinkling of panko bread crumbs, added just before the casserole went into the oven, provided a nice, crunchy contrast to the creamy filling below.

1	pound broccoli florets, cut into 1-inch pieces
1	tablespoon canola oil
1	onion, chopped fine
2	garlic cloves, minced
1	teaspoon minced fresh thyme
	Salt and pepper
1½	cups long-grain white rice
3	cups low-sodium chicken broth
2	(12-ounce) cans 2 percent low-fat evaporated milk
½	cup water
1	tablespoon cornstarch
1½	pounds boneless, skinless chicken breasts, trimmed of all visible fat, halved lengthwise, and cut into ½-inch-thick slices on bias
2	tablespoons Dijon mustard
8	ounces 50 percent light cheddar cheese, shredded (2 cups)
1	cup panko bread crumbs, toasted (see page 18)

1. Adjust oven rack to middle position and heat oven to 400 degrees. Combine broccoli and ¼ cup water in bowl, cover, and microwave until broccoli is just tender, about 5 minutes. Drain broccoli and transfer to 13 by 9-inch baking dish.

2. Meanwhile, heat 2 teaspoons oil in Dutch oven over medium heat until shimmering. Add onion, garlic, thyme, and 1 teaspoon salt and cook until onions are softened and lightly browned, 5 to 7 minutes. Stir in rice and cook until edges of grains begin to turn translucent, about 3 minutes. Whisk in broth and evaporated milk and bring to simmer. Turn heat to medium-low, cover, and cook, stirring often, until rice is just tender, about 15 minutes.

3. Combine water and cornstarch in bowl, then stir into pot. Continue to simmer, stirring constantly, until rice mixture is slightly thickened, about 2 minutes. Stir in chicken and cook until no longer pink (chicken will not be fully cooked), about 4 minutes. Off heat, stir in mustard, ¼ teaspoon pepper, and cheddar, a handful at a time, until melted.

4. Pour rice mixture over broccoli in baking dish. Toss toasted panko with remaining 1 teaspoon oil in bowl, season with salt and pepper to taste, and sprinkle over top. Bake until sauce is bubbling around edges, 15 to 20 minutes. Let cool slightly before serving.

BEFORE → **AFTER**	660 → **430** CALORIES	39 → **10** GRAMS FAT	22 → **3.5** GRAMS SAT FAT

Chicken Florentine

Serves 4

✓ **WHY THIS RECIPE WORKS:** To lighten this retro dish, which is usually weighed down with soggy spinach and too much cream, we started by draining the excess liquid from our cooked spinach by placing it in a colander and pressing on the leaves with a rubber spatula. Searing the chicken breasts first, and then poaching them before broiling our casserole, ensured the meat left flavorful browned bits, or fond, behind, from which we could build our sauce. Cooking the chicken this way also guaranteed every bite was moist and tender. For the sauce, we cut back to just 2 tablespoons of cream for a silky texture; chicken broth gave it a savory flavor, and combining the broth with water prevented the sauce from tasting overly salty. A sprinkling of Parmesan cheese contributed nutty, earthy notes, while a squeeze of lemon juice and a bit of zest added brightness to our fresh take on chicken Florentine. We prefer the tender leaves (and convenience) of bagged baby spinach in this recipe; if using curly-leaf spinach, chop it before cooking. Be sure to drain the spinach well after cooking in step 1 or else the sauce will be watery.

4	teaspoons canola oil
12	ounces (12 cups) baby spinach
1½	pounds boneless, skinless chicken breasts, trimmed of all visible fat
	Salt and pepper
1	shallot, minced
2	garlic cloves, minced
1	tablespoon all-purpose flour
2	cups low-sodium chicken broth
1¼	cups water
2	tablespoons heavy cream
1	teaspoon grated lemon zest plus 1 teaspoon juice
2	tablespoons grated Parmesan cheese

1. Heat 2 teaspoons oil in 12-inch skillet over medium heat until shimmering. Add spinach, a handful at a time, and cook, stirring often, until wilted, about 5 minutes. Transfer spinach to colander and press with rubber spatula to remove excess liquid.

2. Pat chicken dry with paper towels and season with salt and pepper. Wipe out now-empty skillet with paper towels, add remaining 2 teaspoons oil, and heat over medium-high heat until just smoking. Brown chicken lightly on both sides, 4 to 6 minutes; transfer to plate.

3. Add shallot and garlic to oil left in skillet and cook over medium heat until fragrant, about 30 seconds. Stir in flour. Whisk in broth and water, scraping up any browned bits. Add browned chicken and any accumulated juices and bring to simmer. Reduce heat to medium-low and cook until chicken registers 160 degrees, about 10 minutes. Transfer chicken to carving board and tent loosely with aluminum foil.

4. Meanwhile, continue to simmer sauce until slightly thickened and reduced to ¾ cup, about 15 minutes. Off heat, whisk in cream and lemon zest and juice. Season with salt and pepper to taste.

5. Adjust oven rack 5 inches from broiler element and heat broiler. Slice chicken crosswise into ½-inch-thick slices and arrange slices in 2-quart broiler-safe baking dish. Scatter spinach over top, then cover with sauce and sprinkle with Parmesan. Broil until cheese is spotty brown, about 5 minutes. Let cool slightly before serving.

BEFORE → **AFTER**	560 → **340** CALORIES	37 → **13** GRAMS FAT	17 → **3.5** GRAMS SAT FAT

Chicken Tetrazzini

Serves 6

WHY THIS RECIPE WORKS: Most Tetrazzini recipes start with leftover turkey, which is why this dish is so popular right after Thanksgiving, but we wanted it to be an anytime dish, so we swapped in boneless, skinless chicken breasts. An untraditional move—marinating the chicken in soy sauce—added flavor and also helped keep the meat tender. For the creamy sauce, we tried various types of low-fat dairy; in the end, only reduced-fat cream cheese, plus some grated Parmesan, yielded a rich-tasting, full-bodied sauce. You can substitute 2 cups of cooked chopped turkey for the chicken, omitting the soy-sauce marinade in step 1.

12	ounces boneless, skinless chicken breasts, trimmed of all visible fat and cut into ¾-inch pieces
2	tablespoons low-sodium soy sauce
5	ounces spaghetti, broken in half
	Salt and pepper
1	tablespoon unsalted butter
8	ounces white or cremini mushrooms, trimmed and sliced thin
1	onion, chopped fine
2	tablespoons all-purpose flour
1	cup low-sodium chicken broth
2	tablespoons dry sherry
3	ounces ⅓ less fat cream cheese (neufchatel), softened
1	ounce Parmesan cheese, grated (½ cup)
1	cup frozen peas
½	cup panko bread crumbs, toasted (see page 18)

1. Adjust oven rack to upper-middle position and heat oven to 400 degrees. Combine chicken and soy sauce in bowl, cover, and refrigerate for 30 minutes to 1 hour. Bring 2 quarts water to boil in large pot. Add pasta and 1½ teaspoons salt and cook, stirring often, until just al dente. Reserve 1 cup cooking water, then drain pasta and return it to pot.

2. Meanwhile, melt butter in 12-inch skillet over medium-high heat. Add mushrooms, onion, ½ teaspoon salt, and ½ teaspoon pepper and cook until browned, 6 to 8 minutes. Stir in flour and cook until golden, about 2 minutes.

3. Whisk in broth, sherry, and reserved pasta water, scraping up any browned bits, and bring to simmer. Whisk in cream cheese and 6 tablespoons Parmesan and simmer until slightly thickened, about 1 minute. Stir in marinated chicken and peas and simmer gently for 1 minute (chicken will not be fully cooked). Add mixture to cooked pasta and toss to combine.

4. Transfer mixture to 8-inch square baking dish. Toss toasted panko with remaining 2 tablespoons Parmesan in bowl, season with salt and pepper to taste, and sprinkle over top. Bake until hot throughout, 12 to 14 minutes. Let cool slightly before serving.

QUICK PREP TIP
BREAKING LONG-STRAND PASTA IN HALF
To neatly snap noodles in half without having them fly every which way, put them in a zipper-lock bag (or wrap them in a clean kitchen towel), then press against the corner of a counter.

BEFORE → **AFTER**	500 → **290** CALORIES	19 → **8** GRAMS FAT	11 → **4.5** GRAMS SAT FAT

Chicken Pot Pie

Serves 8

✓ **WHY THIS RECIPE WORKS:** With its buttery, flaky crust and tender chicken and vegetables coated in a velvety sauce, what's not to love about chicken pot pie? How about the fact that a single serving can pack in almost 40 grams of fat? To lighten this family-friendly classic, we'd have to cut back on the butter in both the crust and the filling. We started with the sauce, which relies on a butter-flour roux for its thickening power and richness. Fortunately, we found that simply toasting the flour let us ditch the butter; this easy step added deep flavor and allowed us to add the flour to the stew without having it clump. Adding a bit of soy sauce to the filling helped ramp up its flavor even further. Moving on to the topping, we knew pie dough was out. Though puff pastry isn't your standard low-fat fare, we found that one sheet provided the perfect flaky, buttery topping without ratcheting up the fat count significantly. To thaw frozen puff pastry, allow it to sit either in the refrigerator for 24 hours or on the counter for 30 minutes to 1 hour.

1	(9½ by 9-inch) sheet puff pastry, thawed
½	cup all-purpose flour
2	teaspoons canola oil
1	onion, chopped fine
1	celery rib, minced
3½	cups low-sodium chicken broth
1	tablespoon low-sodium soy sauce
2	pounds boneless, skinless chicken breasts, trimmed of all visible fat
3	carrots, peeled, halved lengthwise, and sliced ¼ inch thick
1	cup whole milk
¾	cup frozen peas
2	tablespoons minced fresh parsley
2	teaspoons lemon juice
	Salt and pepper

1. Adjust oven rack to middle position and heat oven to 425 degrees. Roll puff pastry into 13 by 9-inch rectangle on lightly floured counter and transfer to parchment paper–lined rimmed baking sheet. Using tip of paring knife, lightly score pastry in half lengthwise, then into quarters widthwise to create 8 segments, making sure not to cut through pastry completely. Bake pastry until puffed and lightly browned, about 8 minutes; let cool on sheet.

2. Toast flour in 12-inch nonstick skillet over medium-high heat, stirring often, until fragrant and lightly golden, about 5 minutes; transfer to medium bowl and let cool.

3. Meanwhile, heat oil in Dutch oven over medium heat until shimmering. Add onion and celery and cook until softened and lightly browned, 8 to 10 minutes. Stir in broth and soy sauce, scraping up any browned bits. Add chicken and carrots and bring to simmer. Reduce heat to low, cover, and cook until chicken registers 160 degrees, 10 to 15 minutes. Transfer chicken to carving board, let cool slightly, then shred into bite-size pieces.

4. Whisk milk into toasted flour until smooth, then whisk into pot. Bring to simmer and cook, whisking constantly, until sauce thickens, about 2 minutes. Off heat, stir in shredded chicken, peas, parsley, and lemon juice. Season with salt and pepper to taste.

5. Transfer mixture to 13 by 9-inch baking dish. Place baked pastry on top and cut four 1-inch steam vents along center. Bake until pastry is deep golden and sauce is bubbling around edges, about 15 minutes. Let cool slightly before serving.

BEFORE → **AFTER**	610 → **340**	36 → **13**	17 → **5**
	CALORIES	GRAMS FAT	GRAMS SAT FAT

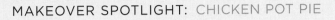

MAKEOVER SPOTLIGHT: CHICKEN POT PIE

1. DITCH THE BUTTERY PIE DOUGH IN FAVOR OF PUFF PASTRY:
We swapped all-butter pie dough for store-bought puff pastry, which is lower in fat and calories and requires only parbaking. After rolling the thawed puff pastry into a 13 by 9-inch rectangle on a lightly floured counter, transfer it to a parchment paper–lined baking sheet. Using a sharp paring knife, lightly score the pastry into 8 equal segments, taking care not to cut all the way through; this makes serving easier. Parbaking the pastry jumpstarts its cooking, so it can start to puff in the oven before finishing on top of the pot pie.

2. MAKE A ROUX WITHOUT BUTTER BY TOASTING THE FLOUR:
A roux is a classic cooked mixture of flour and fat used to thicken a sauce, and it is used in most chicken pot pie fillings. To make our pot pie leaner, we omitted the butter from the roux completely. But you can't just whisk flour into broth to form a sauce because the flour will clump. To ensure a smooth roux, we toasted the flour before mixing it with milk and stirring it into the sauce. The quick step of toasting the flour not only prevented any clumping, but it also lent a nice, roasted flavor and a little color to the sauce as well.

3. POACH THE CHICKEN GENTLY FOR TENDER MEAT: To keep our boneless, skinless chicken breasts from becoming dry and rubbery, we gently poached the chicken in the sauce over low heat. This kept the meat moist and tender. Once the poached chicken has cooled, it can be shredded into tender, bite-size pieces and stirred back into the filling.

4. VENT THE PUFF PASTRY BEFORE BAKING TO KEEP IT CRISP:
To allow steam to escape and prevent the pastry from becoming soggy as the casserole bakes, we found it essential to vent it. After placing the parbaked puff pastry on top of the filling, cut 4 vents, each about 1 inch long, along the center of the pastry.

Tuna Noodle Casserole

Serves 8

✔ **WHY THIS RECIPE WORKS:** Easy to make and economical, tuna noodle casserole was once a go-to supper for families. Sadly, this homey dish has earned a bad rap in recent years. Many recipes are bland and pasty, with mushy noodles and a tinny taste from the laundry list of canned ingredients. To make over this comfort-food classic, we had to lighten it and brighten it. Half-and-half provided richness while cutting back on fat and calories, and two types of cheese (reduced-fat cheddar and American) delivered both cheesy flavor and a creamy texture. We found that cooking the noodles until they were just al dente kept them from becoming mushy in our casserole, and tossing the tuna with a little oil and lemon juice gave the dish a fresh, bright flavor. Frozen peas, which we simply stirred in before baking, added some sweetness. With toasted panko sprinkled over the top, this light casserole was way better than any full-fat version we'd ever tasted. For the American cheese, we found Boar's Head 25 Percent Lower Fat American Cheese worked well; this cheese can be found at the deli counter.

12	ounces (7¾ cups) egg noodles
	Salt and pepper
3	(5-ounce) cans solid white tuna in water, drained thoroughly
4	teaspoons olive oil
2	teaspoons lemon juice
10	ounces white mushrooms, trimmed and sliced ¼ inch thick
1	onion, chopped fine
3	cups low-sodium chicken broth
1½	cups half-and-half
½	cup water
2	tablespoons cornstarch
4	ounces 50 percent light cheddar cheese, shredded (1 cup)
3	ounces reduced-fat American cheese, shredded (¾ cup)
1	cup frozen peas
1	cup panko bread crumbs, toasted (see page 18)

1. Adjust oven rack to middle position and heat oven to 425 degrees. Bring 4 quarts water to boil in Dutch oven. Add noodles and 1 tablespoon salt and cook, stirring often, until just al dente. Drain pasta; set aside.

2. Combine tuna, 2 teaspoons oil, lemon juice, ¼ teaspoon salt, and ¼ teaspoon pepper in bowl and flake tuna into coarse pieces with fork; let sit for 10 minutes.

3. In now-empty pot, heat 1 teaspoon oil over medium-high heat until shimmering. Add mushrooms and onion and cook until liquid evaporates and mushrooms are browned, 6 to 8 minutes. Whisk in broth and half-and-half, scraping up any browned bits, and bring to simmer. Combine water and cornstarch in bowl, then whisk into pot. Continue to simmer, whisking constantly, until sauce is slightly thickened, about 3 minutes. Off heat, whisk in cheddar and American cheese, a handful at a time, until melted. Stir in cooked noodles, tuna mixture, peas, ½ teaspoon salt, and ½ teaspoon pepper.

4. Transfer mixture to 13 by 9-inch baking dish. Toss toasted panko with remaining 1 teaspoon oil in bowl, season with salt and pepper to taste, and sprinkle over top. Bake until sauce is bubbling around edges, 12 to 14 minutes. Let cool slightly before serving.

BEFORE → **AFTER**	690 → **450** CALORIES	40 → **16** GRAMS FAT	21 → **7** GRAMS SAT FAT

Mexican Lasagna

Serves 8

☑ **WHY THIS RECIPE WORKS:** Mexican lasagna keeps the meaty, cheesy layers of its Italian cousin but adds peppers, beans, and corn to the mix. It also ditches the noodles in favor of tortillas for a dish with a distinctly south-of-the-border feel. For ours, we opted to use lean ground turkey, which offered a hearty texture and subtle meaty flavor while also keeping our dish on the leaner side. Doubling the amount of beans made our casserole even heartier. After browning the turkey with the aromatics, we added the beans, plus corn and diced tomatoes, and let it all simmer for 10 minutes so the flavors could meld. Corn tortillas, which we softened slightly in the microwave, contributed a pleasing texture and flavor. A light coating of vegetable oil spray prevented them from becoming mushy when covered with our sauce in the baking dish. Light cheddar cheese worked well in place of the full-fat version, and layering it in the casserole—instead of sprinkling it all on top—ensured every bite offered rich, cheesy flavor. Our Mexican lasagna was pretty good now, but what really put it over the top was a layer of crumbled tortilla chips (baked, not fried); they added a nice crunch and a pleasantly salty bite. Be sure to use 93 percent lean ground turkey, not ground turkey breast (also labeled 99 percent fat free). Serve with salsa, diced avocados, plain Greek yogurt, and/or sliced scallions.

2	teaspoons canola oil
2	red bell peppers, stemmed, seeded, and cut into ½-inch pieces
1	onion, chopped fine
	Salt and pepper
3	garlic cloves, minced
1	tablespoon minced canned chipotle chile in adobo sauce
2	teaspoons chili powder
1	pound 93 percent lean ground turkey
2	tablespoons all-purpose flour
2	cups low-sodium chicken broth
2	(15-ounce) cans pinto beans, rinsed
2	cups frozen corn, thawed
1	(14.5-ounce) can diced tomatoes, drained
6	tablespoons minced fresh cilantro
2	tablespoons lime juice
12	(6-inch) corn tortillas
	Vegetable oil spray
4	ounces 50 percent light cheddar cheese, shredded (1 cup)
2½	ounces baked tortilla chips, crushed (1 cup)

1. Heat oil in Dutch oven over medium heat until shimmering. Add bell peppers, onion, and ½ teaspoon salt, cover, and cook until softened, 8 to 10 minutes. Stir in garlic, chipotle, chili powder, and ¼ teaspoon pepper and cook until fragrant, about 30 seconds. Stir in turkey and cook, breaking up meat with wooden spoon, until no longer pink, 5 to 8 minutes.

2. Stir in flour and cook for 1 minute. Gradually stir in broth and bring to simmer. Stir in beans, corn, and tomatoes and simmer until mixture is slightly thickened and flavors have blended, about 10 minutes. Off heat, stir in ¼ cup cilantro and lime juice and season with salt and pepper to taste.

3. Adjust oven rack to middle position and heat oven to 450 degrees. Spray both sides of tortillas with oil spray. Stack tortillas on plate, cover, and microwave until warm and pliable, 40 to 60 seconds.

4. Spread one-third of turkey mixture into 13 by 9-inch baking dish. Cover with 6 tortillas, overlapping as needed, and sprinkle with ⅓ cup cheddar. Repeat with half of remaining filling, remaining 6 tortillas, and ⅓ cup cheddar. Spread remaining filling over top and sprinkle with crushed chips and remaining ⅓ cup cheddar.

5. Bake until sauce is bubbling around edges, about 10 minutes. Let cool slightly and sprinkle with remaining 2 tablespoons cilantro. Serve.

BEFORE → **AFTER**	660 → **400** CALORIES	37 → **12** GRAMS FAT	15 → **3** GRAMS SAT FAT

Chicken Chilaquiles

Serves 4

☑ **WHY THIS RECIPE WORKS:** Traditionally, the Mexican dish known as chilaquiles starts with fried tortillas, which are covered in a red or green sauce and simmered until softened; then they're topped with shredded meat or eggs, cheese, and *crema* (the Mexican version of sour cream). We wanted a fresher and lighter take on this dish, and opted to bake, not fry, our tortillas; a spritz of vegetable oil spray helped them crisp in the oven. Instead of cooking the vegetables for the sauce in lots of oil, we cut way back and cooked them covered so they would release their moisture, then removed the lid so the moisture would cook off and the flavors would concentrate. Shredded chicken added a nice heartiness to our casserole, so we nixed the eggs. Crumbled *queso fresco* contributed a salty, tangy bite, and low-fat sour cream worked well as a stand-in for the crema. If you cannot find poblano chiles, substitute 2 green bell peppers. To make this dish spicier, add the chile seeds.

10   **(6-inch) corn tortillas, each cut into 8 wedges**
    Vegetable oil spray
2   **poblano chiles, stemmed, seeded, and chopped coarse**
2   **onions, chopped fine**
2   **teaspoons canola oil**
    Salt and pepper
¼   **cup minced fresh cilantro**
6   **garlic cloves, minced**
2   **teaspoons minced canned chipotle chile in adobo sauce**
1   **(14.5-ounce) can whole peeled tomatoes**
¾   **cup low-sodium chicken broth**
1½   **pounds boneless, skinless chicken breasts, trimmed of all visible fat**
3   **ounces crumbled queso fresco or feta cheese (¾ cup)**
¼   **cup low-fat sour cream**
1   **tablespoon lime juice**
1   **tomato, cored, seeded, and chopped**

1. Adjust oven racks to upper-middle and lower-middle positions and heat oven to 350 degrees. Spread tortillas over 2 rimmed baking sheets, spray both sides with oil spray, and bake until brown and dry, 16 to 24 minutes, flipping them halfway through baking; let cool. Increase oven temperature to 500 degrees.

2. Combine poblanos, half of onions, oil, and ¼ teaspoon salt in 12-inch skillet. Cover and cook over medium-low heat until vegetables are softened, 8 to 10 minutes. Uncover, increase heat to medium-high, and cook, stirring occasionally, until lightly browned, 4 to 6 minutes.

3. Stir in 2 tablespoons cilantro, garlic, and chipotle and cook until fragrant, about 30 seconds. Stir in canned tomatoes with their juice and broth. Add chicken and bring to simmer. Reduce heat to low, cover, and cook until chicken registers 160 degrees, 10 to 15 minutes.

4. Transfer chicken to carving board, let cool slightly, then shred into bite-size pieces. Transfer sauce left in skillet to blender and process until smooth, about 1 minute. Return sauce to skillet, season with salt and pepper to taste, and bring to simmer over medium heat. Stir in baked tortillas and cook until they begin to soften, about 2 minutes. Off heat, stir in shredded chicken. Transfer mixture to 8-inch square baking dish and sprinkle with cheese. Bake on lower-middle rack until hot throughout, 5 to 10 minutes.

5. Let casserole cool slightly. Combine sour cream and lime juice and drizzle over top, then sprinkle with tomato, remaining onions, and remaining 2 tablespoons cilantro. Serve.

BEFORE → AFTER	770 → **520**	44 → **13**	15 → **2.5**
	CALORIES	GRAMS FAT	GRAMS SAT FAT

King Ranch Casserole

Serves 8

✓ **WHY THIS RECIPE WORKS:** If you've never had this popular dish from the Lone Star State, you're missing out. This ultra-satisfying casserole takes corn tortillas, tender chicken, and mildly spiced onions and tomatoes and smothers them in a cheesy, creamy sauce before baking it all in the oven. Just to gild the lily, the whole thing is topped with crushed Fritos. But with a single serving clocking in around 630 calories and almost 40 grams of fat, this is a once-in-a-while entrée. So we could enjoy it more often, we decided to make it over, and started by cutting the heavy cream from the ingredient list. Instead, we used a small amount of reduced-fat cream cheese to give our sauce the silky texture of the original version. A moderate amount of grated Colby Jack cheese imparted plenty of cheesy flavor, and flour thickened the sauce nicely. Ground toasted tortillas, sprinkled over the casserole, provided the same subtle crunch and corn flavor of the crushed Fritos—without all the fat and calories. If you can't find Ro-tel tomatoes, substitute 1 (14.5-ounce) can diced tomatoes and 1 (4-ounce) drained can chopped green chiles.

10	**(6-inch) corn tortillas**
	Vegetable oil spray
½	**teaspoon granulated garlic**
½	**teaspoon chili powder**
	Salt and pepper
2	**teaspoons canola oil**
2	**onions, chopped fine**
2	**jalapeño chiles, stemmed, seeded, and minced**
2	**teaspoons ground cumin**
2	**(10-ounce) cans Ro-tel tomatoes**
6	**tablespoons all-purpose flour**
3½	**cups low-sodium chicken broth**
1½	**pounds boneless, skinless chicken breasts, trimmed of all visible fat**
4	**ounces ⅓ less fat cream cheese (neufchatel), cut into ¼-inch pieces**
6	**ounces Colby Jack cheese, shredded (1½ cups)**
2	**tablespoons minced fresh cilantro**

1. Adjust oven racks to upper-middle and lower-middle positions and heat oven to 450 degrees. Spread tortillas over 2 rimmed baking sheets, spray both sides with oil spray, and bake until toasted and crisp, 10 to 12 minutes, flipping them halfway through baking; let cool. Pulse 2 toasted tortillas, granulated garlic, chili powder, and ½ teaspoon salt in food processor until coarsely ground, about 12 pulses; set aside. Break remaining 8 tortillas into bite-size pieces; set aside.

2. Heat oil in Dutch oven over medium-high heat until shimmering. Add onions, jalapeños, and cumin and cook until lightly browned, about 6 minutes. Stir in tomatoes with their juice and cook until most of liquid has evaporated, about 8 minutes. Stir in flour, ½ teaspoon salt, and ½ teaspoon pepper and cook for 1 minute. Slowly whisk in broth and bring to boil. Reduce heat to medium-low and simmer until thickened, about 3 minutes.

3. Add chicken and bring to simmer. Reduce heat to low, cover, and cook until chicken registers 160 degrees, 10 to 15 minutes. Transfer chicken to carving board, let cool slightly, then shred into bite-size pieces. Off heat, stir in cream cheese and Colby Jack, a handful at a time, until melted. Stir in cilantro and shredded chicken.

4. Scatter half of bite-size tortilla pieces into 13 by 9-inch baking dish, then top with half of chicken mixture; repeat with remaining bite-size tortillas and remaining chicken mixture. Sprinkle ground tortilla mixture over top and spray lightly with oil spray. Bake on upper-middle rack until sauce is bubbling around edges, 15 to 20 minutes. Let cool slightly before serving.

BEFORE → **AFTER**	630 → **380**	36 → **16**	19 → **6**
	CALORIES	GRAMS FAT	GRAMS SAT FAT

Chicken Enchiladas

Serves 6

✓ **WHY THIS RECIPE WORKS:** The things that make this Mexican dish so irresistible are the same things that make it so bad for you: the layer of melted cheese, the juicy chicken, and the heavy, rich sauce. For our take on this classic, we determined right off the bat that the dark meat would have to go. Chicken breasts worked well when simmered gently in a potently flavored sauce; the meat was tender and infused with deep flavor. Instead of sprinkling all the cheese on top of the enchiladas, we saved some and mixed it in with the chicken and sauce for ultra-cheesy bites throughout. Pickled jalapeños and minced cilantro added tangy, peppery notes and freshness. When forming our enchiladas, simply rolling the filling in cold tortillas didn't cut it—the enchiladas broke and tore. Heating the tortillas in the microwave helped to make them pliable. Make sure that the cooked chicken is finely shredded, or the edges of large pieces will tear through the tortillas. Serve with lime wedges, plain Greek yogurt, diced avocado, shredded lettuce, and hot sauce.

1	onion, chopped fine
1	teaspoon canola oil
	Salt and pepper
3	garlic cloves, minced
3	tablespoons chili powder
2	teaspoons ground cumin
2	teaspoons sugar
1	(15-ounce) can tomato sauce
1¼	cups water
1	pound boneless, skinless chicken breasts, trimmed of all visible fat
8	ounces 50 percent light cheddar cheese, shredded (2 cups)
1	(4-ounce) can jalapeño chiles, drained and chopped
½	cup minced fresh cilantro
12	(6-inch) corn tortillas
	Vegetable oil spray

1. Adjust oven rack to middle position and heat oven to 350 degrees. Combine onion, oil, and ½ teaspoon salt in large saucepan, cover, and cook over medium-low heat until softened, 8 to 10 minutes. Stir in garlic, chili powder, cumin, and sugar and cook until fragrant, about 30 seconds. Stir in tomato sauce and water, bring to simmer, and cook until slightly thickened, about 5 minutes. Add chicken and bring to simmer. Reduce heat to low, cover, and cook until chicken registers 160 degrees, 10 to 15 minutes.

2. Transfer chicken to carving board, let cool slightly, then shred into small pieces. Strain sauce through medium-mesh strainer into bowl and press to extract as much liquid as possible. Transfer strained bits to large bowl and stir in shredded chicken, ½ cup strained sauce, 1 cup cheddar, jalapeños, and cilantro. Season chicken filling and sauce with salt and pepper to taste.

3. Stack tortillas on plate, cover with damp towel, and microwave until warm and pliable, about 1 minute. Spread warm tortillas over clean counter. Spoon ⅓ cup chicken mixture down center of each tortilla, roll up tortillas tightly, and lay, seam side down, in 13 by 9-inch baking dish.

4. Lightly spray tops of enchiladas with oil spray. Pour sauce over enchiladas, covering tortillas completely. Sprinkle remaining 1 cup cheddar evenly over top. Cover baking dish with aluminum foil and bake until enchiladas are hot throughout, 20 to 25 minutes. Let cool slightly before serving.

BEFORE → **AFTER**	560 → **340** CALORIES	31 → **11** GRAMS FAT	17 → **5** GRAMS SAT FAT

Shepherd's Pie

Serves 6

✔ **WHY THIS RECIPE WORKS:** For a lower-fat shepherd's pie that was still ultra-rich and hearty, we used lean ground beef and handled it gently when cooking so we had big chunks of meat throughout. Tossing the meat with a bit of baking soda was key to keeping it tender and juicy in the finished dish.

1½ **pounds 93 percent lean ground beef**

2 **tablespoons plus 2 teaspoons water**

½ **teaspoon baking soda**
    Salt and pepper

2½ **pounds russet potatoes, peeled and cut into 1-inch chunks**

2 **tablespoons unsalted butter, melted**

½ **cup 2 percent low-fat milk**

1 **large egg yolk**

8 **scallions, green parts only, sliced thin**

2 **teaspoons vegetable oil**

1 **onion, chopped**

4 **ounces white mushrooms, trimmed and chopped**

1 **tablespoon tomato paste**

2 **garlic cloves, minced**

2 **tablespoons Madeira or ruby port**

2 **tablespoons all-purpose flour**

1¼ **cups beef broth**

2 **teaspoons Worcestershire sauce**

1 **bay leaf**

2 **sprigs fresh thyme**

2 **carrots, peeled and chopped**

2 **teaspoons cornstarch**

1. Toss ground beef with 2 tablespoons water, baking soda, 1 teaspoon salt, and ¼ teaspoon pepper in bowl until well combined; let sit for 20 minutes.

2. Meanwhile, place potatoes and 1 tablespoon salt in large saucepan; add water to cover. Bring to boil, then reduce to simmer and cook until potatoes are tender, 8 to 10 minutes. Drain potatoes; return to saucepan over low heat, stirring constantly, to evaporate any remaining moisture, about 1 minute. Off heat, mash potatoes smooth with potato masher. Stir in butter. Whisk milk and egg yolk together in bowl, then stir into potatoes. Stir in scallions; season with salt and pepper to taste. Cover; set aside.

3. Heat oil in broiler-safe 10-inch skillet over medium heat until shimmering. Add onion and mushrooms and cook until vegetables begin to soften, 4 to 6 minutes. Stir in tomato paste and garlic and cook until bottom of skillet is dark brown, about 2 minutes. Stir in Madeira, scraping up any browned bits, and cook until evaporated, about 1 minute. Stir in flour and cook for 1 minute. Stir in broth, Worcestershire, bay leaf, thyme, and carrots; bring to boil, scraping up any browned bits.

4. Reduce heat to medium-low. Pinch beef into 2-inch pieces and lay on top of mixture in skillet. Cover and cook until beef is cooked through, 10 to 12 minutes, stirring and breaking up meat chunks with two forks halfway through cooking time. Combine cornstarch and remaining 2 teaspoons water in bowl, then stir into skillet. Continue to simmer, stirring constantly, until filling is slightly thickened, about 30 seconds. Remove thyme and bay leaf. Season with pepper to taste.

5. Adjust oven rack 6 inches from broiler element and heat broiler. Place mashed potatoes in large zipper-lock bag; snip off corner to create 1-inch opening. Pipe potatoes evenly over filling to cover entire surface. Smooth potato with back of spoon, then use tines of fork to make ridges over surface. Place skillet on rimmed baking sheet; broil until potatoes are golden and sauce is bubbling, 10 to 15 minutes. Let cool slightly; serve.

BEFORE → **AFTER**	710 → **450** CALORIES	40 → **15** GRAMS FAT	19 → **6** GRAMS SAT FAT

Cheeseburger Pie

Serves 6

✔ **WHY THIS RECIPE WORKS:** Although many cheeseburger pies start with pie dough or refrigerated crescent rolls, we knew these were a no-go if we wanted to trim fat and calories from our recipe. So we looked for a low-fat alternative. Our solution? Flour tortillas. We used two for our "pie shell" and sprinkled reduced-fat American cheese in between them so they'd stick together, making a sturdy, yet light, base for our flavorful filling. When it came to the filling, 93 percent lean ground beef gave our cheeseburger pie a hearty texture; to amp up the savory, meaty notes, we added chicken broth and Worcestershire sauce. Simply topped with pickles, tomato slices, and more American cheese, this casserole tasted just like its sandwich cousin, without any of the greasy guilt. For the cheese, we found Boar's Head 25 Percent Lower Fat American Cheese worked well; this cheese can be found at the deli counter.

2　(10-inch) flour tortillas
　　Vegetable oil spray
4　ounces reduced-fat American cheese, shredded (1 cup)
1　teaspoon canola oil
1　onion, chopped fine
2　garlic cloves, minced
1　pound 93 percent lean ground beef
3　tablespoons all-purpose flour
¾　cup low-sodium chicken broth
2　tablespoons ketchup
2　teaspoons Worcestershire sauce
1　teaspoon yellow mustard
　　Salt and pepper
⅓　cup pickle slices
1　tomato, cored, seeded, and sliced thin

1. Adjust oven rack to middle position and heat oven to 400 degrees. Stack tortillas on plate, cover, and microwave until warm and pliable, about 30 seconds. Spray 9-inch pie plate with oil spray. Press 1 warm tortilla into pie plate, sprinkle with ¼ cup cheese, then lay remaining tortilla on top and press into dish. Spray lightly with oil spray and bake until lightly golden and crisp, 10 to 12 minutes, pressing center flat as needed; let cool slightly.

2. Meanwhile, heat oil in 12-inch nonstick skillet over medium heat until shimmering. Add onion, cover, and cook until softened and lightly browned, about 5 minutes. Uncover, stir in garlic, and cook until fragrant, about 1 minute. Stir in ground beef and cook, breaking up meat with wooden spoon, until almost cooked through but still slightly pink, about 5 minutes. Stir in flour and cook for 1 minute.

3. Gradually whisk in broth, ketchup, Worcestershire, and mustard. Bring to simmer over medium-low heat and cook, stirring occasionally, until thickened, 3 to 5 minutes. Season with salt and pepper to taste.

4. Transfer mixture to pie plate and top with pickles, tomato, and remaining ¾ cup cheese. Bake until cheese is melted and edges are browned, 10 to 12 minutes. Let cool slightly before serving.

BEFORE → AFTER	650 → **270**	43 → **12**	19 → **5**
	CALORIES	GRAMS FAT	GRAMS SAT FAT

Meat and Cheese Lasagna

Serves 10

✔ **WHY THIS RECIPE WORKS:** Lasagna is a notorious diet-killer, thanks to all the gooey mozzarella, creamy ricotta, and rich meat sauce. Since the cheese is one of the biggest offenders, it was an obvious place for us to start trimming some fat. Trading the whole-milk mozzarella for the part-skim variety was an easy fix, but when we tried using nonfat or part-skim ricotta in place of the full-fat version, we were disappointed by the texture and flavor of the filling. A surprise ingredient—nonfat cottage cheese—gave us the same smooth texture of full-fat ricotta once processed in the food processor; a few crackers helped absorb the extra moisture from the cottage cheese. As for the meat sauce, ground chicken worked well as a stand-in for the traditional ground beef, delivering a hearty, richly flavored sauce when browned and simmered briefly with tomatoes and aromatics. If the cottage cheese appears watery, drain it through a fine-mesh strainer for 15 minutes before using. Be sure to use ground chicken, not ground chicken breast (also labeled 99 percent fat free), in this recipe. We prefer Barilla no-boil lasagna noodles for their delicate texture.

1	onion, chopped fine
1	teaspoon olive oil
	Salt and pepper
6	garlic cloves, minced
2	tablespoons tomato paste
¼	teaspoon dried oregano
¼	teaspoon red pepper flakes
1	pound ground chicken
1	(28-ounce) can crushed tomatoes
1	(28-ounce) can diced tomatoes, drained
1	cup chopped fresh basil
8	saltines, broken into pieces
16	ounces (2 cups) nonfat cottage cheese, drained if necessary
12	ounces part-skim mozzarella cheese, shredded (3 cups)
1	ounce Parmesan cheese, grated (½ cup)
1	large egg, lightly beaten
12	no-boil lasagna noodles

1. Combine onion, oil, and ½ teaspoon salt in Dutch oven, cover, and cook over medium-low heat until softened, 8 to 10 minutes. Stir in garlic, tomato paste, oregano, and pepper flakes and cook until fragrant, about 30 seconds. Stir in ground chicken and cook, breaking up meat with wooden spoon, until no longer pink, about 4 minutes. Stir in crushed tomatoes and diced tomatoes and simmer until sauce has thickened slightly, about 15 minutes. Off heat, stir in ½ cup basil and season with salt and pepper to taste; cover and set aside.

2. Process saltines in food processor until finely ground, about 7 seconds. Add remaining ½ cup basil, cottage cheese, 2 cups mozzarella, Parmesan, egg, ½ teaspoon salt, and ½ teaspoon pepper and process until smooth, about 20 seconds.

3. Adjust oven rack to middle position and heat oven to 375 degrees. Spread 1½ cups sauce into 13 by 9-inch baking dish. Lay 3 noodles in dish, top each noodle evenly with ⅓ cup cottage cheese mixture, then spoon 1 cup sauce over top; repeat layering twice more.

4. Lay remaining 3 noodles on top. Spread remaining 1½ cups sauce evenly over noodles and sprinkle with remaining 1 cup mozzarella. Spray sheet of aluminum foil with vegetable oil spray, cover baking dish, and bake until sauce is bubbling around edges, about 35 minutes. Remove foil and continue to bake until cheese is lightly browned, 10 to 15 minutes. Let cool slightly before serving.

BEFORE NUMBERS BASED ON: Lasagna Classico from Olive Garden	BEFORE → **AFTER**	580 → **350** CALORIES	32 → **13** GRAMS FAT	18 → **6** GRAMS SAT FAT

MAKEOVER SPOTLIGHT:
MEAT AND CHEESE LASAGNA

1. MAKE A LEANER MEAT SAUCE WITH CHICKEN: By swapping ground chicken for the traditional ground beef, we were able to save substantial fat and calories. But be sure to purchase ground chicken, not ground chicken breast (also labeled 99 percent fat free), or the meat will taste dry and grainy. To help infuse the ground chicken with deep, savory flavor, we simmered it briefly in a quick tomato sauce.

2. PROCESS COTTAGE CHEESE AND SALTINES FOR A CREAMY FILLING THAT'S LOW FAT: Neither nonfat nor part-skim ricotta gave us the creamy consistency we were after, but nonfat cottage cheese, processed until smooth in the food processor, did. A few finely ground saltines helped absorb excess moisture from the cottage cheese. By processing the cheese mixture in the food processor, all of the ingredients became evenly distributed, giving the filling a smooth, creamy texture.

3. MAKE TIDY LAYERS: Be sure to layer the ingredients evenly into the dish, or else you'll have a lumpy lasagna that bakes unevenly and is difficult to cut into servings. Spread 1½ cups of the sauce into the baking dish, then top with 3 noodles. Spread ⅓ cup of the filling mixture onto each noodle and top with 1 cup sauce. Repeat this layering two more times, then top with remaining noodles, sauce, and mozzarella.

4. BAKE COVERED, THEN UNCOVER FOR A NICELY BROWNED, BUBBLING TOP: To prevent the top of the casserole from burning while the interior cooks through, we covered our lasagna with a sheet of aluminum foil for the first 35 minutes of baking. Spraying the foil with vegetable oil spray ensured it didn't stick to the cheese. Uncovering the lasagna and baking it for about 10 minutes longer allowed the edges to brown and the cheese to become gooey and bubbling.

Spinach Lasagna

Serves 8

✔️ **WHY THIS RECIPE WORKS:** Just because spinach is in its name doesn't mean this is a good-for-you dish come dinnertime. For a lighter lasagna, we ditched the butter and flour roux used to thicken the sauce, and reached for cornstarch instead. Low-fat milk provided richness, and whole-milk cottage cheese added a creamy texture and nice tang (nonfat cottage cheese tasted too lean given the mild flavors of this dish). Soaking the noodles in hot water was essential so they'd start to soften; the short cooking time and creamy sauce weren't enough to cook them through. We prefer Barilla no-boil lasagna noodles for their delicate texture. To make the cheese easier to shred, freeze it for 30 minutes to firm it up. If the cottage cheese appears watery, drain it through a fine-mesh strainer for 15 minutes before using; do not substitute nonfat cottage cheese here.

1	onion, chopped fine
1	teaspoon canola oil
	Salt and pepper
4	garlic cloves, minced
3	cups 1 percent low-fat milk
2	bay leaves
½	teaspoon ground nutmeg
2	tablespoons cornstarch
20	ounces frozen spinach, thawed, squeezed dry, and chopped fine
3	ounces Parmesan cheese, grated (1½ cups)
8	ounces (1 cup) whole-milk cottage cheese, drained if necessary
1	large egg
12	no-boil lasagna noodles
6	ounces Italian fontina cheese, shredded (1½ cups)

1. Combine onion, oil, and ⅛ teaspoon salt in large saucepan, cover, and cook over medium-low heat until softened, 8 to 10 minutes. Stir in garlic and cook until fragrant, about 30 seconds. Stir in 2¾ cups milk, bay leaves, and nutmeg; bring to simmer. Combine cornstarch and remaining ¼ cup milk in bowl, then whisk into pot. Continue to simmer, whisking constantly, until sauce is slightly thickened, about 6 minutes. Off heat, remove bay leaves. Stir in spinach and ½ cup Parmesan and season with salt and pepper to taste; cover and set aside.

2. Adjust oven rack to middle position and heat oven to 425 degrees. Process cottage cheese, egg, and ¼ teaspoon salt in food processor until smooth, about 30 seconds. Pour 1 inch boiling water into 13 by 9-inch broiler-safe baking dish. Add lasagna noodles, one at a time, and let noodles soak until pliable, about 5 minutes, separating them with tip of knife to prevent sticking. Remove noodles from water; place in single layer on clean kitchen towels. Discard water in baking dish and wipe dry.

3. Spread ½ cup sauce into now-empty baking dish. Lay 3 noodles in dish, top with ¾ cup sauce, and sprinkle with remaining 1 cup Parmesan. Lay 3 noodles in dish, top with ¾ cup sauce, and sprinkle with ¾ cup fontina. Lay 3 lasagna noodles in dish, top with ¾ cup sauce, and sprinkle with cottage cheese mixture. Lay remaining 3 noodles in dish, top with remaining sauce, and sprinkle with remaining ¾ cup fontina.

4. Spray sheet of aluminum foil with vegetable oil spray, cover baking dish, and bake until bubbling around edges, about 20 minutes. Remove from oven, adjust oven rack 6 inches from broiler element, and heat broiler. Remove foil; broil until cheese is spotty brown, about 5 minutes. Let cool slightly; serve.

BEFORE → **AFTER**	470 → **330**	25 → **13**	15 → **7**
	CALORIES	GRAMS FAT	GRAMS SAT FAT

Baked Manicotti

Serves 8

✔ **WHY THIS RECIPE WORKS:** Manicotti is not only bad for the diet, it can also try your patience. The pasta tubes tend to break when parboiled, making for a frustrating experience. Could we not only lighten but also simplify this recipe? First, we employed the same trick we learned from our meaty lasagna (see page 100): replacing ricotta with nonfat cottage cheese and saltines, which became smooth and creamy in the food processor. To streamline the process, we turned to softened no-boil lasagna noodles, which were much easier to work with than parboiled manicotti shells. Note that you will need 16 no-boil lasagna noodles to make this dish; our favorite brand of noodles, Barilla, has 16 noodles per box, but other brands may contain fewer. If the cottage cheese appears watery, drain it through a fine-mesh strainer for 15 minutes before using.

2	**(28-ounce) cans diced tomatoes**
3	**garlic cloves, minced**
1	**teaspoon olive oil**
¼	**teaspoon red pepper flakes**
	Salt and pepper
¼	**cup chopped fresh basil**
16	**no-boil lasagna noodles**
15	**saltines, broken into pieces**
24	**ounces (3 cups) nonfat cottage cheese, drained if necessary**
12	**ounces part-skim mozzarella cheese, shredded (3 cups)**
1	**ounce Parmesan cheese, grated (½ cup)**
2	**large egg whites**

1. Adjust oven rack to middle position; heat oven to 375 degrees. Working in batches, pulse tomatoes with their juice in food processor until mostly smooth, about 11 pulses; transfer to bowl.

2. Combine garlic, oil, and pepper flakes in large saucepan and cook over medium heat, stirring constantly, until fragrant, about 1 minute. Stir in processed tomatoes and ½ teaspoon salt and simmer until slightly thickened, about 15 minutes. Off heat, stir in 2 tablespoons basil and season with salt and pepper to taste.

3. Meanwhile, pour 1 inch boiling water into 13 by 9-inch baking dish. Add noodles, one at a time, and let soak until pliable, about 5 minutes, separating them with tip of knife to prevent sticking. Remove noodles from water; place in single layer on clean kitchen towels. Discard water in baking dish and wipe dry.

4. Process saltines in clean food processor until finely ground, about 10 seconds. Add cottage cheese, 1½ cups mozzarella, Parmesan, egg whites, remaining 2 tablespoons basil, ½ teaspoon salt, and ½ teaspoon pepper; process until smooth, about 20 seconds.

5. Spread 2 cups sauce into now-empty baking dish. Using spoon, spread ¼ cup cheese filling over bottom three-quarters of each noodle (with short side facing you), leaving top quarter of noodle exposed. Roll up noodle around filling; arrange in baking dish, seam side down. Top with remaining sauce, covering pasta, and sprinkle with remaining 1½ cups mozzarella.

6. Spray sheet of aluminum foil with vegetable oil spray, cover baking dish, and bake until sauce is bubbling around edges, about 40 minutes. Remove foil; continue to bake until cheese is spotty brown, about 5 minutes. Let cool slightly before serving.

BEFORE → **AFTER** 530 → **400** CALORIES 27 → **12** GRAMS FAT 13 → **6** GRAMS SAT FAT

Stuffed Shells with Meat Sauce

Serves 6

✔ **WHY THIS RECIPE WORKS:** A plate of stuffed shells might be incredibly tempting, but after a few bites, we're the ones that are usually stuffed. For a lighter version of this baked pasta dish, we started by swapping out the full-fat cheese. Nonfat ricotta gave the filling a grainy texture, but nonfat cottage cheese made the filling smooth and clean-tasting. Part-skim mozzarella, in lieu of the full-fat stuff, offered plenty of flavor. To bind the filling, which was a bit thin, we added cracker crumbs. Lean ground beef worked well for the sauce; an unusual ingredient, soy sauce, provided ultra-savory notes and boosted the overall beefy flavor of the sauce. With these changes, we'd easily trimmed the fat by half in our stuffed shells, which were still incredibly rich and decadent. If the cottage cheese appears watery, drain it through a fine-mesh strainer for 15 minutes before using.

3	(14.5-ounce) cans diced tomatoes
1	tablespoon olive oil
1	onion, chopped fine
6	ounces 93 percent lean ground beef
2	tablespoons tomato paste
1	tablespoon low-sodium soy sauce
4	garlic cloves, minced
¼	teaspoon red pepper flakes
6	tablespoons chopped fresh basil
	Salt and pepper
12	ounces jumbo pasta shells
12	saltines, broken into pieces
20	ounces (2½ cups) nonfat cottage cheese, drained if necessary
8	ounces part-skim mozzarella cheese, shredded (2 cups)
1	ounce Parmesan cheese, grated (½ cup)

1. Adjust oven rack to upper-middle position and heat oven to 375 degrees. Working in batches, pulse tomatoes with their juice in food processor until coarsely ground, about 6 pulses.

2. Heat oil in large saucepan over medium heat until shimmering. Add onion and cook until softened, about 5 minutes. Stir in ground beef and cook, breaking up meat with wooden spoon, until no longer pink, about 3 minutes. Stir in tomato paste, soy sauce, half of garlic, and pepper flakes and cook until fragrant, about 1 minute. Stir in processed tomatoes and simmer until slightly thickened, about 25 minutes. Off heat, stir in ¼ cup basil and season with salt and pepper to taste.

3. Meanwhile, bring 4 quarts water to boil in large pot. Add shells and 1 tablespoon salt and cook, stirring often, until just al dente. Drain shells and transfer to kitchen towel–lined baking sheet. Reserve 24 shells, discarding any that have broken.

4. Process saltines in clean food processor until finely ground, about 10 seconds. Add cottage cheese, 1½ cups mozzarella, Parmesan, remaining 2 tablespoons basil, remaining garlic, and ½ teaspoon salt and process until smooth, about 20 seconds. Transfer mixture to large zipper-lock bag, cut off one corner of bag using scissors, and pipe 2 tablespoons filling into each shell.

5. Spread half of sauce into 13 by 9-inch baking dish. Arrange filled shells, seam side up, in dish, then top with remaining sauce. Cover baking dish with aluminum foil and bake until sauce is bubbling around edges, 35 to 40 minutes. Remove foil, sprinkle with remaining ½ cup mozzarella, and continue to bake until cheese is melted, about 5 minutes. Let cool slightly before serving.

BEFORE → **AFTER**	600 → **470**	30 → **14**	16 → **6**
	CALORIES	GRAMS FAT	GRAMS SAT FAT

Baked Ziti

Serves 8

✔ **WHY THIS RECIPE WORKS:** A bona fide crowd-pleaser, baked ziti packs in the cheese, sauce, and pasta—and the calories. To revamp this comfort food classic, we started by making a sauce that tasted bright and fresh. The duo of tomato sauce and diced tomatoes gave our sauce the perfect clingy texture and delivered tender bites of tomato. Simmering the sauce briefly provided depth but kept the bright tomato notes intact, and stirring in a good amount of chopped basil reinforced the fresh feel and flavor of our sauce. For the cheese, we replaced full-fat ricotta with nonfat cottage cheese; when processed until smooth, the cottage cheese provided just the right creamy consistency without any off-flavors. Instead of sprinkling grated mozzarella over the top of our casserole, we cut it into chunks and mixed some in with the sauce and pasta for cheesy bites throughout. A final sprinkling of fresh basil underscored the lighter, brighter tone of our made-over baked ziti. If the cottage cheese appears watery, drain it through a fine-mesh strainer for 15 minutes before using.

5	garlic cloves, minced
1	teaspoon olive oil
½	teaspoon dried oregano
1	(28-ounce) can tomato sauce
1	(14.5-ounce) can diced tomatoes
½	cup plus 2 tablespoons chopped fresh basil
	Salt and pepper
1	pound ziti or other short, tubular pasta
8	ounces part-skim mozzarella cheese, cut into ¼-inch cubes
8	saltines, broken into pieces
16	ounces (2 cups) nonfat cottage cheese, drained if necessary
2	ounces Parmesan cheese, grated (1 cup)

1. Adjust oven rack to middle position and heat oven to 400 degrees. Combine garlic, oil, and oregano in 12-inch nonstick skillet over medium heat until garlic is fragrant, about 1 minute. Stir in tomato sauce and diced tomatoes with their juice and simmer until slightly thickened, about 10 minutes. Off heat, stir in ½ cup basil. Season with salt and pepper to taste.

2. Bring 4 quarts water to boil in large pot. Add pasta and 1 tablespoon salt and cook, stirring often, until pasta just begins to soften, about 5 minutes. Reserve 1 cup pasta cooking water, then drain pasta and return it to pot. Stir in tomato sauce and add reserved cooking water as needed to adjust consistency. Stir in ½ cup mozzarella.

3. Process saltines in food processor until finely ground, about 7 seconds. Add cottage cheese, ½ cup Parmesan, ¼ teaspoon salt, and ¼ teaspoon pepper and process until smooth, about 20 seconds.

4. Transfer half of pasta into 13 by 9-inch baking dish. Drop large spoonfuls of cottage cheese mixture evenly over top, then cover with remaining pasta. Sprinkle with remaining 1 cup mozzarella and ½ cup Parmesan.

5. Spray sheet of aluminum foil with vegetable oil spray, cover baking dish, and bake until sauce is bubbling around edges, about 20 minutes. Remove foil and continue to bake until cheese begins to brown, 10 to 15 minutes. Let cool slightly and sprinkle with remaining 2 tablespoons basil. Serve.

BEFORE→ **AFTER**	550→**410** CALORIES	23→**10** GRAMS FAT	9→**5** GRAMS SAT FAT

Ultimate Chili Mac

Serves 8

✔ **WHY THIS RECIPE WORKS:** With its mildly spiced meat sauce, tender pasta, and gooey, cheesy topping, chili mac is a family favorite that satisfies both kids and adults alike. But most recipes for this casual supper deliver a dish that's a bit too greasy and a bit too spicy. For the meat, we preferred 93 percent lean ground beef, which prevented our dish from being overly fatty. To amp up the flavor of the sauce, we turned to a secret weapon we often use in the test kitchen to boost savory, meaty notes: soy sauce. Though it seems unusual here, it added an unmistakable depth of flavor. Using both tomato puree and diced tomatoes gave us a nicely thickened sauce that coated each piece of macaroni, and promised some big bites of tomato. A good amount of chili powder gave this chili mac a subtle potency, while a bit of cayenne ramped up the flavor even further (although it can be omitted, if desired). Finally, for the cheesy topping, we found that light cheddar melted nicely and offered good cheesy flavor.

8   ounces (2 cups) elbow macaroni
      Salt and pepper
1   teaspoon canola oil
2   onions, chopped
1   red bell pepper, stemmed,
      seeded, and chopped
¼   cup chili powder
⅛   teaspoon cayenne (optional)
6   garlic cloves, minced
1   pound 93 percent lean
      ground beef
1   (28-ounce) can tomato puree
1   (14.5-ounce) can diced tomatoes
2   tablespoons low-sodium
      soy sauce
8   ounces 50 percent light cheddar
      cheese, shredded (2 cups)

1. Adjust oven rack to middle position and heat oven to 400 degrees. Bring 2 quarts water to boil in large pot. Add macaroni and 1½ teaspoons salt and cook, stirring often, until just al dente. Reserve ¾ cup cooking water, then drain macaroni; set aside.

2. Heat oil in large saucepan over medium heat until shimmering. Add onions, bell pepper, chili powder, ½ teaspoon salt, and cayenne, if using. Cover and cook until vegetables are softened, about 7 minutes. Stir in garlic and cook until fragrant, about 1 minute. Add ground beef, increase heat to medium-high, and cook, breaking up meat with wooden spoon, until no longer pink, about 5 minutes.

3. Stir in tomato puree, diced tomatoes with their juice, and soy sauce and bring to simmer. Reduce heat to medium-low and cook, stirring occasionally, until flavors have melded, about 30 minutes. Off heat, stir in cooked pasta and add reserved pasta cooking water as needed to adjust consistency. Season with salt and pepper to taste.

4. Transfer mixture to 13 by 9-inch baking dish and sprinkle with cheddar. Bake until cheese is melted and sauce is bubbling around edges, about 15 minutes. Let cool slightly before serving.

BEFORE → **AFTER**	520 → **340**	28 → **11**	12 → **5**
	CALORIES	GRAMS FAT	GRAMS SAT FAT

Baked Macaroni and Cheese

Serves 8

☑ **WHY THIS RECIPE WORKS:** When it comes to comfort foods, mac and cheese sits squarely at the top of the list. There's nothing quite like tender, bite-size pasta coated in a warm, gooey, cheesy sauce and baked with a crunchy topping of buttery bread crumbs. But with over 700 calories and a whopping 40 grams of fat per serving, the standard homemade mac and cheese is less than comforting to our waistlines. Could we keep all the cheesy flavor and creamy texture but lose a significant amount of fat and calories? It all came down to the right selection of milk and cheese. After a number of tests, we hit on low-fat evaporated milk, which gave us a richer, more velvety texture than skim, 1 percent, or 2 percent low-fat milk. Thickening the sauce with cornstarch, instead of the usual roux (a combination of butter and flour), also helped to keep our numbers in check. For the key ingredient, the cheese, we tried different varieties, ultimately landing on a good amount of shredded reduced-fat cheddar, which melted into a smooth coating for our pasta and allowed us to pack in big cheese flavor without a ton of fat. Panko bread crumbs, tossed with just a pat of butter, gave our mac and cheese a golden, crispy crown.

1 pound elbow macaroni
  Salt and pepper
3 (12-ounce) cans 2 percent
  low-fat evaporated milk
¾ teaspoon dry mustard
½ teaspoon garlic powder
  Pinch cayenne pepper
1 tablespoon cornstarch
12 ounces 50 percent light cheddar
  cheese, shredded (3 cups)
1 cup panko bread crumbs,
  toasted (see page 18)
1 tablespoon unsalted butter,
  melted

1. Adjust oven rack to middle position and heat oven to 350 degrees. Bring 4 quarts water to boil in large pot. Add macaroni and 1 tablespoon salt and cook, stirring often, until just al dente. Reserve ½ cup cooking water, then drain macaroni; set aside.

2. Combine evaporated milk, mustard, garlic powder, 1 teaspoon salt, and cayenne in now-empty pot and bring to simmer. Combine ¼ cup reserved pasta water and cornstarch, then whisk into pot. Continue to simmer, whisking constantly, until sauce is slightly thickened, about 3 minutes. Off heat, whisk in cheddar, a handful at a time, until melted. Stir in cooked macaroni and add remaining ¼ cup pasta water as needed to adjust consistency; sauce should be slightly soupy.

3. Transfer mixture to 13 by 9-inch baking dish. Toss toasted panko with melted butter in bowl, season with salt and pepper to taste, and sprinkle over top. Bake until sauce is bubbling around edges, about 20 minutes. Let cool slightly before serving.

BEFORE → **AFTER**	750→**470**	40→**11**	25→**5**
	CALORIES	GRAMS FAT	GRAMS SAT FAT

OVEN-FRIED CHICKEN

Baked Not Fried

Oven-Fried Chicken

Serves 4

✔ **WHY THIS RECIPE WORKS:** The first thing that comes to mind when we think of fried chicken is the shatteringly crisp, ultra-crunchy coating. But one serving of this American classic can weigh in at over 700 calories and 40 grams of fat. To lighten this dish, we ditched the deep-fryer and turned to the oven instead. But would we still be able to get that same crunchy, craggy, golden exterior? After removing the fatty skin from our chicken breasts, we tried a number of potential coatings, including everything from homemade bread crumbs to Melba toast crumbs and even crushed potato and pita chips. Finally, we hit on cornflakes, which stayed crunchy and didn't become soggy the way some of the others did. Garlic powder, cayenne pepper, and poultry seasoning (which adds several spices with just one ingredient) added flavor to the mild cereal, while buttermilk, whisked together with the egg whites, gave our chicken that distinctive buttermilk tang without racking up the fat grams. After coating the sides and top of the chicken, we baked it in a super-hot oven on a wire rack set inside a baking sheet—elevating the chicken allowed the hot air to circulate underneath so it cooked through evenly. Spraying the breaded chicken with vegetable oil spray before baking helped the cornflakes become ultra-crisp without adding much in the way of fat or calories. To crush the cornflakes, place them inside a zipper-lock bag and use a rolling pin or the bottom of a large skillet to break them into fine crumbs. We like to serve this with Macaroni Salad (page 213).

	Vegetable oil spray
½	cup all-purpose flour
4	large egg whites
½	cup buttermilk
1½	teaspoons Dijon mustard
3	cups (3 ounces) Kellogg's Corn Flakes cereal, finely crushed
1	tablespoon canola oil
¼	teaspoon garlic powder
	Salt and pepper
⅛	teaspoon poultry seasoning
	Pinch cayenne pepper
4	(12-ounce) bone-in split chicken breasts, skin removed, trimmed of all visible fat, and halved

1. Adjust oven rack to upper-middle position and heat oven to 425 degrees. Line rimmed baking sheet with aluminum foil, top with wire rack, and spray rack with oil spray. Spread flour into shallow dish. In second shallow dish, whisk egg whites until foamy, then whisk in buttermilk and mustard. In third shallow dish, combine Corn Flakes, oil, garlic powder, ½ teaspoon salt, ¼ teaspoon pepper, poultry seasoning, and cayenne.

2. Pat chicken dry with paper towels and season with salt and pepper. Working with 1 piece at a time and coating top and sides only, dredge chicken in flour, dip in egg white mixture, then coat with Corn Flake mixture, pressing gently to adhere; lay on prepared wire rack with uncoated side of chicken facing down.

3. Spray chicken with oil spray. Bake until crumbs are golden and chicken registers 160 degrees, about 35 minutes. Serve.

BEFORE NUMBERS BASED ON: Original Recipe Fried Chicken from KFC	BEFORE → **AFTER** 1 SERVING = 2 PIECES	720 → **450** CALORIES	42 → **10** GRAMS FAT	10 → **2** GRAMS SAT FAT

MAKEOVER SPOTLIGHT: FRIED CHICKEN

1. REMOVE THE SKIN AND MAKE A CRISPY COATING WITH CORNFLAKES: The first step in making over our recipe was removing the fatty skin, which gets ultra-crisp when fried. Looking to replicate that texture, we tried making the coating with a number of different ingredients, including homemade bread crumbs and potato chips, but cornflakes came out on top. Not only are cornflakes relatively low in fat and calories, but they also provide a super-crisp texture. To crush the cereal into small pieces, we found it best to place them in a zipper-lock bag and crush them with a rolling pin or the bottom of a large skillet.

2. APPLY THE CRUMBS TO THE TOP AND SIDES ONLY: When we coated our chicken all over with the cornflake crumbs, we found that the coating on the bottom became soggy during baking. To avoid this, we simply coated the top and sides only. Given that the bottom of a split chicken breast is mostly bones anyway, we didn't miss the crunchy texture on the underside of the chicken. Plus, using less coating meant less fat and calories. To ensure the crumbs adhere well, be sure to press them onto the sides and top of the chicken.

3. SKIP THE DEEP-FRYER AND BAKE THE CHICKEN INSTEAD: Deep-frying was a nonstarter for our lightened recipe, so we baked our chicken instead—this shaved off a huge amount of fat and calories per serving. To help the chicken cook through more evenly and allow any moisture to drain away, we baked the chicken elevated on a wire rack. Spraying the rack with vegetable oil spray prevented the chicken from sticking.

4. FOR MOIST, TENDER MEAT, CHECK THE TEMPERATURE: The best way to know when the chicken is done is to take its temperature. Be careful not to overbake the chicken, or it will taste dry and stringy. We baked the chicken until the coating was golden and the chicken registered 160 degrees, which took about 35 minutes; this ensured moist, juicy meat.

Crispy Chicken Nuggets

Serves 4

✔ **WHY THIS RECIPE WORKS:** For chicken nuggets that tasted better (and were better for you) than the ones you'd find in a fast-food joint, we started with boneless, skinless chicken breasts and cut them into pieces. A brief stint in a pungent, salty marinade made from Worcestershire sauce, onion powder, and garlic powder ensured our chicken nuggets were both flavorful and moist. Panko bread crumbs made for an ultra-crunchy exterior, especially when toasted beforehand. To keep the coating crispy in the oven, we cooked the chicken nuggets on a wire rack set inside a baking sheet—this allowed the air to circulate all around. And to further ensure a crisp crust, we lightly sprayed the tops of the chicken nuggets with vegetable oil spray. To make cutting the chicken easier, freeze it for 15 minutes.

Vegetable oil spray
1½ pounds boneless, skinless chicken breasts, trimmed of all visible fat
2 tablespoons Worcestershire sauce
2 teaspoons onion powder
½ teaspoon garlic powder
½ teaspoon salt
¼ teaspoon pepper
½ cup all-purpose flour
3 large egg whites
2 cups panko bread crumbs, toasted (see page 18)
1 tablespoon canola oil

1. Adjust oven rack to middle position and heat oven to 475 degrees. Line rimmed baking sheet with aluminum foil, top with wire rack, and spray rack with oil spray. Cut each breast on diagonal into thirds. Slice largest piece crosswise into ½-inch-thick pieces and slice two smaller pieces on diagonal into ½-inch-thick pieces; you should have about 48 nuggets. Toss chicken with Worcestershire, onion powder, garlic powder, salt, and pepper in bowl, cover, and refrigerate for 30 minutes.

2. Spread flour into shallow dish. In second shallow dish, whisk egg whites until foamy. In third shallow dish, combine toasted panko and oil. Pat chicken dry with paper towels. Working in batches, dredge chicken in flour, dip in egg whites, then coat with panko mixture, pressing gently to adhere; lay on prepared wire rack.

3. Spray chicken with oil spray. Bake until chicken registers 160 degrees, 10 to 12 minutes. Serve.

QUICK PREP TIP **CUTTING CHICKEN BREASTS FOR NUGGETS**
Using chef's knife, cut each breast on diagonal into thirds. Then, slice largest piece crosswise into ½-inch-thick pieces and slice two smaller pieces on diagonal into ½-inch-thick pieces.

BEFORE NUMBERS BASED ON: Chicken McNuggets from McDonald's	BEFORE → **AFTER** 1 SERVING = 12 NUGGETS	560 → **420** CALORIES	36 → **10** GRAMS FAT	6 → **1.5** GRAMS SAT FAT

Chicken Chimichangas

Serves 6

✓ **WHY THIS RECIPE WORKS:** Stuffed with tender meat, rice, cheese, and beans, the chimichanga starts out as an ordinary burrito. But what gives it an edge is that it's deep-fried, which renders the shell incredibly crispy and flaky. Unfortunately, this edge comes with loads of calories and fat. Baking was a lower-fat alternative to frying, but now we had to find another way to ensure our chimichangas had the crisp exterior that they're known for. Brushing the tortillas with oil did the trick—now they turned brown and crisped in the oven. Preheating the baking sheet before we set the chimichangas on top also helped, as it ensured the exterior began crisping immediately. For the tortillas, we found it essential to use the 10-inch size, otherwise we ended up with overstuffed chimichangas that broke apart. To liven up our simple filling of shredded chicken, rice, and black beans, we added smoky chipotle chile and fresh cilantro. A mere cup of shredded Mexican cheese contributed richness and flavor and worked to bind the filling.

¼	cup canola oil
1	onion, chopped fine
1½	pounds poached chicken breast, shredded (see page 42)
1	(15-ounce) can black beans, rinsed
2	cups cooked white rice
2	teaspoons minced canned chipotle chile in adobo sauce
4	ounces shredded Mexican cheese blend (1 cup)
½	cup minced fresh cilantro
	Salt and pepper
6	(10-inch) flour tortillas

1. Adjust oven rack to middle position, place rimmed baking sheet on rack, and heat oven to 450 degrees. Heat 2 tablespoons oil in 12-inch nonstick skillet over medium-high heat until shimmering. Add onion and cook until just softened, about 3 minutes. Stir in chicken, beans, rice, and chipotle and cook until heated through, about 3 minutes. Off heat, stir in cheese and cilantro and season with salt and pepper to taste.

2. Stack tortillas on plate, cover, and microwave until warm and pliable, about 1 minute. Lay warm tortillas on clean counter. Spread chicken mixture over bottom half of each tortilla, leaving 1- to 2-inch border at edge. Fold sides of tortilla over filling, then tightly roll bottom of tortilla up around filling into burrito. Brush burritos with remaining 2 tablespoons oil and arrange, seam side down, on preheated sheet. Bake until crisp and golden, 8 to 10 minutes. Serve.

QUICK PREP TIP
MAKING CHIMICHANGAS
Spread chicken mixture over bottom half of each tortilla, leaving 1- to 2-inch border at edge. Fold sides of tortilla over filling, then tightly roll bottom of tortilla up around filling to form burrito.

BEFORE NUMBERS BASED ON:	BEFORE → **AFTER**	1300 → **660**	79 → **25**	24 → **7**
Classic Chicken Chimichanga (without sauce) from On The Border Mexican Grill and Cantina		CALORIES	GRAMS FAT	GRAMS SAT FAT

General Tso's Chicken

Serves 4

✔ **WHY THIS RECIPE WORKS:** Deep-frying and a thick, velvety, spicy-sweet sauce make this Chinese dish incredibly popular, but they also make it incredibly unhealthy. With a single serving clocking in at over 900 calories, we thought it was time to put General Tso on a diet. Swapping the traditional dark meat for white meat was a good start. Moving on to the breading, we started with cornflakes, which gave our Oven-Fried Chicken (page 112) an ultra-crisp exterior. After dredging our chicken pieces in flour and dipping them in egg whites, we coated them with our cornflake crumbs and baked them elevated on a wire rack to allow for even crisping all over. For the sauce, we combined soy sauce, hoisin sauce, vinegar, ginger, and garlic; a bit of cornstarch helped to thicken it. Sugar made the sauce taste overly sweet, so we tried swapping in a number of alternatives. In the end, we opted for apricot jam, which added complexity and made our sauce ultra-clingy. Subbing in balsamic vinegar for the white vinegar ensured a good balance of sweet-and-sour notes. To crush the cornflakes, place them inside a zipper-lock bag and use a rolling pin or the bottom of a large skillet to break them into fine crumbs.

Vegetable oil spray
¼ cup all-purpose flour
3 large egg whites
5 cups (5 ounces) Kellogg's Corn Flakes cereal, finely crushed
1½ pounds boneless, skinless chicken breasts, trimmed of all visible fat, cut into 1-inch pieces
1⅔ cups water
⅓ cup low-sodium soy sauce
¼ cup apricot jam
3 tablespoons hoisin sauce
2 tablespoons cornstarch
1 tablespoon balsamic vinegar
2 teaspoons canola oil
4 garlic cloves, minced
1 tablespoon grated fresh ginger
¼ teaspoon red pepper flakes

1. Adjust oven rack to upper-middle position and heat oven to 475 degrees. Line rimmed baking sheet with aluminum foil, top with wire rack, and spray rack with oil spray. Spread flour into shallow dish. Whisk egg whites until foamy in second shallow dish. Spread Corn Flakes crumbs into third shallow dish. Pat chicken dry with paper towels. Working in batches, dredge chicken in flour, dip in egg whites, then coat with Corn Flakes, pressing gently to adhere; lay on prepared wire rack.

2. Spray chicken with oil spray. Bake until chicken registers 160 degrees and coating is brown and crisp, 12 to 15 minutes.

3. Meanwhile, whisk water, soy sauce, apricot jam, hoisin, cornstarch, and vinegar together in bowl. Heat oil in 12-inch skillet over medium heat until shimmering. Add garlic, ginger, and pepper flakes and cook until fragrant, about 1 minute. Whisk in soy sauce mixture, bring to simmer, and cook until thickened, about 2 minutes. Remove from heat, cover, and keep warm.

4. When chicken is cooked, return sauce to simmer over medium-low heat. Add cooked chicken and toss to coat. Serve.

BEFORE → **AFTER**	910 → **490**	45 → **8**	5 → **1.5**
	CALORIES	GRAMS FAT	GRAMS SAT FAT

Chicken-Fried Steak

Serves 4

✓ **WHY THIS RECIPE WORKS:** Most diners use cube steaks in this Southern dish and pound them ultra-thin before breading and frying them—all of which results in dry, flavorless meat. To cover up these flaws, the steaks are then doused with a heavy, creamy gravy. For our recipe, we decided to cut back on the fatty gravy (and lighten it) and put the focus back on the beef. Rather than use cube steaks, we turned to boneless strip steaks, pounded to ½-inch thickness, which delivered more tender meat and a beefier flavor. Though we normally prefer this cut cooked to a medium level of doneness, in this dish we preferred them well-done. For a crunchy exterior without frying, we tried a number of ingredients before we hit on the right one: Funyuns. Just 2 ounces of these crispy fried onions added a boost of flavor and created a crunchy, crispy coating when paired with panko bread crumbs. Moving on to the gravy, we skipped the standard high-fat roux (made from butter and flour) and simply simmered milk, which we thickened with cornstarch. But this gravy tasted too lean to pass off as comfort food. To add some richness, we included a small amount of preseasoned breakfast sausage, which delivered the savory richness and deep flavor we were looking for. To crush the Funyuns, place them inside a zipper-lock bag and use a rolling pin or the bottom of a large skillet to break them into fine crumbs. When trimming the meat, you may end up trimming as much as 8 ounces of visible fat from the steaks.

½	cup all-purpose flour
4	large egg whites
1	cup panko bread crumbs, toasted (see page 18)
2	ounces Funyuns Onion Flavored Rings, finely crushed (1 cup)
1	tablespoon canola oil
	Salt and pepper
⅛	teaspoon cayenne pepper
2	(1-pound) boneless strip steaks, trimmed of all visible fat, each steak halved
4	ounces turkey breakfast sausage, chopped fine
1½	cups 2 percent low-fat milk
2	teaspoons cornstarch

1. Adjust oven rack to middle position and heat oven to 425 degrees. Line rimmed baking sheet with aluminum foil, top with wire rack, and spray rack with vegetable oil spray. Spread flour into shallow dish. In second shallow dish, whisk egg whites until foamy. In third shallow dish, combine toasted panko, Funyuns, oil, ¼ teaspoon salt, ¼ teaspoon pepper, and cayenne.

2. Pound steaks ½ inch thick with meat pounder, then pat dry with paper towels and season with salt and pepper. Working with 1 steak at a time, dredge in flour, dip in egg whites, then coat with panko mixture, pressing gently to adhere; lay on prepared wire rack. Roast steaks until meat registers 150 to 155 degrees, about 10 minutes.

3. Meanwhile, cook sausage in medium saucepan over medium heat until no longer pink, about 5 minutes. Stir in 1 cup milk and simmer gently for 5 minutes. Combine remaining ½ cup milk and cornstarch, then whisk into pot. Continue to simmer sauce, whisking constantly, until thickened, about 3 minutes. Season with salt and pepper to taste. Spoon sauce over steak and serve.

BEFORE NUMBERS BASED ON: Country-Fried Steak with Country Gravy from Denny's	BEFORE → **AFTER**	993 → **580** CALORIES	65 → **20** GRAMS FAT	23 → **6** GRAMS SAT FAT

Eggplant Parmesan with Spaghetti

Serves 6

✔ **WHY THIS RECIPE WORKS:** Eggplant Parmesan is classic Italian-American comfort food. But once we found out a typical serving contains almost 1,000 calories and more than 50 grams of fat, the idea of eating it became a little less comforting. Instead of frying our eggplant—which soaks up tons of oil due to its porous nature—and smothering it with full-fat mozzarella, we topped it with panko bread crumbs, sprinkled it with shredded part-skim mozzarella, and baked it. Tossing the panko with olive oil, grated Parmesan, and garlic powder guaranteed an ultra-crisp coating and ensured our dish had the same rich flavors found in restaurant versions.

Vegetable oil spray

2   **pounds eggplant, sliced into ⅓-inch-thick rounds**

     Salt and pepper

½   **cup all-purpose flour**

3   **large egg whites**

1½   **cups panko bread crumbs, toasted (see page 18)**

1   **tablespoon extra-virgin olive oil**

1   **ounce Parmesan cheese, grated (½ cup)**

1½   **teaspoons garlic powder**

4   **cups Low-Fat Tomato Sauce (page 135)**

8   **ounces part-skim mozzarella cheese, shredded (2 cups)**

2   **tablespoons chopped fresh basil**

12   **ounces spaghetti**

1. Adjust oven racks to upper-middle and lower-middle positions and heat oven to 475 degrees. Line 2 rimmed baking sheets with aluminum foil, top with wire racks, and spray racks with oil spray. Working with half of eggplant at a time, toss in bowl with ½ teaspoon salt and transfer to large colander (use 1 teaspoon salt total); let drain for 30 minutes. Spread eggplant over several layers of paper towels and pat dry thoroughly.

2. Spread flour into shallow dish. In second shallow dish, whisk egg whites until foamy. In third shallow dish, combine toasted panko, oil, Parmesan, garlic powder, and ½ teaspoon salt.

3. Season eggplant with ½ teaspoon pepper. Working with 1 eggplant slice at a time and coating top only, dredge in flour, dip in egg whites, then coat with panko mixture, pressing gently to adhere; lay on prepared wire racks with breaded side of eggplant facing up. Spray eggplant with oil spray. Bake until eggplant is tender, about 30 minutes.

4. Spread ½ cup tomato sauce over bottom of 13 by 9-inch baking dish. Lay half of eggplant slices in dish, breaded side up, overlapping as needed to fit. Spoon ½ cup sauce over top and sprinkle with 1 cup mozzarella. Layer remaining eggplant over top, breaded side up, and dot with 1 cup sauce, leaving majority of eggplant exposed. Sprinkle with remaining 1 cup mozzarella. Bake until sauce is bubbling and cheese is browned, about 10 minutes. Let cool for 5 minutes, then sprinkle with basil.

5. Meanwhile, bring 4 quarts water to boil in large pot. Add pasta and 1 tablespoon salt and cook, stirring often, until al dente. Reserve ½ cup cooking water, then drain pasta and return it to pot. Stir in remaining 2 cups tomato sauce, season with salt and pepper to taste, and add reserved cooking water as needed to adjust consistency. Serve with eggplant.

BEFORE NUMBERS BASED ON: Eggplant Parmesan from Romano's Macaroni Grill	BEFORE → **AFTER**	950 → **550** CALORIES	56 → **13** GRAMS FAT	12 → **5** GRAMS SAT FAT

Oven-Fried Fish with Tartar Sauce

Serves 4

✔ **WHY THIS RECIPE WORKS:** It shouldn't come as a shock that deep-fried fish, served with a generous amount of tartar sauce on the side, is loaded with fat and calories. But the allure of moist, flaky fish surrounded by a golden, crisp coating is hard to resist, so we set out to lighten this seaside classic. Fresh bread crumbs were our tasters' pick for the breading; tossing the bread crumbs with just a tablespoon of oil and toasting them in a skillet ensured they would be ultra-crisp when the fish came out of the oven. Using firm, meaty halibut also helped; delicate, flaky fish, like cod and haddock, released far too much liquid during cooking, which prevented the crumbs from crisping. Adding a strong barrier of tartar sauce, seasonings, egg whites, and flour to our halibut worked to seal in moisture, keeping the crumb coating crisp. Applying bread crumbs only on the top and sides of the fish maintained the iconic crunch while saving calories and eliminating the problem of a mushy coating on the bottom. We knew that tartar sauce for dipping was a must-have, but we lightened it, too, by using light mayo and low-fat sour cream.

Vegetable oil spray
4 slices hearty white sandwich bread, torn into pieces
1 tablespoon canola oil
½ cup all-purpose flour
¾ cup Low-Fat Tartar Sauce
2 large egg whites
1 tablespoon Dijon mustard
⅛ teaspoon cayenne pepper
2 tablespoons minced fresh parsley
Salt and pepper
1½ pounds skinless halibut fillets, cut into 8 equal portions

1. Adjust oven rack to middle position and heat oven to 450 degrees. Line rimmed baking sheet with aluminum foil, top with wire rack, and spray rack with oil spray. Pulse bread in food processor to coarse crumbs, about 10 pulses. Toast bread crumbs and oil in 12-inch nonstick skillet over medium heat, stirring often, until well browned, about 10 minutes; let cool.

2. Spread ¼ cup flour into shallow dish. In second shallow dish, whisk remaining ¼ cup flour, ¼ cup tartar sauce, egg whites, mustard, and cayenne together. In third shallow dish, combine toasted bread crumbs, parsley, ¼ teaspoon salt, and ⅛ teaspoon pepper.

3. Pat halibut dry with paper towels and season with salt and pepper. Working with 1 piece of halibut at a time and coating top and sides only, dredge in flour, dip in tartar sauce mixture, then coat with bread crumbs, pressing gently to adhere; lay on prepared wire rack with uncoated side of fish facing down.

4. Spray halibut with oil spray. Bake until crumbs are golden and halibut registers 140 degrees, 10 to 12 minutes. Serve with remaining ½ cup tartar sauce.

ON THE SIDE LOW-FAT TARTAR SAUCE
Whisk ½ cup light mayonnaise, 2 tablespoons low-fat sour cream, 4 minced cornichons plus 2 teaspoons cornichon juice, 1 tablespoon drained and minced capers, 2 teaspoons lemon juice, 1 teaspoon minced shallot, and ½ teaspoon Worcestershire sauce together in bowl. Season with salt and pepper to taste. Makes ¾ cup.

BEFORE NUMBERS BASED ON:	BEFORE → **AFTER**	700 → **400**	56 → **15**	9 → **2.5**
Fish & Chips (fried fish and tartar sauce only) from Marie Callender's Restaurant and Bakery		CALORIES	GRAMS FAT	GRAMS SAT FAT

Oven-Fried Shrimp

Serves 4

✔ **WHY THIS RECIPE WORKS:** For crispy, golden fried shrimp that smacked of a seaside shanty—minus the deep-fryer—we baked our shrimp in the oven under a generous blanket of cornflakes and panko bread crumbs. After numerous tests, we found this duo offered an ultra-crisp texture and provided a nice, even coating. To help our crumb coating adhere, we used egg whites, which we combined with Dijon mustard for more flavor; whisking them together aerated the mixture so it was thicker and the breading adhered to it better. A creamy dipping sauce spiked with chipotle chile took our oven-fried shrimp to the next level. To crush the cornflakes, place them inside a zipper-lock bag and use a rolling pin or the bottom of a large skillet to break them into fine crumbs. We like these shrimp with a spritz of lemon juice, or you can serve them with our Creamy Chipotle Chile Sauce.

Vegetable oil spray
½ cup all-purpose flour
4 large egg whites
1 teaspoon Dijon mustard
1 cup panko bread crumbs, toasted (see page 18)
1 cup (1 ounce) Kellogg's Corn Flakes cereal, finely crushed
2 tablespoons canola oil
½ teaspoon salt
¼ teaspoon pepper
¼ teaspoon paprika
32 extra-large shrimp (21 to 25 per pound), peeled and deveined

1. Adjust oven rack to middle position and heat oven to 425 degrees. Line rimmed baking sheet with aluminum foil, top with wire rack, and spray rack with oil spray. Spread flour into shallow dish. In second shallow dish, whisk egg whites and mustard together until foamy. In third shallow dish, combine toasted panko, Corn Flakes, oil, salt, pepper, and paprika.

2. Pat shrimp dry with paper towels. Working in batches, dredge in flour, dip in egg white mixture, then coat with panko mixture, pressing gently to adhere; lay on prepared wire rack. Spray shrimp with oil spray. Bake until shrimp are cooked through, about 10 minutes. Serve.

ON THE SIDE CREAMY CHIPOTLE CHILE SAUCE
Whisk ¼ cup light mayonnaise, 2 tablespoons low-fat sour cream, 1 tablespoon lime juice, 2 teaspoons minced fresh cilantro, 1 minced garlic clove, and ½ teaspoon minced canned chipotle chile in adobo sauce together in bowl. Season with salt and pepper to taste and add water as needed to adjust consistency. Cover and refrigerate for 30 minutes before serving. Makes ½ cup.

BEFORE NUMBERS BASED ON: Golden Fried Shrimp (lunch portion) from LongHorn Steakhouse	BEFORE → **AFTER** 1 SERVING = 8 SHRIMP	620 → **310** CALORIES	34 → **9** GRAMS FAT	6 → **0.5** GRAMS SAT FAT

Chicken and Dumplings

Serves 8

✔ **WHY THIS RECIPE WORKS:** Not surprisingly, chicken and dumplings isn't exactly diet-friendly—after all, the sauce is rich and velvety thanks to a generous amount of cream and butter, and the dumplings aren't exactly skimpy with the butter either. Wanting to create a lighter, healthier version of this classic without losing any of its comfort-food appeal, we focused first on the chicken and stew. Most recipes call for a whole, cut-up chicken or bone-in thighs, but we found bone-in breasts worked just as well and helped trim the fat count once we discarded the skin. But getting rid of the skin meant a serious loss in flavor, so to work around this we simply browned the chicken with the skin on before removing it. To lighten the biscuit-style dumplings, we cut back on the butter significantly; buttermilk gave them a great tangy flavor, and an egg white helped give them structure and kept them together when cooked on top of the stew. To keep our dumplings light and fluffy, we wrapped a towel around the pot's lid as they cooked; this prevented steam droplets from dripping onto the dumplings and making them soggy.

STEW

- 3 pounds bone-in split chicken breasts, trimmed of all visible fat
  Salt and pepper
- 1½ teaspoons canola oil
- 4 carrots, peeled and cut into ¾-inch pieces
- 2 onions, chopped fine
- 1 celery rib, minced
- ¼ cup dry sherry
- 6 cups low-sodium chicken broth
- 1 teaspoon minced fresh thyme or ¼ teaspoon dried
- ½ cup frozen peas
- ¼ cup minced fresh parsley

DUMPLINGS

- 2 cups (10 ounces) all-purpose flour
- 1 teaspoon sugar
- 1 teaspoon salt
- ½ teaspoon baking soda
- ¾ cup buttermilk, chilled
- 2 tablespoons unsalted butter, melted and hot
- 1 large egg white

1. FOR THE STEW: Pat chicken dry with paper towels and season with salt and pepper. Heat oil in large Dutch oven over medium-high heat until just smoking. Brown chicken well, 10 to 12 minutes; transfer to plate and remove skin.

2. Add carrots, onions, celery, and ⅛ teaspoon salt to fat left in pot, cover, and cook over medium-low heat, stirring occasionally, until softened, 8 to 10 minutes. Stir in sherry, scraping up any browned bits. Add broth, thyme, and chicken and any accumulated juices. Bring to simmer, cover, and cook until chicken registers 160 degrees, about 20 minutes.

3. Remove pot from heat; transfer chicken to plate. When cool enough to handle, shred meat into large pieces, discarding bones.

4. FOR THE DUMPLINGS: Whisk flour, sugar, salt, and baking soda together in large bowl. In separate bowl, stir chilled buttermilk and melted butter together until butter forms small clumps, then whisk in egg white. Add buttermilk mixture to flour mixture and stir with rubber spatula until just incorporated.

5. Return stew to simmer and stir in shredded chicken, peas, and parsley. Season with salt and pepper to taste. Using greased tablespoon measure, scoop and drop dumplings on top of stew about 1 inch apart. Wrap lid of Dutch oven with clean kitchen towel (keeping towel away from heat source) and cover pot. Cook over low heat until dumplings have doubled in size, 13 to 16 minutes. Serve.

BEFORE → **AFTER**	500 → **350** CALORIES	21 → **7** GRAMS FAT	8 → **2.5** GRAMS SAT FAT

Deviled Chicken

Serves 4

✓ **WHY THIS RECIPE WORKS:** Deviled chicken not only packs a punch in terms of heat, it also packs a caloric punch. Most recipes we've seen coat chicken breasts with some combination of butter and mayonnaise, plus hot sauce and mustard, before packing on dried stuffing mix or seasoned bread crumbs that create a crunchy layer in the oven. Not only did we want to turn this dish into a lighter entrée, but we also wanted to ditch the stuffing mix and find other ways to boost the flavor of the breading. To ensure the chicken was moist, we kept the mustard, mayo, and hot sauce mixture—sans the butter, and using light mayo in place of the full-fat stuff—and used it to marinate the chicken; lemon juice, garlic, and thyme amped up the flavor without adding much in the way of fat or calories. Instead of swiping off the mustard and mayo mixture and dipping the chicken in an egg wash, we made the marinade pull double duty and used it as the "glue" to keep our breading in place. Homemade bread crumbs tasted much better than the overly seasoned and ultra-salty stuffing mix, and pretoasting them in a single pat of butter added some richness and ensured that our deviled chicken came out of the oven with an ultra-crisp, golden exterior.

3	tablespoons yellow mustard
2	tablespoons light mayonnaise
1½	tablespoons hot sauce
1	tablespoon lemon juice
3	garlic cloves, minced
½	teaspoon minced fresh thyme
	Salt and pepper
4	(6-ounce) boneless, skinless chicken breasts, trimmed of all visible fat
2	slices hearty white sandwich bread, torn into pieces
1	tablespoon unsalted butter
	Vegetable oil spray

1. Adjust oven rack to upper-middle position and heat oven to 450 degrees. Combine mustard, mayonnaise, hot sauce, lemon juice, garlic, thyme, 1 tablespoon pepper, and ¾ teaspoon salt in large bowl. Stir in chicken, cover, and refrigerate for at least 30 minutes or up to 3 hours.

2. Meanwhile, pulse bread, ¼ teaspoon salt, and ¼ teaspoon pepper in food processor to coarse crumbs, about 10 pulses. Melt butter in 12-inch nonstick skillet over medium heat. Add crumbs and toast, stirring often, until golden, 5 to 7 minutes.

3. Line rimmed baking sheet with aluminum foil, top with wire rack, and spray rack with oil spray. Transfer marinated chicken to prepared wire rack. Sprinkle toasted bread crumbs evenly over top, press gently to adhere, and spray chicken with oil spray. Bake until chicken registers 160 degrees, 20 to 25 minutes. Let chicken rest for 5 to 10 minutes before serving.

BEFORE → **AFTER** 540 → **280** CALORIES 23 → **10** GRAMS FAT 4 → **3.5** GRAMS SAT FAT

Nut-Crusted Chicken Breasts

Serves 4

✔ **WHY THIS RECIPE WORKS:** One way to dress up the humble chicken breast for a weeknight dinner is to coat it with a layer of nuts, which adds a welcome crunch factor. But many recipes go overboard on the coating, racking up the fat count on a naturally lean protein. Looking for a way to keep the rich, nutty flavor of this dish intact while cutting back on the fat and calories, we found we could swap in panko bread crumbs for a good portion of the nuts. Not only did this move trim serious fat and calories, but it actually improved the texture of the coating by making it more crisp. Grinding the nuts to fine crumbs before toasting them with the panko ensured the nutty coating stuck to the chicken, and toasting the mixture in a small amount of oil contributed some richness without making it greasy. Salting the chicken before breading it helped it retain moisture as it cooked, and poking holes in the meat with a fork created channels for the salt to reach the interior, making it even juicier.

Vegetable oil spray
4 (6-ounce) boneless, skinless chicken breasts, trimmed of all visible fat
Salt and pepper
⅔ cup sliced almonds
⅔ cup panko bread crumbs
1 shallot, minced
1 tablespoon canola oil
½ cup all-purpose flour
3 large egg whites
2 teaspoons Dijon mustard
1½ teaspoons grated lemon zest
¾ teaspoon minced fresh thyme
⅛ teaspoon cayenne pepper

1. Adjust oven rack to lower-middle position and heat oven to 350 degrees. Line rimmed baking sheet with aluminum foil, top with wire rack, and spray rack with oil spray. Pat chicken dry with paper towels. Using fork, poke thicker half of each breast 5 to 6 times and sprinkle each with ¼ teaspoon salt. Transfer breasts to prepared wire rack and refrigerate, uncovered, while preparing coating.

2. Pulse almonds in food processor until they resemble coarse meal, about 20 pulses. Toast processed almonds, panko, shallot, and oil in 12-inch skillet over medium heat, stirring often, until golden brown, 8 to 10 minute; let cool.

3. Spread flour into shallow dish. In second shallow dish, whisk egg whites and mustard together until foamy. In third shallow dish, combine toasted almond mixture, lemon zest, thyme, cayenne, ¼ teaspoon salt, and ¼ teaspoon pepper. Pat chicken dry with paper towels. Working with 1 piece of chicken at a time, dredge in flour, dip in egg white mixture, then coat with nut mixture, pressing gently to adhere; return to wire rack.

4. Spray chicken with oil spray. Bake until chicken registers 160 degrees, 20 to 25 minutes. Let chicken rest for 5 to 10 minutes before serving.

BEFORE → **AFTER**	670 → **430** CALORIES	33 → **16** GRAMS FAT	10 → **2** GRAMS SAT FAT

Chicken Kiev

Serves 4

✔ **WHY THIS RECIPE WORKS:** Stuffed with butter, breaded, and sautéed in even more butter, chicken Kiev is definitely not on the menu if you're watching your figure. For a lighter version of this classic dish, we tried swapping in a number of low-fat alternatives for the buttery filling—including everything from margarine to sour cream and yogurt—but nothing worked as well as reduced-fat cream cheese, which delivered a rich flavor and creamy texture, plus it melted nicely in the oven. Minced shallot, lemon juice, parsley, and tarragon gave the filling a bright, fresh flavor, and chilling the mixture in the freezer made it easy to roll up in the chicken. Pounding our chicken breasts into thin cutlets, which we could completely wrap around the filling, and refrigerating the stuffed chicken before breading it ensured that the filling didn't leak out during baking. Baking the chicken, rather than sautéing it in butter, saved additional fat and calories. For the breading we liked a mix of toasted panko bread crumbs, for their big crunch, and reduced-fat Ritz cracker crumbs, for their ultra-buttery flavor. To crush the Ritz crackers, place them inside a zipper-lock bag and use a rolling pin or the bottom of a large skillet to break them into fine crumbs.

6	ounces ⅓ less fat cream cheese (neufchatel), softened
1	small shallot, minced
1	tablespoon minced fresh parsley
1	teaspoon lemon juice
½	teaspoon minced fresh tarragon
	Salt and pepper
4	(6-ounce) boneless, skinless chicken breasts, trimmed of all visible fat
	Vegetable oil spray
½	cup all-purpose flour
3	large egg whites
1	teaspoon Dijon mustard
⅔	cup panko bread crumbs, toasted (page 18)
9	Reduced-Fat Ritz Crackers, finely crushed
1	tablespoon unsalted butter, melted

1. Combine cream cheese, shallot, parsley, lemon juice, tarragon, ¼ teaspoon salt, and ¼ teaspoon pepper in bowl. Spread mixture into 3-inch square on sheet of plastic wrap; wrap tightly and freeze until firm, at least 1 hour or up to 4 hours.

2. Using chef's knife, butterfly each chicken breast by slicing it lengthwise almost in half. Open up breast to create single, flat cutlet, then gently pound between sheets of plastic wrap to ¼-inch thickness. Pound edges of cutlets to ⅛-inch thickness. Season chicken with salt and pepper.

3. Cut chilled filling into 4 rectangles and place each on tapered end of cutlet. Roll bottom edge of chicken over filling, then fold in sides and continue to roll chicken up into tidy package; refrigerate, uncovered, to seal edges, about 1 hour.

4. Adjust oven rack to middle position and heat oven to 350 degrees. Line rimmed baking sheet with aluminum foil, top with wire rack, and spray rack with oil spray. Spread flour into shallow dish. In second shallow dish, whisk egg whites and mustard together until foamy. In third shallow dish, combine toasted panko, Ritz crumbs, melted butter, ¼ teaspoon salt, and ¼ teaspoon pepper.

5. Working with 1 piece of chicken at a time, dredge in flour, dip in egg white mixture, then coat with panko mixture, pressing gently to adhere; lay on prepared wire rack. Spray chicken with oil spray. Bake until chicken registers 160 degrees, 40 to 45 minutes. Let chicken rest for 5 to 10 minutes before serving.

BEFORE → **AFTER**	760 → **460**	40 → **18**	18 → **9**
	CALORIES	GRAMS FAT	GRAMS SAT FAT

MAKEOVER SPOTLIGHT: CHICKEN KIEV

1. USE REDUCED-FAT CREAM CHEESE IN THE FILLING: Finding something to replace the usual butter in the filling was the biggest challenge when making over chicken Kiev. We tried a number of options, but reduced-fat cream cheese worked best. It has a rich, creamy flavor and it melts well. After stirring in some minced herbs, shallot, and lemon juice for flavor, we spread the cream cheese mixture into a 3-inch square on a sheet of plastic wrap, wrapped it tightly, and froze it until firm. This step makes it easy to roll up the filling inside the chicken.

2. BUTTERFLY AND POUND THE CHICKEN SO THE FILLING STAYS IN PLACE: Butterflying and pounding the chicken allows you to wrap up the filling securely so it doesn't leak. Using a chef's knife, butterfly each chicken breast by slicing it lengthwise almost in half. Open up the breast to create a single flat cutlet, then gently pound it between sheets of plastic wrap to ¼-inch thickness, starting in the center and working outward; pound the edges to ⅛-inch thickness. Place the filling near the tapered end; roll up the chicken to cover it completely. Fold in the sides and continue rolling to form a cylinder.

3. KEEP THE BREADING LIGHT YET FLAVORFUL WITH REDUCED-FAT RITZ CRACKERS: Traditionally, chicken Kiev is coated with butter-drenched bread crumbs, but using all that butter was out of the question if we wanted to lighten our recipe. Instead, we found we could easily replicate the rich flavor and crisp texture by adding crushed Ritz crackers to panko bread crumbs and tossing it all with a modest amount (just 1 tablespoon) of melted butter.

4. SKIP THE BUTTERY SAUTÉ AND BAKE THE CHICKEN INSTEAD: Most recipes for chicken Kiev sauté the stuffed and breaded chicken in a good amount of butter in a skillet. We turned to the oven instead. To ensure that the crumb coating stayed crisp and to help the chicken cook through evenly, we baked the chicken elevated on a wire rack. Be sure to spray the rack with vegetable oil spray so that the coating sticks to the chicken rather than to the rack. Bake the chicken just until it reaches 160 degrees; don't overcook the chicken or else it will taste dry.

Chicken Fricassee

Serves 4

☑ **WHY THIS RECIPE WORKS:** There's a reason legendary chefs from Auguste Escoffier to Fannie Farmer to James Beard published recipes for chicken fricassee: Made the classic French way, by poaching chicken pieces, mushrooms, and onions in broth and saucing them with a cream-enriched reduction of cooking liquid, this dish captures both richness and intense chicken flavor. Wanting to maintain the flavors and textures of this time-honored dish while lightening its fat and calorie counts, we found the biggest challenge to be finding a substitution for the cream in the sauce. We tried swapping in half-and-half, and while it added richness, it left the sauce thin and watery. Light sour cream was a better choice, but it didn't contribute as much creaminess as we wanted. In the end, we found that reduced-fat cream cheese worked best, adding plenty of body, an ultra-creamy texture, and a pleasant tang. To ensure that our sauce remained satiny-smooth, we found it essential to temper the cream cheese—we added a small amount of the hot broth to it—so it wouldn't curdle when added to the skillet.

4	**(6-ounce) boneless, skinless chicken breasts, trimmed of all visible fat**
	Salt and pepper
2	**teaspoons canola oil**
1	**pound cremini mushrooms, trimmed and sliced ¼ inch thick**
1	**onion, chopped fine**
¼	**cup dry white wine**
1	**tablespoon all-purpose flour**
1	**garlic clove, minced**
1½	**cups low-sodium chicken broth**
2	**ounces ⅓ less fat cream cheese (neufchatel), softened**
2	**teaspoons lemon juice**
2	**teaspoons minced fresh tarragon**
¼	**teaspoon ground nutmeg**

1. Pat chicken dry with paper towels and season with salt and pepper. Heat oil in 12-inch skillet over medium-high heat until just smoking. Brown chicken well on both sides, about 8 minutes; transfer to plate.

2. Add mushrooms, onion, and wine to fat left in skillet and cook over medium heat until liquid has evaporated and mushrooms are browned, 8 to 10 minutes. Stir in flour and garlic and cook for 1 minute. Slowly whisk in broth, scraping up any browned bits, and bring to boil. Return browned chicken and any accumulated juices to skillet. Reduce heat to medium-low, cover, and cook until chicken registers 160 degrees, about 10 minutes.

3. Transfer chicken to serving platter and tent loosely with aluminum foil. Whisk ½ cup of sauce into cream cheese in bowl to temper, then stir cream cheese mixture back into pan. Stir in lemon juice, tarragon, and nutmeg and return sauce to brief simmer. Season with salt and pepper to taste and pour over chicken. Serve.

BEFORE → **AFTER**	500 → **310** CALORIES	26 → **10** GRAMS FAT	10 → **3** GRAMS SAT FAT

Chicken Marsala

Serves 4

✓ **WHY THIS RECIPE WORKS:** A simple yet richly flavored dish, chicken Marsala calls for sautéing chicken breasts before draping them with a mushroom and Marsala wine sauce enriched with a good dose of butter. To lighten the dish, we cut back on the butter to just 1 tablespoon, but that left us with a sauce that was watery and bland. Stirring in a cornstarch slurry toward the end of cooking helped by giving our sauce some much-needed body and a clingy texture. Bumping up the flavor of the sauce was as easy as selecting the right bottle of Marsala—dry Marsala made for a dull, flavorless sauce, but sweet Marsala gave us a sauce with a full, round flavor. To trim the fat count even further, we sautéed our chicken and mushrooms in less oil than most recipes call for. To keep our chicken breasts moist and tender given that we were using less fat, we found it necessary to reduce the heat level when sautéing them. As for the mushrooms, cooking them covered, then uncovered, helped to draw out their moisture so they could brown nicely and add deep flavor to the dish.

½ **cup all-purpose flour**
4 **(6-ounce) boneless, skinless chicken breasts, trimmed of all visible fat**
 Salt and pepper
4 **teaspoons canola oil**
8 **ounces white mushrooms, trimmed and sliced thin**
1 **garlic clove, minced**
2 **teaspoons minced fresh thyme**
1 **cup low-sodium chicken broth**
½ **cup sweet Marsala**
1 **tablespoon water**
1 **teaspoon cornstarch**
1 **tablespoon unsalted butter**

1. Spread flour into shallow dish. Pat chicken dry with paper towels, season with salt and pepper, then lightly dredge in flour. Heat oil in 12-inch skillet over medium heat until just smoking. Add chicken and cook until golden on first side, 6 to 8 minutes. Flip chicken, reduce heat to medium-low, and continue to cook until chicken registers 160 degrees, 6 to 8 minutes; transfer to platter and tent loosely with aluminum foil.

2. Add mushrooms and pinch salt to fat left in skillet, cover, and cook over medium heat until they have released their liquid, about 7 minutes. Uncover, increase heat to medium-high, and cook until mushrooms are well browned, about 7 minutes.

3. Stir in garlic and thyme and cook until fragrant, about 30 seconds. Whisk in broth and Marsala, scraping up any browned bits, and bring to simmer. Whisk water and cornstarch together in bowl, then stir into sauce and simmer until thickened, about 5 minutes. Off heat, whisk in butter and season with salt and pepper to taste. Spoon sauce over chicken and serve.

BEFORE → **AFTER**   670 → **380**   28 → **12**   11 → **3**
CALORIES   GRAMS FAT   GRAMS SAT FAT

Chicken Parmesan with Spaghetti

Serves 6

✔ **WHY THIS RECIPE WORKS:** The best part of chicken Parmesan is its crisp, golden exterior. Unfortunately, this ultra-crunchy coating is the result of frying the chicken in a good amount of oil. We decided to skip the frying and bake our chicken, but initial attempts looked as bland as they tasted. Switching from fresh or dried bread crumbs to panko bread crumbs was a step in the right direction—the panko offered a crunchier texture from the get-go. Toasting it to a golden shade before breading our chicken ensured it was übercrisp, and adding a dash of oil to the toasted crumbs gave them a real "fried" flavor without making our lightened chicken Parmesan greasy or fatty. Part-skim mozzarella made the perfect gooey, yet low-fat, topping.

Vegetable oil spray
½ cup all-purpose flour
3 large egg whites
½ teaspoon garlic powder
1½ cups panko bread crumbs, toasted (see page 18)
1 ounce Parmesan cheese, grated (½ cup)
1 tablespoon olive oil
Salt and pepper
6 (6-ounce) boneless, skinless chicken breasts, trimmed of all visible fat
12 ounces spaghetti
4 cups Low-Fat Tomato Sauce, warmed
4 ounces part-skim mozzarella cheese, shredded (1 cup)
1 tablespoon chopped fresh basil

1. Adjust oven rack to middle position and heat oven to 475 degrees. Line rimmed baking sheet with aluminum foil, top with wire rack, and spray rack with oil spray. Spread flour into shallow dish. In second shallow dish, whisk egg whites and garlic powder together until foamy. In third shallow dish, combine toasted panko, Parmesan, oil, ¼ teaspoon salt, and ¼ teaspoon pepper.

2. Place chicken between 2 sheets of plastic wrap and pound gently to even ½-inch thickness. Season chicken with salt and pepper. Working with 1 piece at a time, dredge chicken in flour, dip in egg white mixture, then coat with panko mixture, pressing gently to adhere; lay on prepared wire rack. Spray chicken with oil spray. Bake until chicken registers 160 degrees, 15 to 20 minutes.

3. Meanwhile, bring 4 quarts water to boil in large pot. Add pasta and 1 tablespoon salt and cook, stirring often, until al dente. Reserve ½ cup cooking water, then drain pasta and return it to pot. Stir in 2 cups tomato sauce, season with salt and pepper to taste, and add reserved cooking water as needed to adjust consistency.

4. Top cutlets with 1 cup tomato sauce and sprinkle with mozzarella. Continue to bake until cheese has melted, 3 to 5 minutes. Sprinkle with basil and serve with pasta, passing remaining 1 cup tomato sauce separately.

ON THE SIDE LOW-FAT TOMATO SAUCE

Pulse 3 (14.5-ounce) cans diced tomatoes with their juice in food processor until mostly smooth, about 15 pulses. Cook 4 minced garlic cloves, 1 tablespoon tomato paste, 1 tablespoon olive oil, ¼ teaspoon dried oregano, and pinch red pepper flakes together in medium saucepan over medium heat until tomato paste begins to brown, about 2 minutes. Stir in processed tomatoes and simmer until sauce is thickened and measures about 4 cups, 20 to 25 minutes. Season with salt, pepper, and sugar to taste. Makes 4 cups.

BEFORE NUMBERS BASED ON: Chicken Parmesan from Romano's Macaroni Grill	BEFORE → **AFTER**	940 → **660** CALORIES	57 → **16** GRAMS FAT	12 → **5** GRAMS SAT FAT

Chicken Piccata with Spaghetti

Serves 4

✔ **WHY THIS RECIPE WORKS:** Chicken piccata might taste light and bright, but it has a surprising amount of fat lurking behind the scenes. Not only is the chicken traditionally cooked in lots of butter so it browns nicely and is moist and flavorful, but the lemon sauce is finished with several pats as well. Sautéing our cutlets in a minimal amount of canola oil—not butter—over medium heat kept our chicken tender and flavorful and cut back on fat, but it was still lacking a nicely browned crust. Flouring one side of each cutlet and cooking the floured side slightly longer ensured the chicken had a picture-perfect, golden brown exterior. For a lean sauce that was ultra-lemony but not bitter, we simmered strips of zest in the sauce, then removed them before serving. Finishing with a single pat of butter enriched the sauce nicely. You can purchase chicken breast cutlets at the supermarket, or make your own by slicing boneless, skinless chicken breasts in half horizontally; you may need to gently pound the cutlets to ensure they are an even thickness.

¼ cup plus 1½ teaspoons all-purpose flour

8 (3-ounce) boneless, skinless chicken breast cutlets, trimmed of all visible fat
Salt and pepper

5 teaspoons canola oil

2 tablespoons capers, rinsed

2 garlic cloves, minced

1½ cups low-sodium chicken broth

¾ cup dry white wine

4 (2-inch) strips lemon zest plus 4 teaspoons juice

8 ounces spaghetti

1½ tablespoons unsalted butter, chilled

1. Spread ¼ cup flour into shallow dish. Pat cutlets dry with paper towels, season with salt and pepper, then lightly dredge 1 side of each cutlet in flour. Heat 1 tablespoon oil in 12-inch skillet over medium heat until shimmering. Add half of cutlets, floured side down, and cook until golden on first side, about 3 minutes. Flip cutlets and continue to cook until no longer pink, about 1 minute; transfer to plate and tent loosely with aluminum foil. Repeat with remaining 2 teaspoons oil and remaining 4 cutlets.

2. Add capers and garlic to fat left in skillet and cook until fragrant, about 30 seconds. Stir in remaining 1½ teaspoons flour. Whisk in broth, wine, and lemon zest strips, scraping up any browned bits. Simmer sauce until slightly thickened and reduced to 1 cup, about 5 minutes.

3. Meanwhile, bring 4 quarts water to boil in large pot. Add pasta and 1 tablespoon salt and cook, stirring often, until al dente. Drain pasta and return it to pot. Stir in ½ tablespoon butter and season with salt and pepper to taste; transfer to individual plates.

4. Return chicken cutlets and any accumulated juices to skillet and simmer until heated through, about 30 seconds. Arrange cutlets on top of pasta. Off heat, remove lemon zest and whisk in lemon juice and remaining 1 tablespoon butter. Spoon sauce over chicken and pasta and serve.

BEFORE NUMBERS BASED ON: **Chicken Piccata from Bertucci's**	BEFORE → **AFTER**	1070 → **560** CALORIES	42 → **15** GRAMS FAT	14 → **4.5** GRAMS SAT FAT

Chicken Cordon Bleu

Serves 4

☑ **WHY THIS RECIPE WORKS:** Stuffed with ham and Swiss cheese, then breaded and sautéed in lots of butter, chicken cordon bleu is nearly as fussy as it is fatty. We wanted to not only lighten this retro classic, but also make it easier to prepare. Focusing first on the fat issue, we switched to low-fat Swiss cheese and baked the breaded chicken instead of cooking it in butter. After testing numerous crumb coatings, we landed on a mixture of panko and crushed reduced-fat Ritz crackers; toasting the panko beforehand ensured that our chicken emerged from the oven with a golden, crisp exterior. To simplify the traditionally finicky assembly method, we simply cut a pocket in the side of each chicken breast and nestled a ham-and-Swiss roll-up inside. Refrigerating the stuffed chicken before breading it ensures that the filling won't leak out during baking. To crush the Ritz crackers, place them inside a zipper-lock bag and use a rolling pin or the bottom of a large skillet to break them into fine crumbs.

2	ounces low-fat Swiss cheese, shredded (½ cup)
8	ounces (8 slices) Black Forest ham
4	(8-ounce) boneless, skinless chicken breasts, trimmed of all visible fat
	Vegetable oil spray
½	cup all-purpose flour
3	large egg whites
2	tablespoons Dijon mustard
⅔	cup panko bread crumbs, toasted (see page 18)
9	Reduced-Fat Ritz Crackers, finely crushed
1	tablespoon unsalted butter, melted
	Salt and pepper

1. Make 4 ham-and-Swiss roll-ups by tightly rolling 2 tablespoons shredded Swiss inside 2 pieces ham, folding in edges as needed. Cut pocket through side of chicken into thickest part of each breast, then stuff each with 1 roll-up. Transfer chicken to plate, cover with plastic wrap, and refrigerate until firm, at least 20 minutes or up to 4 hours.

2. Adjust oven rack to middle position; heat oven to 425 degrees. Line rimmed baking sheet with aluminum foil, top with wire rack, and spray rack with oil spray. Spread flour into shallow dish. In second shallow dish, whisk egg whites and mustard together until foamy. In third shallow dish, combine toasted panko, Ritz crumbs, melted butter, ¼ teaspoon salt, and ¼ teaspoon pepper.

3. Working with 1 piece of chicken at a time, dredge in flour, dip into egg white mixture, then coat with panko mixture, pressing gently to adhere; lay on prepared wire rack. Spray chicken with oil spray. Bake until chicken registers 160 degrees, about 30 minutes. Let chicken rest for 5 to 10 minutes; serve.

QUICK PREP TIP
MAKING CHICKEN CORDON BLEU
Using paring knife, cut small opening in thickest part of chicken breast and work knife back and forth until pocket extends deep into breast. Stuff each pocket with 1 ham-and-Swiss roll-up.

BEFORE → **AFTER**	990 → **500**	47 → **12**	24 → **3.5**
	CALORIES	GRAMS FAT	GRAMS SAT FAT

Cashew Chicken

Serves 4

✔ **WHY THIS RECIPE WORKS:** You'd think that the fat and calories in cashew chicken are due to the nuts, but that's only partially true. Stir-fries are generally quite high in fat thanks to the generous amount of oil that's used to cook the various components of the dish. Yet if you try to cut back or completely eliminate the cooking oil, you're left with dried-out meat and a harsh-tasting sauce. After lots of testing, we learned that the trick is to use just enough oil to coat the chicken and sauté the aromatics—we used ginger and garlic—but the vegetables can simply be cooked in a small amount of water until crisp-tender. For our dish, we were able to cut down the total amount of oil to just 4 teaspoons. As for the nuts, we found a mere ¼ cup of cashews did the trick; chopping them ensured they were more evenly distributed in the dish, offering rich flavor and a nice crunch in every bite. Using toasted sesame oil instead of vegetable oil also helped to reinforce the nutty flavor of our lightened cashew chicken, and marinating the chicken in it ensured the meat itself was richly flavored. Serve with white rice.

¼ cup low-sodium soy sauce

2 tablespoons Chinese rice wine or dry sherry

2 tablespoons cornstarch

1 teaspoon sugar

4 teaspoons toasted sesame oil

12 ounces boneless, skinless chicken breasts, trimmed of all visible fat, halved lengthwise, and sliced thin

¾ cup low-sodium chicken broth

3 garlic cloves, minced

2 teaspoons grated fresh ginger

⅛ teaspoon red pepper flakes

1 red bell pepper, stemmed, seeded, and cut into 2-inch-long matchsticks

¼ cup water

8 ounces snow peas, strings removed and halved crosswise

1 (8-ounce) can water chestnuts, drained and sliced thin

¼ cup roasted unsalted cashews, coarsely chopped

1. Whisk soy sauce, wine, cornstarch, and sugar together in medium bowl. Measure 2 tablespoons of mixture into separate bowl and stir in 2 teaspoons sesame oil and chicken; let marinate for 10 to 30 minutes. Stir broth into remaining soy sauce mixture to make sauce; set aside. In separate bowl, combine garlic, ginger, pepper flakes, and remaining 2 teaspoons sesame oil.

2. Cook bell pepper and water, covered, in 12-inch nonstick skillet over high heat until water is boiling and pepper begins to soften, about 3 minutes. Uncover, add snow peas, and cook until water has evaporated and vegetables are crisp-tender, about 2 minutes; transfer to bowl.

3. Return now-empty skillet to medium-high heat. Add chicken with marinade, breaking up any clumps, and cook until lightly browned on all sides but not fully cooked, about 6 minutes. Clear center of skillet, add garlic mixture, and cook, mashing mixture into pan, until fragrant, 15 to 30 seconds.

4. Stir in cooked vegetables, water chestnuts, and cashews. Whisk sauce to recombine and add to skillet. Simmer until chicken is cooked through and sauce is thickened, 30 seconds to 2 minutes. Serve.

BEFORE → **AFTER**   470 → **280**   25 → **11**   4 → **2**
CALORIES   GRAMS FAT   GRAMS SAT FAT

BAKED STUFFED SHRIMP

Favorites from Land and Sea

Steak au Poivre with Brandied Cream Sauce

Serves 4

✔ **WHY THIS RECIPE WORKS:** Seared and encrusted with peppercorns, steak au poivre makes for an elegant, satisfying dinner. Plus, the filets mignons traditionally called for in this dish are naturally lean, so they're a fine pick for those concerned with fat and calories. The problem is the accompanying sauce that's draped over the steaks—made with brandy and enriched with heavy cream and butter, it's definitely not on the good-for-you list. To lighten our sauce, the cream and butter would have to go. Instead, we started with low-sodium chicken broth; sautéed shallot and thyme amped up its flavor. For a complex profile, we added the brandy twice during cooking. First, we reduced a portion with the aromatics to intensify its flavor and cook off its raw, boozy notes; then, we stirred in a spoonful at the end of cooking to add a final punch to the sauce. A small amount of half-and-half thickened with cornstarch added the "cream" to our cream sauce without racking up the fat count. As for the steaks, we decided to pepper one side only; by searing the unpeppered side first, we were left with richly flavored browned bits that contributed meaty, savory notes to our sauce. Pressing down on the steaks with a cake pan helped ensure the peppercorns stuck to the surface. For perfectly cooked filet mignon, we finished our steaks in a hot oven on a preheated baking sheet. Use a heavy pan to crush the peppercorns against a cutting board in a rocking motion; alternatively, you can place the peppercorns in a zipper-lock bag and whack them with a rolling pin or meat pounder.

4	(6-ounce) center-cut filets mignons, 1½ inches thick, trimmed of all visible fat
	Salt and pepper
1	tablespoon black peppercorns, crushed
1	tablespoon canola oil
1	shallot, minced
1	teaspoon minced fresh thyme
5	tablespoons brandy
1½	cups low-sodium chicken broth
¼	cup half-and-half
2	teaspoons cornstarch

1. Adjust oven rack to middle position, place rimmed baking sheet on oven rack, and heat oven to 450 degrees. Pat steaks dry with paper towels and season with salt. Rub crushed peppercorns over one side of each steak, pressing gently to adhere.

2. Heat oil in 12-inch nonstick skillet over medium-high heat until just smoking. Lay steaks in skillet, peppered side up. Press firmly on steaks with bottom of cake pan and cook until well browned on bottom, about 3 minutes. Flip steaks, reduce heat to medium, and cook, pressing firmly with cake pan, until browned on second side, about 3 minutes. Transfer steaks to hot sheet, peppered side up, and roast until steaks register 120 to 125 degrees (for medium-rare), 4 to 6 minutes. Transfer steaks to carving board, tent loosely with aluminum foil, and let rest for 5 to 10 minutes.

3. Add shallot, thyme, and ¼ teaspoon salt to fat left in skillet and cook over medium heat until softened, about 2 minutes. Off heat, stir in ¼ cup brandy, scraping up any browned bits. Stir in broth and simmer over medium heat until sauce has reduced to ¾ cup, 5 to 7 minutes. Whisk half-and-half and cornstarch together in bowl, then whisk into sauce and continue to simmer until slightly thickened, about 1 minute. Off heat, stir in remaining 1 tablespoon brandy and season with salt and pepper to taste. Spoon sauce over filets and serve.

BEFORE → **AFTER**	720 → **370**	51 → **17**	24 → **5**
	CALORIES	GRAMS FAT	GRAMS SAT FAT

Steak Tips with Mushroom-Onion Gravy

Serves 6

✔ **WHY THIS RECIPE WORKS:** This everyman's classic promises juicy beef and hearty flavors but often delivers overcooked meat in a generic brown sauce or ultra-fatty, gloppy gravy. To rescue this dish, we started with tender sirloin tip steaks (sometimes sold as flap meat). To build flavor without adding any fat, we marinated the tips in a mixture of sugar and soy sauce; the meat absorbed the flavors, and browning them in a skillet left behind plenty of rich, browned bits from which we could build the gravy. Dried porcini intensified the mushroom flavor, and cooking our sliced white mushrooms with a sprinkle of salt in a covered skillet helped them soften and release their liquid without having to use excessive amounts of oil. A sliced onion and some minced garlic and thyme provided serious depth to the sauce. Beef broth amped up the hearty, savory notes of the dish, and the addition of a little flour helped turn our sauce into a full-fledged gravy without making it overly thick. Serve over rice or egg noodles.

1½	pounds sirloin steak tips, trimmed of all visible fat and cut into 1½-inch chunks
1	tablespoon low-sodium soy sauce
1	teaspoon sugar
	Salt and pepper
4	teaspoons canola oil
1	pound white mushrooms, trimmed and sliced thin
1	onion, halved and sliced thin
¼	ounce dried porcini mushrooms, rinsed and minced
1	garlic clove, minced
½	teaspoon minced fresh thyme or ⅛ teaspoon dried
4	teaspoons all-purpose flour
1¾	cups beef broth
1	tablespoon minced fresh parsley

1. Combine steak tips, soy sauce, sugar, and ⅛ teaspoon pepper in bowl; let marinate for 30 minutes to 1 hour. Heat 2 teaspoons oil in 12-inch skillet over medium-high heat until just smoking. Add marinated beef and cook until well browned on all sides, 4 to 6 minutes; transfer to plate.

2. Add remaining 2 teaspoons oil, white mushrooms, onion, porcini, and ⅛ teaspoon salt to fat left in skillet. Cover and cook over medium-low heat until vegetables are softened, 8 to 10 minutes. Uncover, increase heat to medium-high, and continue to cook until vegetables are well browned, 8 to 12 minutes.

3. Stir in garlic and thyme and cook until fragrant, about 30 seconds. Stir in flour and cook for 1 minute. Stir in broth, scraping up any browned bits, and bring to simmer. Add browned beef and any accumulated juices, reduce heat to medium-low, and simmer gently until meat registers 130 to 135 degrees (for medium), 3 to 5 minutes. Season with salt and pepper to taste, sprinkle with parsley, and serve.

BEFORE → **AFTER**	460 → **210**	24 → **6**	8 → **1.5**
	CALORIES	GRAMS FAT	GRAMS SAT FAT

Stir-Fried Beef and Broccoli with Classic Brown Stir-Fry Sauce

Serves 4

✔ **WHY THIS RECIPE WORKS:** In Chinese cooking, stir-fries don't need much oil because they are cooked in well-seasoned woks over intense heat, so the food doesn't stick to the pan. Since few American stoves can attain such heat, most recipes add copious amounts of oil for stir-frying not only the beef but also the vegetables. To avoid the grease trap and keep our stir-fry on the lighter side, we first steamed our vegetables (we liked a mix of broccoli and bell peppers) until they were perfectly done, then we sautéed the beef and aromatics in just 2 teaspoons of oil. Briefly freezing the meat (we liked lean yet beefy flank steak) for 15 minutes made it easy to slice super-thin, and marinating it in soy sauce added big flavor.

SAUCE

- ½   **cup low-sodium chicken broth**
- ¼   **cup hoisin sauce or oyster-flavored sauce**
- 3   **tablespoons Chinese rice wine or dry sherry**
- 1   **tablespoon low-sodium soy sauce**
- 1   **tablespoon cornstarch**
- 1   **teaspoon toasted sesame oil**

STIR-FRY

- 12   **ounces flank steak, trimmed of all visible fat and sliced thinly into 2-inch-long pieces**
- 2   **teaspoons low-sodium soy sauce**
- 3   **scallions, minced**
- 6   **garlic cloves, minced**
- 1   **tablespoon grated fresh ginger**
- 1   **tablespoon canola oil**
- 1   **pound broccoli, florets cut into 1-inch pieces, stalks peeled and sliced thin**
- ⅓   **cup water**
- 2   **red bell peppers, stemmed, seeded, and cut into 2-inch-long matchsticks**

1. FOR THE SAUCE: Whisk all ingredients together in bowl.

2. FOR THE STIR-FRY: Combine beef and soy sauce in bowl; let marinate for 10 to 30 minutes. In separate bowl, combine scallions, garlic, ginger, and 1 teaspoon canola oil.

3. Cook broccoli florets, broccoli stalks, and water together in covered 12-inch nonstick skillet over high heat until water is boiling and broccoli is green and beginning to soften, about 2 minutes. Uncover, add bell peppers, and cook until water has evaporated and vegetables are crisp-tender, about 3 minutes; transfer to colander.

4. Add remaining 2 teaspoons canola oil to now-empty skillet and place over high heat until just smoking. Add beef with marinade, breaking up any clumps, and cook until lightly browned on all sides but not fully cooked, about 2 minutes. Clear center of skillet, add garlic mixture, and cook, mashing mixture into pan, until fragrant, 15 to 30 seconds.

5. Stir in cooked vegetables. Whisk sauce to recombine and add to skillet. Simmer until beef is cooked through and sauce is thickened, about 1 minute. Serve.

BEFORE→ **AFTER**	420→**290** CALORIES	23→**11** GRAMS FAT	6→**2.5** GRAMS SAT FAT

MAKEOVER SPOTLIGHT: STIR-FRIED BEEF

1. USE LEAN YET BEEFY-TASTING FLANK STEAK, SLICE IT THIN, AND MARINATE IT: For our stir-fry, we found that flank steak was the best option. It's readily available and relatively lean, and has a big, beefy flavor that can stand up to the potent ingredients of a stir-fry. Marinating the meat with a little soy sauce for up to half an hour helped it stay moist and tender as it cooked. To make it easier to cut the steak thin, place it in the freezer for 15 minutes. Slice the partially frozen steak lengthwise (with the grain) into 2-inch-wide pieces, then slice each piece across the grain into thin strips.

2. DITCH THE WOK—AND REACH FOR A SKILLET INSTEAD: Though a wok is the traditional cooking vessel for stir-fries, we opted for a 12-inch nonstick skillet because the food browns better in a flat skillet and the nonstick surface means we can use a minimum of oil. Using a 12-inch skillet is important because smaller skillets won't provide enough room and will steam the food rather than stir-fry it. Before adding any ingredients to the pan, be sure to heat the oil—our recipe calls for just 2 teaspoons to cook the beef—in the skillet over high heat until just smoking.

3. STEAM THE VEGETABLES TO CUT BACK ON FAT: Whereas most stir-fry recipes cook the vegetables in batches with big splashes of oil, we found we could simply steam the vegetables using just a small amount of water. Since broccoli is hearty, we gave it a jump start in the skillet, cooking it covered for a few minutes before adding our thinly sliced peppers, which needed just a couple minutes to soften.

4. MAKE YOUR OWN STIR-FRY SAUCE: Store-bought stir-fry sauces not only taste pretty lousy, they also contain loads of hidden fat and sodium. Luckily, homemade sauces are easy to make and require just a handful of ingredients. Using low-sodium chicken broth and low-sodium soy sauce prevented the sauce from tasting too salty, and a mere tablespoon of cornstarch helped the sauce thicken quickly and coat the vegetables and meat nicely without being too gloppy. Add the sauce to the skillet once everything is cooked, and let it just come to a simmer to thicken.

Beef Stroganoff

Serves 6

☑ **WHY THIS RECIPE WORKS:** Ultra-rich and luxurious, Stroganoff starts by browning beef tenderloin in butter before smothering it in a sour cream–enriched mushroom sauce and serving the whole thing over buttered noodles. To make over this dish, we first looked for a way to cut back on the beef. Thinly sliced portobellos, spritzed with vegetable oil spray and roasted, provided big, meaty bites and allowed us to eliminate some of the meat. A bit of tomato paste, added to the sauce, further amped up the savory notes. As for the meat, we swapped the mild (and pricey) tenderloin for beefier sirloin steak; a little baking soda tenderized the tough steak in minutes. To cut calories in the cream sauce, nonfat yogurt proved the best alternative to sour cream, but it curdled instantly when added to the pan. Stirring an egg white into the yogurt solved the problem (the egg white helped to neutralize the acids in the yogurt). Finally, we kept the egg noodles, but switched to the yolk-free variety, which were perfect for sopping up the rich sauce.

Vegetable oil spray
1½ pounds portobello mushroom caps, gills removed, caps halved and sliced thin
Salt and pepper
1 teaspoon baking soda
1¼ pounds sirloin steak, trimmed of all visible fat and sliced thinly into 2-inch-long pieces (see page 145)
10 ounces (6 cups) yolk-free egg noodles
1 tablespoon canola oil
1 onion, chopped fine
4 teaspoons all-purpose flour
2 teaspoons tomato paste
1½ cups beef broth
3 tablespoons white wine
2 teaspoons Dijon mustard
½ cup plain nonfat yogurt
1 large egg white
1 tablespoon minced fresh parsley

1. Adjust oven rack to middle position and heat oven to 425 degrees. Spray rimmed baking sheet with oil spray. Spread sliced mushrooms over prepared baking sheet, spray lightly with oil spray, and sprinkle with ¼ teaspoon salt and ¼ teaspoon pepper. Roast, stirring occasionally, until golden, about 15 minutes.

2. Meanwhile, combine ½ cup cold water and baking soda in large bowl, add beef, and let sit for 15 minutes to tenderize. Bring 4 quarts water to boil in large pot. Add noodles and 1 tablespoon salt and cook, stirring often, until al dente. Drain noodles, return to pot, and cover until needed.

3. Drain and rinse tenderized beef; pat dry with paper towels. Heat 1 teaspoon oil in 12-inch nonstick skillet over high heat until just smoking. Add half of beef and cook without stirring until browned around edges, 1 to 2 minutes. Stir and continue to cook beef until no longer pink, about 30 seconds; transfer to clean bowl. Repeat with 1 teaspoon oil and remaining beef.

4. Add remaining 1 teaspoon oil, onion, and ¼ teaspoon salt to fat left in skillet; cook over medium heat until browned, 6 to 8 minutes. Stir in roasted mushrooms, flour, and tomato paste and cook until tomato paste begins to darken, about 2 minutes. Stir in broth, wine, and mustard, scraping up any browned bits, and bring to boil. Reduce heat to medium-low and simmer gently until sauce is slightly thickened, about 5 minutes.

5. Stir browned beef and any accumulated juices into skillet; simmer gently until heated through, about 1 minute. Off heat, whisk yogurt and egg white together, then stir into skillet. Stir in parsley; season with salt and pepper to taste. Serve over noodles.

BEFORE → **AFTER**	550 → **370** CALORIES	32 → **7** GRAMS FAT	11 → **1.5** GRAMS SAT FAT

Meatloaf

Serves 6

✔ **WHY THIS RECIPE WORKS:** For a lightened all-beef meatloaf that is tender and flavorful—not dry and grainy—we came up with a slew of tricks. Starting with 90 percent lean ground beef, rather than ground chuck or meatloaf mix, helped us lose fat and calories right off the bat; ground chuck proved too fatty for our recipe, as did meatloaf mix, which can vary in composition (it's usually made up of different amounts of ground beef, ground veal, and ground pork) and fat content. For moisture and a flavor boost, we swapped the usual dry bread crumbs for a slice of white bread and added tomato juice to the mix. An untraditional ingredient, soy sauce, also amped up the moisture and flavor of our meatloaf with minimal fat and calories. Sautéed mushrooms, broken down in the food processor so they would blend in with the beef, added even more moisture and gave our meatloaf serious substance and heartiness. Baking the meatloaf elevated on a rimmed baking sheet instead of in a loaf pan eliminated the risk of it becoming soggy. This technique also allowed us to glaze three sides of the meatloaf—rather than just the top—resulting in a pleasantly sticky, browned crust all around.

1	teaspoon canola oil
1	onion, chopped fine
	Salt and pepper
10	ounces cremini or white mushrooms, trimmed and sliced thin
3	garlic cloves, minced
1	teaspoon minced fresh thyme
¼	cup tomato juice
1	slice hearty white sandwich bread, torn into pieces
1½	pounds 90 percent lean ground beef
1	large egg
2	tablespoons minced fresh parsley
1	tablespoon low-sodium soy sauce
1	tablespoon Dijon mustard
⅓	cup ketchup
3	tablespoons cider vinegar
2	tablespoons packed light brown sugar
1	teaspoon hot sauce

1. Adjust oven rack to middle position and heat oven to 375 degrees. Set wire rack inside rimmed baking sheet and arrange 8 by 6-inch piece of aluminum foil in center of rack. Using skewer, poke holes in foil every half-inch.

2. Heat oil in 12-inch nonstick skillet over medium heat until shimmering. Add onion and ¼ teaspoon salt and cook until softened, about 5 minutes. Stir in mushrooms and cook until they have released their liquid and are lightly browned, about 10 minutes. Stir in garlic and thyme and cook until fragrant, about 30 seconds. Stir in tomato juice and cook until thickened, about 1 minute. Let mixture cool for 5 minutes; transfer to food processor, add bread, and process until smooth, about 25 seconds. Add ground beef and pulse to combine, about 20 pulses.

3. Whisk egg, parsley, soy sauce, mustard, ¼ teaspoon salt, and ½ teaspoon pepper in large bowl. Add processed beef mixture and mix with hands until evenly combined. Using hands, shape mixture into 8 by 6-inch loaf on top of prepared foil. Bake until meatloaf registers 160 degrees, about 1 hour.

4. Simmer ketchup, vinegar, sugar, and hot sauce together in small saucepan until thickened, about 5 minutes. Remove meatloaf from oven, adjust oven rack 8 inches from broiler element, and heat broiler. Spread glaze over baked meatloaf and broil until glaze begins to bubble, about 3 minutes. Let rest for 10 minutes. Serve.

BEFORE → **AFTER**	510 → **300** CALORIES	29 → **13** GRAMS FAT	10 → **5** GRAMS SAT FAT

MAKEOVER SPOTLIGHT: MEATLOAF

1. SWAP MUSHROOMS FOR SOME OF THE BEEF: We found that replacing almost a quarter of the meat in our recipe with mushrooms, which have a meaty flavor and a hearty texture similar to that of ground beef when chopped or ground into small pieces, was an easy and seamless way to reduce some of the fat and calories without losing any volume or flavor. Sautéing the mushrooms briefly helped deepen their flavor and worked to drive off some of their moisture before they are combined with the other ingredients.

2. USE LEAN GROUND BEEF AND BOOST THE FLAVOR WITH TOMATO JUICE AND SOY SAUCE: Using 90 percent lean ground beef is an obvious way to trim fat and calories, but we found it to have a dry, mealy quality when packed into a meatloaf. To fix this, we leaned on two pantry ingredients—tomato juice and soy sauce—to help bring the loaf back on track. Not only did they add a tangy, seasoned flavor to the mix, but their extra moisture helped prevent the meat from tasting dry.

3. ADD A SLICE OF BREAD TO KEEP THE MEATLOAF MOIST: Lots of recipes for meatloaf use crackers as a binder, but this move just made our lean loaf taste even drier. Instead, we found a slice of sandwich bread did just as good a job of binding the mixture without robbing the meatloaf of its moisture. To combine the bread, ground beef, and sautéed mushrooms into a uniform mixture, we used the food processor, which makes this task a snap and turns the mushrooms into small enough pieces that they blend into the meatloaf.

4. BAKE THE MEATLOAF ELEVATED ON A WIRE RACK TO AVOID A SOGGY LOAF: Once the meatloaf mixture was assembled, we shaped it into a loaf on top of a wire rack that's been lined with a perforated sheet of aluminum foil to allow extra grease to drain away from the meatloaf as it bakes. Because we used a wire rack, both top and sides of the loaf achieved a nice crust—and as a bonus, the loaf is easier to slice and serve.

Turkey Tacos

Serves 4

✔ **WHY THIS RECIPE WORKS:** So maybe they're not authentic Mexican food, but ground meat tacos boast a comfort-food appeal that's undeniable. Ditching the ground beef in favor of ground turkey helped us slash the fat in our makeover version of this family-friendly dish, but its lean flavor needed a boost. To pump it up, we made a thick, zesty sauce using chicken broth, tomato sauce, cider vinegar, and brown sugar. Chili powder, garlic, and oregano provided the aromatic notes. Crunchy corn taco shells were a given; soft taco shells didn't do nearly as good a job securing the rich, hearty filling. Do not use ground turkey breast here (also labeled 99 percent fat-free) or the filling will be very dry. Serve these tacos with your favorite taco fixings, such as shredded lettuce, diced avocado, chopped tomatoes, minced jalapeños, sliced scallions, cilantro leaves, and/or salsa, or garnish with our simple Fresh Tomato Topping.

1	teaspoon canola oil
1	onion, chopped fine
2	tablespoons chili powder
3	garlic cloves, minced
1	teaspoon dried oregano
1	pound 93 percent lean ground turkey
½	cup canned tomato sauce
½	cup low-sodium chicken broth
2	teaspoons cider vinegar
1	teaspoon packed light brown sugar
	Salt and pepper
8	corn taco shells, warmed

1. Heat oil in 12-inch nonstick skillet over medium-high heat until shimmering. Add onion and cook until softened, about 5 minutes. Stir in chili powder, garlic, and oregano and cook until fragrant, about 30 seconds. Add ground turkey and cook, breaking up meat with wooden spoon, until almost cooked through but still slightly pink, about 2 minutes.

2. Stir in tomato sauce, broth, vinegar, and sugar. Bring to simmer and cook until thickened, about 4 minutes. Season with salt and pepper to taste. Divide filling evenly among taco shells and serve.

ON THE SIDE
FRESH TOMATO TOPPING
Though salsa certainly tastes good on tacos, we also like this simple fresh tomato topping, which doesn't contain any spicy chiles. Though we prefer the sweet flavor of grape tomatoes here, you can substitute cherry tomatoes if desired. Combine 1 cup quartered grape tomatoes, 2 thinly sliced scallions, 1 tablespoon minced fresh cilantro, and ½ tablespoon lime juice in a bowl. Season with salt and pepper to taste. Makes 1 cup.

BEFORE NUMBERS BASED ON: Crispy Tacos with Beef from On the Border Mexican Grill and Cantina	BEFORE → **AFTER**	640 → **320** CALORIES	40 → **14** GRAMS FAT	16 → **3** GRAMS SAT FAT

Stuffed Bell Peppers

Serves 4

✔ **WHY THIS RECIPE WORKS:** Popular since the 1950s, this classic dish usually relies on a mixture of ground beef and rice for the hearty filling and is invariably coated in a thick blanket of tomato sauce. To bring this dish up to date (and get it to toe the nutritional line), we swapped out the ground beef in favor of leaner ground turkey and slashed the amount of oil we used for cooking. Then, we amped up the flavor with sautéed onion and garlic. We found that a small amount of nutty, savory Parmesan was an easy substitute for the larger amounts of cheddar cheese used in many recipes. Diced tomatoes added moisture and sweetness to the filling, and combining some of the tomato juice with ketchup gave us a tangy topping for the peppers. So that our peppers came out of the oven perfectly tender but still holding their shape, we simply boiled them for a few minutes before stuffing and baking them. At last, this retro classic was lighter and brighter in both flavor and feel—and ready for the modern-day dinner table.

4	(6-ounce) red, yellow, or orange bell peppers, ½ inch trimmed off tops, stemmed, and seeded
	Salt and pepper
½	cup long-grain white rice
1	teaspoon olive oil
1	onion, chopped fine
12	ounces 93 percent lean ground turkey
3	garlic cloves, minced
1	(14.5-ounce) can diced tomatoes, drained with ¼ cup juice reserved
2	ounces Parmesan cheese, grated (1 cup)
¼	cup minced fresh parsley
¼	cup ketchup

1. Adjust oven rack to middle position and heat oven to 350 degrees. Bring 4 quarts water to boil in large pot. Add bell peppers and 1 tablespoon salt and cook until peppers just begin to soften, about 3 minutes. Remove peppers from water, drain well, then place cut side up on clean towel to let steam escape. Return water to boil, stir in rice, and boil until tender, about 13 minutes; drain and transfer to large bowl.

2. Combine oil, onion, and ½ teaspoon salt in 12-inch nonstick skillet, cover, and cook over medium-low heat until onion is softened, 8 to 10 minutes. Stir in ground turkey and cook, breaking up meat with wooden spoon, until no longer pink, about 4 minutes. Stir in garlic and cook until fragrant, about 30 seconds. Stir in tomatoes and cook until warmed through, about 2 minutes. Transfer mixture to bowl with rice. Stir in Parmesan and parsley and season with salt and pepper to taste.

3. Drain excess water from peppers, arrange in 8-inch square baking dish, and pack each with filling. Combine ketchup and reserved tomato juice, then spoon over top. Bake until filling is hot, 25 to 30 minutes. Serve.

BEFORE → **AFTER**	570 → **350**	34 → **10**	14 → **3.5**
	CALORIES	GRAMS FAT	GRAMS SAT FAT

Stuffed Pork Chops

Serves 4

✔ **WHY THIS RECIPE WORKS:** Making a lower-fat version of stuffed pork chops started with choosing the right cut of pork. Since bone-in pork chops tend to be fattier than boneless chops, we opted for the latter. But boneless chops are notoriously dry and tough, and while a quick soak in a brine of salt and sugar kept them moist, it didn't improve their texture. Adding a bit of baking soda to the brine was the key, giving us more tender chops. For the stuffing, we hit up our crisper drawer; sautéed spinach and fennel made for a fresher and leaner alternative to the usual sausage and bread crumb combo. Goat cheese gave the filling some richness and helped bind the elements, while lemon zest contributed brightness. A spice rub of coriander, cumin, and crushed fennel seeds added more layers of flavor and echoed the aniselike notes of the sautéed fennel. To cook our chops, we "seared" them on a preheated sheet pan; a spritz of vegetable oil spray ensured they emerged from the oven nicely golden. If you can't find pork chops of the right thickness, purchase a 1½-pound pork loin roast and make your own chops. If the pork is enhanced, do not brine it in step 1.

4	**(6-ounce) boneless pork chops, about 1 inch thick, trimmed of all visible fat**
4	**teaspoons baking soda**
1	**tablespoon sugar**
	Salt and pepper
1	**teaspoon olive oil**
½	**small fennel bulb, stalks discarded, cored, and chopped fine**
1	**shallot, minced**
2	**garlic cloves, minced**
2	**tablespoons dry white wine**
6	**ounces (6 cups) baby spinach**
1½	**ounces goat cheese, crumbled (⅓ cup)**
¼	**teaspoon grated lemon zest**
1	**teaspoon fennel seeds, toasted and crushed**
1	**teaspoon ground coriander**
½	**teaspoon ground cumin**
	Vegetable oil spray

1. Working with 1 chop at a time, use paring knife to cut 1-inch opening in side of chop. Through opening, continue to cut large pocket inside center of chop for filling; use fingers to help enlarge pocket if necessary. Repeat with remaining chops. Combine 2 cups water, baking soda, sugar, and 1 tablespoon salt in large container. Add chops and refrigerate for 30 minutes.

2. Adjust oven rack to upper-middle position, place rimmed baking sheet on rack, and heat oven to 475 degrees. Heat oil in 12-inch nonstick skillet over medium heat until shimmering. Add fennel, shallot, and ¼ teaspoon salt and cook until lightly browned, about 5 minutes. Stir in garlic and cook until fragrant, about 30 seconds. Stir in wine and cook until it evaporates, about 1 minute. Stir in spinach and cook until wilted, about 2 minutes. Transfer to bowl, let cool for 5 minutes, then stir in goat cheese and lemon zest. Season with salt and pepper to taste.

3. Remove chops from brine, rinse, and pat dry with paper towels. Using spoon and your fingers, gently stuff chops with spinach filling. Combine crushed fennel seeds, coriander, cumin, and ½ teaspoon pepper in bowl, then rub evenly over chops. Spray both sides of chops with oil spray. Lay chops on preheated sheet and bake until pork registers 145 degrees, 10 to 14 minutes, flipping chops halfway through cooking. Transfer chops to carving board, tent loosely with aluminum foil, and let rest for 5 to 10 minutes. Serve.

BEFORE → AFTER	690 → **280**	40 → **10**	14 → **3.5**
	CALORIES	GRAMS FAT	GRAMS SAT FAT

Smothered Pork Chops

Serves 4

✔ **WHY THIS RECIPE WORKS:** Some recipes for smothered pork chops take the title a bit too literally, covering the pork with up to a pound of sausage or bacon and using a surfeit of oil to brown the meat. We wanted to give our pork a little breathing room, but keep the accompanying sauce richly flavored and the meat moist and tender. To start, we opted for bacon over sausage, which gave the sauce a savory, smoky backbone. Just one slice provided enough rendered fat that we didn't need any oil at all to sear our chops and sauté the onions; as a bonus, cooking the onions in bacon fat infused them with big flavor. Using beef broth instead of chicken broth for the braising liquid added depth, and 2 tablespoons of flour thickened the sauce nicely. We chose pork rib chops, which provided a balance of dark and light meat, and the moderate amount of fat kept the chops tender throughout braising while also keeping this dish squarely in makeover territory.

4	(8-ounce) bone-in pork rib chops, ½ to ¾ inch thick, trimmed of all visible fat
	Salt and pepper
1	slice bacon, cut into ¼-inch pieces
2	onions, halved and sliced thin
2	tablespoons water
2	garlic cloves, minced
1	teaspoon minced fresh thyme
2	tablespoons all-purpose flour
1¾	cups beef broth
2	bay leaves

1. Pat chops dry with paper towels and season with pepper. Cook bacon in 12-inch nonstick skillet over medium heat until crisp, 5 to 7 minutes; transfer to paper towel–lined plate. Heat bacon fat left in skillet over high heat until just smoking. Add chops and brown well on both sides, about 6 minutes; transfer to plate.

2. Add onions, water, and ¼ teaspoon salt to fat left in skillet and cook over medium heat, scraping up any browned bits, until softened, 5 to 7 minutes. Stir in garlic and thyme and cook until fragrant, about 30 seconds. Stir in flour and cook until golden, about 2 minutes. Whisk in broth, increase heat to medium-high, and bring to boil.

3. Add bay leaves, cooked bacon, and browned chops and any accumulated juices and cover chops with onions and sauce. Cover, reduce heat to low, and simmer gently until pork is very tender, 30 to 35 minutes.

4. Transfer chops to serving platter and tent loosely with aluminum foil. Continue to simmer sauce until thickened, about 5 minutes. Remove bay leaves and season with salt and pepper to taste. Spoon sauce over pork chops and serve.

BEFORE → **AFTER**	630 → **390**	33 → **14**	9 → **4.5**
	CALORIES	GRAMS FAT	GRAMS SAT FAT

Spicy Mexican Shredded Pork Tostadas

Serves 6

✔ **WHY THIS RECIPE WORKS:** Simmered for hours with aromatics and spices and then shredded and browned in oil until crisp, pork tinga is comfort food with a distinctly south-of-the-border feel. Served atop a crunchy tostada with a bevy of garnishes, it's rich and flavorful and offers a variety of appealing textures. Slimming down this heavyweight dish was quite a challenge, since much of its fat comes from the well-marbled pork butt traditionally called for. Switching to pork tenderloin was a nonstarter, since the leaner cut couldn't withstand the lengthy cooking time needed to develop the intense, deep flavor. Instead, we scaled back the pork butt for our leaner take on this satisfying dish and supplemented it with hearty pinto beans. Now just as filling but considerably lighter, our pork tinga still required a few more tweaks. Reducing the amount of oil needed to cook the shredded meat was the next step, and making our own tostadas by coating corn tortillas with vegetable oil spray and baking them in the oven was our final move. In the end, we'd trimmed more than half the fat of the original dish—without sacrificing any of the rich flavors or textures. Garnish the tostadas with chopped scallions, plain Greek yogurt, and lime wedges.

1 **pound boneless pork butt roast, trimmed of all visible fat and cut into 1-inch chunks**

2 **onions, 1 quartered and 1 chopped fine**

5 **garlic cloves, peeled, 3 smashed and 2 minced**

4 **sprigs fresh thyme**

2 **bay leaves**

12 **(6-inch) corn tortillas**
   Vegetable oil spray

2 **teaspoons canola oil**

½ **teaspoon dried oregano**

1 **(15-ounce) can tomato sauce**

1 **(15-ounce) can pinto beans, rinsed**

1 **tablespoon minced canned chipotle chile in adobo sauce**
   Salt and pepper

1. Bring 4 cups water, pork, quartered onion, smashed garlic, thyme, and bay leaves to simmer in large saucepan over medium-high heat, skimming off any foam that rises to surface. Reduce heat to medium-low, partially cover, and cook until meat is tender, 1¼ to 1½ hours.

2. Meanwhile, adjust oven racks to upper-middle and lower-middle positions and heat oven to 450 degrees. Spread tortillas over 2 rimmed baking sheets, spray both sides with oil spray, and bake until brown and crisp, 8 to 10 minutes, switching and rotating sheets halfway through baking.

3. Drain pork, reserving 1 cup of cooking liquid. Remove onion, garlic, thyme, and bay leaves. Return pork to saucepan and, using potato masher, mash until pork is shredded into rough ½-inch pieces.

4. Heat oil in 12-inch nonstick skillet over medium-high heat until just smoking. Add shredded pork and chopped onion and cook until pork is well-browned and crisp, 5 to 7 minutes. Stir in minced garlic and oregano and cook until fragrant, about 30 seconds. Stir in reserved pork cooking liquid, tomato sauce, beans, and chipotle. Bring to simmer and cook until almost all liquid has evaporated, 5 to 7 minutes; season with salt and pepper to taste. Spoon pork mixture onto tostadas and serve.

BEFORE → **AFTER**	500 → **330** CALORIES	30 → **12** GRAMS FAT	7 → **2.5** GRAMS SAT FAT

Jambalaya

Serves 4

✔ **WHY THIS RECIPE WORKS:** This Louisiana classic combines meaty chicken thighs, spicy andouille sausage, and tender shrimp with rice and vegetables for a stick-to-your-ribs one-pot meal. Given the ingredient list (we're looking at you, chicken thighs and andouille), it shouldn't be too surprising that a single serving delivers over 1,000 calories and 60 grams of fat. We wanted to lighten this dish but still keep all the heartiness and flavor. Cutting back on the sausage was our first move, and browning it gave us enough rendered fat to sauté the vegetables, eliminating the need for oil. Ditching the skin-on chicken thighs in favor of leaner skinless chicken breasts, which we poached in a mix of chicken broth, clam juice, and diced tomatoes with their juice, gave us moist, tender bites of meat. To ensure the rice was evenly cooked, we baked it in the oven after setting the chicken aside; this prevented the white meat from overcooking and becoming dry in the oven. For the shrimp, we simply had to add them to the pot for the last few minutes of cooking time, and they were perfectly done. If you can't find andouille, try tasso, chorizo, or linguiça.

2 **(10-ounce) bone-in split chicken breasts, skin removed, trimmed of all visible fat, and halved crosswise**

½ **teaspoon Cajun seasoning**

1 **onion, cut into chunks**

1 **celery rib, cut into chunks**

1 **red bell pepper, stemmed, seeded, and cut into chunks**

5 **garlic cloves, peeled**

6 **ounces andouille sausage, halved lengthwise and sliced ⅛ inch thick**

1 **(14.5-ounce) can diced tomatoes**

1 **cup low-sodium chicken broth**

1 **(8-ounce) bottle clam juice**

2 **bay leaves**

½ **teaspoon minced fresh thyme**

1½ **cups long-grain white rice, rinsed**

1 **pound medium-large shrimp (31 to 40 per pound), peeled, deveined, and tails removed**

2 **tablespoons minced fresh parsley**

Salt and pepper

1. Adjust oven rack to middle position and heat oven to 350 degrees. Rub chicken with Cajun seasoning. Pulse onion, celery, bell pepper, and garlic in food processor until finely chopped, about 6 pulses; do not overprocess.

2. Cook sausage in Dutch oven over medium-high heat until browned, 5 to 8 minutes; transfer to paper towel–lined plate. Add processed vegetables to fat left in pot and cook, scraping up any browned bits, until softened, about 4 minutes. Stir in tomatoes with their juice, broth, clam juice, bay leaves, thyme, and browned sausage. Add chicken and bring to simmer. Cover, reduce heat to low, and cook until chicken registers 160 degrees, 20 to 25 minutes.

3. Transfer chicken to plate, let cool slightly, then shred into bite-size pieces; cover until needed. Meanwhile, stir rice into pot, increase heat to medium-high, and bring to simmer. Cover pot, transfer to oven, and bake until liquid is absorbed and rice is tender, about 25 minutes.

4. Remove pot from oven, fluff rice with fork, and scatter shrimp over top. Cover, return pot to oven, and continue to bake until shrimp are cooked through, 5 to 10 minutes. Remove bay leaves. Stir in parsley and shredded chicken and season with salt and pepper to taste. Serve.

BEFORE NUMBERS BASED ON: Creole Jambalaya from Rock Bottom Restaurant and Brewery	BEFORE → **AFTER**	1054 → **560** CALORIES	62 → **10** GRAMS FAT	26 → **3** GRAMS SAT FAT

Baked Stuffed Shrimp

Serves 4

✔ **WHY THIS RECIPE WORKS:** A seaside classic, baked stuffed shrimp has suffered as much from tired, bready fillings as it has from excessive fat and calories. We decided to revamp the dish with a lighter, healthier filling that was miles from boring. Since we were already working with shrimp, we opted to use a portion of it to build our filling, which amped up the briny, sweet flavor of the dish, while also keeping the ingredient list from getting too long. Sautéing celery and scallions in a small amount of butter added flavor and just enough richness, and light mayonnaise kept the filling moist. Lemon zest and lemon juice contributed a bright acidity to the mixture, and a bit of toasted panko worked to hold it all together. To flavor the shrimp themselves, we used a bit of coriander, sugar, salt, and pepper before stuffing and baking them; a low oven kept them tender and juicy. When shopping, look for shrimp labeled "U15," which indicates that the number of shrimp per pound should be under 15. Serve with lemon wedges.

24	extra jumbo shrimp (U15), peeled and deveined
2	tablespoons unsalted butter
5	scallions, chopped fine
1	large celery rib, chopped fine
2	garlic cloves, minced
¾	teaspoon ground coriander
2	tablespoons dry white wine
5	tablespoons light mayonnaise
¼	cup panko bread crumbs, toasted (see page 18)
3	tablespoons minced fresh parsley
1	teaspoon grated lemon zest plus 4 teaspoons juice
	Salt and pepper
¼	teaspoon sugar

1. Remove and discard tails from 8 shrimp, then pulse in food processor until coarsely chopped, about 4 pulses; transfer to large bowl.

2. Melt butter in 12-inch nonstick skillet over medium heat. Add scallions and celery and cook until softened, about 5 minutes. Stir in garlic and ¼ teaspoon coriander and cook until fragrant, about 30 seconds. Stir in wine and cook until nearly evaporated, about 1 minute; transfer to bowl with processed shrimp. Stir in mayonnaise, panko, parsley, lemon zest and juice, ⅛ teaspoon salt, and ⅛ teaspoon pepper until well combined.

3. Adjust oven rack to middle position and heat oven to 275 degrees. Line rimmed baking sheet with aluminum foil and spray with vegetable oil spray. Combine remaining ½ teaspoon coriander, sugar, pinch salt, and ¼ teaspoon pepper in large bowl. Pat remaining 16 shrimp dry with paper towels and toss with spice mixture. Using paring knife, butterfly shrimp open through vein side. Cut 1-inch slit through center of each shrimp so that they lay flat.

4. Lay shrimp butterflied side down on prepared sheet. Divide filling among shrimp, press gently on filling to compact, then flip tail back to curl around filling. Bake until shrimp are cooked through and filling is hot, 20 to 25 minutes. Serve.

BEFORE → **AFTER**	440 → **230** CALORIES	21 → **11** GRAMS FAT	9 → **4.5** GRAMS SAT FAT

MAKEOVER SPOTLIGHT: STUFFED SHRIMP

1. FOR A LOW-FAT FILLING WITH BIG FLAVOR, INCLUDE SHRIMP: Bread-based fillings for stuffed shrimp are very popular, but they only work when they're loaded with butter for flavor, richness, and moisture. To keep our filling lean, we turned to shrimp—which was already in our ingredient list. With just a few aromatics and seasonings and a bit of light mayo, our shrimp filling was rich, moist, and flavorful. A quick whirl in the food processor was enough to break the shrimp down to small pieces so they could be mixed in with the other ingredients.

2. BUTTERFLY THE SHRIMP BEFORE STUFFING: It's important to butterfly and flatten the shrimp so they can all be stuffed with an even amount of filling. After butterflying the shrimp to slice it open through the vein side, cut a 1-inch slit through the center of each shrimp so that they lie flat.

3. DON'T OVERSTUFF THE SHRIMP: If you overstuff the shrimp, not only will the fat and calorie counts go up, but the filling will require more time to cook through in the oven, and by the time it is done the shrimp will be overcooked. After laying the shrimp butterflied side down on the prepared sheet, divide the filling among the shrimp, about 1 rounded tablespoon of filling per shrimp, press gently on the filling to compact it, then flip the tail back to curl it around the filling.

4. TO KEEP THE LEAN FILLING MOIST, BAKE AT A LOW TEMPERATURE: Cooking the shrimp in a low oven (275 degrees) ensured that the lean filling—and the shrimp itself—retained moisture. Also, the cooler temperature meant that the shrimp cooked through more gently and there was less risk of them overcooking.

Stir-Fried Shrimp and Snow Peas with Coconut Curry Sauce

Serves 4

✔ **WHY THIS RECIPE WORKS:** Sure, curries are loaded with healthy veggies and lean proteins, but it takes just one bite to know they're not as innocent as they seem. After all, most recipes start with a good amount of oil to cook the vegetables and toast the spices, then add a can's worth (or more) of thick, rich coconut milk. Tack on some peanuts or cashews, and all the vegetables in the world can't redeem this high-fat dish. To keep our virtuous shrimp and vegetables from drowning in an overly heavy, fatty sauce, we switched from full-fat coconut milk to light coconut milk; a bit of cornstarch ensured the sauce thickened to just the right consistency. Marinating the shrimp in soy sauce infused it with deep flavor from the get-go. To cook the vegetables, we traded the pool of oil for a small amount of water and covered the pan. With big bites of crisp-tender bell peppers and snow peas in our curry, we didn't even need the fatty nuts. If using smaller or larger shrimp, the cooking times may vary accordingly. Serve with white rice.

SAUCE

- ⅔ cup light coconut milk
- 6 tablespoons low-sodium chicken broth
- 1 tablespoon cornstarch
- 2 teaspoons curry powder
- 1 teaspoon sugar
- ¼ teaspoon salt
- ⅛ teaspoon red pepper flakes

STIR-FRY

- 1 pound extra-large shrimp (21 to 25 per pound), peeled and deveined
- 2 teaspoons low-sodium soy sauce
- 3 scallions, minced
- 3 garlic cloves, minced
- 1 tablespoon grated fresh ginger
- 4 teaspoons canola oil
- 2 red bell peppers, stemmed, seeded, and cut into 2-inch-long matchsticks
- ⅓ cup water
- 12 ounces snow peas, strings removed and halved crosswise

1. FOR THE SAUCE: Whisk all ingredients together in bowl.

2. FOR THE STIR-FRY: Toss shrimp and soy sauce together in bowl; let marinate for 10 to 30 minutes. In separate bowl, combine scallions, garlic, ginger, and 1 teaspoon oil.

3. Cook bell peppers and water together in covered 12-inch nonstick skillet over high heat until water is boiling and peppers begin to soften, about 3 minutes. Uncover, add snow peas, and cook until water has evaporated and vegetables are crisp-tender, about 2 minutes; transfer to colander.

4. Add remaining 1 tablespoon oil to now-empty skillet and place over high heat until just smoking. Add shrimp with marinade and cook until lightly browned on all sides but not fully cooked, about 2 minutes. Clear center of skillet, add garlic mixture, and cook, mashing mixture into pan, until fragrant, 15 to 30 seconds.

5. Stir in cooked vegetables. Whisk sauce to recombine and add to skillet. Simmer until shrimp are cooked through and sauce is thickened, about 1 minute. Serve.

BEFORE → **AFTER**	740 → **210**	53 → **8**	39 → **2**
	CALORIES	GRAMS FAT	GRAMS SAT FAT

Cheesy Shrimp and Grits

Serves 4

✓ **WHY THIS RECIPE WORKS:** A Southern favorite, this dish is often drowning in empty calories, with too much heavy cream, cheese, and butter weighing it down. For our lightened version, we chose to build layers of flavor instead of layers of fat, adding scallions, garlic, and spicy chipotle chile to the hearty grits. Using whole milk instead of heavy cream gave the grits a rich creaminess without making them too dense, and light cheddar cheese pulled double duty, adding flavor to the grits themselves and providing a golden, melted crown on top. As for the shrimp, we simply assembled the grits in a casserole dish and nestled in the shrimp so they could cook through while the cheesy topping browned, eliminating the need for another dish (or extra fat for sautéing or pan-frying the shrimp). We had trimmed more than 40 grams of fat from our made-over shrimp and grits. Do not substitute instant grits here.

1 **tablespoon unsalted butter**

3 **scallions, white parts sliced thin, green parts sliced thin on bias**

2 **garlic cloves, minced**

1 **teaspoon minced canned chipotle chile in adobo sauce**

4 **cups water**

½ **cup whole milk**

1 **cup old-fashioned grits**

4 **ounces 50 percent light cheddar cheese, shredded (1 cup)**
   Salt and pepper

1 **pound extra-large shrimp (21 to 25 per pound), peeled and deveined**

1. Adjust oven rack to middle position and heat oven to 450 degrees. Melt butter in medium saucepan over medium heat. Add scallion whites and cook until softened, about 2 minutes. Stir in garlic and chipotle and cook until fragrant, about 30 seconds. Stir in water and milk and bring to boil. Slowly whisk in grits. Reduce heat to low and cook, stirring often, until grits are thick and creamy, about 15 minutes.

2. Off heat, stir in ½ cup cheese, season with salt and pepper to taste, and transfer to 4½-quart gratin dish. Nestle shrimp into grits, leaving tails exposed. Sprinkle with remaining ½ cup cheddar. Bake until shrimp are cooked through, about 15 minutes. Let cool slightly, then sprinkle with scallion greens. Serve.

QUICK PREP TIP DEVEINING SHRIMP
To devein shrimp, hold shrimp firmly in one hand, then use paring knife to cut down back side of shrimp, about ⅛ to ¼ inch deep, to expose vein. Using tip of knife, gently remove vein. Wipe knife against paper towel to remove vein and discard.

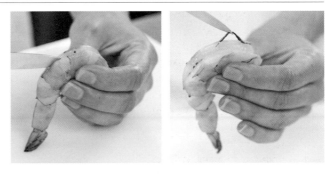

BEFORE → **AFTER**	720 → **310**	53 → **10**	32 → **5**
	CALORIES	GRAMS FAT	GRAMS SAT FAT

Crab-Stuffed Flounder

Serves 4

✔ **WHY THIS RECIPE WORKS:** Packed with an overly dense, bread-crumb-laden stuffing before being drowned in a heavy cream sauce, crab-stuffed flounder takes what should be a light, fresh-tasting entrée into super-fatty territory. For this makeover, not only did we want to slash fat and calories, but we also set out to bring the sweet, fresh flavors of the seafood back to the forefront. Our first step was to jettison the dry, bland bread crumbs that made up the bulk of the filling in favor of a mix of sautéed aromatics. Scallions, celery, and red bell pepper provided the perfect background notes, and combining them with a small amount of reduced-fat cream cheese added richness and helped to bind the filling. Corn amped up its heartiness, and just a bit of Cajun seasoning contributed heat and spice. After stirring our aromatics and cream cheese together, we added the corn and crabmeat; stirring them in gently ensured the crab didn't break apart into small shreds, but instead stayed in big chunks in the finished dish. To stuff our fillets, we simply mounded a bit of the crab mixture in the middle of each piece of flounder, then folded over both ends of the fillet to cover it and placed our stuffed flounder in a baking dish. After just 20 minutes, our stuffed fillets were perfectly done, and the filling was so rich and moist that we were able to do away with the heavy sauce altogether. For finishing touches, we liked a bit of toasted panko and sliced scallions, which added a subtle crunch and a punch of color. Serve with lemon wedges.

1	tablespoon canola oil
3	scallions, white parts chopped fine, green parts sliced thin on bias
1	celery rib, minced
½	red bell pepper, chopped fine
1	garlic clove, minced
¾	teaspoon Cajun seasoning
3	ounces ⅓ less fat cream cheese (neufchatel)
12	ounces lump crabmeat, picked over for shells
½	cup frozen corn, thawed Salt and pepper
8	(3-ounce) skinless flounder fillets, ¼ to ½ inch thick
¼	cup panko bread crumbs, toasted (see page 18)

1. Adjust oven rack to middle position and heat oven to 475 degrees. Heat 2 teaspoons oil in 10-inch nonstick skillet over medium heat until shimmering. Add scallion whites, celery, and bell pepper and cook until softened, about 5 minutes. Stir in garlic and Cajun seasoning and cook until fragrant, about 30 seconds. Off heat, stir in cream cheese until melted; transfer to large bowl. Gently stir in crabmeat and corn, being careful not to break up lumps of crab. Season with salt and pepper to taste.

2. Spray 13 by 9-inch baking dish with vegetable oil spray. Pat flounder dry with paper towels and season with salt and pepper. Place flounder, smooth side down, on cutting board. Mound filling in center of fillets, fold tail end over filling, then fold over thicker end. Lay flounder seam side down in baking dish.

3. Toss panko with remaining 1 teaspoon oil, then sprinkle over flounder. Bake until filling is hot and flounder flakes apart when gently prodded with paring knife, about 20 minutes. Sprinkle with scallion greens and serve.

BEFORE → **AFTER**	510 → **360** CALORIES	32 → **13** GRAMS FAT	13 → **4** GRAMS SAT FAT

Crab Cakes

Serves 4

✔ **WHY THIS RECIPE WORKS:** Order crab cakes at a restaurant and you'll be sorely disappointed. Usually, they're loaded with so much mayonnaise and breading, you'll wonder if the cook forgot the crab. To keep our version light on the binder, we dried the crabmeat with paper towels; this removed some of the moisture so we could use less cracker crumbs. Light mayonnaise and an egg white took the place of the usual full-fat mayo and whole egg as the binder; together, they provided enough moisture to hold the cakes together while also slashing fat. A single pat of melted butter added a touch of richness. Dipping one side of the shaped crab cakes in extra cracker crumbs helped absorb any additional moisture, and chilling the cakes before cooking gave them a chance to set up. To cook our crab cakes, we ditched the skillet and opted for the oven. Broiling them on a baking sheet coated with vegetable oil spray kept the fat count down, and meant we didn't have to bother with flipping our cakes—and running the risk of them breaking apart—to brown the second side. At last, we had golden brown, richly flavored crab cakes that actually tasted like crabmeat—and were low in fat, too. Serve with lemon wedges.

14	**saltines**
1	**pound lump crabmeat, picked over for shells**
3	**scallions, minced**
3	**tablespoons light mayonnaise**
1	**tablespoon unsalted butter, melted**
1	**large egg white**
1½	**teaspoons Dijon mustard**
1	**teaspoon hot sauce**
1	**teaspoon Old Bay seasoning**

1. Process crackers in food processor until finely ground, about 10 seconds. Pat crabmeat dry with paper towels. Using rubber spatula, gently combine crabmeat, ¼ cup processed crackers, scallions, mayonnaise, melted butter, egg white, mustard, hot sauce, and Old Bay in bowl.

2. Divide mixture into 4 equal portions and shape into tight, mounded cakes. Press top of each cake in remaining crumbs; transfer crumb side down to large plate. Cover and refrigerate for 1 to 8 hours.

3. Adjust oven rack 6 inches from broiler element and heat broiler. Line rimmed baking sheet with aluminum foil and spray with vegetable oil spray. Transfer crab cakes to prepared sheet, crumb side down. Broil crab cakes until golden, 12 to 15 minutes. Serve.

QUICK PREP TIP MAKING CRAB CAKES
To get our crab cakes to hold together without too much binder, we dry the crabmeat first with paper towels; this allows us to use fewer crushed crackers for binding. After dipping them in additional cracker crumbs to absorb any extra moisture, we chill the crab cakes so they can set up before broiling them on a baking sheet sprayed with vegetable oil spray.

BEFORE NUMBERS BASED ON: **Crab Cakes from Mimi's Café**	BEFORE → **AFTER**	357 → **250** CALORIES	20 → **8** GRAMS FAT	3 → **2** GRAMS SAT FAT

Fish Meunière

Serves 4

✓ **WHY THIS RECIPE WORKS:** This simple French dish delivers moist, tender fillets napped in a bright, buttery sauce. While we couldn't do away with the butter entirely in our recipe, we could cut back on it. Just a pat, combined with flour to form a paste known as a *beurre manié*, provided ample richness and thickened the sauce nicely. Chicken broth and reduced wine gave us a flavorful base, while capers, parsley, and lemon juice added fresh, bright notes. Thin fillets of sole, flounder, or trout will work well in this dish.

7	teaspoons canola oil
1	shallot, minced
¼	cup dry white wine
1	cup low-sodium chicken broth
1	tablespoon plus ⅓ cup all-purpose flour
1	tablespoon unsalted butter, softened
1	tablespoon capers, rinsed
1	tablespoon minced fresh parsley
1	tablespoon lemon juice
	Salt and pepper
8	(3-ounce) skinless fish fillets, ¼ to ½ inch thick

1. Combine 1 teaspoon oil and shallot in small saucepan, cover, and cook over medium-low heat until softened, about 4 minutes. Stir in wine, increase heat to medium-high, and simmer until pan is almost dry, about 2 minutes. Stir in chicken broth; simmer for 2 minutes. Mash 1 tablespoon flour into softened butter in bowl to form paste, then whisk into pan; simmer until sauce is thickened, about 2 minutes. Stir in capers, parsley, and lemon juice, season with salt and pepper to taste, cover, and set aside.

2. Pat fish fillets dry with paper towels, season with salt and pepper, and let sit until glistening with moisture, about 5 minutes. If using tail-end fillets, score and tuck tail underneath fillet. Spread remaining ⅓ cup flour into shallow dish. Lightly dredge fillets in flour, keeping any tail pieces tucked.

3. Heat 1 tablespoon oil in 12-inch nonstick skillet over high heat until shimmering. Lay half of fillets in pan, reduce heat to medium-high, and cook until golden on bottom, 2 to 3 minutes. Using spatula, gently flip fillets over and continue to cook until fish flakes apart when gently prodded with paring knife, 30 to 60 seconds; transfer to platter and tent loosely with aluminum foil. Repeat with remaining 1 tablespoon oil and remaining fillets. Transfer fish to individual plates, leaving accumulated juices behind on platter. Spoon sauce over top; serve.

QUICK PREP TIP
TUCKING THE TAIL
Using sharp chef's knife, gently score fish crosswise about 2 to 3 inches from tapered tail end; do not cut through fish completely. Gently fold tail underneath at scored line to create evenly thick fillet.

BEFORE → **AFTER**	380 → **300**	27 → **12**	12 → **2.5**
	CALORIES	GRAMS FAT	GRAMS SAT FAT

Spaghetti with Creamy Basil Pesto

Serves 6

✔ **WHY THIS RECIPE WORKS:** Traditionally, pesto is made with basil, garlic, nuts, cheese, and a generous pour of olive oil—all of which amounts to a sauce that's definitely not light. To make over this simple recipe, we started by cutting back on the olive oil and ditching the nuts altogether. To guarantee the same emulsified texture of a full-fat pesto, we kept a couple spoonfuls of olive oil, but we also added in some part-skim ricotta cheese. This duo ensured the ingredients came together in the food processor and gave our low-fat pesto a rich, creamy texture. For deep, complex flavor, we increased the amount of basil, garlic, and grated Parmesan, and tossed in some minced shallot, too. To bring out the basil's flavor, we gently pounded it with a mallet before tossing it in the food processor—this helped to release its flavorful oils. Toasting our garlic in a skillet helped to tame its raw, spicy notes. Do not substitute nonfat ricotta cheese for the part-skim ricotta or the pesto will be dry and a bit gummy.

4   **garlic cloves, unpeeled**
3   **cups fresh basil leaves**
1   **ounce Parmesan cheese, grated (½ cup)**
2   **ounces (¼ cup) part-skim ricotta cheese**
1   **shallot, minced**
2   **tablespoons extra-virgin olive oil**
    Salt and pepper
1   **pound spaghetti**

1. Toast garlic in small skillet over medium heat, shaking pan occasionally, until color of cloves deepens slightly, about 7 minutes; transfer to plate and let cool slightly, then peel and mince.

2. Place basil in heavy-duty zipper-lock plastic bag and pound with meat pounder or rolling pin until leaves are lightly bruised. Process toasted garlic, bruised basil, Parmesan, ricotta, shallot, oil, and ½ teaspoon salt in food processor until smooth, about 30 seconds, scraping down bowl as needed.

3. Bring 4 quarts water to boil in large pot. Add pasta and 1 tablespoon salt and cook, stirring often, until al dente. Reserve 1 cup cooking water, then drain pasta and return it to pot. Stir in pesto, season with salt and pepper to taste, and add reserved cooking water as needed to adjust consistency. Serve.

QUICK PREP TIP
TOASTING GARLIC
To temper the raw bite of fresh garlic, toast the unpeeled cloves in a small skillet over medium heat, shaking the pan occasionally, until the color of the cloves deepens slightly, about 7 minutes. Transfer the garlic to a plate, let cool, then peel the cloves and mince.

BEFORE → AFTER	470 → **360**	22 → **8**	3 → **2**
	CALORIES	GRAMS FAT	GRAMS SAT FAT

Pasta with Sautéed Mushrooms

Serves 6

☑ **WHY THIS RECIPE WORKS:** For an ultra-creamy pasta dish with intense, savory richness but without all the cream, we amped up the flavor with three types of mushrooms. Cremini offered a rich, meaty texture, shiitakes delivered a hearty, deep flavor, and dried porcini added depth and ultra-savory background notes. Cooking the sliced cremini and shiitakes covered ensured they released their liquid, so we didn't need much oil to sauté them—a mere teaspoon did the trick. Once they'd released their juices, we removed the lid to drive off the excess moisture and encourage browning. After trying a number of stand-ins for the heavy cream, we ultimately hit on a little reduced-fat cream cheese, plus some chicken broth; this pair gave us a richly flavored, velvety sauce that was low in fat, and the chicken broth helped to rehydrate and soften the dried porcini. Grated Parmesan amped up the savory flavor and worked to thicken our sauce. To make this dish vegetarian, substitute vegetable broth for the chicken broth.

1	teaspoon extra-virgin olive oil
12	ounces shiitake mushrooms, stemmed and sliced ¼ inch thick
12	ounces cremini mushrooms, trimmed and sliced ¼ inch thick
½	onion, chopped fine
	Salt and pepper
3	garlic cloves, minced
4	teaspoons minced fresh thyme
1¼	cups low-sodium chicken broth
½	ounce dried porcini mushrooms, rinsed and minced
2	ounces ⅓ less fat cream cheese (neufchatel), softened
1	pound farfalle
1	ounce Parmesan cheese, grated (½ cup)
2	tablespoons minced fresh parsley

1. Heat oil in 12-inch skillet over medium heat until shimmering. Add shiitakes, cremini, onion, and ¼ teaspoon salt, cover, and cook until mushrooms have released their liquid, about 8 minutes. Uncover and continue to cook until mushrooms are dry and browned, about 8 minutes. Stir in garlic and thyme and cook until fragrant, about 30 seconds; transfer to bowl and cover.

2. Add broth and porcini to now-empty skillet, scraping up any browned bits, and simmer until porcini are softened, about 2 minutes. Off heat, whisk in cream cheese and season with salt and pepper to taste; cover and set aside.

3. Meanwhile, bring 4 quarts water to boil in large pot. Add pasta and 1 tablespoon salt and cook, stirring often, until al dente. Reserve 1 cup cooking water, then drain pasta and return it to pot. Stir in cooked vegetables, porcini mixture, Parmesan, and parsley, season with salt and pepper to taste, and add reserved cooking water as needed to adjust consistency. Serve.

BEFORE → **AFTER**	510 → **380**	20 → **6**	9 → **2.5**
	CALORIES	GRAMS FAT	GRAMS SAT FAT

Pasta Primavera

Serves 6

✔ **WHY THIS RECIPE WORKS:** Sure, pasta with a mélange of spring vegetables sounds like a light, bright dish, but most recipes turn out a random selection of bland produce weighed down in a dull, thick cream sauce. We set out to do away with the heavy cream and bring back the freshness. First, we narrowed our list of veggies to asparagus and peas; leeks and garlic added aromatic depth and sweetness. After cooking our vegetables, we set them aside while we prepared the pasta. For deep flavor, we toasted the pasta before cooking it right in the sauce (much like a risotto). In this streamlined method, the sauce flavored the pasta and the pasta starch helped thicken the broth into a rich, creamy sauce without any cream or butter. Simmering store-bought vegetable broth with the vegetable trimmings ensured our dish offered pure, fresh vegetable flavor. Lemon juice added bright notes, while olive oil and Parmesan contributed some much-needed richness. Campanelle is our pasta of choice in this dish, but farfalle and penne are acceptable substitutes.

1½ pounds leeks, white and light green parts halved lengthwise, sliced ½ inch thick, and washed thoroughly; 3 cups dark green parts, chopped coarse and washed thoroughly

1 pound asparagus, trimmed, tough ends reserved and chopped coarse, spears sliced ½ inch thick on bias

2 cups frozen baby peas, thawed

4 garlic cloves, minced

4 cups vegetable broth

1 cup water, plus extra as needed

2 tablespoons extra-virgin olive oil
Salt and pepper

⅛ teaspoon red pepper flakes

1 pound campanelle

1 cup dry white wine

2 tablespoons minced fresh mint

2 tablespoons minced fresh chives

½ teaspoon grated lemon zest plus 1 tablespoon juice

1 ounce Parmesan cheese, grated (½ cup)

1. Place dark green leek trimmings, asparagus trimmings, 1 cup peas, half of garlic, vegetable broth, and water in large saucepan. Bring to simmer and cook gently for 10 minutes. Strain broth through fine-mesh strainer into 8-cup liquid measuring cup, pressing on solids to extract as much liquid as possible; discard solids. (You should have 5 cups broth; add water as needed to measure 5 cups.) Return broth to saucepan, cover, and keep warm over low heat.

2. Combine sliced leeks, 1 teaspoon oil, and ⅛ teaspoon salt in Dutch oven. Cover and cook over medium-low heat, stirring occasionally, until just beginning to brown, about 5 minutes. Stir in asparagus pieces and cook until crisp-tender, 4 to 6 minutes. Stir in remaining garlic and pepper flakes and cook until fragrant, about 30 seconds. Stir in remaining 1 cup peas and cook for 1 minute; transfer vegetables to plate.

3. Wipe now-empty pot clean, add 2 teaspoons oil, and place over medium heat until shimmering. Add pasta and cook, stirring frequently, until just beginning to brown, about 5 minutes. Stir in wine and cook until absorbed, about 2 minutes. Stir in warm broth, increase heat to medium-high, and bring to boil. Cook, stirring often, until most of liquid is absorbed and pasta is al dente, 8 to 10 minutes. Meanwhile, combine mint, chives, and lemon zest in bowl.

4. Off heat, stir in cooked vegetables, remaining 1 tablespoon oil, half of herb mixture, lemon juice, and Parmesan. Season with salt and pepper to taste and serve, passing remaining herb mixture separately.

BEFORE → **AFTER**	550 → **450** CALORIES	24 → **7** GRAMS FAT	14 → **1.5** GRAMS SAT FAT

Everyday Macaroni and Cheese

Serves 5

✔ **WHY THIS RECIPE WORKS:** Weighing in at more than 650 calories and nearly 40 grams of fat, a bowl of mac and cheese really should be a once-in-a-while treat. But given that it's such a crowd-pleaser—who doesn't love mac and cheese?—it's a popular dish that shows up on many restaurant and diner menus, often overloaded with butter and cheese. So that we could enjoy it more often, we set out to seriously lighten it, while still keeping its rich, creamy, cheesy appeal intact. Our first move was swapping in 50 percent light cheddar cheese for the full-fat cheese in the sauce, which provided big, cheesy flavor and allowed us to trim significant fat. Rather than use whole milk in our sauce, we opted for 2 percent low-fat milk; skim milk and 1 percent low-fat milk gave us a sauce that was too thin and watery and didn't coat the pasta well. To thicken the sauce, most mac and cheese recipes call for a roux, which is a mixture of butter and flour, but we found that a small amount of cornstarch did the trick and kept our nutritional counts in check. For an even creamier sauce, we substituted a can of low-fat evaporated milk for some of the milk. Every bit as good as its full-fat counterpart, our lightened mac and cheese now boasted both rich, cheesy flavor and a velvety, smooth sauce. Don't be tempted to use either preshredded or nonfat cheddar cheese in this dish—the texture and flavor of the mac and cheese will suffer substantially.

8	ounces (2 cups) elbow macaroni
	Salt and pepper
1	(12-ounce) can 2 percent low-fat evaporated milk
¾	cup 2 percent low-fat milk
¼	teaspoon dry mustard
⅛	teaspoon garlic powder
	Pinch cayenne pepper
2	teaspoons cornstarch
8	ounces 50 percent light cheddar cheese, shredded (2 cups)

1. Bring 2½ quarts water to boil in large saucepan. Add macaroni and 1½ teaspoons salt and cook, stirring often, until al dente. Drain pasta; set aside.

2. Combine evaporated milk, ½ cup milk, mustard, garlic powder, cayenne, and ½ teaspoon salt in now-empty saucepan and bring to simmer. Whisk together remaining ¼ cup milk and cornstarch, then whisk into sauce. Continue to simmer, whisking constantly, until sauce is thickened and smooth, about 2 minutes.

3. Off heat, gradually whisk in cheddar until melted and smooth. Stir in macaroni and let mixture sit off heat until slightly thickened, 2 to 5 minutes. Season with salt and pepper to taste and serve.

BEFORE NUMBERS BASED ON: **Mac 'n Cheese from Ruby Tuesday**	BEFORE → **AFTER**	680 → **350** CALORIES	37 → **10** GRAMS FAT	N/A → **5** GRAMS SAT FAT

Pasta ai Quattro Formaggi

Serves 6

☑ **WHY THIS RECIPE WORKS:** Pasta ai quattro formaggi is the Italian take on mac and cheese. Loaded up with four cheeses and a big pour of heavy cream, it offers great flavor and richness, but (no surprise here) it's even worse for your diet than its American cousin. We sought to bring this intensely flavored, creamy dish to the dinner table—but in a lighter form. Since cheese is the star of the show, we couldn't sacrifice too much or substitute low- or reduced-fat cheeses without compromising significant flavor and texture. Instead, we chose varieties with bold flavor and cut back on the amounts. The combination of Italian fontina, Gorgonzola, Pecorino Romano, and Parmesan gave us the best flavor and a creamy texture, and using a mixture of milk and evaporated milk (both 2 percent low-fat) in our sauce ensured it was smooth and velvety. A bit of cornstarch worked to thicken the sauce nicely. Combining the hot sauce and pasta with the cheese—and not cooking the cheese in the sauce—preserved the fresh flavor of the cheeses. Be sure to use Italian fontina rather than bland and rubbery Danish or American fontina. To make the cheese easier to shred, freeze it for 30 minutes to firm it up.

3   **ounces fontina cheese, shredded (¾ cup)**

1   **ounce Gorgonzola cheese, crumbled (¼ cup)**

1   **ounce Parmesan cheese, grated (½ cup)**

¼   **cup grated Pecorino Romano cheese**

1   **(12-ounce) can 2 percent low-fat evaporated milk**

½   **cup 2 percent low-fat milk**
     Salt and pepper

1   **tablespoon cornstarch**

1   **pound penne**

1. In large bowl, combine fontina, Gorgonzola, Parmesan, and Pecorino. In medium saucepan, combine evaporated milk, ¼ cup milk, ½ teaspoon salt, and ¼ teaspoon pepper and bring to simmer. Whisk together remaining ¼ cup milk and cornstarch, then whisk into sauce. Continue to simmer, whisking constantly, until sauce is thickened and smooth, about 2 minutes.

2. Meanwhile, bring 4 quarts water to boil in large pot. Add pasta and 1 tablespoon salt and cook, stirring often, until just al dente. Drain pasta, then add to bowl of cheese. Immediately pour hot milk mixture over pasta, cover, and let stand 5 minutes.

3. Stir pasta mixture with rubber spatula, scraping up cheeses from bottom of bowl, until cheese has melted and sauce thickly coats pasta. Season with salt and pepper to taste and serve.

BEFORE NUMBERS BASED ON: **Five Cheese Ziti al Forno** (lunch portion) from Olive Garden	BEFORE→**AFTER**	770→**430** CALORIES	32→**10** GRAMS FAT	17→**5** GRAMS SAT FAT

Spaghetti Carbonara

Serves 6

☑ **WHY THIS RECIPE WORKS:** This Roman classic marries pasta with an indulgent sauce comprised of cheese, eggs, cream, and bacon, resulting in a dish that's definitely not what we'd call light. To revamp our carbonara, we started by figuring out which ingredients could stay and which had to go. First up for consideration: the bacon. Rather than cut it from our recipe entirely, we simply dialed back on the amount—just 2 slices provided ample smoky flavor—and supplemented it with relatively lean Canadian bacon for more meaty bites. Next up: the eggs. Most recipes call for at least three eggs to add richness, but we cut this in half, scaling down to just a single egg, plus a white. The cream was definitely a no-go if we wanted to slash fat from our recipe; fortunately, we found that fat-free evaporated milk gave us a surprisingly silky sauce. However, we found that now the pasta was soaking up all the sauce, which made our carbonara dry. In full-fat versions of carbonara, all the fat from the cream, butter, and bacon works to coat the pasta, preventing it from absorbing too much sauce. Looking for another ingredient that would play the same role, we landed on mayonnaise, which created a protective coating on the pasta and fooled tasters into thinking they were getting the real deal. To increase the sauce's volume without adding more ingredients (and more fat!), we simply included some of the pasta cooking water and combined it with the rest of the sauce ingredients in a food processor. The result was an emulsified, creamy sauce that perfectly coated our spaghetti. Parmesan can be substituted for the Pecorino Romano if necessary. Do not substitute low-fat or nonfat mayonnaise in this dish.

1⅓   **ounces Pecorino Romano cheese, grated (⅔ cup)**
¼   **cup fat-free evaporated milk**
2   **tablespoons mayonnaise**
1   **large egg plus 1 large white**
2   **ounces Canadian bacon, chopped**
2   **slices bacon, chopped**
3   **garlic cloves, minced**
      Salt and pepper
⅓   **cup dry white wine**
1   **pound spaghetti**
1   **tablespoon minced fresh parsley**

1. Process Pecorino, evaporated milk, 1½ tablespoons mayonnaise, and egg and white in food processor until smooth, about 15 seconds; leave in processor.

2. Cook Canadian bacon and bacon together in 12-inch non-stick skillet over medium heat until fat has rendered and bacon is browned, about 7 minutes; transfer to paper towel–lined plate. Add garlic and 1 teaspoon pepper to fat left in skillet and cook over medium heat until fragrant, about 30 seconds. Stir in wine and simmer until thickened slightly, about 1 minute; cover and set aside.

3. Meanwhile, bring 4 quarts water to boil in large pot. Add pasta and 1 tablespoon salt and cook, stirring often, until al dente. Reserve ½ cup pasta cooking water, then drain pasta and return it to pot. Stir in remaining 1½ teaspoons mayonnaise.

4. With processor running, slowly add wine mixture and ¼ cup reserved cooking water to cheese mixture and process until smooth and frothy, about 1 minute. Immediately stir mixture into pasta, season with salt and pepper to taste, and add remaining cooking water as needed to adjust consistency. Stir in crisp bacon, sprinkle with parsley, and serve.

BEFORE → **AFTER**	630 → **430** CALORIES	33 → **11** GRAMS FAT	10 → **3.5** GRAMS SAT FAT

Fettuccine Alfredo

Serves 4

✔ **WHY THIS RECIPE WORKS:** Though fettuccine Alfredo isn't terribly tough to make, most folks reserve it for a rare splurge when dining out—and since it weighs in at 800 calories and almost 50 grams of fat (30 of them saturated), that's probably a good thing! We wanted to know if we could jettison the cream and most of the butter from this classic dish, but keep its rich, indulgent character. After trying a number of substitutions for the cream, we found that a combination of whole milk and half-and-half worked best, giving our sauce a creamy texture and rich flavor. To replicate the thickness of Alfredo sauce made with heavy cream, we turned to a roux, a mixture of butter and flour. With just 1½ tablespoons of butter and 1 tablespoon of flour, we were able to thicken the sauce nicely. As for the cheese, a full cup of Parmesan added nutty, complex flavor but minimal fat. For more savory oomph, we included a pinch of nutmeg and simmered a crushed garlic clove in the sauce. Finally, we found that serving Alfredo immediately in freshly warmed bowls was crucial; this ensured it stayed hot, rich, and creamy, all the way to the table. Our lightened Alfredo now offered all the rich, creamy allure of the full-fat version, but with a fraction of the fat and calories.

1½ **tablespoons unsalted butter**
1 **tablespoon all-purpose flour**
1 **cup whole milk**
⅓ **cup half-and-half**
1 **garlic clove, peeled and lightly crushed**
Salt and pepper
Pinch nutmeg
2 **ounces Parmesan cheese, grated (1 cup)**
1 **pound fresh fettuccine**

1. Bring 4 quarts water to boil in large pot. Using ladle, fill 4 individual serving bowls with about ½ cup boiling water; set aside.

2. Melt butter in large saucepan over medium heat. Whisk in flour until smooth and cook until golden, 1 to 2 minutes. Whisk in milk, half-and-half, garlic, ½ teaspoon salt, ½ teaspoon pepper, and nutmeg and bring to simmer. Reduce heat to medium-low and simmer gently until sauce is slightly thickened, 1 to 2 minutes. Off heat, remove garlic and stir in Parmesan; cover and set aside.

3. Return water to boil, add pasta and 1 tablespoon salt and cook, stirring often, until al dente. Reserve 1 cup cooking water, then drain pasta. Return sauce to low heat and stir in cooked pasta and ⅓ cup reserved cooking water. Cook gently, tossing pasta with tongs, until everything is heated through and sauce nicely coats pasta, about 1 minute. Season with salt and pepper to taste and add remaining cooking water as needed to adjust consistency. Working quickly, empty water from serving bowls, fill with pasta, and serve immediately.

BEFORE NUMBERS BASED ON: Fettuccine Alfredo (lunch portion) from Olive Garden	BEFORE → **AFTER**	800 → **540** CALORIES	48 → **17** GRAMS FAT	30 → **9** GRAMS SAT FAT

Weeknight Sausage Ragu

Serves 6

✓ **WHY THIS RECIPE WORKS:** Pasta with ragu is a classic Italian-American supper, but it typically calls for simmering several cuts of fatty meat for hours. We wanted a sauce that had all the heartiness and big flavor of the long-simmered version—but without all the fat or time spent on the stovetop. To streamline our shopping list, we scaled back to just one type of meat: hot Italian turkey sausage, which is preseasoned (so we didn't need a laundry list of spices and herbs) and offered plenty of meaty flavor and heartiness but not much fat. Going up on the amount of aromatics helped us ratchet up the flavor of our sauce exponentially; a tablespoon of olive oil provided ample moisture for sautéing. A red bell pepper provided a slight sweetness and helped add substance to the sauce. Tomato paste amped up the savory notes of our ragu in lieu of the long simmering time, while red wine contributed depth and complexity. For the tomatoes, we used two cans of diced; processed until nearly smooth in the food processor, they cooked down to just the right clingy consistency on the stovetop. Ready in under an hour, our revamped ragu was now set to join the weeknight rotation—and since we'd trimmed so much fat from our recipe, we could still afford dessert, too.

2   **(28-ounce) cans diced tomatoes**
1   **tablespoon olive oil**
2   **onions, chopped**
    Salt and pepper
5   **garlic cloves, minced**
1   **tablespoon tomato paste**
¼   **cup red wine**
1   **red bell pepper, stemmed, seeded, and chopped**
12 **ounces hot Italian turkey sausage, casings removed**
1   **pound penne**
¼   **cup chopped fresh basil**

1. Working in batches, pulse tomatoes with their juice in food processor until mostly smooth, about 10 pulses; transfer to bowl. Heat oil in large saucepan over medium-high heat until shimmering. Add onions and ¼ teaspoon salt and cook until golden brown, about 7 minutes.

2. Stir in garlic and tomato paste and cook until fragrant, about 1 minute. Stir in wine, scraping up any browned bits. Stir in bell pepper and sausage and cook, breaking up meat with wooden spoon, until sausage is no longer pink, about 4 minutes. Stir in processed tomatoes and simmer sauce until thickened, about 45 minutes.

3. Meanwhile, bring 4 quarts water to boil in large pot. Add pasta and 1 tablespoon salt and cook, stirring often, until al dente. Reserve ½ cup pasta cooking water, then drain pasta and return it to pot. Stir in sauce and basil, season with salt and pepper to taste, and add reserved cooking water as needed to adjust consistency. Serve.

BEFORE → AFTER	610 → **440** CALORIES	19 → **7** GRAMS FAT	6 → **1.5** GRAMS SAT FAT

Spaghetti and Meatballs

Serves 6

✔ **WHY THIS RECIPE WORKS:** The epitome of comfort food, spaghetti and meatballs is a longtime family favorite that unfortunately comes with a high nutritional price tag. Our goal was to create an ultra-flavorful dish that kept the fat and calories in check. From the outset, we knew the traditional meatloaf mix called for would have to go if we wanted to slash the fat. Switching to ground turkey gave us leaner meatballs that still had a meaty flavor and a hearty texture. To ensure they stayed tender and moist, we included a small amount of milk; bread crumbs gave our meatballs structure and ensured they held together during cooking. Minced garlic, grated Parmesan, and fresh parsley guaranteed they were well-seasoned. Browning the meatballs in a minimal amount of oil, then finishing them in the sauce, ensured they were cooked through and lent our simple tomato sauce a rich, meaty flavor. Do not use ground turkey breast meat (also labeled 99 percent fat-free); it will make meatballs that are dry and grainy. You will need a 12-inch nonstick skillet with at least 2-inch sides to accommodate both the meatballs and the sauce; the skillet will be quite full.

½ cup panko bread crumbs
¼ cup skim milk
1 ounce Parmesan cheese, grated (½ cup)
¼ cup minced fresh parsley
6 garlic cloves, minced
Salt and pepper
1 pound 93 percent lean ground turkey
3 (14.5-ounce) cans diced tomatoes
2 teaspoons olive oil
1 onion, chopped fine
¼ teaspoon red pepper flakes
1 pound spaghetti
3 tablespoons chopped fresh basil

1. Mix panko, milk, Parmesan, parsley, one-third of garlic, ½ teaspoon salt, and ½ teaspoon pepper together in bowl. Add turkey and mix with hands until evenly combined. Lightly shape mixture into twelve 1½-inch meatballs.

2. Pulse 2 cans tomatoes with their juice in food processor until mostly smooth, about 10 pulses. Heat oil in 12-inch nonstick skillet over medium heat until just smoking. Brown meatballs well on all sides, about 10 minutes; transfer to paper towel–lined plate.

3. Add onion and ⅛ teaspoon salt to fat left in skillet, cover, and cook over medium-low heat until softened, 8 to 10 minutes. Stir in remaining garlic and pepper flakes and cook until fragrant, about 30 seconds. Stir in processed tomatoes and remaining 1 can diced tomatoes with their juice and simmer for 10 minutes. Return meatballs to skillet, cover, and simmer until meatballs are cooked through, about 10 minutes.

4. Meanwhile, bring 4 quarts water to boil in large pot. Add pasta and 1 tablespoon salt and cook, stirring often, until al dente. Reserve ½ cup cooking water, then drain pasta and return it to pot. Stir in several large spoonfuls of tomato sauce, season with salt and pepper to taste, and add reserved cooking water as needed to adjust consistency. Divide pasta among 6 individual bowls, top with meatballs and remaining sauce, and sprinkle with basil. Serve.

| BEFORE NUMBERS BASED ON: Spaghetti with Meatballs (lunch portion) from Olive Garden | BEFORE → **AFTER** | 680 → **490** CALORIES | 30 → **9** GRAMS FAT | 12 → **2.5** GRAMS SAT FAT |

MAKEOVER SPOTLIGHT:
SPAGHETTI AND MEATBALLS

1. SWAP IN LEAN GROUND TURKEY FOR THE FATTY MEATLOAF MIX: Most meatball recipes call for meatloaf mix, which is a combination of ground beef, veal, and pork. But while meatloaf mix is convenient, it's definitely not low in fat. Instead, we opted for 93 percent lean ground turkey, which is much lower in fat but still meaty tasting. Adding skim milk to the meatballs kept them moist, and panko bread crumbs gave the meatballs structure and helped them hold together. For flavor, we also added Parmesan, parsley, and garlic to the mix.

2. BROWN THE MEATBALLS, THEN USE THE DRIPPINGS TO MAKE THE SAUCE: Using the rendered fat and fond to sauté our aromatics ensured we were able to capture all of the rich flavor of the meatballs in our sauce. Also, we didn't have to use any additional oil to cook our aromatics. To brown the meatballs, we needed only 2 teaspoons of olive oil. After browning the meatballs on all sides, we set them aside and sautéed the aromatics before adding the tomatoes to the skillet.

3. PULSE CANNED DICED TOMATOES FOR A QUICK AND FLAVORFUL SAUCE: Diced tomatoes were the best choice when it came to canned tomato products—they delivered bright, fresh flavor and didn't require a long cooking time. Pulsing some of the tomatoes until almost smooth and simmering the sauce briefly ensured it had just the right consistency, and still provided some hearty chunks of tomato throughout.

4. FOR BIG FLAVOR, SIMMER THE MEATBALLS RIGHT IN THE SAUCE: To instill both the meatballs and the sauce with robust flavor, we finished the meatballs right in the sauce. After letting the sauce simmer for 10 minutes, we returned the meatballs to the pan and simmered them until they were cooked through. Be careful not to overcook the meatballs or they will taste dry.

Linguine with Bolognese

Serves 6

✔ **WHY THIS RECIPE WORKS:** With its hearty combination of tender meat in a thick, full-bodied, dairy-enriched tomato sauce, Bolognese is considered the king of Italian meat sauces. But we didn't think this rich, tempting dish should be written off the menu, so we set out to find a way for Bolognese to keep its crown—and all the comfort-food appeal and great flavors—but lose the fat. Ditching the usual meat-loaf mix in favor of ground turkey was an easy fix, but now we had to find a way to bump up the savory notes. We found our answer in the triple whammy of pancetta, dried porcini, and anchovy; after processing these glutamate-rich ingredients, we sautéed them in butter for the base of our sauce. We also doubled the amount of tomato paste, which is high in glutamates, too. Swapping low-fat milk for the whole milk helped trim additional fat while still delivering tender, moist turkey. Finally, cooking the pasta right in the sauce transformed this king of Italian sauces into an easy, one-pot supper. When adding the linguine in step 5, stir gently to avoid breaking the noodles; after a minute or two they will soften enough to be stirred more easily. Make sure to stir the noodles often to prevent scorching. If necessary, add hot water, 1 tablespoon at a time, to adjust the consistency of the sauce before serving. Do not use ground turkey breast meat (also labeled 99 percent fat-free) here. Serve with grated Parmesan cheese if desired.

2	carrots, peeled and cut into 1-inch pieces
1	onion, cut into 1-inch pieces
2	ounces pancetta, cut into 1-inch pieces
½	ounce dried porcini mushrooms, rinsed
1	anchovy fillet, rinsed
1	(28-ounce) can whole tomatoes
1	tablespoon unsalted butter
	Salt and pepper
1	teaspoon sugar
1	garlic clove, minced
1	pound 93 percent lean ground turkey
1½	cups 2 percent low-fat milk
2	tablespoons tomato paste
½	cup dry white wine
4	cups water
1	pound linguine

1. Pulse carrots and onion in food processor until finely chopped, 10 to 15 pulses; transfer to bowl. Process pancetta, mushrooms, and anchovy in now-empty food processor until finely chopped, 30 to 35 seconds; transfer to separate bowl. Pulse tomatoes with their juice in now-empty food processor until mostly smooth, about 8 pulses; transfer to separate bowl.

2. Melt butter in Dutch oven over medium heat. Add processed pancetta mixture and cook until browned, about 2 minutes. Stir in processed carrot mixture and 1 teaspoon salt, cover, and cook over medium-low heat, stirring occasionally, until softened, 8 to 10 minutes.

3. Stir in sugar and garlic and cook until fragrant, about 30 seconds. Stir in turkey, breaking up meat with wooden spoon, and cook for 1 minute. Stir in milk, scraping up any browned bits, and simmer, stirring occasionally, until nearly evaporated, 18 to 20 minutes.

4. Stir in tomato paste and cook for 1 minute. Stir in wine and simmer, stirring occasionally, until nearly evaporated, 8 to 10 minutes.

5. Stir in processed tomatoes, water, and linguine and bring to simmer over medium-high heat. Cover and cook, stirring often, until pasta is tender and sauce is thickened, 12 to 16 minutes. Off heat, season with salt and pepper to taste and serve.

BEFORE → **AFTER**	670 → **530** CALORIES	24 → **12** GRAMS FAT	11 → **4.5** GRAMS SAT FAT

Pasta O's with Meatballs

Serves 5

✔ **WHY THIS RECIPE WORKS:** For a tastier and lighter version of this longtime kid favorite, we started with the sauce. Replicating its slightly thickened consistency was easy—we simmered and pureed a combination of canned tomatoes and chicken broth, flavored with a handful of aromatics. Cooking our onion, carrot, and celery covered ensured they released their moisture and we didn't need to use a ton of oil to sauté them. To make this a hearty, flavorful supper, we made mini meatballs and simmered them right in the sauce. Ground chicken kept our meatballs on the leaner side, and seasoning them with a few spoonfuls of store-bought reduced-fat pesto guaranteed a dinner that was big in flavor but low in fat and calories. You can use any bite-size pasta in this recipe; alphabet pasta is fun if you can find it. Do not use ground chicken breast here (also labeled 99 percent fat-free) or the meatballs will taste dry and grainy. Serve with grated Parmesan cheese.

6	ounces ground chicken
2½	tablespoons reduced-fat pesto
2	tablespoons panko bread crumbs
	Salt and pepper
1	teaspoon olive oil
1	onion, chopped coarse
1	carrot, peeled and chopped coarse
1	small celery rib, chopped coarse
3	garlic cloves, minced
1	(28-ounce) can diced tomatoes
1½	cups low-sodium chicken broth
4	ounces (1 cup) ditalini

1. Combine chicken, pesto, panko, ⅛ teaspoon salt, and pinch pepper in bowl and mix with hands until uniform. Using heaping teaspoon, lightly shape mixture into ¾-inch round meatballs (about 28 meatballs); place on plate, cover, and refrigerate until needed.

2. Combine oil, onion, carrot, and celery in large saucepan, cover, and cook over medium heat until onion is softened, 5 to 7 minutes. Stir in garlic and cook until fragrant, about 30 seconds. Stir in tomatoes with their juice and broth, cover, and simmer gently until carrot is softened, 15 to 20 minutes.

3. Working in batches, process mixture in blender until very smooth, 1 to 2 minutes. Return pureed mixture to clean pot, cover, and bring to simmer over medium heat. Stir in pasta and meatballs, cover, and simmer gently until pasta is tender and meatballs are cooked through, 12 to 15 minutes. Season with salt and pepper to taste and serve.

BEFORE → **AFTER**   420 → **230** CALORIES   15 → **6** GRAMS FAT   4 → **1.5** GRAMS SAT FAT

Pasta with Chicken and Broccoli

Serves 6

✔ **WHY THIS RECIPE WORKS:** Though it sounds light, this dish usually tops the scales when it comes to fat and calories—probably thanks to the generous amounts of butter or cream (or sometimes both) in the sauce. We wanted a fresh take on this dish that didn't rely on tons of fat for flavor. For a richly flavored sauce, we started with chicken broth and added a bit of flour to make it clingy and saucy; sun-dried tomatoes, minced anchovies, red pepper flakes, and a whopping 8 cloves of garlic gave the sauce some punch. To keep things easy, we simply sautéed our chicken (we used boneless, skinless chicken breasts), then set it aside while we used the same pan to make the sauce; this prevented the meat from becoming overcooked and dry in the finished dish. And before we cooked our pasta, we used the same water to simmer our broccoli until it was just crisp-tender. Once the broccoli and pasta were done, we combined them with our chicken and sauce, plus a good amount of grated Asiago for richness and a savory boost. We prefer to use a pasta with lots of nooks and crannies, such as campanelle or rotini, to keep the flavors on the pasta, and not at the bottom of your bowl.

1	pound boneless, skinless chicken breasts, trimmed of all visible fat, halved lengthwise and sliced crosswise into ¼-inch-thick pieces
	Salt and pepper
1	tablespoon olive oil
1	onion, chopped fine
½	cup oil-packed sun-dried tomatoes, rinsed, patted dry, and sliced ¼ inch thick
8	garlic cloves, minced
3	anchovy fillets, rinsed and minced
¼	teaspoon red pepper flakes
2	tablespoons all-purpose flour
3	cups low-sodium chicken broth
1	pound broccoli florets, cut into 1-inch pieces
1	pound campanelle
1	ounce Asiago or Pecorino Romano cheese, grated (½ cup)
¼	cup chopped fresh basil

1. Pat chicken dry with paper towels and season with salt and pepper. Heat 2 teaspoons oil in 12-inch skillet over medium-high heat until just smoking. Add chicken and cook until browned and cooked through, about 5 minutes; transfer to bowl.

2. Add onion, sun-dried tomatoes, garlic, anchovies, pepper flakes, and remaining 1 teaspoon oil to fat left in skillet, cover, and cook over medium-low heat until onion begins to soften, about 5 minutes. Uncover, stir in flour, and cook for 1 minute. Slowly whisk in broth and simmer, covered, until tomatoes are softened, about 2 minutes. Remove lid and simmer until sauce has thickened, about 5 minutes. Off heat, stir in cooked chicken; cover until needed.

3. Meanwhile, bring 4 quarts water to boil in large pot. Add broccoli and 1 tablespoon salt and cook until broccoli is bright green and tender but still crisp in center, about 2 minutes; using slotted spoon, transfer to large paper towel–lined plate.

4. Return water to boil, stir in pasta, and cook, stirring often, until al dente. Reserve ½ cup cooking water, then drain pasta and return it to pot. Stir in chicken mixture, cooked broccoli, Asiago, and basil. Cover and let sit for 1 minute. Add reserved cooking water as needed to adjust consistency and season with salt and pepper to taste. Serve.

BEFORE → **AFTER**	780 → **480** CALORIES	27 → **9** GRAMS FAT	13 → **2** GRAMS SAT FAT

Shrimp Scampi with Pasta

Serves 6

✔ **WHY THIS RECIPE WORKS:** Shrimp scampi is a deceptively fatty dish. Sure, it looks innocent enough, boasting tender shrimp in a bright, piquant sauce flavored with garlic and lemon. But the big problem with scampi lies in the generous amounts of oil and butter used to cook the shrimp and enrich the sauce. Lightening our version of this classic dish would take some ingenuity. First, we looked to bump up the flavor, and increased the amount of garlic to 8 cloves and the lemon juice to a full ½ cup. A chopped onion further rounded out the flavor profile, and sautéing it covered ensured it released its moisture so we needed just a teaspoon of oil to cook it. For a balanced sauce, we used a mix of chicken broth and clam juice, but it was too thin to coat the pasta. A bit of cornstarch worked to thicken it nicely, but without any butter our sauce still tasted fairly lean. After testing a variety of low-fat ingredients, we hit on reduced-fat cream cheese, which practically melted into the sauce and imparted an undertone of richness and creaminess without dulling the brightness of our scampi or making it a full-fledged cream sauce. Finally, for perfectly tender shrimp, we simply added them to the finished sauce and let them cook through in the residual heat while we simmered our pasta. Take care not to overcook the shrimp or they will be tough. To make this dish spicier, increase the amount of red pepper flakes.

1   onion, chopped fine
1   teaspoon olive oil
    Salt and pepper
8   garlic cloves, minced
2   teaspoons minced fresh thyme
⅛   teaspoon red pepper flakes
2   cups low-sodium chicken broth
2   (8-ounce) bottles clam juice
1   bay leaf
2   tablespoons cornstarch
2   tablespoons water
½   cup lemon juice (3 lemons)
1½ ounces ⅓ less fat cream cheese
    (neufchatel), softened
1½ pounds extra-large shrimp
    (21 to 25 per pound), peeled,
    deveined, and tails removed
1   pound linguine
2   tablespoons minced fresh
    parsley

1. Combine onion, oil, and ⅛ teaspoon salt in 12-inch nonstick skillet, cover, and cook over medium-low heat until softened, 8 to 10 minutes. Stir in garlic, thyme, and pepper flakes and cook until fragrant, about 30 seconds. Stir in broth, clam juice, and bay leaf and simmer until sauce has reduced to about 2 cups, 7 to 10 minutes.

2. Whisk cornstarch and water together in bowl, then whisk into sauce. Continue to simmer, whisking constantly, until thickened, about 2 minutes. Off heat, whisk in lemon juice and cream cheese until smooth. Stir in shrimp, cover, and let sit off heat until shrimp are cooked through, 7 to 10 minutes. Remove bay leaf.

3. Meanwhile, bring 4 quarts water to boil in large pot. Add pasta and 1 tablespoon salt and cook, stirring often, until al dente. Reserve ½ cup cooking water, then drain pasta and return it to pot. Stir in shrimp mixture and parsley, cover, and let sit for 1 minute. Add reserved cooking water as needed to adjust consistency and season with salt and pepper to taste. Serve.

BEFORE → **AFTER**	580 → **400**	20 → **4.5**	3 → **1.5**
	CALORIES	GRAMS FAT	GRAMS SAT FAT

American Chop Suey

Serves 6

✔ **WHY THIS RECIPE WORKS:** This retro classic combines ground beef, macaroni, and tomato sauce for a dish that's incredibly homey, hearty, and appealing. But what's not appealing about most versions of this dish is the greasy slick of fat outlining the bowl. For an American chop suey that was lighter but still every bit as flavorful, we bypassed the usual 85 and 90 percent lean ground beef in favor of 93 percent lean ground beef, which helped us trim the fat substantially. For more heartiness and meaty flavor—without adding more meat—we included mushrooms; when finely ground in the food processor, they practically disappeared into our chop suey. To further ramp up the savory notes of the sauce, we reached for one of our makeover secret weapons: soy sauce. A generous 2 tablespoons of this glutamate-rich ingredient gave our dish more oomph without adding any fat whatsoever. Three types of tomato products—paste, sauce, and diced—added big tomato flavor and body. Cooking the macaroni right in the sauce helped the pasta absorb all the rich, meaty flavors and ensured the sauce thickened to just the right consistency.

8	ounces white mushrooms, trimmed and chopped coarse
1	tablespoon canola oil
1	onion, chopped fine
1	red bell pepper, stemmed, seeded, and chopped
1	celery rib, chopped
	Salt and pepper
2	garlic cloves, minced
2	tablespoons low-sodium soy sauce
1	tablespoon tomato paste
1	pound 93 percent lean ground beef
1	(15-ounce) can tomato sauce
1	(14.5-ounce) can diced tomatoes
1½	cups low-sodium chicken broth
8	ounces (2 cups) elbow macaroni

1. Pulse mushrooms in food processor until finely ground, about 10 pulses. Heat oil in Dutch oven over medium heat until shimmering. Add processed mushrooms, onion, bell pepper, celery, and ¼ teaspoon salt and cook until vegetables begin to soften, about 5 minutes.

2. Stir in garlic, soy sauce, and tomato paste and cook until fragrant, about 1 minute. Stir in beef, breaking up meat with wooden spoon, and cook until no longer pink, about 5 minutes. Stir in tomato sauce, diced tomatoes with their juice, and broth, scraping up any browned bits. Cover, reduce heat to low, and simmer until beef and vegetables are tender, about 20 minutes.

3. Stir in macaroni, cover, and cook, stirring often, until macaroni is tender, about 20 minutes. Season with salt and pepper to taste and serve.

BEFORE → **AFTER**	490 → **340** CALORIES	21 → **9** GRAMS FAT	7 → **2.5** GRAMS SAT FAT

Pork Lo Mein

Serves 6

✔ **WHY THIS RECIPE WORKS:** Order this classic Chinese dish at a restaurant, and along with the tender noodles, pork, and vegetables cloaked in a salty-sweet sauce, you'll be taking in almost 800 calories and 25 grams of fat. Could we find a way to slash the fat and calories but keep the great flavors and textures of this satisfying dish? Replacing the usual pork shoulder with lean pork tenderloin was a good start. Marinating the thinly sliced pork in a potent mixture of oyster sauce, soy sauce, hoisin sauce, toasted sesame oil, and five-spice powder ensured it was flavorful. Mushrooms, cabbage, and scallions added freshness, and grated ginger and Sriracha sauce contributed spice and heat. Rather than let the noodles take center stage (we'd opted for spaghetti, which proved a great stand-in for the traditional fresh Chinese noodles), we swapped the proportions and put the emphasis on the pork and vegetables, making this a better-for-you and more flavorful take on the full-fat, high-calorie original.

4½ tablespoons low-sodium soy sauce

3 tablespoons oyster sauce

3 tablespoons hoisin sauce

1½ tablespoons toasted sesame oil

¼ teaspoon five-spice powder

1 (1½-pound) pork tenderloin, trimmed of all visible fat, halved lengthwise, and sliced crosswise into ⅛-inch-thick pieces

¾ cup low-sodium chicken broth

1½ teaspoons cornstarch

12 ounces spaghetti
 Salt

4½ teaspoons canola oil

6 tablespoons Chinese rice wine or dry sherry

12 ounces shiitake mushrooms, stemmed and halved if small or quartered if large

½ head napa cabbage, cored and sliced crosswise into ½-inch-thick pieces (6 cups)

8 scallions, white parts sliced thin, green parts cut into 1-inch pieces

1 tablespoon grated fresh ginger

3 garlic cloves, minced

1 teaspoon Sriracha sauce

1. Combine soy sauce, oyster sauce, hoisin, sesame oil, and five-spice powder together in bowl. Measure ¼ cup sauce mixture into separate bowl and stir in pork; cover and refrigerate, 30 to 60 minutes. Whisk broth and cornstarch into remaining sauce mixture.

2. Bring 4 quarts water to boil in large pot. Add pasta and 1 tablespoon salt and cook, stirring often, until al dente. Drain pasta; set aside.

3. Meanwhile, heat 1½ teaspoons canola oil in Dutch oven over high heat until just smoking. Add half of pork, breaking up any clumps, and cook until lightly browned but not fully cooked, about 3 minutes. Stir in 3 tablespoons wine and cook until liquid is nearly evaporated, about 1 minute. Transfer to clean bowl. Repeat with 1½ teaspoons canola oil, remaining pork, and remaining 3 tablespoons wine.

4. Wipe now-empty pot clean, add remaining 1½ teaspoons canola oil, and place over high heat until shimmering. Add mushrooms and cook until lightly browned, 4 to 6 minutes. Stir in cabbage and cook until wilted, about 2 minutes. Stir in scallions, ginger, and garlic and cook until fragrant, about 30 seconds.

5. Whisk sauce to recombine and add to pot. Stir in cooked pork and any accumulated juices and simmer until sauce has thickened slightly and pork is heated through, about 1 minute. Stir in cooked pasta and Sriracha. Serve.

BEFORE NUMBERS BASED ON:	BEFORE → **AFTER**	760 → **500**	25 → **11**	5 → **2**
Pork Lo Mein from P.F. Chang's China Bistro		CALORIES	GRAMS FAT	GRAMS SAT FAT

Peanut Noodle Salad

Serves 6

✓ **WHY THIS RECIPE WORKS:** With its crisp vegetables and tender noodles coated in a velvety, mildly spicy peanut sauce, this salad offers a refreshing change of pace—but a peek at the fat and calorie counts reveals that it's a nutritional nightmare. Scaling back on the peanut butter, to ⅓ cup from the full cup called for in many recipes, helped cut calories and fat but ensured there was still plenty of nutty flavor. A spoonful of toasted sesame oil, which we added to our cooked noodles to prevent them from sticking to each other, ramped up the nuttiness of our dish even more. Rinsing the cooked pasta with cold water kept it from overcooking and helped to remove some of the starch so it wouldn't become pasty. And putting more emphasis on the vegetables in this dish—we added an extra carrot and bell pepper to the mix—promised a peanut noodle salad that was low in fat but still ultra-satisfying. Use a milder hot sauce, such as the test kitchen's favorite, Frank's RedHot Original Cayenne Pepper Sauce, in this recipe. If using a hotter sauce, such as Tabasco, reduce the amount to ½ teaspoon.

⅓	cup chunky peanut butter
5	tablespoons low-sodium soy sauce
2	tablespoons rice vinegar
2	tablespoons packed light brown sugar
1	tablespoon grated fresh ginger
2	garlic cloves, minced
1	teaspoon hot sauce
1	pound spaghetti
	Salt and pepper
1	tablespoon toasted sesame oil
2	red bell peppers, stemmed, seeded, and sliced thin
2	carrots, peeled and shredded
1	cucumber, peeled, halved lengthwise, seeded, and sliced thin
⅓	cup minced fresh cilantro

1. Whisk peanut butter, soy sauce, vinegar, sugar, ginger, garlic, and hot sauce together in bowl until smooth.

2. Bring 4 quarts water to boil in large pot. Add pasta and 1 tablespoon salt and cook, stirring often, until tender. Reserve ¾ cup cooking water, then drain pasta and rinse with cold water until cool. Drain pasta well, transfer to large bowl, and stir in sesame oil.

3. Stir in peanut butter mixture, bell peppers, carrots, cucumber, and cilantro and season with salt and pepper to taste. Add reserved cooking water as needed to adjust consistency. Serve.

BEFORE → **AFTER**	550 → **430**	24 → **11**	4 → **2**
	CALORIES	GRAMS FAT	GRAMS SAT FAT

Pad Thai

Serves 4

☑ **WHY THIS RECIPE WORKS:** We'd had enough of the soggy noodles, overcooked shrimp, and greasy sauce we experienced when ordering takeout. For noodles that weren't flabby, we soaked them first in hot water to soften them slightly, then stir-fried them in the sauce so they were perfectly tender. Cooking the shrimp briefly in a small amount of oil and setting them aside while we made the sauce kept them from becoming rubbery. Cutting back on the oil in the sauce helped to trim fat grams without adversely affecting the bright, bold flavor of our dish. Finally, a sprinkling of chopped peanuts added crunch—but not a ton of fat. For an accurate measurement of boiling water, bring a full kettle of water to a boil, then measure out the desired amount. Because this dish comes together very quickly, make sure all your ingredients are prepped before you start cooking. If you can't find tamarind paste, you can substitute 1 tablespoon tamarind concentrate mixed with ⅔ cup hot water, or ⅓ cup lime juice mixed with ⅓ cup water. If using lime juice, substitute brown sugar for the granulated sugar in the sauce and omit the lime wedges.

8	ounces (¼-inch-wide) rice noodles
2	tablespoons tamarind paste
¾	cup boiling water
3	tablespoons fish sauce
3	tablespoons sugar
2	tablespoons canola oil
1	tablespoon rice vinegar
¼	teaspoon cayenne pepper
12	ounces medium shrimp (41 to 50 per pound), peeled, deveined, and tails removed
1	shallot, minced
3	garlic cloves, minced
2	large eggs, lightly beaten
6	ounces (3 cups) bean sprouts
4	scallions, sliced thin on bias
	Salt
¼	cup minced fresh cilantro
2	tablespoons roasted, unsalted peanuts, chopped
	Lime wedges

1. Cover noodles with very hot tap water in large bowl and stir to separate. Let noodles soak until softened, pliable, and limp but not fully tender, about 20 minutes; drain.

2. Meanwhile, soak tamarind paste in boiling water in bowl until softened, about 10 minutes. Push mixture through fine-mesh strainer into medium bowl, removing seeds and fibers and extracting as much pulp as possible. Whisk fish sauce, sugar, 1 tablespoon oil, vinegar, and cayenne into tamarind liquid.

3. Heat 1½ teaspoons oil in 12-inch nonstick skillet over high heat until just smoking. Add shrimp and cook, stirring occasionally, until shrimp are pink, curled, and browned around edges, about 3 minutes; transfer to bowl.

4. Add remaining 1½ teaspoons oil to skillet and return to medium heat until shimmering. Add shallot and garlic and cook until lightly browned, about 1½ minutes. Stir in eggs and cook, stirring constantly, until scrambled but still moist, about 20 seconds. Stir in softened noodles and sauce mixture; increase heat to high and cook, tossing gently, until noodles are evenly coated, about 1 minute.

5. Stir in cooked shrimp, sprouts, and scallions and cook until shrimp are heated through and noodles are tender, about 2 minutes. Season with salt to taste. Sprinkle with cilantro and peanuts. Serve, passing lime wedges separately.

BEFORE → **AFTER**	600 → **470**	24 → **13**	4 → **1.5**
	CALORIES	GRAMS FAT	GRAMS SAT FAT

Broccoli with Cheese Sauce

Serves 4

✓ **WHY THIS RECIPE WORKS:** This family favorite has enticed kids to eat their veggies for years, but only because there's so much of the ultra-cheesy, buttery sauce compared to the good-for-you broccoli. We wanted a healthier take on this classic so we could feel good about not only eating it, but also serving it to loved ones. Most versions start the sauce with a roux (a mixture of flour and butter) before adding half-and-half or whole milk and tons of cheese. For a lighter, but no less flavorful, cheese sauce, we nixed the roux and used cornstarch as the thickener. Chicken broth, in place of the fatty dairy, spiked with Dijon mustard and cayenne pepper provided a savory, full-bodied backbone, but our sauce was still lacking in richness. We tried a variety of low-fat dairy ingredients, but only reduced-fat cream cheese gave us the smooth, creamy texture and rich flavor we sought. For deep cheesy flavor, we liked cheddar; the light variety offered good flavor and helped us slash fat. When it came to the broccoli, boiling gave us wet, limp florets, while steaming resulted in a flavorless vegetable. Roasting, however, delivered broccoli with a distinct, nutty flavor that was the perfect match for the rich, creamy cheese sauce.

1½	pounds broccoli florets, cut into 1-inch pieces
	Vegetable oil spray
1	cup low-sodium chicken broth
	Pinch cayenne pepper
1	tablespoon cornstarch
½	teaspoon Dijon mustard
1	ounce ⅓ less fat cream cheese (neufchatel)
3	ounces 50 percent light cheddar cheese, shredded (¾ cup)
	Hot water
	Salt and pepper

1. Adjust oven rack to lower-middle position, place rimmed baking sheet on rack, and heat oven to 450 degrees. Spray broccoli lightly with oil spray, then arrange in single layer on preheated baking sheet. Roast until spotty brown, 15 to 18 minutes, stirring halfway through roasting time.

2. Meanwhile, combine ¾ cup broth and cayenne in small saucepan and bring to simmer. Whisk remaining ¼ cup broth, cornstarch, and mustard together, then whisk into simmering broth. Bring to boil, whisking constantly, until sauce is slightly thickened, about 2 minutes. Turn heat to low and whisk in cream cheese until melted. Whisk in cheddar, a handful at a time, until smooth. (If sauce becomes too thick, stir in hot water, 1 tablespoon at a time, to loosen.) Season with salt and pepper to taste. Transfer broccoli to large platter, pour sauce over top, and serve.

BEFORE → **AFTER**	260 → **150**	19 → **6**	9 → **3.5**
	CALORIES	GRAMS FAT	GRAMS SAT FAT

Everyday Green Bean Casserole

Serves 6

✔ **WHY THIS RECIPE WORKS:** A staple on the holiday table, green bean casserole sure packs in the fat and calories, with its ultra-creamy sauce and crunchy, buttery, oniony topping. Not only did we want to lighten the load when it came to this classic dish, but we also hoped to streamline the recipe so we could enjoy it more often. To start, we left the casserole dish on the shelf and turned to our skillet instead, transforming this recipe into an easy one-pan side. After steaming the green beans until tender, which took about 6 minutes, we set them aside and built the sauce in the same pan. Cooking the mushrooms covered helped to draw out their moisture and allowed us to cut back to just a teaspoon of oil; after about 10 minutes, we uncovered the pan so they could brown. Chicken broth provided a rich, savory backbone, while a small amount of flour helped to thicken the sauce. Minced garlic and fresh thyme helped bump up the flavors. In lieu of the fatty cream, we found that reduced-fat cream cheese gave our sauce the richness and creaminess it was missing, plus it imparted a nice, tangy flavor. For the finishing touch, we reached for canned fried onions. Just a cup, sprinkled around the edge of the pan, gave our casserole a traditional look and provided good crunch and flavor.

1	pound green beans, trimmed and cut into 2-inch lengths
½	cup water
1	teaspoon canola oil
1	small onion, chopped fine
6	ounces white mushrooms, trimmed and sliced thin
3	garlic cloves, minced
½	teaspoon minced fresh thyme
1	tablespoon all-purpose flour
2	cups low-sodium chicken broth
1	ounce ⅓ less fat cream cheese (neufchatel) Pepper
2	ounces (1 cup) canned fried onions

1. Adjust oven rack to middle position and heat oven to 425 degrees. Combine green beans and water in 12-inch ovensafe skillet, cover, and cook over medium-high heat until green beans are tender and bright green, about 6 minutes; drain green beans and set aside.

2. Combine oil, onion, and mushrooms in now-empty skillet. Cover and cook over medium-low heat until onions have softened and mushrooms have released their liquid, 8 to 10 minutes. Uncover, increase heat to medium, and cook until mushrooms and onion are well browned, about 5 minutes. Stir in garlic and thyme and cook until fragrant, about 30 seconds. Stir in flour and cook until golden, about 1 minute.

3. Increase heat to medium-high, whisk in broth, scraping up any browned bits, and simmer until sauce is thickened, 5 to 7 minutes. Off heat, whisk in cream cheese and season with pepper to taste. Return cooked green beans to skillet and toss with sauce to coat. Sprinkle fried onions around edge of skillet and bake until hot throughout and onions are toasted, about 8 minutes. Let cool slightly and serve.

BEFORE → **AFTER**	270 → **130**	21 → **7**	11 → **2**
	CALORIES	GRAMS FAT	GRAMS SAT FAT

Creamed Spinach

Serves 4

✓ **WHY THIS RECIPE WORKS:** For our lightened take on this restaurant staple, we wanted the spinach to be the star of the show, so we started by increasing the amount we included in our recipe. Looking for the right ingredients to give us a cheesy, rich sauce that was low in fat and not too heavy, we hit on the duo of low-fat milk and light herb-flavored Boursin cheese. Leave some water clinging to the spinach leaves to help encourage steam when cooking. Two and a half pounds of flat-leaf spinach (about 4 bunches) can be substituted for the curly-leaf spinach, but do not use baby spinach because it is much too delicate.

¼ cup water

3 (10-ounce) bags curly-leaf spinach, stemmed and chopped coarse

¼ cup 2 percent low-fat milk

4 ounces (½ cup) Boursin Gourmet Light Garlic and Herbs Spreadable Cheese

Salt and pepper

1. Add water to Dutch oven and place over medium-high heat. Stir in spinach, a handful at a time, and cook until fully wilted, glossy, and tender, 30 seconds to 1 minute. Transfer spinach to colander and squeeze with tongs or press firmly with back of large spoon to remove excess liquid.

2. Wipe now-empty pot dry with paper towels and add milk. Whisk in Boursin and simmer over medium heat until slightly thickened, about 1 minute. Off heat, stir in drained spinach until evenly coated with sauce. Season with salt and pepper to taste. Serve.

BEFORE → **AFTER**   440 → **120** CALORIES   28 → **6** GRAMS FAT   15 → **3.5** GRAMS SAT FAT

Creamed Corn

Serves 6

✓ **WHY THIS RECIPE WORKS:** Creamed corn is usually more about the cream than about the corn. For a dish that tasted of fresh, sweet corn but still offered serious richness, we ditched the cream in favor of whole milk and reduced-fat cream cheese. Scraping the pulp off the cobs with the back of a knife after cutting off the kernels amped up the flavor of the dish significantly. It is important to use fresh, not frozen, corn in this recipe. For additional information on cutting corn kernels from the cob, see page 68.

5 ears corn, husks and silk removed

1 tablespoon canola oil

¾ cup whole milk

2 ounces ⅓ less fat cream cheese (neufchatel)

Salt and pepper

Cut kernels from ears of corn into bowl. Using back of butter knife, scrape any remaining pulp from cobs into bowl. Heat oil in large saucepan over medium-high heat until shimmering. Add corn and cook until softened, about 2 minutes. Stir in milk and cream cheese and simmer until corn is tender and mixture has thickened, 3 to 6 minutes. Season with salt and pepper to taste. Serve.

BEFORE → **AFTER**   310 → **140** CALORIES   25 → **7** GRAMS FAT   10 → **2** GRAMS SAT FAT

Cheesy Cauliflower Bake

Serves 10

✔ **WHY THIS RECIPE WORKS:** To revamp this retro casserole, we jettisoned the cream in the sauce and used low-fat milk, thickened with cornstarch, instead. Reduced-fat cream cheese gave the illusion of creaminess and richness without all the calories or fat. A small amount of extra-sharp cheddar provided an assertive bite, and tossing our bread crumbs with a bit of cheddar and Parmesan ensured the topping offered big flavor. Make sure to gently simmer the cauliflower, partially covered, so the milk does not boil over and separate.

3 slices hearty white sandwich bread, torn into pieces

2 teaspoons olive oil

2 ounces Parmesan cheese, grated (1 cup)

3 ounces extra-sharp cheddar cheese, shredded (¾ cup)

3 garlic cloves, minced
   Salt and pepper

1¼ cups 2 percent low-fat milk

¾ cup low-sodium chicken broth

2 teaspoons dry mustard

1 teaspoon minced fresh thyme

2 heads cauliflower (4 pounds), cored and cut into ¾-inch florets

1 tablespoon cornstarch

1 tablespoon water

3 tablespoons ⅓ less fat cream cheese (neufchatel)

1. Adjust oven rack to middle position and heat oven to 450 degrees. Pulse bread in food processor to coarse crumbs, about 10 pulses. Toast bread crumbs and oil in 12-inch nonstick skillet over medium heat, stirring often, until well browned, about 10 minutes; let cool. Combine cooled crumbs, ¼ cup Parmesan, 2 tablespoons cheddar, 1 teaspoon garlic, ¼ teaspoon salt, and ¼ teaspoon pepper in bowl.

2. Whisk remaining garlic, milk, broth, mustard, thyme, ¼ teaspoon salt, and ¼ teaspoon pepper together in Dutch oven. Add cauliflower and bring to simmer over medium-high heat. Reduce heat to low, partially cover, and simmer, stirring occasionally, until cauliflower is nearly tender, 5 to 7 minutes.

3. Whisk cornstarch and water together in bowl, then add to pot, bring to simmer, and cook, stirring constantly, until sauce has thickened slightly, about 2 minutes. Off heat, stir in remaining ¾ cup Parmesan, remaining cheddar, and cream cheese until fully incorporated.

4. Pour cauliflower mixture into 13 by 9-inch baking dish and top evenly with toasted crumb mixture. Bake until bubbling around edges and crumbs are crisp, 8 to 12 minutes. Let cool for 10 minutes before serving.

QUICK PREP TIP
CUTTING CAULIFLOWER
Holding cauliflower upside down with stem facing up, cut around core with sharp knife and remove. Separate cauliflower florets from inner stem, then cut into smaller pieces as needed.

BEFORE → **AFTER**   310 → **160** CALORIES   24 → **8** GRAMS FAT   15 → **4** GRAMS SAT FAT

Mashed Potatoes

Serves 6

✔ **WHY THIS RECIPE WORKS:** Creamy mashed potatoes are notoriously fat-laden, thanks to copious amounts of butter and heavy cream. Not surprisingly, a single serving of this crowd-pleaser can contain almost 350 calories and over 20 grams of fat. Our goal was to move mashed potatoes into the realm of lighter fare without any sacrifice in flavor or texture. We started by selecting the right variety of potato; Yukon Golds won out in our tests, as they delivered a nice, buttery flavor and creamy mash. Next, we set out to trim fat where we could. While we couldn't cut the butter completely from the ingredient list without a loss in flavor, we found we could get away with using just 3 tablespoons. Heavy cream was a no-go in our recipe if we wanted to lighten it, but we had to find another way to ensure our mashed potatoes were richly flavored and boasted a satisfyingly creamy texture. After trying a whole roster of ingredients, we landed on the duo of buttermilk and low-fat sour cream, which delivered spuds that were smooth and creamy and had a nice, tangy flavor without racking up the fat and calories. To achieve the proper texture, it is important to cook the potatoes thoroughly; they are done if they break apart when a knife is inserted and gently wiggled. To reduce the chance of curdling, the buttermilk must be at room temperature when mixed with the cooled melted butter.

2	pounds Yukon Gold potatoes, peeled and sliced ½ inch thick
	Salt and pepper
⅔	cup buttermilk, room temperature
3	tablespoons unsalted butter, melted and cooled
¼	cup low-fat sour cream, room temperature

1. Place potatoes and 1 tablespoon salt in large saucepan and add water to cover potatoes by 1 inch. Bring to boil over high heat, then reduce to medium-low and simmer gently until potatoes are tender but not falling apart, 15 to 18 minutes.

2. Drain potatoes, then return to saucepan on still-warm stovetop. Using potato masher, mash potatoes smooth. Gently stir buttermilk and cooled butter together in bowl until combined. Gently fold buttermilk mixture and sour cream into potatoes until just incorporated. Season with salt and pepper to taste and serve.

BEFORE NUMBERS BASED ON: Mashed Potatoes from LongHorn Steakhouse	BEFORE→**AFTER**	340→**200** CALORIES	22→**6** GRAMS FAT	12→**3.5** GRAMS SAT FAT	

MAKEOVER SPOTLIGHT: MASHED POTATOES

1. PICK THE RIGHT POTATOES AND SIMMER THEM GENTLY:
Yukon Gold potatoes have a naturally buttery flavor and
creamy texture that are perfect for making low-fat mashed
potatoes. To ensure that the potatoes cooked evenly and didn't
become overly soft and waterlogged, we sliced them ½ inch
thick instead of cutting them into chunks. We also started
cooking them in cold water and simply simmered them gently;
when we cooked them in boiling water, they started to break
down too much and dissolve.

2. RETURN THE SPUDS TO THE PAN AND MASH THEM BY HAND:
After draining the potatoes, we returned them to the hot saucepan over the still-warm burner. The residual heat helped keep
the potatoes warm and drive off excess moisture that would
otherwise water down the mash. Using a food processor or
electric mixer to mash the potatoes made them gluey. Instead,
we used a potato masher to break down our spuds. The potato
masher makes this task easy—you can mash the potatoes right
in the pot—but it will leave a few lumps behind. For an absolutely smooth puree, use a food mill or ricer.

**3. CUT BACK ON THE BUTTER AND USE BUTTERMILK INSTEAD
OF HEAVY CREAM:** Most recipes for mashed potatoes call for a
good amount of butter and heavy cream to deliver an ultra-rich
flavor and creamy texture. But we found we could cut back on
the butter significantly, and used just 3 tablespoons. Instead
of using heavy cream, we turned to buttermilk, which is naturally lean and offers a nice tangy flavor. But given its leanness,
buttermilk can curdle easily when it hits the hot potatoes. To
avoid this, we mixed our room-temperature buttermilk with the
melted and cooled butter before adding it to the potatoes.

**4. USE LOW-FAT SOUR CREAM TO AMP UP THE RICHNESS AND
FLAVOR:** To ensure a lightened mash with an ultra-rich flavor
and creamy texture, we added a little low-fat sour cream to
the potatoes. Not only did the sour cream enrich our mashed
potatoes, but it also helped boost the tangy flavor added by
the buttermilk. To prevent the spuds from becoming gummy,
we gently folded the buttermilk-butter mixture and sour cream
into the potatoes.

Twice-Baked Potatoes

Serves 8

✔️ **WHY THIS RECIPE WORKS:** These stuffed spuds are usually loaded up with whole milk, sour cream, and cheddar cheese—making them far from low-fat fare. Replacing the whole milk and sour cream with lighter versions still gave us a creamy, rich filling, and slashed enough fat that we could keep the full-fat cheddar.

4	**(8-ounce) russet potatoes, unpeeled**
1	**teaspoon canola oil**
1	**tablespoon unsalted butter**
1	**onion, chopped fine**
1	**garlic clove, minced**
4	**ounces sharp cheddar cheese, shredded (1 cup)**
½	**cup low-fat sour cream, room temperature**
¼	**cup skim milk**
½	**teaspoon dry mustard**
	Salt and pepper
2	**scallions, sliced thin**

1. Adjust oven racks to upper-middle and middle positions and heat oven to 400 degrees. Rub potatoes with oil, place directly on upper oven rack, and bake until skins are crisp and deep brown and skewer glides easily through flesh, about 1 hour, flipping them over halfway through baking.

2. Meanwhile, melt butter in 10-inch nonstick skillet over medium heat. Add onion and cook until softened and lightly browned, 5 to 7 minutes. Stir in garlic and cook until fragrant, about 30 seconds; transfer to bowl and cover.

3. Line rimmed baking sheet with aluminum foil; top with wire rack. Transfer baked potatoes to rack; let cool slightly, about 10 minutes. Increase oven temperature to 500 degrees.

4. Cut each potato in half lengthwise, through narrow side, so that halved potatoes lie flat. Carefully scoop flesh from each potato half into medium bowl, leaving ⅛-inch thickness of flesh in each shell. Mash potato flesh with potato masher or fork until smooth, then stir in ½ cup cheddar, sour cream, milk, mustard, cooked onion mixture, ¾ teaspoon salt, and ⅛ teaspoon pepper. Spoon mixture into potato shells, mounding it slightly at center. Sprinkle with remaining ½ cup cheddar.

5. Bake potatoes on middle rack until shells are crisp and cheese is melted and spotty brown, 10 to 15 minutes. Sprinkle with scallions and serve.

QUICK PREP TIP

MAKING TWICE-BAKED POTATOES
Russet potatoes have two wide, flat sides and two narrow, curved sides. To ensure the twice-baked potatoes rest on their flat sides once stuffed and don't topple over, be sure to halve them lengthwise through the curved side. Using a spoon, scoop out the flesh of the hot potato into a medium bowl, leaving ⅛ inch of flesh in each shell.

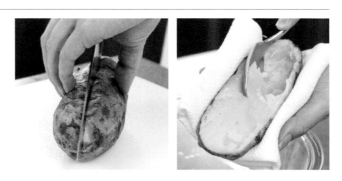

BEFORE → **AFTER**	370 → **250**	20 → **8**	10 → **4.5**
	CALORIES	GRAMS FAT	GRAMS SAT FAT

Scalloped Potatoes

Serves 6

✔ **WHY THIS RECIPE WORKS:** Ultra-rich and cheesy, with a crisp, golden crown hiding tender, creamy bites, scalloped potatoes are the ultimate comfort food. Unfortunately, since they can weigh in at almost 500 calories and over 30 grams of fat, they are generally reserved for special occasions. In an effort to make this comforting classic something we could feel better about enjoying more often, we had to do some serious ingredient swapping. The first thing to go was the butter, which we traded for just 1 tablespoon of canola oil. Our next target was the heavy cream. We eliminated it by using 2 percent low-fat milk, thickened and stabilized with cornstarch, which gave our potatoes the requisite creaminess. Adding some reduced-fat cream cheese and replacing the full-fat cheddar with a little Parmesan—its sharp, bold flavor meant we could use less of it—were the final adjustments needed to lighten this dish without sacrificing its characteristic creamy richness. Do not substitute 1 percent low-fat or skim milk or else the sauce will curdle during baking.

1   tablespoon canola oil
1   onion, minced
      Salt and pepper
1   garlic clove, minced
1   teaspoon minced fresh thyme
2½   pounds russet potatoes, peeled and sliced ⅛ inch thick
2   cups 2 percent low-fat milk
2   bay leaves
2   teaspoons cornstarch
1   tablespoon water
3   tablespoons ⅓ less fat cream cheese (neufchatel)
2   ounces Parmesan cheese, grated (1 cup)

1. Adjust oven rack to middle position and heat oven to 450 degrees. Heat oil in Dutch oven over medium heat until shimmering. Add onion and ½ teaspoon salt and cook until softened, 5 to 7 minutes. Stir in garlic and thyme and cook until fragrant, about 30 seconds.

2. Add potatoes, milk, and bay leaves and bring to simmer. Cover, reduce heat to low, and simmer until potatoes are partially tender (tip of paring knife can be slipped into center of potato with some resistance), about 10 minutes.

3. Remove bay leaves. Whisk cornstarch and water together in bowl, then add to pot and bring to simmer. Off heat, stir in cream cheese, 2 tablespoons Parmesan, and ¼ teaspoon pepper, being careful not to break up potatoes. Transfer mixture to 8-inch square baking dish.

4. Sprinkle with remaining Parmesan. Cover dish with aluminum foil and bake until bubbling around edges, about 20 minutes. Remove foil and continue to bake until potatoes are completely tender and top is golden brown, 10 to 15 minutes. Let cool for 10 minutes before serving.

BEFORE → **AFTER**	480 → **270** CALORIES	34 → **7** GRAMS FAT	21 → **3.5** GRAMS SAT FAT

MAKEOVER SPOTLIGHT:
SCALLOPED POTATOES

1. SLICE THE POTATOES EVENLY: This crucial step ensures that the potatoes will cook at the same rate. The ideal thickness is ⅛ inch; any thicker and the potatoes will take too long to cook through, any thinner and the potatoes may dissolve during cooking. The quickest way to slice them evenly is in a food processor fitted with a slicing blade. A mandoline or V-slicer, however, also works well.

2. SKIP THE BUTTER AND USE OIL INSTEAD: Rather than add a few pats of butter to the pot to cook our aromatics and add richness, we used a small amount of canola oil, which is much lower in saturated fat. All we needed to sauté our onion, garlic, and thyme was a tablespoon.

3. DITCH THE HEAVY CREAM IN FAVOR OF LOW-FAT MILK: Most scalloped potatoes go heavy on the heavy cream—but this racks up the fat and calories in a heartbeat. So we used 2 percent low-fat milk to simmer our potatoes instead; a small amount of cornstarch helped to thicken it. Simmering the potatoes gently on the stovetop helped jump-start their cooking and reduced the baking time substantially, preventing the lightened casserole from drying out in the oven.

4. ADD REDUCED-FAT CREAM CHEESE AND A BIT OF PARMESAN: To ramp up the creamy richness of our casserole without using heavy cream, we added a few tablespoons of reduced-fat cream cheese, which ensured the sauce was rich and silky—but still low in fat. And rather than add lots of shredded cheddar, we opted for a conservative amount of grated Parmesan, which is highly flavorful but low in fat. Mixing some in with the casserole gave it a savory, nutty flavor, and sprinkling the rest over the dish guaranteed a nicely browned top.

Sweet Potato Casserole

Serves 8

✔ **WHY THIS RECIPE WORKS:** A given on any holiday table, sweet potato casserole is usually too sweet, loaded with lots of sugar and an abundance of marshmallows. Unfortunately, not only do these ingredients make for one saccharine-sweet dish, they also rack up the calories. We were shocked to find just one serving can clock in at close to 500 calories! In an effort to lighten this iconic dish, we began by swapping the white sugar for brown sugar, which contributed a richer, deeper flavor and allowed us to use less. After a number of tests, we learned that ½ cup was all we needed to provide ample sweetness. To cook the sweet potatoes, we simply cut them into small pieces and simmered them in a bit of water, with the brown sugar and a few pats of butter for richness, until tender. Then we mashed them until they were smooth and moved them to our casserole dish. Sprinkled with a mere 2 cups of mini marshmallows—mini marshmallows covered more ground than their larger cousins—and broiled for a few minutes, our lightened sweet potato casserole had the look, feel, and flavor of the original version—but without all the calories. For a more intense molasses flavor, use dark brown sugar instead of light brown sugar.

3	tablespoons unsalted butter, cut into 1-inch pieces
3¾	pounds sweet potatoes, peeled, quartered, and cut crosswise into 1-inch pieces
½	cup packed brown sugar
1	teaspoon salt
¼	teaspoon pepper
½	cup water
2	cups mini marshmallows

1. Melt butter in Dutch oven over medium-high heat. Stir in sweet potatoes, sugar, salt, pepper, and water and bring to simmer. Cover, reduce heat to medium-low, and cook, stirring often, until potatoes are completely tender, 35 to 45 minutes. Off heat, mash sweet potato mixture with potato masher until smooth.

2. Adjust oven rack 6 inches from broiler element and heat broiler. Transfer potato mixture to 13 by 9-inch broiler-safe casserole dish and top with marshmallows. Broil until marshmallows are slightly melted and golden, 3 to 4 minutes. Serve.

BEFORE NUMBERS BASED ON:
Sweet Potato Casserole from Boston Market

BEFORE → **AFTER**   480 → **290**   14 → **4**   4.5 → **2.5**
CALORIES   GRAMS FAT   GRAMS SAT FAT

Potato Salad

Serves 6

✓ **WHY THIS RECIPE WORKS:** How do you cut the fat in a salad when the dressing is mostly mayonnaise? Simply switching from full-fat mayo to the lower-fat variety was an obvious move, but this reduced the numbers only slightly. For substantial slimming down, we made a low-fat dressing using some of the potatoes themselves. Mashing some of the cooked spuds with a small amount of their cooking water, then stirring in the mayo and seasonings (chopped celery, sweet relish, and Dijon mustard), gave us a thick, nicely clingy dressing. To slash the fat even further, we swapped out some of the light mayo in favor of nonfat Greek yogurt. White vinegar added a much-needed acidic note and helped instill our potatoes with big flavor from the get-go. Dill pickle relish can be substituted for the sweet pickle relish if desired.

2	pounds red potatoes, unpeeled, cut into ¾-inch pieces
	Salt and pepper
2	tablespoons white vinegar
¼	cup light mayonnaise
¼	cup 0 percent Greek yogurt
1	celery rib, chopped fine
1½	tablespoons sweet pickle relish
1	tablespoon Dijon mustard
2	scallions, green parts only, sliced thin

1. Place potatoes and 2 teaspoons salt in large saucepan and add water to cover potatoes by 1 inch. Bring to boil over high heat, then reduce to medium and simmer gently until potatoes are just tender, about 10 minutes.

2. Reserve ¼ cup cooking water. Drain potatoes thoroughly, then transfer to large bowl. Drizzle vinegar over hot potatoes and gently toss to coat. Transfer ¾ cup potatoes to medium bowl; reserve for sauce. Refrigerate remaining potatoes until cooled, about 30 minutes.

3. Using potato masher, mash reserved ¾ cup potatoes with 3 tablespoons cooking water until smooth, adding remaining cooking water as needed. Stir in mayonnaise, yogurt, celery, relish, mustard, ½ teaspoon salt, and ¼ teaspoon pepper. Refrigerate until cool, about 15 minutes.

4. Gently combine cooled potatoes with cooled dressing to coat. Stir in scallions, cover, and refrigerate for 30 minutes. Serve.

QUICK PREP TIP
MASHING POTATOES FOR POTATO SALAD
For a flavorful low-fat potato salad, we supplement the light mayonnaise and nonfat Greek yogurt in the dressing with cooked potatoes, mashed with a little of their cooking water.

BEFORE NUMBERS BASED ON: Potato Salad from KFC	BEFORE → **AFTER**	210 → **140** CALORIES	11 → **2.5** GRAMS FAT	2.5 → **0** GRAMS SAT FAT

Macaroni Salad

Serves 10

✔ **WHY THIS RECIPE WORKS:** What makes this cookout and barbecue staple so appealing is the cool and creamy dressing and the crunchy vegetables, which contrast nicely with the tender pasta. We had no problem keeping the vegetables (we preferred a simpler dish, with just red onion and celery) in our made-over macaroni salad. But the dressing—a generous amount of mayonnaise, plus a few seasonings—was a definite problem. Switching to light mayo helped cut the fat and calories, but to ensure our lightened salad wasn't dry and flavorless, we found it was key to cook the pasta until just tender—not all the way—and leave a little moisture on it. This way, the pasta absorbed the water rather than the creamy dressing (which could have left our salad dry and bland). A fair amount of lemon juice helped to brighten the salad and counter the richness of the dressing. For seasonings, we liked a bit of Dijon mustard and cayenne pepper. Minced parsley added a fresh, herbal note. Though we usually prefer minced garlic, we opted for garlic powder in this recipe because its flavor wasn't as sharp and the powder could dissolve into the smooth dressing. To ensure the pasta was well-seasoned and flavorful, we tossed it with the vegetables and seasonings first, then stirred in the mayo. Don't drain the macaroni too well before adding the other ingredients—a little extra moisture will keep the salad from drying out. If you've made the salad ahead of time, simply stir in a little warm water to loosen the texture before serving.

1	**pound elbow macaroni**
	Salt and pepper
½	**small red onion, minced**
1	**celery rib, minced**
¼	**cup minced fresh parsley**
2	**tablespoons lemon juice**
1	**tablespoon Dijon mustard**
⅛	**teaspoon garlic powder**
	Pinch cayenne pepper
1½	**cups light mayonnaise**

1. Bring 4 quarts water to boil in large pot. Add macaroni and 1 tablespoon salt and cook, stirring often, until tender. Drain macaroni, rinse with cold water until cool, then drain again briefly, leaving macaroni slightly wet. Transfer to large bowl.

2. Stir in onion, celery, parsley, lemon juice, mustard, garlic powder, and cayenne and let sit until flavors are absorbed, about 2 minutes. Stir in mayonnaise and let sit until salad texture is no longer watery, 5 to 10 minutes. Season with salt and pepper to taste. Serve.

BEFORE → **AFTER**	410 → **250**	27 → **9**	4 → **1.5**
	CALORIES	GRAMS FAT	GRAMS SAT FAT

Pasta Salad

Serves 6

✓ **WHY THIS RECIPE WORKS:** Though it might have "salad" in its title, this deli classic is rarely good-for-you dining. Most versions we've seen are weighed down with a heavy dressing and compensate for bland vegetables and pasta by loading up on the cheese. We were after a lively, fresh pasta salad that included lots of vegetables and was dressed with a zippy, bright-tasting vinaigrette. For the vegetables, we liked a mix of green beans, halved cherry tomatoes, and shredded carrot, which delivered nice, crunchy bites. To streamline our recipe, we used the same water to cook our pasta that we'd used to cook our green beans. For the dressing, we found that a light red wine vinaigrette, flavored with Dijon mustard, garlic, and red pepper flakes, added just the right amount of sweetness and bright acidity. Looking for ways to infuse the vegetables with big flavor, we tossed them with a little salt and a tablespoon of vinegar and let them marinate for a short time while the pasta cooked. Once the pasta was ready, we drained it and added it to the vegetables to take on some flavor, too. Right before serving, we tossed everything with our potent vinaigrette. Our perky pasta salad offered such bright, fresh flavors that we didn't even need to gussy up the dish with a lot of cheese—just ½ cup grated Parmesan did the trick. Instead of penne, other short, bite-size pasta such as fusilli or campanelle can be substituted. This recipe can easily be doubled to serve a crowd.

Salt and pepper
4 ounces green beans, trimmed and cut into 2-inch lengths
4 ounces cherry tomatoes, halved
1 carrot, peeled and shredded
2 tablespoons minced red onion
3 tablespoons red wine vinegar
8 ounces (2½ cups) penne
¼ cup chopped fresh basil
2 teaspoons minced fresh parsley
2 tablespoons extra-virgin olive oil
2 teaspoons Dijon mustard
1 garlic clove, minced
⅛ teaspoon red pepper flakes
1 ounce Parmesan cheese, grated (½ cup)

1. Bring 4 quarts water to boil in large pot. Fill large bowl with ice water. Add 1 tablespoon salt and green beans to boiling water and cook until tender, about 3 minutes. Using slotted spoon, transfer green beans to ice water and let chill for 3 minutes; drain green beans and pat dry with paper towels. In separate large bowl, combine cooked green beans, tomatoes, carrot, onion, 1 tablespoon vinegar, and ¼ teaspoon salt.

2. Return water to boil, stir in pasta, and cook, stirring often, until al dente. Drain pasta and rinse under cold water until cool. Drain pasta well and transfer it to bowl with vegetables. Add basil and parsley and toss to combine.

3. Before serving, whisk remaining 2 tablespoons vinegar, oil, mustard, garlic, and pepper flakes together in small bowl, then pour over salad and toss to combine. Stir in Parmesan and season with salt and pepper to taste. Serve.

BEFORE → **AFTER**   590 → **220** CALORIES   38 → **7** GRAMS FAT   14 → **1.5** GRAMS SAT FAT

Cheese Bread

Makes one 8½-inch loaf; serves 12

✔ **WHY THIS RECIPE WORKS:** The ultimate cheese bread is hearty and addictive, with a tender crumb and moist bites of cheese throughout. But given that cheese, butter, and sour cream are all in the ingredient list, this savory baked good can be off-limits if you're watching fat and calories. Fortunately, we found a way to work this quick bread into the weekly rotation by giving it a makeover. Substituting low-fat cheese and sour cream for the full-fat versions gave us a rubbery bread with zero flavor, so we tried another approach. We kept the full-fat cheese, but reduced the amount slightly, then we swapped the butter for a tablespoon of canola oil and used buttermilk in place of the sour cream. Now our bread boasted a tender crumb and big, cheesy flavor. Adding shredded Parmesan to the batter amped up the savory notes even further, and coating the oiled loaf pan with more Parmesan guaranteed a crisp, cheesy exterior. Shredding the Parmesan on the large holes of a box grater and sprinkling it over the top of this bread adds a nice texture and helps prevent the cheese from burning; do not grate it fine or use pregrated Parmesan. The texture of this bread improves as it cools, so resist the urge to slice the loaf while it is piping hot.

2	ounces Parmesan cheese, shredded (⅔ cup)
2½	cups (12½ ounces) all-purpose flour
1	tablespoon baking powder
1	teaspoon salt
¼	teaspoon dry mustard
⅛	teaspoon cayenne pepper
⅛	teaspoon pepper
3	ounces extra-sharp cheddar cheese, cut into ¼-inch cubes (¾ cup)
1¼	cups buttermilk
1	tablespoon canola oil
1	large egg

1. Adjust oven rack to middle position and heat oven to 350 degrees. Lightly coat 8½ by 4½-inch loaf pan with vegetable oil spray, then sprinkle 3 tablespoons Parmesan evenly over bottom of pan.

2. Whisk flour, baking powder, salt, mustard, cayenne, and pepper together in large bowl. Stir in cheddar and 3 tablespoons Parmesan, breaking up any clumps. In separate bowl, whisk buttermilk, oil, and egg together until smooth. Gently fold buttermilk mixture into flour mixture. (Do not overmix.) Batter will be heavy and thick.

3. Scrape batter into prepared pan and smooth top. Sprinkle remaining Parmesan evenly over top. Bake until golden brown and toothpick inserted into center comes out clean, 45 to 50 minutes, rotating pan halfway through baking. Let loaf cool in pan on wire rack for 5 minutes. Remove loaf from pan and let cool completely on rack, about 1 hour. Serve.

BEFORE → **AFTER**	270 → **160**	12 → **6**	7 → **2.5**
1 SERVING = ⅔-INCH SLICE	CALORIES	GRAMS FAT	GRAMS SAT FAT

Cheesy Garlic Bread

Serves 8

✓ **WHY THIS RECIPE WORKS:** For a light garlic bread that kept the garlicky bite and big crunch, we cooked minced garlic over low heat with just a pat of butter and a bit of water so it would turn into a sticky, golden, spreadable paste. Instead of slathering the bread with a stick of butter, we found a secret ingredient—light mayo—imparted an übercreamy texture. Scoring the bread first ensured our garlic-mayo mixture really soaked in. Shredded reduced-fat Italian cheese offered cheesy flavor and melted nicely under the broiler. To cut the finished garlic bread, place it cheese side down on a cutting board and slice through the crust (rather than the cheese) with a serrated knife; this will ensure the cheesy layer stays in place and doesn't slide off.

5   garlic cloves, minced
1   tablespoon unsalted butter
1   tablespoon plus ½ teaspoon water
½   cup light mayonnaise
¼   teaspoon pepper
1   (16-ounce) loaf Italian bread
6   ounces shredded low-fat Italian cheese blend (1½ cups)

1. Adjust oven rack to lower-middle position and heat oven to 400 degrees. Cook garlic, butter, and ½ teaspoon water together in 8-inch nonstick skillet over low heat, stirring occasionally, until garlic is sticky and straw-colored, 7 to 10 minutes. Transfer to bowl; stir in mayonnaise, pepper, and remaining 1 tablespoon water.

2. Using serrated knife, slice loaf in half horizontally, then score interior crumb crosswise at 1-inch intervals, about ¾-inch deep; do not cut through crust. Spread garlic mixture over cut sides of bread.

3. Sandwich bread halves back together and wrap in aluminum foil. Place on baking sheet; bake for 15 minutes. Unwrap bread and lay, cut sides up, on baking sheet. Continue to bake until just beginning to brown, about 10 minutes longer. Remove bread from oven. Adjust oven rack 8 inches from broiler element and heat broiler.

4. Sprinkle cheese over cut sides of bread; broil until cheese has melted and bread is crisp, 1 to 2 minutes. Transfer bread, cheese side down, to cutting board, cut evenly into 16 pieces, and serve.

QUICK PREP TIP MAKING CHEESY GARLIC BREAD
To help the garlic mixture soak into the bread without using lots of butter, we score the bread. Using a serrated knife, slice the loaf in half horizontally, then score the interior crosswise at 1-inch intervals, about ¾-inch deep; do not cut through the side or bottom of the crust.

BEFORE → **AFTER**	450 → **250**	22 → **9**	13 → **4**
1 SERVING = 2 PIECES	CALORIES	GRAMS FAT	GRAMS SAT FAT

CINNAMON ROLLS

Breakfast and Brunch

Denver Omelets

Serves 2

✔ **WHY THIS RECIPE WORKS:** With its colorful, veggie-laden filling, this hearty omelet might appear to be good-for-you dining. But take one bite, and you'll know this rich, meaty, cheesy affair couldn't possibly be light. To keep the heartiness of this breakfast dish, but lose a significant amount of fat and calories, we started by adjusting the ratio of egg whites to egg yolks. In the end, 3 egg whites to 1 whole egg worked best; though this combination might seem overly lean, it offered a nice, firm texture and full, eggy flavor. A mix of red and green bell peppers gave us both sweetness and vegetal flavor, while garlic and onion provided the aromatic background; sautéing the vegetables in a teaspoon of canola oil helped to build their flavor and soften their texture. Just 2 ounces of ham steak, which we cooked briefly with the vegetables, provided plenty of meaty flavor and salty, savory notes. Adding a dash of hot sauce to the pan with the ham and veggies punched things up a bit. Finally, for the cheese, we opted for Parmesan, which is low in fat and offers such bold flavor that we needed only 2 tablespoons to make an impact. The filling can be doubled if you are making more than two omelets; be sure to have all your ingredients prepared so that you can make the omelets one right after the other. You can substitute ¾ cup of store-bought egg whites for the 6 large whites called for in the recipe.

1	tablespoon canola oil
½	red bell pepper, chopped fine
½	green bell pepper, chopped fine
¼	cup finely chopped onion
	Salt and pepper
2	ounces ham steak, chopped
1	tablespoon minced fresh parsley
1	garlic clove, minced
½	teaspoon hot sauce
2	large eggs plus 6 large whites
2	tablespoons grated Parmesan cheese

1. Heat 1 teaspoon oil in 8-inch nonstick skillet over medium-high heat until shimmering. Add red bell pepper, green bell pepper, onion, and ⅛ teaspoon salt and cook until vegetables are softened, about 5 minutes. Stir in ham and cook until vegetables are lightly browned, about 2 minutes. Stir in parsley, garlic, and hot sauce and cook until fragrant, about 30 seconds; transfer to bowl.

2. Whisk eggs and whites, ⅛ teaspoon salt, and ⅛ teaspoon pepper together in bowl. Wipe now-empty skillet clean, add 1 teaspoon oil, and place over medium heat until shimmering. Add half of egg mixture and stir gently until just beginning to set, 5 to 10 seconds. Using rubber spatula, gently pull cooked eggs back from one edge of skillet and tilt pan, allowing any uncooked egg to run to cleared edge of skillet. Repeat this process until egg on top is mostly set but still moist, about 2 minutes.

3. Remove skillet from heat, sprinkle with 1 tablespoon Parmesan, and let it melt partially, about 10 seconds. Spoon half of ham mixture over half of omelet. Carefully slide filling-topped half of omelet onto plate and, with firm grip, tilt skillet slightly so that remaining omelet folds over top to make half-moon shape. Serve immediately; wipe now-empty skillet clean and repeat with remaining 1 teaspoon oil, egg mixture, Parmesan, and ham mixture.

BEFORE NUMBERS BASED ON: **Western Omelet from Denny's**	BEFORE→**AFTER**	450→**260** CALORIES	32→**14** GRAMS FAT	10→**3** GRAMS SAT FAT

Frittata with Asparagus, Mushrooms, and Goat Cheese

Serves 6

✔ **WHY THIS RECIPE WORKS:** For a light frittata that was moist and hearty and boasted an appealing filling that didn't make the fat and calorie counts spike, we took a cue from our Denver Omelets (page 220) and started by testing various amounts of eggs. A combination of 6 egg whites and 6 whole eggs, plus a few tablespoons of low-fat milk, gave us a frittata that was moist and rich tasting, but it was lacking in the looks department—the resulting frittata was flat and thin. To amp up its volume, we used a two-step cooking method—we jump-started the cooking of the frittata on the stovetop, then finished it under the broiler. This yielded a beautifully puffed, golden brown frittata. For the filling, we skipped the fatty bacon and sausage and opted for more healthful yet still hearty mushrooms and asparagus, which we cooked in a modest amount of olive oil. For a creamy, cheesy element, we included some crumbled goat cheese, which is low in fat but big on flavor. Do not substitute skim milk here. You can substitute ¾ cup of store-bought egg whites for the 6 large whites called for in the recipe. You will need an ovensafe nonstick skillet for this recipe.

6   **large eggs plus 6 large whites**
2   **ounces goat cheese, crumbled (½ cup)**
3   **tablespoons 1 percent low-fat milk**
2   **tablespoons minced fresh parsley**
2   **teaspoons grated lemon zest**
½   **teaspoon salt**
¼   **teaspoon pepper**
2   **teaspoons olive oil**
4   **ounces white mushrooms, trimmed and sliced thin**
1   **small onion, chopped fine**
4   **asparagus spears, trimmed and cut into ¼-inch lengths**
1   **garlic clove, minced**

1. Adjust oven rack 6 inches from broiler element and heat broiler. Whisk eggs and whites, goat cheese, milk, parsley, lemon zest, salt, and pepper together in bowl.

2. Heat oil in 10-inch ovensafe nonstick skillet over medium-high heat until shimmering. Add mushrooms and onion, cover, and cook until mushrooms have released their liquid, about 5 minutes. Uncover, add asparagus, and continue to cook until vegetables are tender and dry, about 2 minutes. Stir in garlic and cook until fragrant, about 30 seconds.

3. Add egg mixture and cook, gently pushing, lifting, and folding it from one side of skillet to other, until large, very wet curds form, about 2 minutes. Shake skillet to distribute eggs evenly and continue to cook, without stirring, until bottom is lightly browned, about 2 minutes. Transfer skillet to oven and broil until frittata has risen and surface is puffed and spotty brown, about 4 minutes.

4. Being careful of hot skillet handle, remove skillet from oven and let stand until eggs in center are cooked but still moist (yet not runny), 1 to 3 minutes. Loosen edges of frittata from skillet with rubber spatula, then gently slide out onto serving platter. Serve warm or at room temperature.

BEFORE → **AFTER**	290 → **150**	18 → **8**	8 → **3**
	CALORIES	GRAMS FAT	GRAMS SAT FAT

Breakfast Strata

Serves 6

✓ **WHY THIS RECIPE WORKS:** Most stratas are rich, cheesy, and ultra-fatty, loaded with butter, eggs, and cream or half-and-half. In our efforts to lighten this popular brunch dish, we first tried using egg whites and a mix of more whites than yolks, plus skim milk. But these versions were all disappointingly lean and unsatisfying. Sticking with whole eggs proved best, and whole milk kept the custard just rich enough. Incorporating chopped spinach provided additional heartiness to the dish, and feta cheese, which is naturally low in fat, was a great alternative to full-fat cheeses and lent our strata a pleasant tangy flavor. Reduced white wine and sautéed aromatics also helped to bump up the flavor. Do not substitute oil for the butter in this recipe as it provides important richness. Do not substitute low-fat or skim milk here.

½   **loaf (6 ounces) French or Italian bread, cut into ½-inch pieces**

1   **tablespoon unsalted butter**

1   **onion, chopped fine**

1   **garlic clove, minced**

10   **ounces frozen spinach, thawed, squeezed dry, and chopped coarse**

½   **cup dry white wine**

6   **large eggs**

1¾   **cups whole milk**

1   **teaspoon salt**

¼   **teaspoon pepper**

6   **ounces feta cheese, crumbled (1½ cups)**

1. Adjust oven rack to middle position and heat oven to 275 degrees. Spread bread pieces out over rimmed baking sheet and bake until thoroughly dry and crisp, 30 to 40 minutes.

2. Melt butter in 10-inch nonstick skillet over medium heat. Add onion and cook until softened, about 5 minutes. Stir in garlic and cook until fragrant, about 30 seconds. Stir in spinach and cook until spinach is heated through, about 2 minutes; transfer to bowl. Add wine to now-empty skillet, bring to simmer over medium-high heat, and cook until it has reduced to ¼ cup, about 3 minutes; set aside to cool separately.

3. Spray 8-inch square baking dish with vegetable oil spray. Whisk eggs, milk, reduced wine, salt, and pepper together in large bowl. Stir in dried bread, spinach mixture, and 1 cup feta until well combined. Pour mixture into prepared baking dish and cover with plastic wrap. Weight strata down with large zipper-lock bag filled with sugar. Refrigerate for 1 to 24 hours.

4. Adjust oven rack to middle position and heat oven to 325 degrees. Remove weight from strata and let stand at room temperature for 20 minutes. Unwrap, sprinkle with remaining ½ cup feta, and bake until surface is puffed and edges pull away slightly from dish, 50 to 55 minutes. Let cool slightly before serving.

BEFORE→**AFTER**	480→**330**	32→**16**	18→**8**
	CALORIES	GRAMS FAT	GRAMS SAT FAT

MAKEOVER SPOTLIGHT: STRATA

1. USE BREAD CUBES RATHER THAN SLICES AND TOAST THEM: Strata is traditionally made with layers of sliced, dried bread; however, we found this didn't work with a lightened custard—the slices weighed the custard down and tasted dense. Dried cubes of bread, on the other hand, didn't overwhelm the delicate texture of the custard and allowed the strata to soufflé slightly during baking. Also, drying the bread helped keep it from disintegrating into the custard. To dry the bread cubes, spread them out over a rimmed baking sheet and bake them in a 275-degree oven until dry and crisp.

2. DITCH THE FATTY CREAM IN FAVOR OF MILK AND TOSS THE BREAD IN THE CUSTARD: For a low-fat yet still creamy and rich custard, we ditched the heavy cream in favor of whole milk. Reduced white wine and sautéed onion and garlic boosted the flavor of our leaner strata. Whereas traditional stratas are built in layers in a baking dish (like a lasagna), we found it best to toss all of the custard, bread cubes, and aromatics together, then pour the mixture into the dish. This helped the bread become evenly soaked through and prevented any pockets of dry bread.

3. WEIGHT THE STRATA AND LET IT REST FOR A CUSTARDY TEXTURE THROUGHOUT: Pressing the strata and letting it sit for at least an hour was key; this gave the dry bread time to absorb the custard so the strata baked up with an even, creamy texture. We found that a large zipper-lock bag full of sugar or dried beans made a great weight. The weighted strata can be refrigerated for up to 24 hours before baking—in fact, the longer the strata rests, the more delicate and flavorful it will be.

4. USE FLAVORFUL, BUT LOWER-FAT, FETA FOR THE CHEESE: Utilizing feta, a flavorful yet less fatty cheese, helped us cut a lot of fat and calories from the dish without sacrificing any flavor. For evenly distributed bites of cheese throughout, we stirred some of the feta into the strata and sprinkled the rest over the top just before baking.

Quiche Lorraine

Serves 8

✔ **WHY THIS RECIPE WORKS:** A buttery, flaky crust paired with a bacony, cheesy custard are what make quiche Lorraine great. They're also what packs each serving with 43 grams of fat. For a rich yet low-fat version, we tried replacing the heavy cream in the custard with a variety of light dairy ingredients. In the end, only buttermilk delivered an ultra-silky texture. A bit of whole milk ensured rich flavor, and some cornstarch helped the custard set. Bacon and cheese are a given in quiche Lorraine, but we had to cut back seriously on the amounts. Four slices of bacon provided plenty of richness and flavor, and a mere ¼ cup of Gruyère added a subtle nutty, cheesy flavor. For a low-fat crust, we tried replacing the butter with fat-free dairy or canola oil mixed with water, but these tests were a flop. Instead, we swapped in olive oil for the butter to cut back on saturated fat and used a tablespoon of rendered bacon fat and grated Parmesan for flavor.

CRUST

4	slices bacon, chopped
1¼	cups (6¼ ounces) all-purpose flour
¼	cup grated Parmesan cheese
1	tablespoon sugar
½	teaspoon salt
½	teaspoon pepper
3	tablespoons olive oil
¼	cup ice water

FILLING

1⅓	cups buttermilk
⅓	cup whole milk
5	large eggs
4	teaspoons cornstarch
½	teaspoon salt
¼	teaspoon pepper
1	ounce Gruyère cheese, shredded (¼ cup)

1. FOR THE CRUST: Spray 9-inch pie plate with vegetable oil spray. Cook bacon in 10-inch skillet over medium-high heat until crisp, about 5 minutes; transfer to paper towel–lined plate and set aside for filling. Measure out and reserve 1 tablespoon rendered bacon fat; discard remaining fat.

2. Adjust oven rack to lowest position and heat oven to 350 degrees. Process flour, 1 tablespoon Parmesan, sugar, salt, and pepper in food processor until combined, about 5 seconds. Add oil and reserved bacon fat and pulse until mixture resembles coarse cornmeal, about 12 pulses. Add water and process until dough begins to clump into large pieces, about 10 seconds. Transfer dough to prepared pie plate and press evenly over bottom using heel of your hand. Using your fingertips, work dough evenly up sides of pie plate until even with plate. Wrap loosely in plastic wrap and freeze until firm, about 30 minutes.

3. Remove plastic wrap, line crust with 12-inch square of greased aluminum foil, and fill with pie weights. Bake until top edge of crust begins to color, about 30 minutes. Remove foil and weights from crust, sprinkle remaining 3 tablespoons Parmesan evenly over top, and continue to bake until cheese melts, about 7 minutes longer; let crust cool for 10 minutes.

4. FOR THE FILLING: Whisk buttermilk, milk, eggs, cornstarch, salt, and pepper together in bowl until smooth. Stir in crisp bacon and Gruyère. Transfer mixture to 4-cup liquid measuring cup. Place warm pie shell on oven rack and carefully pour in filling. Bake until knife inserted about 1 inch from edge comes out clean and center is set but still soft, 40 to 45 minutes. Let cool on wire rack for 15 minutes before serving.

BEFORE NUMBERS BASED ON:	BEFORE → **AFTER**	508 → **250**	43 → **14**	22.5 → **4.5**
Marie's Classic Quiche from Marie Callender's		CALORIES	GRAMS FAT	GRAMS SAT FAT

Corned Beef Hash with Poached Eggs

Serves 4

✔ **WHY THIS RECIPE WORKS:** What's the key to a truly great hash with deep, hearty flavor? Getting a well-browned, crisp exterior on the potatoes. To achieve the perfect crust without a lot of oil, we jump-started the cooking of our spuds by microwaving them. Once they were softened, we added them to the skillet with some chopped corned beef—for convenience's sake, we started with thin slices from the deli counter—and sautéed aromatics so they would brown. Chicken broth and low-fat sour cream helped add flavor, moisture, and richness without a lot of fat. Packing the hash down in the skillet, then flipping it a few minutes later, guaranteed it had a nice crust on all sides. For the eggs, we simply made a few indentations in our hash, nestled them in, covered the pan, and cooked it all until the eggs were just set.

2	pounds russet potatoes, peeled and cut into ½-inch pieces
1	tablespoon olive oil
	Salt and pepper
1	onion, chopped fine
2	garlic cloves, minced
12	ounces thinly sliced deli corned beef, chopped
⅓	cup low-sodium chicken broth
⅓	cup low-fat sour cream
½	teaspoon hot sauce
4	scallions, sliced thin
4	large eggs

1. Toss potatoes with 1 teaspoon oil, ¼ teaspoon salt, and ¼ teaspoon pepper in bowl. Cover and microwave until potatoes are softened, about 8 minutes, stirring halfway through cooking.

2. Heat remaining 2 teaspoons oil in 12-inch nonstick skillet over medium-high heat until shimmering. Add onion and cook until softened and lightly browned, about 5 minutes. Stir in garlic and cook until fragrant, about 30 seconds. Stir in microwaved potatoes and corned beef. Whisk broth, sour cream, and hot sauce together in bowl, then add to skillet. Using back of spatula, gently pack potato mixture into skillet and cook undisturbed, until liquid has nearly evaporated, about 5 minutes. Flip hash, one portion at a time, and lightly repack into skillet. Repeat flipping process every few minutes until hash is nicely browned, 6 to 8 minutes.

3. Stir in scallions and lightly repack hash into pan. Make four indentations (about 2 inches wide) in surface of hash. Crack 1 egg into each indentation and season with salt and pepper. Cover, reduce heat to medium-low, and cook until eggs are just set, 3 to 5 minutes. Remove from heat and serve.

QUICK PREP TIP
POACHING EGGS ON HASH
Make four indentations (about 2 inches wide) in surface of hash. Crack 1 egg into each indentation and season with salt and pepper. Cover, reduce heat to medium-low, and cook until eggs are just set.

BEFORE → **AFTER**	580 → **420**	31 → **12**	12 → **3.5**
	CALORIES	GRAMS FAT	GRAMS SAT FAT

Eggs Benedict

Serves 4

✔ **WHY THIS RECIPE WORKS:** It's no surprise this brunch classic is a nutritional nightmare. After all, it's topped off with hollandaise sauce, which is made from egg yolks and butter. For a low-fat yet light and creamy sauce, we cut back on both and tried adding skim milk, low-fat milk, buttermilk, and even chicken broth. Only buttermilk, plus a single egg and one pat of butter, gave us an ultra-flavorful sauce that was luxurious and creamy. A small amount of cornstarch worked to thicken the mixture nicely.

- 4 English muffins, split in half, toasted, and still warm
- 8 (½-ounce) slices Canadian bacon, about ⅛ inch thick
- ¾ cup buttermilk
- 9 large eggs
- 2 teaspoons cornstarch
   Salt
   Pinch cayenne pepper
- 1 tablespoon unsalted butter
- ½ teaspoon lemon juice
- 2 tablespoons white vinegar

1. Adjust oven rack to middle position and heat oven to 250 degrees. Arrange toasted English muffins and ham on baking sheet separately and keep warm in oven.

2. Whisk buttermilk, 1 egg, cornstarch, ¼ teaspoon salt, and cayenne together in small saucepan until smooth. Bring to simmer over medium-low heat, whisking often, and cook until sauce is thickened, about 30 seconds. Off heat, whisk in butter and lemon juice; cover and keep warm. (If necessary, thin sauce with a few drops of warm water before serving.)

3. Fill 12-inch skillet nearly to rim with water. Add vinegar and 1 teaspoon salt and bring to boil. Meanwhile, crack remaining 8 eggs into four teacups (2 eggs per cup). Reduce water to simmer. Gently tip cups so eggs slide into skillet simultaneously. Remove skillet from heat, cover, and poach eggs until whites are set but yolks are still slightly runny, about 4 minutes (poach 30 seconds longer for firm yolks).

4. When eggs are cooked, arrange 1 ham slice on top of each English muffin half. Using slotted spoon, gently separate and lift poached eggs from water and let drain before laying them on top of ham. Spoon 2 tablespoons hollandaise over each egg. Serve immediately.

QUICK PREP TIP
POURING EGGS INTO A SKILLET
Crack two eggs into each of four teacups and tip cups, simultaneously, into simmering water.

BEFORE NUMBERS BASED ON:
Eggs Benedict from IHOP

BEFORE → **AFTER**   700 → **390** CALORIES   37 → **17** GRAMS FAT   18.5 → **6** GRAMS SAT FAT

Sausage, Egg, and Cheese Breakfast Sandwiches

Serves 4

✔️ **WHY THIS RECIPE WORKS:** A staple on the menu of any fast-food restaurant or greasy spoon, breakfast sandwiches, though small and compact, pack a nutritional wallop. Typically loaded with eggs, sausage, and cheese, this heavyweight clocks in at over 500 calories and almost 35 grams of fat. For a lighter, but just as satisfying, start to our day, we began by cutting out some of the egg yolks. Two whole eggs plus 6 egg whites delivered a flavorful but substantially lighter sandwich; cutting back on the yolks any further gave us a sandwich with rubbery, flavorless eggs. Cooking the eggs in canola oil rather than butter helped to trim the saturated fat count. Swapping out the fatty pork sausage patties for the leaner turkey variety, and full-fat American cheese for reduced-fat cheese, also worked to lighten the sandwich; since turkey sausage patties tend to be small, we used 1½ patties per sandwich to guarantee they were big, thick, and meaty. Because there are multiple components, putting together a batch of hot egg sandwiches was a bit tricky to navigate. To simplify assembly, we toasted our English muffins and cooked our sausage patties, then kept them warm in the oven while we cooked the eggs. This ensured our breakfast sandwiches hit the table nice and toasty—just like they would at the local diner. We use Jimmy Dean Heat 'N Serve Turkey Sausage Patties in the test kitchen because they are available locally; other brands of turkey sausage may affect the nutritional information. For the cheese, we like Boar's Head 25 Percent Lower Fat American Cheese, which can be found at the deli counter. You can substitute ¾ cup of store-bought egg whites for the 6 large whites called for in the recipe.

4	English muffins, split in half, toasted, and still warm
6	(1-ounce) turkey breakfast sausage patties, prepared according to package instructions and halved
2	large eggs plus 6 large whites
¼	teaspoon salt
¼	teaspoon pepper
1	teaspoon canola oil
4	slices reduced-fat American cheese

1. Adjust oven rack to middle position and heat oven to 250 degrees. Arrange toasted English muffins and sausage on baking sheet separately and keep warm in oven.

2. Whisk eggs and whites, salt, and pepper together in bowl. Heat oil in 10-inch nonstick skillet over medium-high heat until shimmering. Add egg mixture and cook, gently pushing, lifting, and folding it from one side of skillet to other, until large, very wet curds form, about 2 minutes. Reduce heat to low and shake skillet to distribute eggs evenly. Cover and continue to cook until top of omelet is set, about 5 minutes.

3. Using rubber spatula, loosen edge of omelet from skillet and gently slide it out onto cutting board. Cut omelet into quarters, then fold in corners to make portions that fit nicely on English muffins. Assemble sandwiches by layering 1 portion omelet, 1 slice cheese, and 3 sausage halves between toasted English muffins. Serve immediately.

BEFORE NUMBERS BASED ON: Sausage, Egg, and Cheese English-Muffin Breakfast Sandwich from Dunkin' Donuts	BEFORE → **AFTER**	510 → **340** CALORIES	33 → **14** GRAMS FAT	12 → **5** GRAMS SAT FAT

Crumb Coffee Cake

Serves 9

✔ **WHY THIS RECIPE WORKS:** A great greeting for weekend brunch guests is a slice of moist, tender coffee cake boasting a buttery, crunchy topping. But if that greeting contains 19 grams of fat and 440 calories, it doesn't seem as friendly, does it? We wanted to make over our coffee cake so it still tasted rich and buttery—but wasn't a calorie bomb. A lot of recipes go overboard on the topping, which is typically made of butter, white and brown sugars, flour, and cinnamon, so that's where we started cutting back. We also tried cutting back on the white sugar in the cake, but this led to a dry cake. Adding in a small amount of brown sugar kept the cake moist, and allowed us to get away with a smaller amount of white sugar. Slashing the butter to just 4 tablespoons helped trim fat, but we had to find another way to add back some moisture and tenderness. We tried a number of low-fat dairy substitutes, but only buttermilk did the trick, contributing the perfect richness as well as a nice, tangy flavor. Since many coffee shop crumb cakes include a rich, cinnamony swirl in the middle of the cake, we opted to do the same. But rather than ratchet up the fat count with more butter, we opted for a simple filling of apple butter, which contributed more moisture and echoed the warm spice notes of our cake.

 2 cups (10 ounces) all-purpose flour
 ¾ cup packed (5¼ ounces) light brown sugar
 ½ cup (3½ ounces) granulated sugar
 ½ teaspoon salt
 ½ teaspoon baking powder
 ¼ teaspoon baking soda
 ¾ cup buttermilk
 4 tablespoons unsalted butter, melted and cooled
 1 large egg
 1 teaspoon vanilla extract
 ⅓ cup apple butter
 1 teaspoon ground cinnamon

1. Adjust oven rack to middle position and heat oven to 350 degrees. Spray 8-inch square baking pan with vegetable oil spray.

2. Whisk flour, ½ cup brown sugar, granulated sugar, salt, baking powder, and baking soda together in large bowl. Measure out and reserve ¼ cup of mixture separately for topping. In separate bowl, whisk buttermilk, 3 tablespoons melted butter, egg, and vanilla together. Gently fold buttermilk mixture into remaining flour mixture with rubber spatula until just combined; do not overmix. Smooth half of batter into prepared pan, then spread apple butter evenly over top. Dollop remaining batter into pan and smooth top.

3. Stir cinnamon and remaining ¼ cup brown sugar into reserved mixture for topping. Add remaining 1 tablespoon melted butter and toss with fork to make streusel; sprinkle over top of cake.

4. Bake until streusel is golden and toothpick inserted into center of cake comes out clean, 30 to 35 minutes, rotating pan halfway through baking. Let cake cool completely in pan on wire rack, about 2 hours. Serve.

BEFORE NUMBERS BASED ON: **Classic Coffee Cake from Starbucks** | BEFORE→**AFTER** 440→**290** CALORIES | 19→**6** GRAMS FAT | 11→**3.5** GRAMS SAT FAT

Blueberry Muffins

Makes 12 muffins

✓ **WHY THIS RECIPE WORKS:** Compared with popular breakfast treats like doughnuts or sausage-and-egg biscuit sandwiches, blueberry muffins certainly seem like a healthful option—after all, they're full of berries. But the truth is that one of these super-sized muffins from the corner coffee shop can contain almost 500 calories. We knew we could do better. Cutting back on the butter trimmed fat and calories, but it also made our muffins a bit bland and tough. Switching up the mixing method gave us muffins with a more delicate crumb; instead of simply stirring the wet ingredients into the dry, we creamed the butter with the sugar, then beat in the eggs and dry ingredients. This made for a lighter and more airy batter. To enhance the muffins' texture further, we also swapped in lower-protein cake flour for a portion of the all-purpose flour and included a full tablespoon of baking powder and ½ teaspoon of baking soda for plenty of lift. When it came to the dairy, we needed something that would give our muffins a moist crumb and nice tang. Low-fat sour cream produced gummy muffins, but low-fat yogurt did the trick. Once the blueberries were folded in and the batter was portioned, we finished them off with a sprinkling of sugar to help with browning and give the muffin tops a pleasant bakery-style crunch. Frozen blueberries can be substituted for the fresh blueberries; rinse and dry the frozen berries (do not thaw) before folding into batter.

2	cups (10 ounces) all-purpose flour
1	cup (4 ounces) cake flour
1	tablespoon baking powder
½	teaspoon baking soda
¾	teaspoon salt
1	cup (7 ounces) plus 1 tablespoon sugar
4	tablespoons unsalted butter, softened
2	large eggs
1	teaspoon grated lemon zest plus 2 teaspoons juice
1	teaspoon vanilla extract
1½	cups plain low-fat yogurt
10	ounces (2 cups) blueberries

1. Adjust oven rack to upper-middle position and heat oven to 425 degrees. Spray 12-cup muffin tin with vegetable oil spray. Whisk all-purpose flour, cake flour, baking powder, baking soda, salt, and ¼ cup sugar together in bowl.

2. Using stand mixer fitted with paddle, beat butter and ¾ cup sugar on medium-high speed until pale and fluffy, 3 to 6 minutes. Add eggs, 1 at a time, and beat until combined. Add lemon zest and juice and vanilla and beat until combined. Reduce speed to low and add flour mixture in 3 additions, alternating with 3 additions of yogurt, scraping down bowl as needed; do not overmix. Using rubber spatula, give batter final stir by hand, then gently fold in blueberries.

3. Using greased ½-cup measure, portion batter into prepared muffin cups (batter should fill cups completely; divide any remaining batter evenly between cups). Sprinkle remaining 1 tablespoon sugar over tops.

4. Bake until golden brown and toothpick inserted in center comes out clean, 17 to 19 minutes, rotating pan halfway through baking. Let muffins cool in pan on wire rack for 5 minutes, then flip out onto rack and let cool for 10 minutes before serving.

BEFORE NUMBERS BASED ON: **Blueberry Muffin from Dunkin' Donuts**	BEFORE → **AFTER**	460 → **250** CALORIES	15 → **5** GRAMS FAT	3 → **3** GRAMS SAT FAT

Buttermilk Biscuits

Makes 12 biscuits

✔ **WHY THIS RECIPE WORKS:** A tender, golden buttermilk biscuit fresh from the oven is its own advertisement. But even without a slather of butter or jam, one average-sized biscuit racks up the fat and calories, thanks to generous amounts of butter and shortening. To lighten ours significantly, we started by cutting back on the butter and looking for a stand-in for the shortening. We tried several options, including canola oil, low-fat sour cream, low-fat yogurt, and reduced-fat cream cheese. The latter worked best, giving our biscuits an underlying rich and creamy flavor. For an ultra-fluffy texture, we froze the butter and cream cheese for an hour; this way, when combined with the flour and other dry ingredients in the food processor, the butter and cream cheese broke into small pieces but didn't disappear completely. When the biscuits were baked, these bits of fat melted and created pockets of steam that contributed to their fluffy, flaky charm.

4	tablespoons unsalted butter, cut into ½-inch pieces
1½	ounces ⅓ less fat cream cheese (neufchatel), cut into ½-inch pieces
3	cups (15 ounces) all-purpose flour
1	tablespoon sugar
1	tablespoon baking powder
½	teaspoon baking soda
¾	teaspoon salt
1¼	cups buttermilk

1. Place butter and cream cheese on plate and freeze until cheese is solid, about 1 hour; do not overfreeze. Adjust oven rack to middle position and heat oven to 450 degrees. Line baking sheet with parchment paper.

2. Process flour, sugar, baking powder, baking soda, and salt together in food processor until combined, about 5 seconds. Scatter frozen butter and cream cheese evenly over top and pulse until mixture resembles coarse cornmeal, about 15 pulses; transfer to large bowl.

3. Stir in buttermilk with rubber spatula until dough comes together. Turn dough out onto lightly floured counter and knead until just smooth and no longer shaggy, 8 to 10 times. Pat dough into 9-inch circle, about ¾ inch thick.

4. Using floured 2½-inch biscuit cutter, stamp out 12 biscuits, gently patting dough scraps back into uniform ¾-inch-thick piece as needed. Arrange biscuits upside down on prepared baking sheet, spaced 1½ inches apart.

5. Bake until biscuits begin to rise, about 5 minutes. Rotate sheet, reduce oven temperature to 400 degrees, and continue to bake until tops and bottoms are golden brown, 12 to 15 minutes longer. Transfer biscuits to wire rack and let cool for 10 minutes before serving.

BEFORE → **AFTER**	300 → **160** CALORIES	16 → **4.5** GRAMS FAT	9 → **3** GRAMS SAT FAT

Cinnamon Rolls

Makes 12 rolls

✓ **WHY THIS RECIPE WORKS:** With their rich dough, buttery cinnamon filling, and gooey cream cheese icing, what's not to love about cinnamon rolls? Well, there is the hefty fat and calorie count to consider—around 15 grams of fat and at least 410 calories in every roll. For a low-fat version, we cut back on the butter. Just 2 tablespoons provided ample richness and moisture in our dough when combined with skim milk and maple syrup. Brown sugar kept our filling moist so we could slash the butter to a pat. Finally, for the icing, we omitted the butter altogether and turned to reduced-fat cream cheese.

3¾ cups (18¾ ounces) all-purpose flour

2¼ teaspoons instant or rapid-rise yeast
Salt

1⅓ cups skim milk, heated to 110 degrees, plus 1 tablespoon

3 tablespoons maple syrup

3 tablespoons unsalted butter, melted

½ cup packed (3½ ounces) dark brown sugar

¼ cup (1¾ ounces) granulated sugar

2 teaspoons ground cinnamon

1 cup (4 ounces) confectioners' sugar

2 ounces ⅓ less fat cream cheese (neufchatel)

½ teaspoon vanilla extract

1. Combine 3½ cups flour, yeast, and 1 teaspoon salt in stand mixer fitted with dough hook. Combine 1⅓ cups warm milk, maple syrup, and 2 tablespoons melted butter in liquid measure. With stand mixer on low speed, slowly add milk mixture to flour mixture until dough forms, about 2 minutes. Increase speed to medium-low and knead until dough is shiny and smooth, 4 to 6 minutes. (If dough appears very sticky after 4 minutes of kneading, add remaining ¼ cup flour as needed.)

2. Transfer dough to floured counter and knead briefly by hand into smooth ball. Place dough in large greased bowl, cover with plastic wrap, and let rise at room temperature until doubled, 2 to 2½ hours. Meanwhile, combine brown sugar, granulated sugar, cinnamon, ⅛ teaspoon salt, and remaining 1 tablespoon melted butter in separate bowl.

3. Spray 13 by 9-inch baking dish with vegetable oil spray. Transfer dough to floured counter and roll into 18 by 12-inch rectangle, long side facing you. Mist dough with water and sprinkle with sugar mixture, leaving ½-inch border at top edge; press on sugar to adhere. Using bench scraper, roll dough into tight 18-inch log. Pinch seam closed and roll seam side down; even ends and reshape as needed.

4. Using serrated knife, slice dough crosswise into 12 rolls; lay cut side up in prepared dish. Cover loosely with greased plastic wrap and let rolls rise at room temperature until nearly doubled, 1 to 1½ hours.

5. Adjust oven rack to middle position and heat oven to 350 degrees. Bake rolls until deep golden, 20 to 25 minutes. Flip rolls onto wire rack, let cool for 10 minutes, and invert rolls. Whisk confectioners' sugar, cream cheese, vanilla, and remaining 1 tablespoon milk together until smooth; spread over tops of rolls. Serve.

BEFORE NUMBERS BASED ON: Iced Cinnamon Roll from Au Bon Pain	BEFORE → **AFTER**	410 → **280** CALORIES	15 → **4** GRAMS FAT	8 → **2.5** GRAMS SAT FAT

MAKEOVER SPOTLIGHT:
CINNAMON ROLLS

1. CUT BACK ON THE BUTTER IN THE DOUGH AND ADD MAPLE SYRUP FOR MOISTURE: Most cinnamon rolls start with a rich yeast dough that's been loaded up with butter, but we found we could cut back to just 2 tablespoons in our dough. Substituting maple syrup for the usual granulated sugar helped add back some moisture, and swapping out the whole milk for skim allowed us to trim even more fat from our recipe.

2. MAKE A FLAVORFUL, MOIST FILLING—WITHOUT A LOT OF BUTTER—BY ADDING BROWN SUGAR AND WATER: Cinnamon rolls also call for lots of butter in the filling to help keep it moist and adhere it to the dough. To cut back on the butter, we added brown sugar, which kept the filling moist. Misting the dough lightly with water ensured the filling stuck to it. After rolling the dough into an 18 by 12-inch rectangle, mist it with water and sprinkle it with the sugar mixture, leaving a ½-inch border at the top edge. Press on the sugar to adhere, then roll the dough into a tight 18-inch log.

3. SLICE THE LOG INTO 12 EVEN ROLLS AND BAKE: Cutting the filled log into 12 even rolls ensured that they cooked through evenly; if some are larger or smaller, they will bake up unevenly and the nutritional information will be inaccurate. To slice the log, we used a serrated knife; when we tried to use any other type of knife, we crushed the soft dough. Because the rolls are fragile, it's important to use a light hand. Once they are sliced, arrange them cut side up in a greased 13 by 9-inch baking dish.

4. FOR A CREAMY YET LOW-FAT ICING, DITCH THE BUTTER AND USE REDUCED-FAT CREAM CHEESE: The creamy blanket of frosting is traditionally made with butter, cream cheese, and confectioners' sugar. The butter was quick to go in our lightened version, but replacing the full-fat cream cheese took more effort. We tried several options, but reduced-fat cream cheese, which offered a creamy texture and tangy flavor, worked best. We also used far less than most recipes call for and made the icing easier to spread by adding a little skim milk. After the baked rolls have cooled, spread the icing over the top.

Banana Bread

Serves 12

✔ **WHY THIS RECIPE WORKS:** Good banana bread is soft, moist, and full of flavor—thanks in part to a lot of butter or vegetable oil. For a leaner take on this easy quick bread, we opted for butter, which offered more flavor than oil, and cut back, pat by pat, until we were down to just 3 tablespoons. To help maintain a tender loaf without adding more fat, we swapped out some of the all-purpose flour for lower-protein cake flour. Adding a good helping of baking powder and baking soda provided plenty of lift. Next, we tried incorporating various dairy ingredients—we tested everything from milk and buttermilk to low-fat sour cream and low-fat yogurt—to ensure our banana bread was plenty moist. Low-fat yogurt came out on top; it let the banana flavor (three bananas provided enough tropical punch) take center stage in our loaf and helped give it structure. At last, we had a moist, rich banana bread that was loaded with banana flavor—and tasters couldn't even tell it was light.

1½ cups (7½ ounces) all-purpose flour

½ cup (2 ounces) cake flour

¾ cup (5¼ ounces) sugar

1 teaspoon baking powder

1 teaspoon baking soda

½ teaspoon salt

3 very ripe bananas, peeled and mashed well (1½ cups)

3 tablespoons unsalted butter, melted and cooled

2 large eggs

¼ cup plain low-fat yogurt

1 teaspoon vanilla extract

¼ cup walnuts, toasted and chopped coarse

1. Adjust oven rack to middle position and heat oven to 325 degrees. Spray 8½ by 4½-inch loaf pan with vegetable oil spray.

2. Whisk all-purpose flour, cake flour, sugar, baking powder, baking soda, and salt together in large bowl. In separate bowl, whisk mashed bananas, melted butter, eggs, yogurt, and vanilla together. Gently fold banana mixture and walnuts into flour mixture with rubber spatula until just combined; do not overmix.

3. Scrape batter into prepared pan and smooth top. Bake until golden brown and toothpick inserted into center comes out clean, 55 to 65 minutes, rotating pan halfway through baking. Let loaf cool in pan on wire rack for 10 minutes, then turn out onto rack and let cool for 1 hour before serving.

BEFORE → **AFTER**	280 → **200**	13 → **5**	4.5 → **2**
1 SERVING = ⅔-INCH SLICE	CALORIES	GRAMS FAT	GRAMS SAT FAT

Granola

Makes 6 cups; serves 12

☑ **WHY THIS RECIPE WORKS:** Nuts, grains, and dried fruit sound virtuous enough, but when they're combined to make granola, they turn into something that is anything but innocent. Most granolas contain so much butter and oil, they should be sold in the cookie aisle at the supermarket, not in the cereal aisle. We set out to create a recipe with big, crunchy clusters of granola, with just the right amount of sweetness and with a ratio of grains to nuts that didn't tip the scale. We started by narrowing our ingredient list to oats, which retained their hearty texture even after a stint in the oven, and a moderate amount of almonds and walnuts. We also included ¼ cup of sunflower seeds. First, we toasted our ingredients in a skillet in just 3 tablespoons of oil—not ½ cup, as other recipes do. Adding our nuts, oats, and seeds to the pan in stages gave us a jump start on the intense, toasted flavor we were after. Once mixed with a little honey to bind everything together, our granola needed just 20 minutes in the oven to finish cooking. To our already flavor-packed granola, we added raisins for some extra contrast and chew. Do not substitute quick-cooking or instant rolled oats in this recipe, or the granola will taste sandy rather than crunchy.

¼	**cup slivered almonds**
¼	**cup walnuts, chopped coarse**
3	**cups (9 ounces) old-fashioned rolled oats**
3	**tablespoons canola oil**
¼	**cup sunflower seeds**
½	**cup honey**
¼	**teaspoon salt**
1	**cup raisins**

1. Adjust oven rack to middle position and heat oven to 325 degrees. Toast almonds and walnuts in 12-inch skillet over medium heat, stirring often, until fragrant and beginning to darken, about 5 minutes. Stir in oats and oil and continue to toast until oats begin to turn golden, about 2 minutes. Stir in sunflower seeds and continue to toast until mixture turns golden, about 2 minutes.

2. Off heat, stir in honey and salt until granola is well coated. Spread granola evenly over rimmed baking sheet. Bake, stirring every few minutes, until light golden brown, 15 to 20 minutes.

3. Stir in raisins. With spatula, push granola onto one half of baking sheet and press gently into ½-inch-thick slab. Let granola cool to room temperature, about 30 minutes. Loosen dried granola with spatula, break into small clusters, and serve.

BEFORE → **AFTER**	320 → **230**	16 → **8**	1.5 → **1**
1 SERVING = ½ CUP	CALORIES	GRAMS FAT	GRAMS SAT FAT

CHOCOLATE CUPCAKES

Chocolate Desserts

Chewy Chocolate Cookies

Makes 24 cookies

✔ **WHY THIS RECIPE WORKS:** These cookies get their ultra-rich, intense chocolate flavor and chewy, moist texture from lots of chocolate and butter—which makes for one fatty cookie. Once we cut back on the fat in our lightened cookies, however, we found we had some serious gaps to fill in. To bring back the big chocolate flavor, we went up to a full cup of cocoa powder, which amped up the rich flavor without adding much in the way of fat. In addition, stirring just 2 ounces of finely chopped chocolate into the dough ensured that every bite offered nice bursts of chocolate. For the right texture, we found using melted butter and a good dose of dark brown sugar (twice the amount of the granulated sugar) delivered moist cookies with a good amount of chew. Plus, the brown sugar offered a hint of caramel flavor that enhanced the chocolate taste without overwhelming it. Pressing the cookies flat before baking proved key because there isn't any extra fat in the dough to help them spread on their own in the oven. Finally, underbaking the cookies slightly ensures that they don't taste dry and tough; the cookies will finish baking and set up as they cool.

1   **cup (5 ounces) all-purpose flour**
1   **cup (3 ounces) cocoa**
½   **teaspoon baking soda**
¼   **teaspoon salt**
1   **cup packed (7 ounces) dark brown sugar**
½   **cup (3½ ounces) granulated sugar**
2   **large eggs**
5   **tablespoons unsalted butter, melted and cooled**
1   **teaspoon vanilla extract**
2   **ounces bittersweet chocolate, chopped fine**

1. Adjust oven racks to upper-middle and lower-middle positions and heat oven to 375 degrees. Line 2 baking sheets with parchment paper. Whisk flour, cocoa, baking soda, and salt together in bowl.

2. In large bowl, whisk brown sugar, granulated sugar, eggs, melted butter, and vanilla together until well combined and smooth. Gently stir in flour mixture with rubber spatula until soft dough forms. Stir in chopped chocolate.

3. Working with generous 1 tablespoon dough at a time, roll dough into balls using wet hands and place 2 inches apart on prepared sheets, 12 cookies per sheet. Using bottom of slightly wet drinking glass, press cookies ½ inch thick.

4. Bake cookies until edges are just set but centers are still soft and look underdone, 10 to 12 minutes, switching and rotating sheets halfway through baking. Let cookies cool slightly on sheets. Serve warm or at room temperature.

BEFORE → **AFTER**	210 → **110**	13 → **3.5**	8 → **2**
	CALORIES	GRAMS FAT	GRAMS SAT FAT

Fudgy Brownies

Makes 16 brownies

✔ **WHY THIS RECIPE WORKS:** Most low-fat brownie recipes deliver dry, flavorless squares, so we set out to develop our own recipe for a great brownie that was rich and fudgy—and low in fat. First, we scaled back on the chocolate to just 2 ounces; increasing the amount of cocoa helped to boost the flavor in the absence of a lot of chocolate. We also reduced the amount of butter significantly by replacing some of it with low-fat sour cream. While not a typical brownie ingredient, the sour cream proved a great substitute for excess butter, adding moisture without affecting the flavor. Eliminating an egg yolk helped slash even more fat without adversely affecting the texture. Finally, we found a secret ingredient in our pantry that helped our brownies taste ultra-fudgy without costing us a lot of extra fat or calories: chocolate syrup. Just 1 tablespoon ensured our brownies were moist and fudgy, not dry and cakey. Be sure not to overbake the brownies or else they will lose their fudgy texture. For more information on making a foil sling, see page 267.

2 ounces bittersweet chocolate, chopped
2 tablespoons unsalted butter
¾ cup (3¾ ounces) all-purpose flour
⅓ cup (1 ounce) cocoa
½ teaspoon baking powder
¼ teaspoon salt
1 cup (7 ounces) sugar
2 tablespoons low-fat sour cream
1 tablespoon chocolate syrup
1 large egg plus 1 large white
2 teaspoons vanilla extract

1. Adjust oven rack to middle position and heat oven to 350 degrees. Make foil sling for 8-inch square baking pan by folding 2 long sheets of aluminum foil so each is 8 inches wide. Lay sheets of foil in pan perpendicular to each other, with extra foil hanging over edges of pan. Push foil into corners and up sides of pan, smoothing foil flush to pan. Spray pan with vegetable oil spray.

2. Microwave chocolate and butter together in covered bowl, stirring occasionally, until melted and smooth, 1 to 3 minutes; transfer to large bowl and let cool slightly. In separate bowl, whisk flour, cocoa, baking powder, and salt together.

3. Whisk sugar, sour cream, chocolate syrup, egg, egg white, and vanilla into melted chocolate. Fold in flour mixture until just incorporated. Scrape batter into prepared pan and smooth top.

4. Bake brownies until toothpick inserted in center comes out with few moist crumbs attached, 20 to 25 minutes, rotating pan halfway through baking. Let brownies cool completely in pan on wire rack, about 2 hours. Remove brownies from pan using foil sling, cut into 16 squares, and serve.

BEFORE → **AFTER**	220 → **110** CALORIES	11 → **3** GRAMS FAT	7 → **1.5** GRAMS SAT FAT

Whoopie Pies

Makes 8 whoopie pies

✔ **WHY THIS RECIPE WORKS:** With one whoopie pie clocking in at 740 calories and 42 grams of fat, this classic dessert is a definite diet-killer. To lighten our whoopie pies, we started with the cookie, which should be cakey and tender. Since we had just developed a recipe for low-fat chocolate cookies, we began there; swapping in more flour for some of the sugar and adding a splash of water made the texture plenty cakey. Finding a replacement for the creamy filling, however, was much trickier and took dozens of tests to get right. Most recipes call for butter or shortening, confectioners' sugar, and Marshmallow Fluff, but we knew trimming serious fat and calories from this dessert would require scaling back on the butter and sugar. We tried a number of combinations, including everything from Marshmallow Fluff and melted marshmallows to reduced-fat cream cheese, whipped topping, and a confectioners' sugar–milk mixture, plus varying amounts of butter. In the end, we found three ingredients that delivered the perfect low-fat whoopie pie filling: reduced-fat cream cheese, store-bought vanilla frosting, and whipped topping. The cream cheese offered a subtle tangy flavor, the frosting (which is surprisingly low in fat) gave our filling a rich, creamy texture, and the whipped topping guaranteed it was light and fluffy. For one final tweak, we stirred in a dash of vanilla, which boosted the flavor of the filling so it could stand up to the ultra-chocolaty cookies.

1 **cup (3 ounces) cocoa**
1 **cup warm tap water**
1½ **cups (7½ ounces) all-purpose flour**
½ **teaspoon baking soda**
¼ **teaspoon salt**
1 **cup packed (7 ounces) dark brown sugar**
5 **tablespoons unsalted butter, melted and cooled**
1¼ **teaspoons vanilla extract**
2 **large eggs**
2 **ounces ⅓ less fat cream cheese (neufchatel)**
⅔ **cup store-bought vanilla frosting**
⅔ **cup Cool Whip Whipped Topping**

1. Adjust oven racks to upper-middle and lower-middle positions and heat oven to 375 degrees. Line 2 baking sheets with parchment paper. Whisk cocoa and water together in bowl. In separate bowl, whisk flour, baking soda, and salt together.

2. In large bowl, whisk sugar, melted butter, and 1 teaspoon vanilla together until incorporated. Whisk in eggs and cocoa mixture until smooth. Gently stir in flour mixture with rubber spatula until soft dough forms.

3. Using greased ¼-cup measure, drop scant ¼-cup scoops of batter 2 inches apart on prepared baking sheets (you should have 16 cakes total). Bake cakes until toothpick inserted in center comes out clean, about 14 minutes, switching and rotating sheets halfway through baking. Let cakes cool completely on sheets.

4. Meanwhile, microwave cream cheese in covered bowl until very soft, about 20 seconds, then transfer to large bowl. Whisk in frosting and remaining ¼ teaspoon vanilla, then gently fold in Cool Whip until well combined. Cover and refrigerate until stiff, about 30 minutes. Assemble 8 sandwich cookies by spreading about 2½ tablespoons of filling between 2 cookies. Serve.

BEFORE → **AFTER**	740 → **390**	42 → **15**	9 → **8**
	CALORIES	GRAMS FAT	GRAMS SAT FAT

Chocolate Cupcakes

Makes 12 cupcakes

✓ **WHY THIS RECIPE WORKS:** A cupcake piled high with creamy chocolate buttercream frosting is the perfect single-serving dessert, yet on average it packs in more than 25 grams of fat, leaving plenty of room for improvement. To start, we tried a number of low-fat cupcake recipes that included "alternative" ingredients like prunes or applesauce, but they were overwhelmingly disappointing, giving us dry, crumbly cakes. Instead, we worked with a more traditional recipe and trimmed the fat by reducing the amount of chocolate and switching from butter to canola oil, which is lower in saturated fat. Adding a hefty dose of cocoa along with a bit of instant espresso powder boosted the chocolate flavor immensely, and swapping in bread flour for the all-purpose flour provided plenty of lift and structure to our lean batter. Finally, topping the cakes with a simple yet ultra-creamy frosting made of confectioners' sugar instead of an over-the-top buttercream frosting helped to make these cupcakes a reasonable, yet still indulgent, treat. You can substitute ¾ cup hot coffee for the boiling water and instant espresso powder. For an accurate measurement of boiling water, bring a full kettle of water to a boil, then measure out the desired amount.

2	ounces bittersweet chocolate, chopped fine
⅓	cup (1 ounce) cocoa
¾	teaspoon instant espresso powder
¾	cup boiling water
¾	cup (4⅛ ounces) bread flour
¾	cup (5¼ ounces) sugar
½	teaspoon salt
½	teaspoon baking soda
5	tablespoons canola oil
2	large eggs
2	teaspoons white vinegar
1	teaspoon vanilla extract
2	cups Low-Fat Chocolate Frosting (recipe follows)

1. Adjust oven rack to middle position and heat oven to 350 degrees. Line 12-cup muffin tin with paper or foil liners.

2. Combine chocolate, cocoa, and espresso powder in large bowl. Pour boiling water over top, cover, and let sit for 5 minutes to melt chocolate; whisk smooth, then set aside to cool slightly. In separate bowl, whisk flour, sugar, salt, and baking soda together.

3. Whisk oil, eggs, vinegar, and vanilla into cooled chocolate mixture until smooth. Whisk in flour mixture until smooth. Using greased ¼-cup measure, portion batter into prepared muffin cups.

4. Bake cupcakes until toothpick inserted in center comes out with few moist crumbs attached, 17 to 19 minutes, rotating pan halfway through baking. Let cupcakes cool in pan on wire rack for 10 minutes. Remove cakes from pan and let cool completely on rack, about 1 hour. Using small icing spatula, frost each cupcake with about 2½ tablespoons frosting. Serve.

ON THE SIDE LOW-FAT CHOCOLATE FROSTING
Pulse 3½ cups confectioners' sugar and ½ cup cocoa together in food processor until combined, about 5 pulses. Add 7 tablespoons 1 percent low-fat milk, 2 tablespoons softened unsalted butter, 1 ounce melted bittersweet chocolate, and 1 teaspoon vanilla extract; process until smooth, about 15 seconds. Makes 2 cups.

BEFORE → **AFTER**	420 → **340**	28 → **11**	18 → **3**
	CALORIES	GRAMS FAT	GRAMS SAT FAT

MAKEOVER SPOTLIGHT:
CHOCOLATE CUPCAKES

1. CUT BACK ON THE CHOCOLATE AND RAMP UP THE FLAVOR WITH COCOA AND ESPRESSO POWDER: There's no doubt about it—chocolate is a fatty ingredient. But after we trimmed the chocolate from our cupcakes, they were light on flavor. To ramp it up without adding lots of fat and calories, we increased the amount of cocoa and added instant espresso powder, which adds depth and complexity. To help these ingredients meld seamlessly into the batter and to bloom their flavor, we combined them with boiling water, which works to melt the chocolate.

2. DITCH THE BUTTER IN FAVOR OF CANOLA OIL, AND USE BREAD FLOUR FOR STRUCTURE: Swapping canola oil for the butter not only lowers the amount of saturated fat in these little cakes, but it also helps keep the cakes moist and allows the bold flavor of the chocolate to really shine through. We also found that bread flour helped prevent these leaner cakes from falling flat because it has more protein than all-purpose flour, and the additional protein gives the cakes extra lift and structure.

3. DON'T OVERBAKE THE CUPCAKES: This rule applies to all low-fat cakes because they are quick to turn dry and crumbly when overbaked. When testing the cakes, aim for slightly underdone because they will continue to bake after you remove them from the oven. To test for doneness, insert a toothpick or bamboo skewer into the center of the cake. When you remove it there should be some moist crumbs attached, but not any raw batter.

4. SKIP THE BUTTERCREAM FROSTING AND MAKE A RICH YET LOW-FAT FROSTING WITH CONFECTIONERS' SUGAR: Buttercream frosting, made with lots of butter and egg yolks or cream, was a no-go for our lightened cupcakes. Instead, we opted for a frosting made with confectioners' sugar, milk, and just 2 tablespoons of butter. A half-cup of cocoa and an ounce of chocolate gave our lightened frosting an intense, chocolaty flavor and a creamy, silky texture. Adjusting its consistency is easy; if it's too loose, add extra confectioners' sugar to tighten it up, and if it's too dry, add small drops of milk to loosen it.

Chocolate Sheet Cake

Serves 16

✔ **WHY THIS RECIPE WORKS:** You might feel like this birthday-party favorite is off-limits once you learn that a single slice packs a whopping 600 calories and almost 50 grams of fat. To make over this crowd-pleaser, we began by reducing the amounts of the worst offenders in our lineup—the butter and chocolate. To compensate for the missing butter, we turned to buttermilk, which is naturally low in fat; it added both flavor and moisture to our cake. Increasing the amount of cocoa and adding chocolate syrup and instant espresso powder to the mix guaranteed a cake with deep flavor. Even with low-fat chocolate frosting, our made-over chocolate cake slashed the calorie count in half and cut the fat to under 10 grams—meaning we'd never have to pass up a slice again.

3	ounces semisweet chocolate, chopped
2	tablespoons chocolate syrup
1½	cups (7½ ounces) all-purpose flour
¾	cup (2¼ ounces) cocoa
1	teaspoon baking powder
1	teaspoon baking soda
¼	teaspoon salt
6	tablespoons unsalted butter, cut into 1-inch pieces and softened
1¼	cups (8¾ ounces) sugar
2	large eggs
1	teaspoon vanilla extract
2	teaspoons instant espresso powder
1½	cups buttermilk
2	cups Low-Fat Chocolate Frosting (see page 246)

1. Adjust oven rack to middle position and heat oven to 350 degrees. Spray 13 by 9-inch baking pan with vegetable oil spray and line bottom with parchment paper. Microwave chocolate in covered bowl, stirring occasionally, until melted and smooth, 1 to 3 minutes; stir in chocolate syrup and let cool slightly. In separate bowl, whisk flour, cocoa, baking powder, baking soda, and salt together.

2. Using stand mixer fitted with paddle, beat butter and sugar on medium-high speed until pale and fluffy, about 3 minutes. Add melted chocolate mixture and beat until mixture looks thick and grainy, about 1 minute. Add eggs, vanilla, and espresso powder and beat until fluffy and pale brown, 2 minutes. Reduce speed to low and add flour mixture in 3 additions, alternating with 2 additions of buttermilk, scraping down bowl as needed. Give batter final stir by hand.

3. Pour batter into prepared pan and smooth top. Bake until toothpick inserted in center comes out with few moist crumbs attached, 25 to 30 minutes. Let cake cool completely in pan on wire rack, about 1½ hours. Spread frosting over top of cake and cut into 16 pieces. Serve.

BEFORE → **AFTER**	640 → **320**	44 → **9**	27 → **5**
	CALORIES	GRAMS FAT	GRAMS SAT FAT

Glazed Chocolate Bundt Cake

Serves 16

✔ **WHY THIS RECIPE WORKS:** Chocolate Bundt cake offers an elegant yet easy dessert fix. After all, it doesn't require frosting or fussy finishing techniques—just a simple glaze, and it's good to go. But given that a single slice can add 400 calories to your day's total, we decided it was time for a makeover. We started our testing by cutting back on the chocolate, using only 3 ounces as well as some cocoa; blooming the cocoa in hot water ratcheted up the flavor. Many chocolate Bundt cakes include sour cream for flavor and tenderness, but we found the low-fat and nonfat varieties made the cake taste dry and bland and obscured the flavor of the chocolate. Switching to buttermilk or low-fat milk had the same effect. In the end, we opted for water; now our cake was moist and had a bolder chocolate flavor. Swapping the granulated sugar for brown sugar helped to increase the moistness of our cake. Wondering if the butter was also working to hold back the rich flavor of our Bundt cake, we tried nixing it in favor of canola oil. At last, we had a lightened Bundt cake with a super-rich chocolate flavor and texture. Drizzled with a simple glaze, this revamped dessert tasted every bit as good as it looked. For an accurate measurement of boiling water, bring a full kettle of water to a boil, then measure out the desired amount.

CAKE

- 3 ounces bittersweet chocolate, chopped fine
- ¾ cup (2¼ ounces) cocoa
- 1 teaspoon instant espresso powder
- 1 cup boiling water
- 1¾ cups (8¾ ounces) all-purpose flour
- 1 teaspoon baking soda
- 1 teaspoon salt
- 2 cups packed (14 ounces) light brown sugar
- ½ cup canola oil
- 2 large eggs, room temperature
- 1 tablespoon vanilla extract

VANILLA GLAZE

- 1 cup (4 ounces) confectioners' sugar
- 1 tablespoon skim milk
- 1 tablespoon vanilla extract
  Pinch salt

1. FOR THE CAKE: Adjust oven rack to lower-middle position and heat oven to 350 degrees. Spray inside of 12-cup Bundt pan thoroughly with vegetable oil spray.

2. Combine chocolate, cocoa, and instant espresso powder in large bowl, pour boiling water over top, and cover; let sit for 5 minutes to melt chocolate, then whisk smooth. In separate bowl, whisk flour, baking soda, and salt together.

3. Process melted chocolate mixture, sugar, oil, eggs, and vanilla together in food processor until combined, about 1 minute; transfer to clean large bowl. Sift one-third of flour mixture over batter and whisk until just few streaks of flour remain. Repeat twice more with remaining flour mixture, then continue to whisk batter gently until most lumps are gone (do not overmix).

4. Scrape batter into prepared pan and smooth top. Wipe any drops of batter off sides of pan and gently tap pan on counter to settle batter. Bake until toothpick inserted in center comes out clean, 50 to 60 minutes, rotating pan halfway through baking. Let cake cool in pan on wire rack for 10 minutes. Remove cake from pan and let cool completely on rack, about 2 hours.

5. FOR THE VANILLA GLAZE: Whisk all ingredients together in bowl until smooth, then drizzle evenly over top of cooled cake, letting it drip down sides. Let glaze set for 15 minutes before serving.

BEFORE → **AFTER**	400 → **280** CALORIES	17 → **10** GRAMS FAT	10 → **1.5** GRAMS SAT FAT

German Chocolate Cake

Serves 12

☑ **WHY THIS RECIPE WORKS:** This over-the-top triple-layer cake garnished with shredded coconut and pecans was just begging for a makeover. For our first move, we cut back from three layers to two—and even then, a single slice still provided a generous serving. Ditching the traditional German's chocolate, we opted for milk chocolate and cocoa powder, which provided more flavor and a better texture. Fat-free evaporated milk and a little cornstarch helped thicken the frosting, and toasting the nuts and coconut intensified their flavors so we could use less. For an accurate measurement of boiling water, bring a full kettle of water to a boil, then measure out the desired amount.

CAKE

- 3 **ounces milk chocolate, chopped**
- 3 **tablespoons cocoa**
- ⅓ **cup boiling water**
- 1⅓ **cups (6⅔ ounces) all-purpose flour**
- ½ **teaspoon baking soda**
- 3 **tablespoons unsalted butter, softened**
- ½ **cup packed (3½ ounces) brown sugar**
- ⅓ **cup (2⅓ ounces) granulated sugar**
- ½ **teaspoon salt**
- 3 **large eggs, room temperature**
- 1 **teaspoon vanilla extract**
- ½ **cup low-fat sour cream, room temperature**

FROSTING

- ⅔ **cup packed (4⅔ ounces) brown sugar**
- 1 **cup fat-free evaporated milk**
- 3 **tablespoons cornstarch**
- 2 **tablespoons unsalted butter**
- ¼ **teaspoon salt**
- 1 **tablespoon vanilla extract**
- ½ **cup (1½ ounces) sweetened shredded coconut, toasted**
- ⅓ **cup pecans, toasted and chopped fine**

1. FOR THE CAKE: Adjust oven rack to lower-middle position and heat oven to 350 degrees. Grease two 9-inch round cake pans, line with parchment paper, grease parchment, then flour pans. Combine chocolate and cocoa together in medium bowl, pour boiling water over top, and cover; let sit for 5 minutes to melt chocolate, then whisk smooth. In separate bowl, whisk flour and baking soda together.

2. Using stand mixer fitted with paddle, beat butter, brown sugar, granulated sugar, and salt on medium-high speed until pale and fluffy, about 3 minutes. Add eggs, 1 at a time, and beat until combined. Reduce speed to low and add chocolate mixture and vanilla until incorporated. Add flour mixture in 3 additions, alternating with 2 additions of sour cream, scraping down bowl as needed. Give batter final stir by hand.

3. Divide batter evenly between pans; bake until toothpick inserted in center comes out clean, 10 to 15 minutes. Let cool in pans on wire rack for 10 minutes. Remove cakes from pans, discard parchment, and let cool completely on rack, about 2 hours.

4. FOR THE FROSTING: Combine sugar, evaporated milk, cornstarch, butter, and salt together in small saucepan. Bring to simmer over medium-high heat and cook, whisking constantly, until just thickened, about 1 minute. Off heat, stir in vanilla and all but 1 tablespoon each coconut and pecans; let cool to room temperature.

5. Cover edges of cake platter with strips of parchment. Place 1 cake layer on platter. Spread half of frosting evenly over top, right to edge of cake. Top with second cake layer, press lightly to adhere, then spread remaining frosting evenly over top of cake, leaving sides unfrosted. Sprinkle with remaining coconut and pecans. Carefully remove parchment strips before serving.

BEFORE → **AFTER**	580 → **320**	33 → **12**	17 → **6**
	CALORIES	GRAMS FAT	GRAMS SAT FAT

Chocolate Cream Pie

Serves 8

✔ **WHY THIS RECIPE WORKS:** With its chocolate-cookie crust, ultra-rich filling, and decadent topping of whipped cream, this diner favorite definitely pulls out all the stops. To revamp this heavyweight dessert—a single slice offers over 650 calories and 50 grams of fat—we started with the crust, ditching the high-fat chocolate cookies in favor of chocolate graham crackers, which are low in fat, and reducing the amount of butter as much as we could. A little reduced-fat cream cheese helped to bind the mixture and add more flavor. For the filling, we nixed the heavy cream and opted for whole milk thickened with cornstarch. Cocoa plus bittersweet chocolate delivered intense flavor, and adding an egg ensured our pie was firm enough to slice. For the topping, we tried all manner of whipped cream substitutes but were disappointed every time—after all, a cream pie just isn't a cream pie without whipped cream. Even with a modest layer on top, our revamped chocolate cream pie managed to trim over 300 calories and 30 grams of fat per slice—and it still tasted every bit as rich and creamy as the original. Do not substitute low-fat or skim milk in the pie.

CRUST

- 8 chocolate graham crackers (4½ ounces), broken into 1-inch pieces
- 3 tablespoons sugar
- 3 tablespoons unsalted butter, melted and cooled
- 1 ounce ⅓ less fat cream cheese (neufchatel), softened

PIE

- ½ cup (3½ ounces) granulated sugar
- 3 tablespoons cornstarch
- 2 tablespoons cocoa
- ⅛ teaspoon salt
- 2½ cups whole milk
- 1 large egg, lightly beaten
- 4 ounces bittersweet chocolate, chopped fine
- 2½ teaspoons vanilla extract
- ½ cup heavy cream
- 1 tablespoon confectioners' sugar

1. FOR THE CRUST: Adjust oven rack to middle position and heat oven to 350 degrees. Spray 9-inch pie plate with vegetable oil spray. Process graham crackers and sugar in food processor to fine crumbs, about 10 seconds. Add butter and cream cheese and pulse until combined, about 8 pulses. Press crumbs into bottom and up sides of prepared pie plate. Bake until top edge is slightly lighter in color and crust is set, about 15 minutes. Let cool completely, about 30 minutes.

2. FOR THE PIE: Combine granulated sugar, cornstarch, cocoa, and salt in bowl. Whisk milk and egg together in medium saucepan, then whisk in sugar mixture. Add chocolate and bring to boil over medium heat, whisking constantly. Reduce heat to low and cook, whisking constantly, until mixture becomes thick and glossy, about 3 minutes. Off heat, stir in 2 teaspoons vanilla.

3. Strain mixture through fine-mesh strainer into cooled crust. Place plastic wrap directly on surface of pudding to prevent skin from forming. Refrigerate until completely cool, 3 to 24 hours.

4. Using stand mixer fitted with whisk, whip cream, confectioners' sugar, and remaining ½ teaspoon vanilla on medium-low speed until foamy, about 1 minute. Increase speed to high and whip until soft peaks form, 1 to 3 minutes. Spread whipped topping evenly over pie and cut pie into 8 pieces. Serve.

BEFORE → **AFTER**	660 → **320** CALORIES	53 → **18** GRAMS FAT	30 → **11** GRAMS SAT FAT

Warm Chocolate Fudge Cakes

Serves 8

✔ **WHY THIS RECIPE WORKS:** With warm, oozing, fudgy centers, an easy, no-fuss procedure, and a short baking time, these little cakes make the perfect finale for any weeknight supper—unless you're thinking about fat and calories. Wanting to knock the nutritional counts down a little so we could enjoy this chocolaty dream of a dessert more often, we took a close look at all of the ingredients to see where we could lighten the load. First, we reduced the total amount of canola oil traditionally called for in this easy dump-and-stir batter. Next, we went up on the cocoa; a whopping 1 cup ensured our cakes were deeply chocolaty, but didn't add much in the way of fat. Dark brown sugar made for a dessert with complexity and rich, caramel notes, and adding a little extra milk kept our cakes moist. To ensure that each cake had a super-fudgy center, we simply pressed a small piece of chocolate into the middle of each ramekin before baking. Our cakes needed just 20 minutes in the oven until they were nicely gooey and had risen slightly. Served warm, these rich little desserts are the perfect sweet treat after dinner. Not only have they been seriously lightened from the original full-fat version, but they are also a snap to make and can be ready in record time.

1½ cups (6 ounces) cake flour
1 cup (3 ounces) cocoa
1 teaspoon baking powder
½ teaspoon baking soda
½ teaspoon salt
1¼ cups 2 percent low-fat milk
1½ cups packed (10½ ounces) dark brown sugar
¼ cup canola oil
2 large eggs
1 teaspoon vanilla extract
2 ounces bittersweet chocolate, broken into 8 equal pieces

1. Adjust oven rack to middle position and heat oven to 350 degrees. Grease and flour eight 6-ounce ramekins and arrange on rimmed baking sheet. Whisk flour, cocoa, baking powder, baking soda, and salt together in bowl. In large bowl, whisk milk, sugar, oil, eggs, and vanilla together. Slowly whisk flour mixture into milk mixture until combined.

2. Portion batter into prepared ramekins and gently tap ramekins on counter to release air bubbles. Gently press 1 piece chocolate into center of each ramekin to submerge. Bake until cakes rise, tops turn glossy, and center is gooey when pierced with skewer, about 20 minutes, rotating sheet halfway through baking. (Do not overbake.) Serve warm.

BEFORE → **AFTER**   560 → **380**   33 → **12**   12 → **3**
CALORIES   GRAMS FAT   GRAMS SAT FAT

Chocolate Mousse

Serves 6

👍 **WHY THIS RECIPE WORKS:** For a creamy mousse without the cream, we used an Italian meringue. A trio of chocolates delivered big chocolate flavor. If desired, ⅔ cup semisweet chips can be substituted for the semisweet chocolate. For an elegant finish, top with white chocolate shavings if desired.

4	ounces semisweet chocolate, broken into pieces
⅓	cup white chocolate chips
2	tablespoons cocoa
6	tablespoons plus ⅓ cup water
1	teaspoon vanilla extract
⅓	cup (2⅓ ounces) sugar
3	large egg whites, room temperature
¼	teaspoon cream of tartar

1. Combine semisweet chocolate, white chocolate chips, cocoa, 6 tablespoons water, and vanilla in medium bowl set over large saucepan of barely simmering water, making sure water does not touch bottom of bowl. Heat mixture, whisking often, until chocolate is melted and mixture is smooth, about 2 minutes; set aside to cool slightly.

2. Bring remaining ⅓ cup water and sugar to boil in small saucepan over medium-high heat; cook until mixture is slightly thickened and syrupy (about 235 degrees on candy thermometer), 3 to 4 minutes. Remove from heat; cover to keep warm.

3. Using stand mixer fitted with whisk, whip egg whites and cream of tartar together on medium-low speed until foamy, about 1 minute. Increase speed to medium-high and whip until soft peaks form, 2 to 3 minutes.

4. Reduce speed to medium and slowly add hot syrup, avoiding whisk and sides of bowl. Increase mixer speed to medium-high and continue to whip until meringue has cooled slightly (just warm) and is very thick and shiny, 2 to 5 minutes.

5. Gently whisk one-third of meringue into chocolate mixture until combined, then gently whisk in remaining meringue. Divide mousse evenly among six 4-ounce ramekins or pudding cups. Cover tightly with plastic wrap and refrigerate until set, at least 12 hours or up to 3 days. Serve.

QUICK PREP TIP **MAKING AN ITALIAN MERINGUE**

An Italian meringue is made by whipping egg whites with a sugar syrup; we use it to give our chocolate mousse a creamy lushness without adding any fat. To make an Italian meringue, pour hot sugar syrup into the whipped egg whites, but avoid touching either the beater or the sides of the bowl. If the syrup hits the beater or bowl, it will stick to them rather than be incorporated into the eggs.

BEFORE → **AFTER**   270 → **200**   22 → **9**   13 → **5**
CALORIES   GRAMS FAT   GRAMS SAT FAT

Chocolate Pudding

Serves 4

✔ **WHY THIS RECIPE WORKS:** Rich and chocolaty, with a thick, creamy texture, chocolate pudding is the ideal after-school snack—until you check the label. We envisioned an anytime afternoon treat that wasn't quite so high in calories or fat. A blend of bittersweet chocolate and cocoa worked to trim the fat level while still keeping our pudding richly flavored, and adding the chocolate at the outset of cooking—rather than stirring it in at the end—intensified its flavor. We also found that whole milk thickened with cornstarch delivered the same creamy texture as the heavy cream called for in most full-fat pudding recipes. You can substitute 2 percent low-fat milk for the whole milk to reduce fat and calories further; however, do not substitute 1 percent low-fat or skim milk or else the pudding will have a very weak, shallow flavor.

½ cup (3½ ounces) sugar

2½ tablespoons cornstarch

2 tablespoons cocoa

⅛ teaspoon salt

2½ cups whole milk

2 ounces bittersweet chocolate, chopped

2 teaspoons vanilla extract

1. Combine sugar, cornstarch, cocoa, and salt together in bowl. Whisk milk and sugar mixture together in medium saucepan. Add chocolate and bring to boil over medium heat, whisking constantly. Reduce heat to low and cook, whisking constantly, until mixture becomes thick and glossy, about 3 minutes.

2. Off heat, stir in vanilla. Strain mixture through fine-mesh strainer into bowl. Place plastic wrap directly on surface of pudding to prevent skin from forming. Refrigerate until well chilled, at least 4 hours or up to 2 days. Gently stir pudding before serving.

QUICK PREP TIP
CHOPPING CHOCOLATE
Some chocolate is sold in thick bars, which can make chopping difficult. To make this task easier, hold a large knife at a 45-degree angle to one corner and bear down evenly. After cutting about an inch from the corner, repeat with the other corners.

BEFORE → **AFTER**   390 → **280**   28 → **9**   17 → **5**
                     CALORIES   GRAMS FAT   GRAMS SAT FAT

Chocolate Milkshake

Serves 1

✔️ **WHY THIS RECIPE WORKS:** Can you get a thick, creamy milkshake—without any ice cream? Absolutely. After trying a variety of low-fat and light ice creams (chocolate or vanilla, plus assorted flavorings), and even chocolate sorbet, we hit on nonfat chocolate frozen yogurt plus a bit of whole milk; this duo delivered a rich flavor and lush, creamy texture. Hot fudge sauce amped up the deep, chocolaty notes, and a dash of vanilla rounded out the flavor, while a few ice cubes prevented our fro-yo shake from melting too quickly.

⅓ cup whole milk

3 (2-ounce) ice cubes

1 tablespoon hot fudge sauce

¼ teaspoon vanilla extract

2 cups nonfat chocolate frozen yogurt

Process milk, ice cubes, hot fudge sauce, and vanilla together in blender until smooth, about 20 seconds. Add frozen yogurt and blend until incorporated, about 10 seconds. Pour into chilled 16-ounce drinking glass. Serve with drinking straw.

BEFORE NUMBERS BASED ON: Original Chocolate Shake from Johnny Rockets	BEFORE → **AFTER**	920 → **510** CALORIES	51 → **4.5** GRAMS FAT	30 → **3.5** GRAMS SAT FAT

Mocha Frappé

Serves 1

✔️ **WHY THIS RECIPE WORKS:** A mocha frappé makes for the ultimate cool-down treat on a hot day, but we were shocked to see that hidden underneath all that icy goodness was 400 calories and 15 grams of fat. Although light versions are common, they usually disappoint with their watery texture and saccharine-sweet aftertaste. We knew we could do better. Nonfat chocolate frozen yogurt and a little low-fat milk gave us an ultra-creamy texture. Rather than use regular brewed coffee, we opted for instant espresso powder, which was more convenient and offered a stronger, more intense flavor. Last but not least, we topped our revamped frappé with a dollop of whipped cream—just like they do at the coffeehouse—for an ultra-creamy finish.

⅓ cup 2 percent low-fat milk

2 teaspoons instant espresso powder

1½ cups (8 ounces) ice cubes

2 teaspoons sugar

¼ teaspoon vanilla extract

1 cup nonfat chocolate frozen yogurt

2 tablespoons Fat-Free Reddi-wip

Blend milk and espresso powder together in blender until espresso dissolves, about 5 seconds. Add ice, sugar, and vanilla and blend until smooth, about 20 seconds. Add frozen yogurt and blend until incorporated, about 10 seconds. Pour into chilled 16-ounce drinking glass and top with Reddi-wip. Serve with drinking straw.

BEFORE NUMBERS BASED ON: Grande Mocha Frappuccino from Starbucks	BEFORE → **AFTER**	400 → **290** CALORIES	15 → **2** GRAMS FAT	9 → **1** GRAMS SAT FAT

CHOCOLATE CHIP COOKIES

Cookies and Bars

Chocolate Chip Cookies

Makes 18 cookies

✔ **WHY THIS RECIPE WORKS:** Cutting the fat and calories in chocolate chip cookies while ending up with a treat we'd still want to eat wasn't as easy as just reducing the amount of butter—this move left our cookies hard as rocks after they cooled. After trying a barrage of "healthy" substitutes, from applesauce to mashed bananas, we landed on homemade date puree, made from cooking and mashing dried dates. After replacing three-quarters of the butter in our favorite full-fat recipe with date puree, we were greeted with moist cookies boasting a rich, sweet flavor. Browning the butter also added depth to our reduced-fat cookies, and pressing a few of the chocolate chips into the tops of the cookies made it look like they were chock-full of chocolate. Our revamped chocolate chip cookies looked as good as they tasted, and thanks to our butter substitute they were flavorful and tender for days, not hours. Be sure to buy dates that are still supple.

1	cup water
¼	cup finely chopped dates
3	tablespoons unsalted butter
2	cups (10 ounces) all-purpose flour
½	teaspoon baking soda
½	teaspoon salt
1¼	cups packed (8¾ ounces) light brown sugar
1	large egg
2	teaspoons vanilla extract
½	cup (3 ounces) semisweet chocolate chips

1. Bring water and dates to boil in small saucepan over medium-high heat; reduce to simmer and cook until dates are tender and most of water has evaporated, about 20 minutes. Using rubber spatula, press mixture through fine-mesh strainer set over bowl to make date puree. Scrape any dates left in strainer into puree (you should have ¼ cup puree).

2. Meanwhile, adjust oven rack to middle position; heat oven to 325 degrees. Line 2 baking sheets with parchment paper. Melt butter in small saucepan over medium heat and cook until nutty brown, about 4 minutes; transfer to small bowl and let cool.

3. Whisk flour, baking soda, and salt together in bowl. Using stand mixer fitted with paddle, beat date puree, browned butter, and sugar on medium speed until blended, about 2 minutes. Beat in egg and vanilla until combined. Reduce speed to low and beat in flour mixture until just incorporated. Give batter final stir by hand, then stir in all but 2 tablespoons of chocolate chips.

4. Working with 2 tablespoons of dough at a time, roll dough into balls, then tear each ball in half and press halves back together with torn side facing up. Space cookies, torn side up, about 2 inches apart on prepared baking sheets, 9 cookies per sheet. Press remaining 2 tablespoons chips evenly into tops of cookies.

5. Bake cookies, one tray at a time, until edges are light golden brown and centers are soft and puffy, 15 to 18 minutes, rotating sheet halfway through baking. Let cookies cool on sheet for 10 minutes, then serve warm or transfer to wire rack and let cool completely.

BEFORE → **AFTER**	310 → **160**	15 → **4**	9 → **2.5**
	CALORIES	GRAMS FAT	GRAMS SAT FAT

MAKEOVER SPOTLIGHT:
CHOCOLATE CHIP COOKIES

1. CUT THE FAT BY REPLACING SOME OF THE BUTTER WITH DATE PUREE: Simply slashing the amount of butter in our dough left us with hard, dry cookies. So we looked for a substitute that would add moisture without contributing off-flavors. Pureed dates added a moist, sweet texture with just a hint of fruitiness. For a fine puree that we could incorporate easily into the dough, we boiled the dates until they were tender, then worked them through a fine-mesh strainer using a rubber spatula. Be sure to use dried dates that are still supple, or the puree will be difficult to strain and have a coarse consistency.

2. BROWN THE BUTTER FOR DEEP FLAVOR: To make the most of the small amount of butter in our recipe, we found it best to brown it to bring out its nutty, caramel flavors before adding it to the dough. Be sure to use a stainless steel pan when browning the butter, as the dark surface of a nonstick pan will make it difficult to gauge the color of the butter. Also, keep your eye on the butter as it begins to brown because it can go from browned to burnt quickly.

3. TEAR THE COOKIES AND TOP WITH CHOCOLATE CHIPS FOR AN APPEALING, CRAGGY APPEARANCE: Most of the recipes we tried for low-fat chocolate chip cookies resulted in unappealing cookies once baked—they were flat and smooth, with no visible chips. For a nice, craggy surface, we tore our dough balls in half, then pressed them back together again with the craggy surface facing up. Also, we reserved a few chocolate chips and pressed them into the tops of the cookies before baking. This guaranteed our cookies looked like the real deal and ensured the chips were evenly distributed in the dough.

4. FOR MOIST, CHEWY COOKIES, UNDERBAKE THEM: It was essential to remove our cookies from the oven at just the right time. That's because there is no extra fat in the dough to keep them moist and chewy if they are overbaked. We pulled the cookies from the oven when they were slightly underdone and let them finish baking on the hot sheet. When the cookies are ready to be removed from the oven, their edges will be firm and set but the centers will look slightly underdone when you peer through the cracks.

Peanut Butter Cookies

Makes 24 cookies

✔ **WHY THIS RECIPE WORKS:** Most cookies get their fat and calories from sugar, eggs, and a whole lot of butter. This classic lunchbox cookie takes things one step further by adding at least a cup of peanut butter to the mix. To lighten ours, we started by cutting back on the namesake ingredient; just ½ cup ensured our cookies still had a nice, nutty flavor. Swapping out some of the butter for canola oil and omitting an egg trimmed even more fat grams. To ensure our lean dough baked up into soft, moist, and chewy cookies, we added corn syrup and traded some of the white sugar for light brown sugar; the brown sugar also contributed a subtle caramel flavor. To reinforce the peanut flavor, we sprinkled some chopped dry-roasted peanuts on top of our cookies before baking them. The dough is quite soft, so keep it chilled until you are ready to form and bake the cookies. These cookies are best eaten on the day they are baked.

1¼ cups (6¼ ounces) all-purpose flour

¾ teaspoon baking soda

½ teaspoon salt

½ cup creamy peanut butter

½ cup packed (3½ ounces) light brown sugar

⅓ cup light corn syrup

¼ cup (1¾ ounces) granulated sugar

3 tablespoons canola oil

2 tablespoons unsalted butter, melted and cooled

1 large egg

1 teaspoon vanilla extract

3 tablespoons unsalted, dry-roasted peanuts, chopped fine

1. Adjust oven racks to upper-middle and lower-middle positions and heat oven to 350 degrees. Line 2 baking sheets with parchment paper. Whisk flour, baking soda, and salt together in bowl.

2. In large bowl, whisk peanut butter, brown sugar, corn syrup, granulated sugar, oil, melted butter, egg, and vanilla together until smooth. Gently stir in flour mixture with rubber spatula until combined. Divide dough in half, wrap in plastic wrap, and refrigerate until firm, about 1 hour.

3. Working with 2 tablespoons dough at a time, roll dough into balls and place 2 inches apart on prepared sheets, 12 cookies per sheet. Press dough to ¾-inch thickness using bottom of greased measuring cup. Press chopped peanuts evenly into tops of cookies.

4. Bake cookies until puffed and edges are lightly browned, 12 to 14 minutes, switching and rotating sheets halfway through baking. Let cookies cool on sheets for 10 minutes then serve warm or transfer to wire rack to cool completely.

BEFORE → **AFTER**	190 → **130** CALORIES	11 → **6** GRAMS FAT	4 → **1.5** GRAMS SAT FAT

Cheesecake Bars

Makes 16 bars

✔ **WHY THIS RECIPE WORKS:** While these dessert bars may not pack the same fatty punch as whole slices of cheesecake, they're not exactly diet food either. We wanted to cut the fat from this rich, decadent treat, but still keep the creamy texture and luscious flavor. Ditching the full-fat cream cheese in favor of the reduced-fat variety was a good start, but the filling wasn't as smooth and creamy as we expected. After trying a variety of low-fat and nonfat dairy ingredients, we landed on nonfat cottage cheese, which we processed to an ultra-smooth texture in the food processor. For the crust, we combined graham cracker crumbs with just a few pats of butter and a small amount of brown sugar for moisture and flavor. Now our revamped cheesecake bars offered all the great textures and flavors of a slice of cheesecake—without any of the guilt. For more information on making a foil sling, see page 267.

CRUST

7   **whole graham crackers, broken into 1-inch pieces**

3   **tablespoons unsalted butter, melted and cooled**

3   **tablespoons packed light brown sugar**

⅛   **teaspoon salt**

FILLING AND TOPPING

8   **ounces (1 cup) nonfat cottage cheese, drained if necessary**

8   **ounces ⅓ less fat cream cheese (neufchatel), softened**

⅔   **cup (4⅔ ounces) granulated sugar**

2   **teaspoons lemon juice**

1   **teaspoon vanilla extract**

2   **large eggs**

5   **small strawberries, hulled and sliced thin**

1. FOR THE CRUST: Adjust oven rack to middle position and heat oven to 350 degrees. Make foil sling for 8-inch square baking pan by folding 2 long sheets of aluminum foil so each is 8 inches wide. Lay sheets of foil in pan perpendicular to each other, with extra foil hanging over edges of pan. Push foil into corners and up sides of pan, smoothing foil flush to pan. Lightly coat foil with vegetable oil spray.

2. Process graham crackers in food processor to fine, even crumbs, about 30 seconds. Add melted butter, sugar, and salt and pulse to incorporate, about 5 pulses. Transfer mixture to prepared pan and press firmly into even layer using wide metal spatula. Bake until crust is fragrant and beginning to brown, 12 to 15 minutes, rotating pan halfway through baking. Let cool on wire rack for at least 15 minutes.

3. FOR THE FILLING AND TOPPING: Process cottage cheese in food processor until smooth and no visible lumps remain, about 30 seconds, scraping down bowl as needed. Add cream cheese and process until smooth, about 1 minute. Add sugar, lemon juice, and vanilla and process until smooth, about 1 minute, scraping down bowl as needed. With processor running, add eggs one at a time and process until smooth, about 30 seconds. Pour filling over baked crust. Bake bars until edges are set but center still jiggles slightly, 30 to 35 minutes, rotating pan halfway through baking.

4. Let bars cool completely in pan on wire rack, about 2 hours. Cover loosely with plastic wrap and refrigerate until thoroughly chilled, 3 to 24 hours. Remove from pan using foil sling and cut into 16 squares. Garnish each with strawberry slice and serve.

BEFORE → **AFTER**	220 → **130** CALORIES	16 → **6** GRAMS FAT	9 → **3.5** GRAMS SAT FAT

Pecan Bars

Makes 16 bars

✓ **WHY THIS RECIPE WORKS:** Pecan bars boast a nutty, caramel flavor and a gooey, crunchy texture, but with 17 grams of fat each they are a diet-slaying treat. To lighten up this dessert, we replaced a portion of the nuts with Honey Nut Cheerios, which stayed crunchy when baked and provided big, nutty flavor.

CRUST

- ¾   cup (3¾ ounces) all-purpose flour
- ⅓   cup packed (2⅓ ounces) light brown sugar
- ¼   cup pecans, toasted and chopped coarse
- ¼   teaspoon salt
- ¼   teaspoon baking powder
- 3   tablespoons unsalted butter, cut into ½-inch pieces and chilled

FILLING

- ⅓   cup packed (2⅓ ounces) light brown sugar
- ⅓   cup light corn syrup
- 2   tablespoons unsalted butter, melted and cooled
- 1   tablespoon bourbon or dark rum
- 2   teaspoons vanilla extract
- ¼   teaspoon salt
- 1   large egg
- 1   cup Honey Nut Cheerios, crushed
- ¾   cup pecans, chopped coarse

1. FOR THE CRUST: Adjust oven rack to middle position and heat oven to 350 degrees. Make foil sling for 8-inch square baking pan by folding 2 long sheets of aluminum foil so each is 8 inches wide. Lay sheets of foil in pan perpendicular to each other, with extra foil hanging over edges of pan. Push foil into corners and up sides of pan, smoothing foil flush to pan. Spray foil with vegetable oil spray.

2. Pulse flour, sugar, pecans, salt, and baking powder together in food processor until combined, about 5 pulses. Sprinkle butter over top and pulse until mixture is pale yellow and resembles coarse cornmeal, about 8 pulses. Transfer mixture to prepared pan and press firmly into even layer using wide metal spatula. Bake until crust is fragrant and beginning to brown, about 20 minutes, rotating pan halfway through baking. Let cool on wire rack for at least 15 minutes.

3. FOR THE FILLING: Whisk sugar, corn syrup, melted butter, bourbon, vanilla, and salt together in large bowl until sugar dissolves. Whisk in egg until combined. Stir in Cheerios and pecans. Spread filling evenly over crust. Bake until top is golden brown, 22 to 25 minutes, rotating pan halfway through baking.

4. Let bars cool completely in pan on wire rack, about 2 hours. Remove from pan using foil sling and cut into 16 squares. Serve.

QUICK PREP TIP
MAKING A FOIL SLING
To make it easy to remove bar cookies from the baking pan, line it with an aluminum foil sling. Fold 2 long sheets of foil so they are as wide as the pan. Lay them perpendicular to each other in the pan, with some hanging over the edges. Push the foil into the corners and up the sides, smoothing out wrinkles.

BEFORE → **AFTER**	240 → **170** CALORIES	17 → **9** GRAMS FAT	5 → **2.5** GRAMS SAT FAT

Raspberry Streusel Bars

Makes 16 bars

✔ **WHY THIS RECIPE WORKS:** For low-fat raspberry streusel bars with big flavor, we started with fresh fruit. Mashing the raspberries with a bit of jam gave our filling just the right texture, and adding a dash of lemon juice brightened the fruit flavor. Reducing the amount of butter in both the crust and the topping helped us lower the fat count of our raspberry bars, while substituting brown sugar for white sugar added moisture and flavor. Nuts contributed a good crunch factor to the crust, and oats amped up the heartiness of our streusel. Thawed frozen raspberries can be substituted for the fresh berries. We prefer the texture and flavor of old-fashioned rolled oats; however, quick oats can be substituted. Do not use instant oats. For more information on making a foil sling, see page 267.

CRUST

- ¾ cup (3¾ ounces) all-purpose flour
- ⅓ cup packed (2⅓ ounces) light brown sugar
- ¼ cup pecans, toasted and chopped coarse
- ½ teaspoon salt
- ¼ teaspoon baking powder
- 3 tablespoons unsalted butter, cut into ½-inch pieces and chilled

FILLING

- ¾ cup raspberry jam
- 2½ ounces (½ cup) raspberries
- 1 tablespoon lemon juice
- ½ cup (1½ ounces) old-fashioned rolled oats
- ¼ cup packed (1¾ ounces) light brown sugar
- 2 tablespoons all-purpose flour
- ¼ teaspoon ground cinnamon
- ⅛ teaspoon salt
- 2 tablespoons unsalted butter, melted and cooled

1. FOR THE CRUST: Adjust oven rack to middle position and heat oven to 350 degrees. Make foil sling for 8-inch square baking pan by folding 2 long sheets of aluminum foil so each is 8 inches wide. Lay sheets of foil in pan perpendicular to each other, with extra foil hanging over edges of pan. Push foil into corners and up sides of pan, smoothing foil flush to pan. Lightly coat foil with vegetable oil spray.

2. Pulse flour, sugar, pecans, salt, and baking powder in food processor until combined, about 5 pulses. Sprinkle butter over top and pulse until mixture is pale yellow and resembles coarse cornmeal, about 8 pulses. Transfer mixture to prepared pan; press firmly into even layer using wide metal spatula. Bake until crust is fragrant and beginning to brown, 20 to 24 minutes, rotating pan halfway through baking. Let cool on wire rack for at least 15 minutes.

3. FOR THE FILLING: Increase oven temperature to 375 degrees. Mash jam, raspberries, and lemon juice together in bowl with fork until just a few pieces of raspberry remain. In separate bowl, combine oats, sugar, flour, cinnamon, and salt, then add melted butter and toss gently with fork. Spread berry mixture evenly over baked crust, then sprinkle with oat mixture. Bake bars until filling is bubbling and topping is deep golden brown, 22 to 25 minutes, rotating pan halfway through baking.

4. Let bars cool completely in pan on wire rack, about 2 hours. Remove from pan using foil sling and cut into 16 squares. Serve.

BEFORE → **AFTER**	200 → **150** CALORIES	10 → **5** GRAMS FAT	5 → **2.5** GRAMS SAT FAT

Lemon Squares

Makes 9 squares

✓ **WHY THIS RECIPE WORKS:** Standard recipes for this treat pack in over 20 grams of fat and almost 400 calories per square—and that's assuming you can stop at one. We knew the key to a slimmer bar that didn't taste like diet food was all in the crust. We tried a variety of fats (butter, oil, margarine, reduced-fat cream cheese) in different quantities in the shortbread crust, but there was no good substitute for butter. Fortunately, we found that we could bake a successful, buttery crust with only 4 tablespoons of butter. Milk helped the crust hold together, but it was still on the gummy side until we thought to add cornstarch, which brought back the crispness. Lemon zest and sugar helped improve the flavor, and a bit of baking powder gave the crust just the lift it needed. Lightening the basic lemon curd was a bit easier; we omitted an egg yolk with no loss in flavor or texture, and we cut back on the sugar until the flavor was just sweet enough to balance the tartness of the lemons. Press the crust dough snugly against the pan edges to keep the lemon topping from running beneath the crust. For more information on making a foil sling, see page 267.

CRUST

- ¾ cup (3¾ ounces) all-purpose flour
- ⅓ cup (1⅓ ounces) confectioners' sugar
- 3 tablespoons cornstarch
- 1 teaspoon grated lemon zest
- ½ teaspoon baking powder
- ¼ teaspoon salt
- 4 tablespoons unsalted butter, cut into ½-inch pieces and chilled
- 1 tablespoon milk

FILLING

- ¾ cup (5¼ ounces) granulated sugar
- 1 large egg plus 1 large white
- 2 tablespoons all-purpose flour
- ⅛ teaspoon salt
- 1 tablespoon grated lemon zest plus 6 tablespoons juice (2 lemons)
- 1 tablespoon confectioners' sugar

1. FOR THE CRUST: Adjust oven rack to middle position and heat oven to 350 degrees. Make foil sling for 8-inch square baking pan by folding 2 long sheets of aluminum foil so each is 8 inches wide. Lay sheets of foil in pan perpendicular to each other, with extra foil hanging over edges of pan. Push foil into corners and up sides of pan, smoothing foil flush to pan. Lightly coat foil with vegetable oil spray.

2. Process flour, sugar, cornstarch, lemon zest, baking powder, and salt in food processor until combined, about 10 seconds. Add chilled butter and milk and pulse until mixture resembles coarse meal, about 10 pulses. Transfer mixture to prepared pan and press firmly into even layer using wide metal spatula. Bake until edges are lightly browned, 16 to 20 minutes, rotating pan halfway through baking. Let cool on wire rack for at least 15 minutes.

3. FOR THE FILLING: Reduce oven temperature to 325 degrees. Whisk granulated sugar, egg and white, flour, and salt together in bowl until smooth. Stir in lemon zest and juice. Pour filling over baked crust. Bake until filling is set, 15 to 20 minutes. Let bars cool completely in pan on wire rack, about 1 hour. Remove from pan using foil sling, cut into 9 squares, and dust with confectioners' sugar. Serve.

BEFORE → **AFTER**	390 → **190** CALORIES	22 → **6** GRAMS FAT	13 → **3.5** GRAMS SAT FAT

Key Lime Bars

Makes 16 bars

✓ **WHY THIS RECIPE WORKS:** Great Key lime bars are a balancing act of tart and creamy, soft and crisp. Could we cut the fat and calories without disrupting this harmony? For our first move, we lightened the custard by using reduced-fat cream cheese and low-fat sweetened condensed milk instead of their full-fat counterparts, and by swapping an egg white for the yolk. Next, we bypassed the bottled lime juice; though convenient, bottled juice is harsh, bitter, and light on the lime flavor. For Key lime bars with a big citrus punch, we used both fresh-squeezed lime juice and lime zest. While many recipes insist on using only tiny, tart Key limes, we found that everyday limes worked just fine. Graham cracker crumbs, held together with just a few pats of butter and sweetened with a small amount of sugar, made the perfect complement to our creamy, tangy filling. If you use Key limes, note that you'll need about 20 Key limes to yield ½ cup of juice. For more information on making a foil sling, see page 267.

CRUST

- **8** whole graham crackers, broken into 1-inch pieces
- **4** tablespoons unsalted butter, melted and cooled
- **3** tablespoons sugar
-    Pinch salt

FILLING

- **1½** ounces ⅓ less fat cream cheese (neufchatel), softened
- **1** tablespoon grated lime zest plus ½ cup juice (4 limes)
-    Pinch salt
- **1** (14-ounce) can low-fat sweetened condensed milk
- **1** large egg white

1. FOR THE CRUST: Adjust oven rack to middle position and heat oven to 325 degrees. Make foil sling for 8-inch square baking pan by folding 2 long sheets of aluminum foil so each is 8 inches wide. Lay sheets of foil in pan perpendicular to each other, with extra foil hanging over edges of pan. Push foil into corners and up sides of pan, smoothing foil flush to pan. Lightly coat foil with vegetable oil spray.

2. Process graham crackers in food processor to fine, even crumbs, about 30 seconds. Add melted butter, sugar, and salt and pulse to incorporate, about 5 pulses. Transfer mixture to prepared pan and press firmly into even layer using wide metal spatula. Bake until crust is fragrant and beginning to brown, 12 to 16 minutes, rotating pan halfway through baking. Let cool on wire rack for at least 15 minutes.

3. FOR THE FILLING: Combine cream cheese, lime zest, and salt in medium bowl. Whisk in condensed milk until smooth, then whisk in egg white, followed by lime juice. Pour filling over baked crust and smooth top. Bake until center is firm and edges begin to pull away slightly from sides, 15 to 20 minutes.

4. Let bars cool completely in pan on wire rack, about 1 hour. Cover loosely with plastic wrap and refrigerate until thoroughly chilled, 2 to 3 hours. Remove from pan using foil sling and cut into 16 squares. Serve.

BEFORE → **AFTER**   190 → **130** CALORIES   9 → **4.5** GRAMS FAT   6 → **3** GRAMS SAT FAT

Blondies

Makes 24 blondies

✅ **WHY THIS RECIPE WORKS:** Chewy, rich, and dotted with chocolate chips, blondies rely on a good dose of brown sugar for their irresistible flavor. To make over our blondies but keep all the rich flavor and moist, chewy texture, we started by cutting back on the butter and chocolate chips. Unfortunately, we were met with flavorless, dry squares. Substituting corn syrup for some of the brown sugar ensured our blondies were moist, and letting the batter rest after we whisked it together helped the sugar dissolve and gave our low-fat blondies the chew they were missing. By switching to mini chocolate chips, we were able to get away with using less but were still guaranteed a bit of chocolate in every bite. For even more flavor, and to amp up the caramel notes of our blondies, we added butterscotch chips to the mix. If you prefer, you can substitute white chocolate chips for the butterscotch chips, or you can use a combination of the two. For more information on making a foil sling, see page 267.

1 cup packed (7 ounces) light brown sugar

½ cup light corn syrup

6 tablespoons unsalted butter, melted and cooled

½ teaspoon salt

2 large eggs

2 teaspoons vanilla extract

1¼ cups (6¼ ounces) all-purpose flour

½ cup (3 ounces) mini semisweet chocolate chips

⅓ cup (2 ounces) butterscotch chips

1. Adjust oven rack to middle position and heat oven to 350 degrees. Make foil sling for 13 by 9-inch baking pan by folding 2 long sheets of aluminum foil; first sheet should be 13 inches wide and second sheet should be 9 inches wide. Lay sheets of foil in pan perpendicular to each other, with extra foil hanging over edges of pan. Push foil into corners and up sides of pan, smoothing foil flush to pan. Lightly coat foil with vegetable oil spray.

2. Whisk sugar, corn syrup, melted butter, and salt together in large bowl. Whisk in eggs and vanilla until no lumps remain, about 30 seconds. Let mixture stand 3 minutes, then whisk constantly for 30 seconds. Repeat process of resting and whisking 2 more times until mixture is thick, smooth, and shiny. Gently stir in flour with rubber spatula until combined.

3. Scrape batter into prepared pan, smooth top, and sprinkle with chocolate chips and butterscotch chips. Bake until toothpick inserted into center comes out with few moist crumbs attached, 22 to 25 minutes, rotating pan halfway through baking.

4. Let blondies cool completely in pan on wire rack, about 2 hours. Remove from pan using foil sling and cut into 24 squares. Serve.

BEFORE → **AFTER**	200 → **140** CALORIES	11 → **5** GRAMS FAT	5 → **3** GRAMS SAT FAT

Oatmeal Fudge Bars

Makes 16 bars

✔ **WHY THIS RECIPE WORKS:** For lightened oatmeal fudge bars that didn't compromise on the fudgy texture, we ditched the butter, sugar, and eggs altogether in favor of marshmallows. When melted in the microwave with a cup of chocolate chips, the marshmallows gave our filling volume and ample sweetness without adding any fat. Some skim milk helped us thin out the mixture to the right consistency, while a little bit of flour provided structure. To add intensity and ramp up the deep, chocolaty notes, we added instant espresso powder to the mix. To trim the fat count even more, we reduced the amount of butter in the crust and topping by half, and melted it so that it would evenly coat the oats in both and make them crisp. Old-fashioned rolled oats may be substituted for the quick oats, although the bars will be more chewy. For more information on making a foil sling, see page 267.

CRUST AND TOPPING

- ½ cup (2½ ounces) all-purpose flour
- ½ cup (1½ ounces) quick oats
- ⅓ cup packed (2⅓ ounces) light brown sugar
- ¼ teaspoon baking powder
- ⅛ teaspoon salt
- 4 tablespoons unsalted butter, melted and cooled

FILLING

- ½ cup (2½ ounces) all-purpose flour
- 1½ teaspoons instant espresso powder or instant coffee powder
- ¼ teaspoon salt
- 1 cup (6 ounces) semisweet chocolate chips
- 4 ounces (2 cups) marshmallows
- ¼ cup skim milk
- 1 teaspoon vanilla extract
  Vegetable oil spray

1. FOR THE CRUST AND TOPPING: Adjust oven rack to middle position and heat oven to 325 degrees. Make foil sling for 8-inch square baking pan by folding 2 long sheets of aluminum foil so each is 8 inches wide. Lay sheets of foil in pan perpendicular to each other, with extra foil hanging over edges of pan. Push foil into corners and up sides of pan, smoothing foil flush to pan. Spray foil with vegetable oil spray.

2. Whisk flour, oats, sugar, baking powder, and salt together in bowl. Stir in melted butter until combined. Measure out and reserve ¼ cup of mixture for topping. Transfer remaining mixture to prepared pan and press firmly into even layer using wide metal spatula. Bake crust until fragrant and beginning to brown, 20 to 24 minutes, rotating pan halfway through baking. Let cool on wire rack for at least 15 minutes.

3. FOR THE FILLING: Whisk flour, espresso powder, and salt together in bowl. Microwave chocolate chips, marshmallows, and milk together in large bowl, stirring often, until melted and smooth, 1 to 3 minutes. Let cool slightly, then stir in vanilla and flour mixture until just incorporated.

4. Spread filling evenly over baked crust. Sprinkle with reserved oat mixture and spray lightly with vegetable oil spray. Bake until edges are set but center is still slightly soft, about 20 minutes, rotating pan halfway through baking.

5. Let bars cool completely in pan on wire rack, about 2 hours. Remove from pan using foil sling and cut into 16 squares. Serve.

BEFORE → AFTER	260 → **160** CALORIES	12 → **6** GRAMS FAT	7 → **3.5** GRAMS SAT FAT

NEW YORK-STYLE CHEESECAKE

More Sweet Treats

Apple Crisp

Serves 6

✔ **WHY THIS RECIPE WORKS:** Most apple crisp recipes load up the baking dish with too much sugar and too much butter, leading to a dessert that packs in almost 30 grams of fat and 600 calories per serving. For a lighter dessert that put the fruit front and center, we started by cooking and mashing a portion of the apples with apple juice and cinnamon to create a sauce that would help thicken the filling. Since the apples and juice provided plenty of sweetness, we were able to cut down on the sugar substantially. Apple slices, cooked down slightly before baking, gave our filling a hearty texture. To cut down on the fat in the crispy topping, we kept the oats but traded the usual nuts for Grape-Nuts cereal, which provided a satisfying crunch with significantly less fat. We tried cutting back on the butter in the topping, but this made it dry and too crumbly. Switching to melted butter helped because it coated the oats evenly and kept them moist, and adding some of the mashed apples ensured the topping stuck together. Instant or quick oats will make the topping sandy, so be sure to use old-fashioned oats.

TOPPING

- ⅔ cup (2 ounces) old-fashioned rolled oats
- ⅓ cup (1½ ounces) Grape-Nuts cereal
- 5 tablespoons packed (2¼ ounces) light brown sugar
- ¼ cup (1¼ ounces) all-purpose flour
- 3 tablespoons unsalted butter, melted and cooled
- ½ teaspoon ground cinnamon
- ⅛ teaspoon salt

FILLING

- 4 pounds Golden Delicious apples, peeled, cored, and halved
- 1 cup apple juice
- 2 tablespoons packed light brown sugar
- ¾ teaspoon ground cinnamon
- 2 teaspoons lemon juice

1. FOR THE TOPPING: Process ⅓ cup oats in food processor until finely ground, about 20 seconds. Transfer processed oats to medium bowl and stir in remaining topping ingredients.

2. FOR THE FILLING: Adjust oven rack to upper-middle position and heat oven to 400 degrees. Cut half of apples into 1-inch chunks. Slice remaining apples into ¼-inch-thick wedges.

3. Bring apple chunks, juice, sugar, and cinnamon to simmer in 12-inch nonstick skillet over medium heat. Cover and cook, stirring occasionally, until apples are tender, about 15 minutes. Transfer mixture to large bowl and mash smooth with potato masher. Measure out and reserve 1 tablespoon of mashed apple for topping. Return remaining mashed apple mixture to skillet and add sliced apples. Cover and cook over medium heat until slices begin to soften, 3 to 4 minutes. Off heat, stir in lemon juice.

4. Scrape filling into 8-inch square baking dish and smooth into even layer. Stir reserved mashed apple into topping mixture until topping is crumbly. Sprinkle topping over filling. Bake until juices are bubbling and topping is deep golden brown, about 25 minutes. Cool on wire rack until warm, about 15 minutes. Serve.

BEFORE → **AFTER**	600 → **330**	29 → **6**	13 → **3.5**
	CALORIES	GRAMS FAT	GRAMS SAT FAT

Strawberry Shortcakes

Serves 8

✓ **WHY THIS RECIPE WORKS:** Sure, this dessert makes the perfect showcase for ripe, fresh, in-season fruit. But though this dish might seem virtuous, the buttery shortcakes, sweetened berries, and overload of whipped cream all add up quickly when it comes to fat and calories. To trim the fat from our shortcakes, we cut the amount of butter in half and used a combination of low-fat milk and low-fat yogurt in place of the standard heavy cream. To give the cakes a little more heft so they would hold up better under the weight of the fruit, we added an egg to the dough. Melting the butter and stirring it into our chilled milk and yogurt ensured they puffed nicely and were tender. For a thick, saucy filling that boasted big bites of berries, we crushed a portion of the fruit with some sugar, then stirred in the remaining berries and let it sit so the sugar could dissolve and the berries could release their juice. Finally, to cut some fat from the topping but still keep it rich and creamy, we swapped in ¼ cup low-fat sour cream for the same amount of heavy cream. As an added bonus, the tang provided by the sour cream made a great counterpoint to the sweet fruit.

BISCUITS

- **2 cups (10 ounces) all-purpose flour**
- **2 tablespoons sugar**
- **2 teaspoons baking powder**
- **¾ teaspoon salt**
- **½ cup plain low-fat yogurt, chilled**
- **6 tablespoons 1 percent low-fat milk, chilled**
- **1 large egg**
- **4 tablespoons unsalted butter, melted and hot**

STRAWBERRIES AND WHIPPED CREAM

- **2½ pounds strawberries, hulled (8 cups)**
- **7 tablespoons sugar**
- **¼ cup heavy cream**
- **½ teaspoon vanilla extract**
- **¼ cup low-fat sour cream**

1. FOR THE BISCUITS: Adjust oven rack to upper-middle position and heat oven to 425 degrees. Line baking sheet with parchment paper. Whisk flour, 4 teaspoons sugar, baking powder, and salt together in large bowl. In separate bowl, whisk yogurt, milk, and egg together, then stir in hot melted butter until it forms small clumps. Stir yogurt mixture into flour mixture until dough comes together and no dry bits remain.

2. Using greased ¼-cup measure, scoop out and drop 8 mounds of dough onto prepared sheet, spaced about 1½ inches apart. Sprinkle remaining 2 teaspoons sugar over top. Bake shortcakes until golden brown and crisp, about 15 minutes, rotating sheet halfway through baking. Transfer biscuits to wire rack and let cool for 15 minutes.

3. FOR THE STRAWBERRIES AND WHIPPED CREAM: Using potato masher, crush 3 cups strawberries with 6 tablespoons sugar in large bowl. Thinly slice remaining 5 cups strawberries, then stir into mashed strawberries. Let sit at room temperature until sugar has dissolved and berries are juicy, about 30 minutes.

4. Just before serving, use stand mixer fitted with whisk to whip cream, vanilla, and remaining 1 tablespoon sugar on medium-low speed until foamy, about 1 minute. Increase speed to high and whip until soft peaks form, 1 to 3 minutes. Gently fold in sour cream by hand. Split shortcakes in half. Spoon berry mixture over shortcake bottoms, dollop with whipped cream, and replace shortcake tops. Serve.

BEFORE → **AFTER**	460 → **320**	25 → **10**	16 → **6**
	CALORIES	GRAMS FAT	GRAMS SAT FAT

Lemon Pound Cake

Serves 8

✔ **WHY THIS RECIPE WORKS:** Pick up a slice of this rich, buttery cake at the local bake shop and you'll also be picking up about 500 calories and 25 grams of fat—which is a lot for a simple afternoon snack. We wanted to slash the fat from our pound cake so it didn't have to be a once-in-a-while treat. We cut back on the butter as low as we could go, then looked for other ways to keep our loaf moist. Low-fat sour cream worked perfectly and added a subtle tangy flavor. A bit of vegetable shortening also amped up the moistness and tender texture of our cake and ensured it domed nicely. Although we used two fewer eggs than are called for in most low-fat pound cake recipes, the cake had plenty of structure and richness. For the sugar, we stuck with a full cup—any less and the cake wasn't sweet enough. The one-two punch of lemon juice and lemon zest infused our cake with bright, citrusy notes, and a thin layer of lemon glaze added a final blast of fresh citrus flavor. The cake becomes moister when it sits on the counter, tightly wrapped in plastic, for a day or two.

CAKE

- 1½ cups (7½ ounces) all-purpose flour
- ½ teaspoon baking powder
- ¼ teaspoon salt
- ⅓ cup low-fat sour cream
- 1½ tablespoons grated lemon zest plus 1½ tablespoons juice (2 lemons)
- ½ teaspoon vanilla extract
- 1 cup (7 ounces) granulated sugar
- 5 tablespoons unsalted butter, softened
- 1 tablespoon vegetable shortening
- 3 large eggs, room temperature

GLAZE

- ⅓ cup (1⅓ ounces) confectioners' sugar
- 1 tablespoon lemon juice

1. FOR THE CAKE: Adjust oven rack to middle position and heat oven to 300 degrees. Grease and flour 8½ by 4½-inch loaf pan. Whisk flour, baking powder, and salt together in bowl. In separate bowl, whisk sour cream, lemon juice, and vanilla together. In another bowl, whisk sugar and lemon zest together until well combined.

2. Using stand mixer fitted with paddle, beat butter, shortening, and sugar-zest mixture on medium-high speed until pale and fluffy, about 3 minutes. Add eggs, one at a time, and mix until combined (batter may look slightly curdled). Reduce speed to low and add flour mixture in 3 additions, alternating with sour cream mixture in 2 additions, scraping down bowl as needed. Give batter final stir by hand.

3. Scrape batter into prepared pan and smooth top. Gently tap pan on counter to release air bubbles. Bake until cake is golden brown and toothpick inserted in center comes out with few moist crumbs attached, 60 to 70 minutes, rotating pan halfway through baking. Let cake cool in pan on wire rack for 10 minutes. Remove cake from pan and let cool completely, about 2 hours.

4. FOR THE GLAZE: Whisk sugar and lemon juice together in bowl until smooth. Brush glaze over cake and let sit for 10 minutes. Serve.

BEFORE NUMBERS BASED ON: Lemon Pound Cake from Au Bon Pain	BEFORE → **AFTER** 1 SERVING = 1-INCH SLICE	490 → **310** CALORIES	25 → **11** GRAMS FAT	5 → **5** GRAMS SAT FAT

Key Lime Pie

Serves 8

✔ **WHY THIS RECIPE WORKS:** Key lime pie tastes light, bright, and refreshing—so it's surprising to learn that a single slice clocks in at 21 grams of fat and 410 calories. Swapping out the traditional full-fat cream cheese for the reduced-fat variety helped us slash fat right off the bat, and adding nonfat Greek yogurt to the filling ensured our lightened pie offered the same rich texture of the original version. The tanginess from the yogurt also enhanced the lime flavor, letting us cut back on the number of limes. Sweetened condensed milk is another common ingredient in this pie; fortunately, we found switching from full-fat to fat-free didn't compromise the flavor or texture at all. To further cut calories and fat from the crust, we eliminated half the sugar and swapped in some light cream cheese for a portion of the butter. In the end, we trimmed more than half the fat in our revamped Key lime pie, yet it still delivered an ultra-creamy texture, serious tang, and a richly flavored crust.

8	whole graham crackers, broken into 1-inch pieces
1	tablespoon sugar
3	tablespoons unsalted butter, melted and cooled
4	ounces (8 tablespoons) ⅓ less fat cream cheese (neufchatel), softened
1¼	teaspoons unflavored gelatin
1	tablespoon grated lime zest plus ¾ cup juice (6 limes)
1	(14-ounce) can fat-free sweetened condensed milk
½	cup 0 percent Greek yogurt
1	teaspoon vanilla extract

1. Adjust oven rack to middle position and heat oven to 325 degrees. Process graham crackers and sugar together in food processor to fine, even crumbs, about 30 seconds. Add melted butter and 2 tablespoons cream cheese and pulse to incorporate, about 5 pulses.

2. Sprinkle mixture into 9-inch pie plate. Using bottom of measuring cup, press crumbs into even layer on bottom and sides of pie plate. Bake crust until fragrant and beginning to brown, 12 to 14 minutes. Let cool completely on wire rack, about 45 minutes.

3. Sprinkle gelatin over 3 tablespoons lime juice in bowl and let sit until gelatin softens, about 5 minutes. Microwave until mixture is bubbling around edges and gelatin dissolves, about 30 seconds. Process remaining 6 tablespoons cream cheese, condensed milk, and yogurt in now-empty food processor until smooth, about 1 minute. With processor running, add gelatin mixture, remaining 9 tablespoons lime juice, lime zest, and vanilla and process until thoroughly combined, about 1 minute.

4. Scrape mixture into cooled pie shell and smooth top. Cover with plastic wrap and refrigerate until firm, at least 3 hours or up to 2 days. Cut pie into 8 pieces and serve.

BEFORE → **AFTER**	410 → **250**	21 → **8**	13 → **4.5**
	CALORIES	GRAMS FAT	GRAMS SAT FAT

Pineapple Upside-Down Cake

Serves 8

✔ **WHY THIS RECIPE WORKS:** This retro classic boasts a tender, buttery cake topped with sugar-glazed pineapple. Light and healthy? Probably not. For our makeover, we ditched the canned pineapple rings and jarred cherries that we've spotted on most iterations of this dessert (the cherries offered calories but no flavor) and opted for frozen pineapple, which delivered consistently sweet results every time. For a leaner cake, we decreased the butter and used fat-free sour cream rather than the full-fat variety or the whole milk called for in many recipes. Typically, pineapple upside-down cake calls for brown sugar in the topping and white sugar in the cake, but we decided to swap out some of the white sugar in the cake for brown, which delivered a moister texture and deeper flavor. Merely tossing our pineapple with brown sugar before topping it with the batter resulted in a finished upside-down cake that was a soggy, runny mess. To combat the problem, we first sautéed the fruit in the sugar to caramelize the pineapple and reduce some of the juices, then we topped it with the batter. Once inverted, our lightened cake both looked and tasted every bit as good as its full-fat cousin. If you can't find frozen pineapple, you can substitute fresh.

PINEAPPLE

4	cups (24 ounces) frozen pineapple, thawed and cut into ½-inch pieces
⅓	cup packed (2⅓ ounces) dark brown sugar
1½	tablespoons unsalted butter
2	teaspoons lemon juice
½	teaspoon vanilla extract

CAKE

1	cup (5 ounces) all-purpose flour
1	teaspoon baking powder
½	teaspoon salt
½	cup nonfat sour cream
½	cup (3½ ounces) granulated sugar
¼	cup packed (1¾ ounces) dark brown sugar
2	large eggs
1½	teaspoons vanilla extract
4	tablespoons unsalted butter, melted and cooled

1. FOR THE PINEAPPLE: Adjust oven rack to middle position and heat oven to 350 degrees. Grease 9-inch round cake pan. Cook pineapple and sugar in 12-inch skillet over medium-high heat, stirring often, until pineapple is light brown and juices are nearly evaporated, 12 to 15 minutes. Off heat, stir in butter, lemon juice, and vanilla. Transfer pineapple mixture to prepared pan and smooth into even layer.

2. FOR THE CAKE: Whisk flour, baking powder, and salt together in bowl. In large bowl, whisk sour cream, granulated sugar, brown sugar, eggs, and vanilla together until smooth. Slowly whisk in melted butter until incorporated. Whisk in flour mixture until just incorporated (do not overmix).

3. Scrape batter evenly into pan, covering pineapple completely. Bake until cake is golden and toothpick inserted into center comes out clean, 25 to 30 minutes, rotating pan halfway through baking. Let cake cool in pan on wire rack for 10 minutes. Turn cake out onto platter and let cool for at least 1 hour before serving.

BEFORE → **AFTER**	460 → **310**	17 → **9**	10 → **5**
	CALORIES	GRAMS FAT	GRAMS SAT FAT

Red Velvet Cupcakes

Makes 12 cupcakes

✔ **WHY THIS RECIPE WORKS:** Granted, the cakes themselves aren't exactly good for you, but the real guilty party in this dessert is the thick, rich layer of cream cheese frosting, which most bakeries just pile on. But before we set about lightening the ultra-fatty frosting, we looked to trim some fat grams from the cakes. We started by scaling back on the butter and increasing the amount of buttermilk, which is naturally lean. Switching to cake flour, which has less protein than all-purpose, ensured our low-fat cakes stayed tender. A small amount of food coloring gave them the deep red hue this dessert is known for. Finally, for a cupcake that really tasted of chocolate, we bumped up the cocoa powder from the usual tablespoon or two to a full ¼ cup, giving our cupcake an identity and richer flavor. Moving on to the frosting, we first switched to reduced-fat cream cheese, but cream cheese and confectioners' sugar alone resulted in a heavy, dense topping for our tender little cakes. After experimenting with a number of ingredients, we hit on Cool Whip. When folded in, it made our frosting light and fluffy without adding a ton of fat. Two tablespoons of frosting per cupcake provided plenty of richness and a tangy flavor. Finally, we had a red velvet cupcake worthy of its name—and it made just a dent in our daily fat count.

CUPCAKES

- 1½ cups (6 ounces) cake flour
- ¼ cup (¾ ounce) cocoa
- 1 teaspoon baking powder
- ½ teaspoon salt
- 1¼ cup (8¾ ounces) granulated sugar
- ⅔ cup buttermilk, room temperature
- 4 tablespoons unsalted butter, melted and cooled
- 1 large egg
- 1 tablespoon (½ ounce) red food coloring
- 1½ teaspoons vanilla extract

FROSTING

- ¾ cup (3 ounces) confectioners' sugar, sifted
- 4 ounces ⅓ less fat cream cheese (neufchatel), softened
- ½ teaspoon vanilla extract
- 1¾ cups Cool Whip Whipped Topping

1. FOR THE CUPCAKES: Adjust oven rack to middle position and heat oven to 350 degrees. Line 12-cup muffin tin with paper or foil liners. Whisk flour, cocoa, baking powder, and salt together in bowl.

2. In large bowl, whisk sugar, buttermilk, melted butter, egg, food coloring, and vanilla together until combined. Whisk in flour mixture until just incorporated (do not overmix).

3. Using greased ¼-cup measure, fill muffin cups evenly with batter. Bake cupcakes until toothpick inserted in center comes out clean, 15 to 20 minutes, rotating pan halfway through baking. Let cupcakes cool in pan on wire rack for 10 minutes. Remove cupcakes from pan and let cool completely, about 1 hour.

4. FOR THE FROSTING: Whisk sugar, cream cheese, and vanilla together in medium bowl until smooth and free of lumps. Fold in Cool Whip with rubber spatula until incorporated. Cover and refrigerate frosting until chilled and spreadable, about 30 minutes. Spread 2 tablespoons frosting over top of each cupcake. Serve.

BEFORE NUMBERS BASED ON: Red Velvet Cupcake from Au Bon Pain	BEFORE → **AFTER**	400 → **280** CALORIES	22 → **8** GRAMS FAT	7 → **6** GRAMS SAT FAT

Carrot Cake

Serves 15

☑ **WHY THIS RECIPE WORKS:** Sure, carrots are a healthy snack, but that doesn't mean the same can be said of carrot cake. At around 500 calories and over 30 grams of fat per serving, this dessert is far from healthy fare. To revamp our recipe, we started by nixing the nuts and raisins, which contributed too much fat and sugar. Reducing the amount of oil and eggs by more than half resulted in a dry cake, but the calories we saved in the process were too important to ignore. Since carrots contribute moisture, we tried adding more, but found that too many made the batter difficult to spread and the cake heavy. Instead of using oil substitutes, we found that pureed carrots—in the form of baby food—contributed moisture and just the right flavor. For the frosting, light cream cheese offered the right amount of heft and tang. And instead of just cutting back on the butter, we replaced it with Marshmallow Fluff. Made with egg whites, corn syrup, and sugar, it blended easily with the cream cheese and gave us a rich, thick frosting that tasted even more delicious than its full-fat counterpart.

CAKE

- 2½ cups (12½ ounces) all-purpose flour
- 2 teaspoons baking powder
- 1 teaspoon baking soda
- 1½ teaspoons ground cinnamon
- ½ teaspoon ground nutmeg
- ½ teaspoon salt
- ⅛ teaspoon ground cloves
- 2 large eggs
- 1 (4-ounce) jar carrot baby food
- 1 cup packed (7 ounces) dark brown sugar
- ½ cup canola oil
- 1 pound carrots, peeled and shredded

FROSTING

- 8 ounces ⅓ less fat cream cheese (neufchatel), softened
- 1 cup Marshmallow Fluff
- 1½ teaspoons vanilla extract
- ¼ cup (1 ounce) confectioners' sugar

1. FOR THE CAKE: Adjust oven rack to middle position and heat oven to 350 degrees. Grease 13 by 9-inch baking pan, then line bottom of pan with parchment paper.

2. Whisk flour, baking powder, baking soda, cinnamon, nutmeg, salt, and cloves together in bowl. Using stand mixer fitted with paddle, beat eggs, baby food, and sugar on medium speed until smooth and creamy, 1 to 2 minutes. Slowly add oil and mix until thoroughly incorporated, about 1 minute. Reduce speed to low and add flour mixture in 2 additions, scraping down bowl as needed, until batter is nearly smooth, about 30 seconds. Gently fold in carrots by hand.

3. Scrape batter into prepared pan and smooth top. Gently tap pan on counter to release air bubbles. Bake cake until toothpick inserted into center comes out with few moist crumbs attached, 24 to 28 minutes, rotating pan halfway through baking. Let cake cool completely in pan on wire rack, about 1½ hours.

4. FOR THE FROSTING: Using stand mixer fitted with paddle, beat cream cheese, Marshmallow Fluff, and vanilla on medium-high speed until combined, about 1 minute. Sift sugar over cream cheese mixture and beat on low speed until mixture is smooth, about 1 minute. Spread frosting evenly over top of cake. Cut into 15 squares and serve.

BEFORE → **AFTER**	520 → **280** CALORIES	33 → **12** GRAMS FAT	8 → **3** GRAMS SAT FAT

New York–Style Cheesecake

Serves 10

✔ **WHY THIS RECIPE WORKS:** Reduced-fat cream cheese, low-fat cottage cheese, and low-fat yogurt cheese gave us a light cheesecake that rivaled the real deal and boasted a tangy, rich flavor and silky texture. If yogurt cheese is unavailable, place 2 cups of plain low-fat yogurt in a fine-mesh strainer lined with a double layer of cheesecloth and set it over a large bowl. Cover tightly with plastic wrap and refrigerate until it has the texture of cream cheese, at least 10 hours or up to 2 days. Serve with mixed berries.

CRUST

- 8 whole graham crackers, broken into 1-inch pieces
- 4 tablespoons unsalted butter, melted and cooled
- 1 tablespoon sugar

FILLING

- 1 pound (2 cups) 1 percent cottage cheese
- 1 pound ⅓ less fat cream cheese (neufchatel), room temperature
- 8 ounces (1 cup) low-fat yogurt cheese
- 1½ cups (10½ ounces) sugar
- 1 tablespoon vanilla extract
- 1 teaspoon grated lemon zest
- ¼ teaspoon salt
- 3 large eggs, room temperature

1. FOR THE CRUST: Adjust oven rack to middle position and heat oven to 325 degrees. Process graham crackers in food processor to crumbs, about 30 seconds. Add melted butter and sugar and pulse to incorporate, about 5 pulses. Sprinkle mixture into 9-inch springform pan. Using bottom of measuring cup, press crumbs into even layer over pan bottom. Bake until crust is fragrant and looks set, 10 to 15 minutes; let cool completely.

2. FOR THE FILLING: Increase oven temperature to 500 degrees. Line medium bowl with clean dish towel. Spoon cottage cheese into bowl; let drain 30 minutes. Process drained cottage cheese in now-empty food processor until smooth and no visible lumps remain, about 1 minute. Add cream cheese and yogurt cheese; process until smooth, 1 to 2 minutes, scraping down bowl as needed. Add sugar, vanilla, lemon zest, and salt; continue to process until smooth, about 1 minute. With processor running, add eggs, one at a time, and continue to process until smooth.

3. Lightly spray sides of prepared pan containing crust with vegetable oil spray and set on rimmed baking sheet. Pour processed cheese mixture into pan and bake for 10 minutes. Without opening oven door, reduce oven temperature to 200 degrees and continue to bake until center of cheesecake registers 150 degrees, about 1½ hours, rotating pan halfway through baking.

4. Transfer cake to wire rack and run paring knife around edge of cake. Let cool until barely warm, 2½ to 3 hours, running paring knife around edge of cake every hour. Wrap pan tightly in plastic wrap and refrigerate until cold, about 3 hours.

5. To serve, wrap wet, hot kitchen towel around pan and let stand 1 minute. Remove sides of pan. Blot any excess moisture from top of cheesecake with paper towels. Let cheesecake stand at room temperature about 30 minutes; serve.

BEFORE NUMBERS BASED ON: Original Cheesecake from The Cheesecake Factory	BEFORE → **AFTER**	620 → **360** CALORIES	38 → **17** GRAMS FAT	26 → **10** GRAMS SAT FAT

MAKEOVER SPOTLIGHT:
NEW YORK–STYLE CHEESECAKE

1. MAKE A GRAHAM CRACKER CRUST WITH LESS BUTTER:
Graham cracker crusts have a surprising amount of fat, but we found we could easily lower it by simply axing some of the butter. This move worked well with our cheesecake because the crust was only on the bottom of the pan (not the sides), and the weight of the cheesecake kept it firmly in place. To ensure it stayed crisp, we parbaked the crust before adding the filling. Be sure to press the crust firmly into the pan using the bottom of a measuring cup so it doesn't crumble apart when served.

2. SWITCH TO REDUCED-FAT CREAM CHEESE AND ADD IN LOW-FAT COTTAGE CHEESE AND YOGURT CHEESE: Not surprisingly, cream cheese is an ultra-fatty ingredient. Swapping in reduced-fat cream cheese was an obvious move, but we wanted to bring down the fat and calories further. So we substituted some low-fat cottage cheese and yogurt cheese for a portion of the cream cheese; the cottage cheese provided a neutral-tasting base, while the yogurt cheese offered serious tanginess. Be sure to drain the cottage cheese for 30 minutes before using or the filling will be too loose.

3. PROCESS THE FILLING FOR AN ULTRA-SMOOTH TEXTURE:
To ensure our low-fat filling was perfectly smooth and had a rich and creamy texture, we ran it through the food processor. Not only did the food processor make quick work of de-lumping the cottage cheese, but it also guaranteed the three cheeses were thoroughly combined with the eggs and other flavorings.

4. CHECK THE TEMPERATURE FOR A MOIST CHEESECAKE WITH NICELY BROWNED EDGES: Not surprisingly, our low-fat cheesecake turned dry and mealy if overbaked. We found that the only way to accurately test its doneness was to use an instant-read thermometer. Also, to achieve that picture-perfect, well-browned top, we found two oven temperatures worked better than one. We started the cake in a hot 500-degree oven to jump-start the browning, then reduced the oven temperature to 200 degrees (without opening the oven door) and baked the cake until it registered 150 degrees in the center.

Tiramisù

Serves 6

✔ **WHY THIS RECIPE WORKS:** The name of this dessert is Italian for "pick-me-up." So why do we feel so full and heavy after a few spoonfuls? Maybe because it includes an ultra-fatty mixture of mascarpone, whipped cream, and whipped egg yolks, which are layered with liqueur-and-coffee-brushed ladyfingers. To lighten our recipe, we traded the high-fat mascarpone and eggs for a combination of low-fat cottage cheese, reduced-fat cream cheese, and nonfat Greek yogurt; processing this trio together in the food processor gave us a creamy, smooth, nicely thickened mixture. To tone down the boozy flavor, we cut back on the rum, but maximized its punch by soaking the ladyfingers directly in it. A little extra vanilla rounded out the flavor of the creamy filling and masked any tanginess from the cheeses. Be sure to use hard ladyfingers, like those found in the cookie or international aisle, not the fresh, cakelike ladyfingers found in the bakery department. Depending on the brand, 5 ounces is equivalent to 26 to 30 ladyfingers. Be sure to mix the cottage cheese before measuring if any moisture has separated out. You can substitute ¾ cup brewed coffee for the hot water and espresso powder.

¾	cup hot water
2	tablespoons dark rum
1½	tablespoons instant espresso powder
8	ounces ⅓ less fat cream cheese (neufchatel), softened
1½	cups (6 ounces) confectioners' sugar
8	ounces (1 cup) low-fat cottage cheese
½	cup 0 percent Greek yogurt
1	tablespoon vanilla extract
5	ounces dried ladyfingers (savoiardi)
1½	teaspoons cocoa

1. Combine hot water, 4 teaspoons rum, and espresso powder in bowl and let sit for 5 minutes. Process cream cheese, sugar, cottage cheese, yogurt, vanilla, and remaining 2 teaspoons rum in food processor until completely smooth, about 20 seconds.

2. Arrange half of ladyfingers in single layer over bottom of 8-inch square baking dish (some small gaps are OK). Pour half of rum-espresso mixture over top and let sit until most liquid has been absorbed, about 1 minute. Spread half of cream cheese mixture evenly over top. Repeat with remaining ladyfingers, remaining rum-espresso mixture, and remaining cream cheese mixture.

3. Cover with plastic wrap and refrigerate for at least 3 hours or up to 24 hours. Just before serving, dust with cocoa. Serve.

BEFORE → **AFTER**	530 → **350** CALORIES	36 → **10** GRAMS FAT	19 → **5** GRAMS SAT FAT

Peanut Butter Pie

Serves 8

✔️ **WHY THIS RECIPE WORKS:** With its ultra-rich peanut butter filling and buttery, chocolaty crust, what's not to love about this dessert? Maybe the fat count—a single slice of this decadent treat weighs in at almost 60 grams of fat! Working from the bottom up, we replaced the traditional chocolate sandwich cookies in the crust with chocolate wafers, which are much lower in fat but still plenty flavorful and crunchy. We experimented with cutting back on the butter and stopped when we were down to just one tablespoon. A single pat, plus a little water, was enough to hold our cookie crumbs together. For the filling, we swapped the full-fat peanut butter for the reduced-fat variety, but finding a substitute for the heavy cream that traditionally gives the filling its ultra-smooth, creamy texture was more challenging. After trying a number of ingredients, we found the combination of Marshmallow Fluff and Cool Whip did the trick, ensuring our pie tasted every bit as rich as its ultra-fatty cousin. As a bonus, the marshmallow crème offered enough sweetness that we could cut back on the sugar without any loss of flavor. To gild the lily, we topped our pie with more Cool Whip, for a rich-tasting dessert that was worlds away from diet food.

CRUST

5½ ounces (25 cookies) chocolate wafer cookies
5 teaspoons water
1 tablespoon unsalted butter, melted and cooled
1 teaspoon granulated sugar

FILLING

¾ cup Marshmallow Fluff
¾ cup reduced-fat creamy peanut butter
3 cups Cool Whip Whipped Topping
2 tablespoons confectioners' sugar
1 teaspoon vanilla extract
¼ teaspoon salt

1. FOR THE CRUST: Adjust oven rack to middle position and heat oven to 350 degrees. Process cookies in food processor until finely ground, about 15 seconds. Add water, melted butter, and sugar and pulse to incorporate, about 5 pulses.

2. Sprinkle mixture into 9-inch pie plate. Using bottom of measuring cup, press crumbs into even layer on bottom and sides of pie plate. Bake until crust is fragrant and looks set, 13 to 15 minutes. Let cool completely on wire rack, about 45 minutes.

3. FOR THE FILLING: Using stand mixer fitted with whisk, whip Marshmallow Fluff, peanut butter, ¼ cup Cool Whip, sugar, vanilla, and salt on medium speed until combined and smooth, about 1 minute. Reduce speed to medium-low, add 2¼ cups Cool Whip, and whip until incorporated and no streaks remain, 1 to 2 minutes.

4. Scrape mixture into cooled pie shell and smooth top. Cover with plastic wrap and refrigerate until filling is chilled and set, at least 8 hours or up to 1 day. Cut pie into 8 pieces, dollop each piece with 1 tablespoon Cool Whip, and serve.

BEFORE → **AFTER**	720 → **360**	59 → **17**	27 → **8**
	CALORIES	GRAMS FAT	GRAMS SAT FAT

Chilled Lemon Mousse with Raspberry Sauce

Serves 6

✔ **WHY THIS RECIPE WORKS:** Lemon mousse has a light, ethereal texture and delicate lemon flavor that belies the fact that it's traditionally made by combining an egg yolk–heavy lemon curd with whipped heavy cream. To lighten things up, we started by losing the yolks in favor of gelatin, which helped to thicken our mousse. We tried ditching the heavy cream altogether, but at least a little was crucial for mousse with a rich flavor and creamy texture. Instead, we decided to replace some of the cream with whole-milk Greek yogurt. Not only did the yogurt slash the fat count, but it also contributed a rich, tangy flavor that complemented the citrus notes. To give the mousse some lift and volume, we whipped a few egg whites before adding the cream, yogurt, gelatin, and lemon juice. For a fuller, rounder citrus flavor, we added a bit of lemon zest. A simple raspberry sauce made the perfect finishing touch, offering a sweet, slightly tart bite that paired well with the brightly flavored mousse. Do not substitute 2 percent or 0 percent Greek yogurt in the mousse. You can substitute frozen raspberries for the fresh berries in the sauce.

SAUCE

- 3¾ ounces (¾ cup) raspberries
- 2 tablespoons sugar
- 2 tablespoons water
  Pinch salt

MOUSSE

- ¾ teaspoon unflavored gelatin
- 3 tablespoons water
- ½ cup whole Greek yogurt
- ¼ cup heavy cream
- 1½ teaspoons grated lemon zest plus 3 tablespoons juice
- 1 teaspoon vanilla extract
- ⅛ teaspoon salt
- 3 large egg whites
- ¼ teaspoon cream of tartar
- 6 tablespoons (2⅔ ounces) sugar

1. FOR THE SAUCE: Simmer all ingredients together in medium saucepan over medium heat until sugar is dissolved, 2 to 4 minutes. Transfer mixture to blender and process until smooth, about 15 seconds. Strain mixture through fine-mesh strainer; you should have ½ cup sauce. Spoon sauce into six 4-ounce ramekins and refrigerate until chilled, about 20 minutes.

2. FOR THE MOUSSE: Sprinkle gelatin over water in bowl and let sit until gelatin softens, about 5 minutes. In separate bowl, whisk yogurt, heavy cream, lemon zest and juice, vanilla, and salt together until smooth.

3. Whisk egg whites, cream of tartar, and sugar together in bowl of stand mixer. Set bowl over large saucepan of barely simmering water; make sure water does not touch bottom of bowl. Heat mixture, whisking constantly, until tripled in size and mixture registers about 160 degrees, 5 to 10 minutes.

4. Off heat, quickly whisk in gelatin mixture until melted. Using stand mixer fitted with whisk, whip warm mixture on medium-high speed until it forms stiff, shiny peaks, 4 to 6 minutes. Add yogurt mixture and continue to whip until just combined, 30 to 60 seconds. Spoon mousse evenly into chilled ramekins on top of sauce, cover tightly with plastic wrap, and refrigerate until chilled and set, 6 to 8 hours. Serve chilled.

BEFORE → **AFTER**	410 → **150**	29 → **6**	16 → **4**
	CALORIES	GRAMS FAT	GRAMS SAT FAT

Crème Brûlée

Serves 8

✓ **WHY THIS RECIPE WORKS:** For this makeover, we swapped the heavy cream for whole milk and half-and-half and cut back on the egg yolks. Cornstarch ensured the custard was plenty thick and stood up to the heat of the torch, and white chocolate added a luxurious feel without contributing too much fat.

2   ounces white chocolate, chopped
1   vanilla bean, cut in half lengthwise, seeds scraped out and reserved
2   cups half-and-half
1½ cups whole milk
⅓   cup (2⅓ ounces) granulated sugar
¼   teaspoon salt
5   large egg yolks
3   tablespoons cornstarch
8   teaspoons turbinado sugar

1. Adjust oven rack to middle position and heat oven to 300 degrees. Place white chocolate in 8-cup liquid measuring cup. Combine vanilla bean, seeds, half-and-half, milk, granulated sugar, and salt in large saucepan. Whisk egg yolks and cornstarch together in bowl until combined, then whisk into saucepan. Bring to boil over medium heat, stirring constantly, then reduce heat to medium-low; simmer until thickened, about 1 minute. Strain through fine-mesh strainer into liquid measuring cup with chocolate; whisk together until chocolate is melted and custard is completely smooth.

2. Bring 2 quarts water to boil. Place kitchen towel in bottom of roasting pan; arrange eight 4- to 5-ounce ramekins (or fluted dishes) on towel. Divide custard mixture evenly among ramekins. Carefully place pan on oven rack and pour boiling water into pan until water comes halfway up sides of ramekins. Bake until custard is just set and center registers 170 degrees, about 30 minutes (about 20 minutes if using shallow fluted dishes).

3. Carefully transfer ramekins to wire rack; cool to room temperature, about 2 hours. Cover with plastic wrap; refrigerate until well chilled and set, at least 4 hours or up to 2 days.

4. Gently blot away any condensation using paper towels. Sprinkle 1 teaspoon turbinado sugar evenly over each custard. Caramelize sugar with torch until deep golden brown. Serve.

QUICK PREP TIP   BROWNING CRÈME BRÛLÉE
After sprinkling the surface of each custard with turbinado sugar, tilt and tap the ramekin to distribute the sugar in a thin, even layer. Pour out any excess sugar and wipe the inside rim clean. To caramelize the sugar, sweep the flame from the perimeter of the custard toward the middle, keeping it about 2 inches above the ramekin. The sugar is properly caramelized when bubbling and deep golden brown. Be sure to burn the sugar topping on the crème brûlée just before serving. If done too far in advance (more than a half-hour or so), the caramelized sugar topping will soften and eventually turn to liquid caramel.

BEFORE → **AFTER**   580 → **240**   51 → **13**   30 → **8**
CALORIES   GRAMS FAT   GRAMS SAT FAT

Bread Pudding

Serves 6

✔ **WHY THIS RECIPE WORKS:** Cubes of bread, heavy cream, a touch of sugar, and a few egg yolks—combine and bake and you've got bread pudding: a borderline minimalist dessert. But don't be fooled—the calories and fat in this homey classic are hardly negligible. Just one serving of this diet-buster can add 800 calories and 36 grams of fat to your daily tally. To revamp this simple dessert, we started by trading out the egg yolks for whole eggs, which provided structure and significantly reduced the calorie count. Replacing the heavy cream with skim milk slashed the fat, but did nothing to help thicken the custard. A few tablespoons of instant pudding mix solved that problem while also contributing rich flavor without adding a lot of extra calories. As for the bread, the reduced-calorie variety dissolved into the custard and turned our pudding to mush, but we found that cinnamon swirl sandwich bread was sturdy enough to stay firm and also worked to amp up the flavor of our low-fat dessert with its warm spice notes. Both instant and "cook and serve" pudding mixes work here, but avoid sugar-free pudding, which gives the bread pudding a chemical aftertaste.

2	cups skim milk
3	large eggs
5	tablespoons (2¼ ounces) sugar
3	tablespoons vanilla pudding mix
2	teaspoons vanilla extract
¼	teaspoon salt
12	slices cinnamon swirl sandwich bread, cut into ¾-inch pieces
¼	teaspoon ground cinnamon

1. Adjust oven rack to middle position and heat oven to 375 degrees. Lightly spray 8-inch square baking dish with vegetable oil spray.

2. Whisk milk, eggs, ¼ cup sugar, pudding mix, vanilla extract, and salt together in large bowl until combined. Gently stir in bread. Let mixture sit, tossing occasionally, until liquid is mostly absorbed, about 10 minutes.

3. Combine remaining 1 tablespoon sugar and cinnamon in small bowl. Transfer soaked bread mixture to prepared baking dish and sprinkle with cinnamon sugar. Bake bread pudding until just set and surface is golden brown, 35 to 40 minutes. Let bread pudding cool on wire rack for 15 minutes. Serve.

BEFORE → **AFTER**	810 → **320**	36 → **8**	21 → **2**
	CALORIES	GRAMS FAT	GRAMS SAT FAT

Rich and Creamy Banana Pudding

Serves 12

✔ **WHY THIS RECIPE WORKS:** Creamy, sweet, and fruity, banana pudding is a Southern mainstay and road-side restaurant classic. For a lightened version that did the original justice, we bypassed the whole milk in favor of low-fat milk, swapped out a few egg yolks for fat-free sweetened condensed milk, and thickened the mixture with cornstarch for a low-fat yet rich and creamy pudding. Roasting the bananas concentrated their flavor and offered a big, banana-y punch. Low-fat vanilla wafers provided a flavorful cookie layer, while a little whipped cream, plus a bit of nonfat Greek yogurt, made the perfect light yet creamy topping.

PUDDING

7	slightly underripe large bananas
½	cup (3½ ounces) sugar
3	tablespoons cornstarch
4	large egg yolks
4½	cups 1 percent low-fat milk
1	(14-ounce) can fat-free sweetened condensed milk
½	teaspoon salt
1	tablespoon vanilla extract
3	tablespoons lemon juice
1	(11-ounce) box reduced-fat vanilla wafers

TOPPING

½	cup heavy cream, chilled
¼	cup (1¾ ounces) sugar
1½	teaspoons vanilla extract
½	cup 0 percent Greek yogurt

1. FOR THE PUDDING: Adjust oven rack to upper-middle position and heat oven to 325 degrees. Place 3 unpeeled bananas on baking sheet and bake until skins are completely black, about 20 minutes. Let cool for 5 minutes, then peel bananas.

2. Meanwhile, whisk ¼ cup sugar, cornstarch, and egg yolks together in medium bowl until smooth. Whisk remaining ¼ cup sugar, milk, condensed milk, and salt together in large saucepan. Bring to simmer over medium heat. Whisk ½ cup of simmering milk mixture into egg yolk mixture to temper, then slowly whisk yolk mixture into saucepan. Cook, whisking constantly, until mixture is thick and large bubbles appear at surface, about 2 minutes. Off heat, whisk in vanilla.

3. Transfer pudding to food processor. Add warm roasted bananas and 2 tablespoons lemon juice and process until smooth, about 30 seconds. Transfer pudding to large bowl and press lightly greased parchment paper directly against surface of pudding. Refrigerate until slightly cool, about 45 minutes.

4. Cut remaining 4 bananas into ¼-inch slices and toss with remaining 1 tablespoon lemon juice in bowl. Layer one-quarter of chilled pudding, 12 cookies, one-third of sliced bananas, then 12 more cookies evenly into 3-quart trifle dish. Repeat this layering process twice more, then spread remaining pudding over top. (Reserve remaining cookies for garnish.) Press lightly greased parchment paper against surface of pudding and refrigerate until wafers have softened, at least 8 hours or up to 2 days.

5. FOR THE TOPPING: Using stand mixer fitted with whisk, whip cream, sugar, and vanilla on medium-low speed until foamy, about 1 minute. Increase speed to high and whip until soft peaks form, 1 to 3 minutes. Gently fold in yogurt. Top banana pudding with whipped topping, garnish with reserved cookies, and serve.

BEFORE → **AFTER**	600 → **420** CALORIES	31 → **8** GRAMS FAT	17 → **3.5** GRAMS SAT FAT

Nutritional Information

Here you'll find the complete nutritional information for all the recipes in this book; serving size information has been included when the amount is not readily apparent from the recipe. See page 9 for more information on how we calculated the nutritional values of our recipes.

	CAL	FAT	SAT FAT	CHOL	CARB	PROTEIN	FIBER	SODIUM
APPETIZERS AND SNACKS								
Nachos (for 6 nachos)	270	8 g	3.5 g	15 mg	35 g	15 g	5 g	590 mg
Fresh Tomato Salsa (for ¼ cup)	15	0 g	0 g	0 mg	3 g	1 g	1 g	0 mg
Buffalo Wings (for 6 wings)	370	25 g	8 g	105 mg	4 g	31 g	0 g	2190 mg
Coconut Shrimp with Orange Dipping Sauce (for 6 shrimp with sauce)	290	5 g	2 g	120 mg	25 g	19 g	1 g	820 mg
Mozzarella Sticks (for 4 pieces)	230	7 g	4 g	25 mg	19 g	21 g	1 g	700 mg
Herbed Deviled Eggs (for 2 pieces)	60	3.5 g	1 g	95 mg	1 g	6 g	0 g	200 mg
Crab Rangoon (for 2 pieces)	80	3 g	1.5 g	20 mg	7 g	5 g	0 g	180 mg
Stuffed Jalapeños (for 3 pieces)	120	7 g	4.5 g	20 mg	7 g	9 g	0 g	360 mg
Vegetable Egg Rolls (for 1 roll)	100	3.5 g	0 g	5 mg	14 g	3 g	1 g	250 mg
Clams Casino (for 4 clams)	160	9 g	4.5 g	45 mg	7 g	11 g	0 g	580 mg
Hot Spinach Dip (for ⅓ cup)	120	9 g	3 g	15 mg	7 g	4 g	1 g	300 mg
Roasted Artichoke Dip (for ¼ cup)	150	11 g	3.5 g	15 mg	10 g	5 g	3 g	590 mg
Seven-Layer Dip (for ⅓ cup)	130	7 g	0.5 g	5 mg	11 g	4 g	5 g	270 mg
Pita Chips (for 6 chips)	80	0 g	0 g	0 mg	17 g	3 g	1 g	310 mg
Caramelized Onion Dip (for 3 tablespoons)	60	3.5 g	0 g	5 mg	2 g	3 g	0 g	190 mg
Ranch Dip (for 3 tablespoons)	50	2.5 g	0 g	5 mg	1 g	3 g	0 g	140 mg
Bacon-Scallion Cheese Ball (for 2 tablespoons)	80	6 g	4 g	15 mg	1 g	4 g	0 g	140 mg
Pimento Cheese (for ¼ cup)	120	8 g	4.5 g	20 mg	3 g	12 g	0 g	80 mg
Parmesan Popcorn (for 2⅓ cups)	90	2 g	1 g	5 mg	13 g	4 g	3 g	420 mg
SALADS, SANDWICHES, AND PIZZA								
Spinach Salad with Warm Bacon Dressing	150	9 g	3 g	105 mg	9 g	8 g	3 g	390 mg
Chicken Caesar Salad	390	18 g	4 g	120 mg	13 g	42 g	2 g	1110 mg
Low-Fat Croutons (for ½ cup)	40	1.5 g	0 g	0 mg	6 g	1 g	0 g	360 mg
Classic Wedge Salad with Blue Cheese Dressing	130	8 g	2.5 g	15 mg	6 g	6 g	1 g	470 mg
Chinese Chicken Salad	350	14 g	2 g	75 mg	27 g	29 g	4 g	1020 mg
Buffalo Chicken Salad	470	17 g	5 g	130 mg	34 g	43 g	4 g	2070 mg
Classic Cobb Salad	320	19 g	4.5 g	160 mg	8 g	27 g	2 g	650 mg
Classic Cobb Salad (with avocado)	400	27 g	6 g	160 mg	13 g	28 g	5 g	650 mg
Beef Taco Salad	500	19 g	6 g	80 mg	47 g	38 g	7 g	1110 mg
Niçoise Salad	410	21 g	3.5 g	125 mg	32 g	25 g	6 g	760 mg

	CAL	FAT	SAT FAT	CHOL	CARB	PROTEIN	FIBER	SODIUM
Open-Faced Tuna Melts	320	13 g	5 g	80 mg	16 g	33 g	1 g	1210 mg
Drive-Through Cheeseburgers	360	14 g	6 g	80 mg	26 g	31 g	1 g	680 mg
Philly Cheesesteaks	400	15 g	6 g	65 mg	37 g	35 g	3 g	900 mg
Sloppy Joes	310	9 g	2.5 g	45 mg	35 g	21 g	3 g	950 mg
Reuben Sandwiches	430	15 g	5 g	80 mg	34 g	37 g	4 g	2330 mg
Broccoli and Sausage Calzones	540	15 g	5 g	45 mg	68 g	32 g	3 g	1490 mg
Thin-Crust Cheese Pizza (for 2 slices)	350	10 g	4.5 g	15 mg	47 g	16 g	2 g	690 mg

THE SOUP BOWL

	CAL	FAT	SAT FAT	CHOL	CARB	PROTEIN	FIBER	SODIUM
French Onion Soup (for 1½ cups with 1 crouton)	250	3.5 g	1.5 g	10 mg	44 g	10 g	7 g	1010 mg
Creamless Creamy Tomato Soup (for 1½ cups)	190	10 g	1.5 g	0 mg	19 g	3 g	3 g	700 mg
Creamy Mushroom Soup (for 1⅓ cups)	130	5 g	2.5 g	15 mg	12 g	6 g	1 g	690 mg
Classic Corn Chowder (for 1½ cups)	320	12 g	2.5 g	15 mg	51 g	12 g	5 g	370 mg
Loaded Baked Potato Soup (for 1⅓ cups)	270	13 g	6 g	30 mg	28 g	11 g	2 g	590 mg
Broccoli-Cheddar Soup (for 1½ cups)	260	11 g	6 g	30 mg	28 g	13 g	5 g	660 mg
New England Clam Chowder (for 1¼ cups)	240	8 g	3.5 g	40 mg	28 g	13 g	2 g	700 mg
Shrimp Bisque (for 1 cup)	190	6 g	3.5 g	80 mg	12 g	9 g	2 g	690 mg
All-American Chili (for 1½ cups)	320	10 g	2 g	65 mg	29 g	30 g	8 g	910 mg
Beef and Vegetable Stew (for 1½ cups)	440	10 g	2 g	75 mg	45 g	34 g	9 g	780 mg
Pork and Hominy Stew (for 1½ cups)	290	9 g	1.5 g	75 mg	25 g	28 g	5 g	810 mg
Creole-Style Gumbo (for 1¾ cups)	300	8 g	2 g	140 mg	19 g	34 g	3 g	1430 mg

CLASSIC CASSEROLES

	CAL	FAT	SAT FAT	CHOL	CARB	PROTEIN	FIBER	SODIUM
Chicken Divan	430	10 g	3.5 g	85 mg	50 g	37 g	2 g	820 mg
Chicken Florentine	340	13 g	3.5 g	120 mg	14 g	41 g	4 g	980 mg
Chicken Tetrazzini	290	8 g	4.5 g	55 mg	31 g	22 g	3 g	890 mg
Chicken Pot Pie	340	13 g	5 g	75 mg	25 g	30 g	3 g	590 mg
Tuna Noodle Casserole	450	16 g	7 g	90 mg	48 g	29 g	3 g	890 mg
Mexican Lasagna	400	12 g	3 g	40 mg	52 g	24 g	9 g	710 mg
Chicken Chilaquiles	520	13 g	2.5 g	120 mg	51 g	44 g	6 g	800 mg
King Ranch Casserole	380	16 g	6 g	85 mg	31 g	27 g	4 g	1060 mg
Chicken Enchiladas	340	11 g	5 g	70 mg	33 g	32 g	6 g	750 mg
Shepherd's Pie	450	15 g	6 g	115 mg	49 g	30 g	5 g	850 mg
Cheeseburger Pie	270	12 g	5 g	60 mg	15 g	22 g	1 g	640 mg
Meat and Cheese Lasagna	350	13 g	6 g	85 mg	32 g	26 g	4 g	1040 mg
Spinach Lasagna	330	13 g	7 g	70 mg	32 g	21 g	2 g	690 mg
Baked Manicotti	400	12 g	6 g	40 mg	47 g	27 g	5 g	1560 mg
Stuffed Shells with Meat Sauce	470	14 g	6 g	50 mg	51 g	34 g	5 g	1640 mg
Baked Ziti	410	10 g	5 g	25 mg	58 g	25 g	4 g	1380 mg
Ultimate Chili Mac	340	11 g	5 g	50 mg	40 g	27 g	6 g	990 mg
Baked Macaroni and Cheese	470	11 g	5 g	45 mg	66 g	28 g	1 g	600 mg

	CAL	FAT	SAT FAT	CHOL	CARB	PROTEIN	FIBER	SODIUM
BAKED NOT FRIED								
Oven-Fried Chicken (for 2 pieces)	450	10 g	2 g	145 mg	31 g	55 g	1 g	1120 mg
Crispy Chicken Nuggets (for 12 nuggets)	420	10 g	1.5 g	110 mg	34 g	45 g	2 g	710 mg
Chicken Chimichangas	660	25 g	7 g	115 mg	60 g	46 g	5 g	900 mg
General Tso's Chicken	490	8 g	1.5 g	110 mg	62 g	44 g	2 g	1410 mg
Chicken-Fried Steak	580	20 g	6 g	130 mg	42 g	55 g	1 g	800 mg
Eggplant Parmesan with Spaghetti	550	13 g	5 g	25 mg	83 g	29 g	12 g	1510 mg
Oven-Fried Fish with Tartar Sauce	400	15 g	2.5 g	90 mg	26 g	37 g	1 g	1180 mg
Low-Fat Tartar Sauce (for 1 tablespoon)	25	2.5 g	0 g	0 mg	1 g	0 g	0 g	125 mg
Oven-Fried Shrimp (for 8 shrimp)	310	9 g	0.5 g	145 mg	33 g	23 g	1 g	1100 mg
Creamy Chipotle Chile Sauce (for 2 tablespoons)	45	4 g	0.5 g	5 mg	2 g	0 g	0 g	135 mg
A CHICKEN IN EVERY POT								
Chicken and Dumplings (for 1½ cups stew with 3 dumplings)	350	7 g	2.5 g	80 mg	36 g	30 g	3 g	1130 mg
Deviled Chicken	240	10 g	3.5 g	120 mg	9 g	37 g	1 g	1130 mg
Nut-Crusted Chicken Breasts	430	16 g	2 g	110 mg	23 g	45 g	3 g	620 mg
Chicken Kiev	460	18 g	9 g	145 mg	25 g	47 g	1 g	1130 mg
Chicken Fricassee	310	10 g	3 g	120 mg	11 g	41 g	2 g	770 mg
Chicken Marsala	380	12 g	3 g	115 mg	18 g	39 g	1 g	670 mg
Chicken Parmesan with Spaghetti	660	16 g	5 g	125 mg	72 g	57 g	6 g	1420 mg
Low-Fat Tomato Sauce (for ½ cup)	50	1.5 g	0 g	0 mg	9 g	1 g	3 g	400 mg
Chicken Piccata with Spaghetti	560	15 g	4.5 g	120 mg	51 g	45 g	2 g	980 mg
Chicken Cordon Bleu	500	12 g	3.5 g	185 mg	26 g	68 g	1 g	1530 mg
Cashew Chicken	280	11 g	2 g	55 mg	20 g	23 g	3 g	800 mg
FAVORITES FROM LAND AND SEA								
Steak au Poivre with Brandied Cream Sauce (for 1 filet plus ¼ cup sauce)	370	17 g	5 g	115 mg	5 g	39 g	0 g	750 mg
Steak Tips with Mushroom-Onion Gravy	210	6 g	1.5 g	55 mg	8 g	28 g	1 g	380 mg
Stir-Fried Beef and Broccoli with Classic Brown Stir-Fry Sauce (for 1½ cups)	290	11 g	2.5 g	55 mg	24 g	24 g	5 g	640 mg
Beef Stroganoff	370	7 g	1.5 g	45 mg	45 g	29 g	5 g	550 mg
Meatloaf (for 1¼-inch slice)	300	13 g	5 g	105 mg	17 g	26 g	1 g	670 mg
Turkey Tacos (for 2 tacos without garnishes)	320	14 g	3 g	65 mg	28 g	26 g	5 g	550 mg
Fresh Tomato Topping for Tacos (for ¼ cup)	10	0 g	0 g	0 mg	3 g	1 g	1 g	0 mg
Stuffed Bell Peppers (for 1 pepper)	350	10 g	3.5 g	60 mg	41 g	26 g	6 g	1150 mg
Stuffed Pork Chops	280	10 g	3.5 g	100 mg	12 g	36 g	4 g	500 mg
Smothered Pork Chops (for 1 chop plus ½ cup onion mixture)	390	14 g	4.5 g	130 mg	10 g	53 g	2 g	590 mg
Spicy Mexican Shredded Pork Tostadas (for 2 tostadas)	330	12 g	2.5 g	35 mg	41 g	16 g	6 g	570 mg
Jambalaya	560	10 g	3 g	205 mg	66 g	50 g	4 g	1540 mg
Baked Stuffed Shrimp (for 6 shrimp)	230	11 g	4.5 g	195 mg	10 g	20 g	1 g	1100 mg
Stir-Fried Shrimp and Snow Peas with Coconut Curry Sauce (for 1¼ cup)	210	8 g	2 g	105 mg	18 g	15 g	4 g	790 mg
Cheesy Shrimp and Grits	310	10 g	5 g	135 mg	32 g	24 g	3 g	500 mg

	CAL	FAT	SAT FAT	CHOL	CARB	PROTEIN	FIBER	SODIUM
Crab-Stuffed Flounder (for 2 pieces)	360	13 g	4 g	190 mg	11 g	45 g	1 g	1350 mg
Crab Cakes (for 1 cake)	250	8 g	2 g	140 mg	11 g	29 g	0 g	770 mg
Fish Meunière (for 2 fillets plus ¼ cup sauce)	300	12 g	2.5 g	80 mg	11 g	32 g	0 g	590 mg

PASTA NIGHT

	CAL	FAT	SAT FAT	CHOL	CARB	PROTEIN	FIBER	SODIUM
Spaghetti with Creamy Basil Pesto (for 1½ cups)	360	8 g	2 g	5 mg	59 g	14 g	3 g	390 mg
Pasta with Sautéed Mushrooms (for 1½ cups)	380	6 g	2.5 g	10 mg	66 g	17 g	5 g	450 mg
Pasta Primavera (for 2 cups)	450	7 g	1.5 g	5 mg	75 g	15 g	6 g	520 mg
Everyday Macaroni and Cheese (for 1 cup)	350	10 g	5 g	40 mg	44 g	24 g	2 g	440 mg
Pasta ai Quattro Formaggi (for 1½ cups)	430	10 g	5 g	35 mg	64 g	21 g	2 g	640 mg
Spaghetti Carbonara (for 1½ cups)	430	11 g	3.5 g	50 mg	59 g	18 g	3 g	530 mg
Fettuccine Alfredo (for 2 cups)	540	17 g	9 g	135 mg	71 g	26 g	3 g	1000 mg
Weeknight Sausage Ragu (for 1¾ cups)	440	7 g	1.5 g	25 mg	77 g	20 g	8 g	1180 mg
Spaghetti and Meatballs (for 1½ cups spaghetti with sauce and 2 meatballs)	490	9 g	2.5 g	45 mg	76 g	30 g	7 g	1010 mg
Linguine with Bolognese (for 1¾ cups)	530	12 g	4.5 g	60 mg	73 g	32 g	5 g	950 mg
Pasta O's with Meatballs (for 1 cup)	230	6 g	1.5 g	25 mg	32 g	12 g	5 g	740 mg
Pasta with Chicken and Broccoli (for 2 cups)	480	9 g	2 g	55 mg	69 g	32 g	6 g	950 mg
Shrimp Scampi with Pasta (for 1⅔ cups)	400	4.5 g	1.5 g	115 mg	65 g	24 g	3 g	1030 mg
American Chop Suey (for 1½ cups)	340	9 g	2.5 g	50 mg	41 g	24 g	5 g	1030 mg
Pork Lo Mein (for 1⅔ cups)	500	11 g	2 g	75 mg	62 g	35 g	5 g	1050 mg
Peanut Noodle Salad (for 1¾ cups)	430	11 g	2 g	0 mg	71 g	16 g	6 g	660 mg
Pad Thai (for 1½ cups)	470	13 g	1.5 g	180 mg	74 g	18 g	4 g	970 mg

ON THE SIDE

	CAL	FAT	SAT FAT	CHOL	CARB	PROTEIN	FIBER	SODIUM
Broccoli with Cheese Sauce	150	6 g	3.5 g	15 mg	15 g	12 g	4 g	230 mg
Everyday Green Bean Casserole	130	7 g	2 g	5 mg	14 g	4 g	3 g	280 mg
Creamed Spinach (for ½ cup)	120	6 g	3.5 g	15 mg	10 g	10 g	5 g	340 mg
Creamed Corn (for ½ cup)	140	7 g	2 g	10 mg	17 g	5 g	2 g	55 mg
Cheesy Cauliflower Bake	160	8 g	4 g	20 mg	16 g	9 g	4 g	420 mg
Mashed Potatoes (for ⅔ cup)	200	6 g	3.5 g	20 mg	28 g	5 g	2 g	140 mg
Twice-Baked Potatoes	250	8 g	4.5 g	20 mg	36 g	8 g	3 g	330 mg
Scalloped Potatoes	270	7 g	3.5 g	20 mg	42 g	12 g	3 g	450 mg
Sweet Potato Casserole	290	4 g	2.5 g	10 mg	61 g	4 g	7 g	420 mg
Potato Salad	140	2.5 g	0 g	0 mg	27 g	4 g	3 g	590 mg
Macaroni Salad (for 1 cup)	250	9 g	1.5 g	5 mg	37 g	6 g	2 g	410 mg
Pasta Salad (for ¾ cup)	220	7 g	1.5 g	5 mg	32 g	8 g	2 g	430 mg
Cheese Bread (for ⅔-inch slice)	160	6 g	2.5 g	25 mg	19 g	7 g	1 g	490 mg
Cheesy Garlic Bread (for 2 pieces)	250	9 g	4 g	15 mg	30 g	11 g	2 g	560 mg

	CAL	FAT	SAT FAT	CHOL	CARB	PROTEIN	FIBER	SODIUM
BREAKFAST AND BRUNCH								
Denver Omelets	260	14 g	3 g	200 mg	7 g	25 g	2 g	950 mg
Frittata with Asparagus, Mushrooms, and Goat Cheese	150	8 g	3 g	190 mg	4 g	13 g	1 g	360 mg
Breakfast Strata	330	16 g	8 g	225 mg	24 g	16 g	2 g	1060 mg
Quiche Lorraine	250	14 g	4.5 g	130 mg	19 g	11 g	1 g	530 mg
Corned Beef Hash with Poached Eggs	420	12 g	3.5 g	235 mg	47 g	28 g	4 g	900 mg
Eggs Benedict	390	17 g	6 g	445 mg	31 g	26 g	0 g	950 mg
Sausage, Egg, and Cheese Breakfast Sandwiches	340	14 g	5 g	110 mg	28 g	24 g	0 g	650 mg
Crumb Coffee Cake	290	6 g	3.5 g	35 mg	54 g	4 g	1 g	220 mg
Blueberry Muffins (for 1 muffin)	250	5 g	3 g	45 mg	45 g	5 g	1 g	340 mg
Buttermilk Biscuits (for 1 biscuit)	160	4.5 g	3 g	15 mg	24 g	4 g	1 g	350 mg
Cinnamon Rolls (for 1 roll)	280	4 g	2.5 g	10 mg	55 g	6 g	1 g	250 mg
Banana Bread (for ⅔-inch slice)	200	5 g	2 g	40 mg	35 g	4 g	2 g	250 mg
Granola (for ½ cup)	230	8 g	1 g	0 mg	37 g	4 g	3 g	50 mg
CHOCOLATE DESSERTS								
Chewy Chocolate Cookies (for 1 cookie)	110	3.5 g	2 g	20 mg	19 g	1 g	2 g	60 mg
Fudgy Brownies (for 1 brownie)	110	3 g	1.5 g	15 mg	21 g	2 g	1 g	60 mg
Whoopie Pies	390	15 g	8 g	70 mg	61 g	6 g	5 g	220 mg
Chocolate Cupcakes	340	11 g	3 g	35 mg	62 g	3 g	3 g	170 mg
Low-Fat Chocolate Frosting (for 1 tablespoon)	70	1 g	0.5 g	0 mg	15 g	0 g	1 g	0 mg
Chocolate Sheet Cake	320	9 g	5 g	40 mg	61 g	4 g	3 g	180 mg
Glazed Chocolate Bundt Cake	280	10 g	1.5 g	25 mg	50 g	3 g	2 g	250 mg
German Chocolate Cake	320	12 g	6 g	60 mg	47 g	5 g	1 g	260 mg
Chocolate Cream Pie	320	18 g	11 g	65 mg	38 g	5 g	2 g	125 mg
Warm Chocolate Fudge Cakes	380	12 g	3 g	50 mg	70 g	6 g	5 g	320 mg
Chocolate Mousse	200	9 g	5 g	5 mg	30 g	4 g	2 g	40 mg
Chocolate Pudding	280	9 g	5 g	15 mg	48 g	6 g	2 g	140 mg
Chocolate Milkshakes (for 2 cups)	510	4.5 g	3.5 g	10 mg	98 g	20 g	5 g	310 mg
Mocha Frappé (for 2 cups)	290	2 g	1 g	10 mg	57 g	11 g	2 g	160 mg

	CAL	FAT	SAT FAT	CHOL	CARB	PROTEIN	FIBER	SODIUM
COOKIES AND BARS								
Chocolate Chip Cookies (for 1 cookie)	160	4 g	2.5 g	15 mg	30 g	2 g	1 g	110 mg
Peanut Butter Cookies (for 1 cookie)	130	6 g	1.5 g	10 mg	16 g	3 g	1 g	120 mg
Cheesecake Bars (for 1 bar)	130	6 g	3.5 g	40 mg	14 g	4 g	0 g	150 mg
Pecan Bars (for 1 bar)	170	9 g	2.5 g	20 mg	21 g	2 g	1 g	105 mg
Raspberry Streusel Bars (for 1 bar)	150	5 g	2.5 g	10 mg	25 g	1 g	1 g	100 mg
Lemon Squares (for 1 square)	190	6 g	3.5 g	35 mg	34 g	2 g	0 g	135 mg
Key Lime Bars (for 1 bar)	130	4.5 g	3 g	15 mg	19 g	3 g	0 g	70 mg
Blondies (for 1 blondie)	140	5 g	3 g	25 mg	23 g	2 g	0 g	65 mg
Oatmeal Fudge Bars (for 1 bar)	160	6 g	3.5 g	10 mg	25 g	2 g	0 g	70 mg
MORE SWEET TREATS								
Apple Crisp (for 1 cup)	330	6 g	3.5 g	15 mg	73 g	3 g	8 g	60 mg
Strawberry Shortcakes	320	10 g	6 g	50 mg	49 g	6 g	4 g	390 mg
Lemon Pound Cake (for 1-inch slice)	310	11 g	5 g	90 mg	47 g	5 g	1 g	140 mg
Key Lime Pie	250	8 g	4.5 g	30 mg	38 g	7 g	0 g	140 mg
Pineapple Upside-Down Cake	310	9 g	5 g	70 mg	52 g	4 g	2 g	230 mg
Red Velvet Cupcakes	280	8 g	6 g	35 mg	46 g	4 g	1 g	200 mg
Carrot Cake	280	12 g	3 g	35 mg	40 g	5 g	2 g	320 mg
New York-Style Cheesecake	360	17 g	10 g	105 mg	38 g	14 g	0 g	490 mg
Tiramisù	350	10 g	5 g	50 mg	52 g	12 g	1 g	330 mg
Peanut Butter Pie	360	17 g	8 g	5 mg	42 g	7 g	2 g	400 mg
Chilled Lemon Mousse with Raspberry Sauce	150	6 g	4 g	20 mg	20 g	4 g	1 g	115 mg
Crème Brûlée	240	13 g	8 g	145 mg	25 g	5 g	0 g	130 mg
Bread Pudding	320	8 g	2 g	95 mg	50 g	12 g	4 g	440 mg
Rich and Creamy Banana Pudding	420	8 g	3.5 g	85 mg	79 g	9 g	2 g	280 mg

Conversions & Equivalencies

Some say cooking is a science and an art. We would say that geography has a hand in it, too. Flour milled in the United Kingdom and elsewhere will feel and taste different from flour milled in the United States. So we cannot promise that the loaf of bread you bake in Canada or England will taste the same as a loaf baked in the States, but we can offer guidelines for converting weights and measures. We also recommend that you rely on your instincts when making our recipes. Refer to the visual cues provided. If the bread dough hasn't "come together in a ball," as described, you may need to add more flour—even if the recipe doesn't tell you to. You be the judge.

The recipes in this book were developed using standard U.S. measures following U.S. government guidelines. The charts below offer equivalents for U.S., metric, and imperial (U.K.) measures. All conversions are approximate and have been rounded up or down to the nearest whole number.

EXAMPLE:

| 1 teaspoon | = | 4.9292 milliliters, rounded up to 5 milliliters |
| 1 ounce | = | 28.3495 grams, rounded down to 28 grams |

VOLUME CONVERSIONS

U.S.	METRIC
1 teaspoon	5 milliliters
2 teaspoons	10 milliliters
1 tablespoon	15 milliliters
2 tablespoons	30 milliliters
¼ cup	59 milliliters
⅓ cup	79 milliliters
½ cup	118 milliliters
¾ cup	177 milliliters
1 cup	237 milliliters
1¼ cups	296 milliliters
1½ cups	355 milliliters
2 cups (1 pint)	473 milliliters
2½ cups	591 milliliters
3 cups	710 milliliters
4 cups (1 quart)	0.946 liter
1.06 quarts	1 liter
4 quarts (1 gallon)	3.8 liters

WEIGHT CONVERSIONS

OUNCES	GRAMS
½	14
¾	21
1	28
1½	43
2	57
2½	71
3	85
3½	99
4	113
4½	128
5	142
6	170
7	198
8	227
9	255
10	283
12	340
16 (1 pound)	454

CONVERSIONS FOR INGREDIENTS COMMONLY USED IN BAKING

Baking is an exacting science. Because measuring by weight is far more accurate than measuring by volume, and thus more likely to achieve reliable results, in our recipes we provide ounce measures in addition to cup measures for many ingredients. Refer to the chart below to convert these measures into grams.

INGREDIENT	OUNCES	GRAMS
1 cup all-purpose flour*	5	142
1 cup cake flour	4	113
1 cup whole-wheat flour	5½	156
1 cup granulated (white) sugar	7	198
1 cup packed brown sugar (light or dark)	7	198
1 cup confectioners' sugar	4	113
1 cup cocoa powder	3	85
4 tablespoons butter† (½ stick, or ¼ cup)	2	57
8 tablespoons butter† (1 stick, or ½ cup)	4	113
16 tablespoons butter† (2 sticks, or 1 cup)	8	227

* U.S. all-purpose flour, the most frequently used flour in this book, does not contain leaveners, as some European flours do. These leavened flours are called self-rising or self-raising. If you are using self-rising flour, take this into consideration before adding leavening to a recipe.

† In the United States, butter is sold both salted and unsalted. We generally recommend unsalted butter. If you are using salted butter, take this into consideration before adding salt to a recipe.

OVEN TEMPERATURES

FAHRENHEIT	CELSIUS	GAS MARK (IMPERIAL)
225	105	¼
250	120	½
275	135	1
300	150	2
325	165	3
350	180	4
375	190	5
400	200	6
425	220	7
450	230	8
475	245	9

CONVERTING TEMPERATURES FROM AN INSTANT-READ THERMOMETER

We include doneness temperatures in many of the recipes in this book. We recommend an instant-read thermometer for the job. Refer to the above table to convert Fahrenheit degrees to Celsius. Or, for temperatures not represented in the chart, use this simple formula:

Subtract 32 degrees from the Fahrenheit reading, then divide the result by 1.8 to find the Celsius reading.

EXAMPLE:
"Roast chicken until thighs register 175 degrees." To convert:

175°F − 32 = 143°
143° ÷ 1.8 = 79.44°C, rounded down to 79°C

Index